the lost girls

the lost girls

three friends. four continents.
one unconventional detour around the world.

JENNIFER BAGGETT

HOLLY C. CORBETT

AMANDA PRESSNER

HARPER

An Imprint of HarperCollins*Publishers*
www.harpercollins.com

Disclaimer: When we finished our first draft of *The Lost Girls*, we realized that in order to print it in a typeface you didn't need a magnifying glass to read—and make it light enough to carry on a plane without incurring excess baggage fees—we'd probably have to cut things down a little. And so we set out to streamline our tale, a task that required numerous late-night brainstorming sessions over red wine and sushi and a few workdays when we never changed out of our pajamas at all.

And though we've stuck to the real story of our adventures as closely and accurately as we can recall (cowriters have a wonderful way of keeping you honest!), we occasionally merged characters, reordered events, and condensed time to keep your eyes from glazing over. Many names of people and places (including the Indian ashram) have been changed and some of the identifying details altered to protect the innocent—and not so innocent—but the characters and stories themselves are entirely authentic. We really did bribe our way across the Cambodian border, really did sleep with cockroaches in Kenya, and really did get on a plane together and embark on a journey around the world. The trip turned out to be the greatest adventure of our lives—and that's the most important truth of them all.

But now we'll stop our rambling and let you read about it for yourself.

FIRST EDITION

Maps by Maureen Rubin Pressner

Designed by William Ruoto

Library of Congress Cataloging-in-Publication Data

Baggett, Jennifer.
    The lost girls : three friends, four continents, one unconventional detour around the world / Jennifer Baggett, Holly C. Corbett, and Amanda Pressner.
—1st ed.
        p. cm.
    ISBN 978-0-06-168906-2
    1. Baggett, Jennifer—Travel. 2. Corbett, Holly C.—Travel. 3. Pressner, Amanda—Travel. 4. Voyages and travels. 5. Backpacking. 6. Women travelers—Biography. 7. Women adventurers—Biography. 8. Young Women—New York (State)—New York—Biography. 9. Friends—New York (State)—New York—Biography. 10. Travelers' writings, American. I. Title.
    G465.B335 2010
    910.4'1—dc22
                                                                    2009054294

10 11 12 13 14 OV/RRD 10 9 8 7 6 5 4 3 2 1

To our parents, for always supporting us on our journeys, no matter how far-fetched or far-flung.

And to all the other Lost Girls out there trying to find their way.

"The world is round and the place which may seem like the end may also be the beginning."

—IVY BAKER PRIEST

Contents

the lost girls

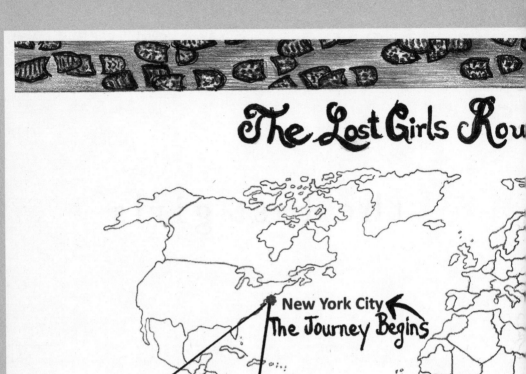

The Lost Girls Rou

New York City
The Journey Begins

N

W   E

S

Peru
Bolivia   Brazil

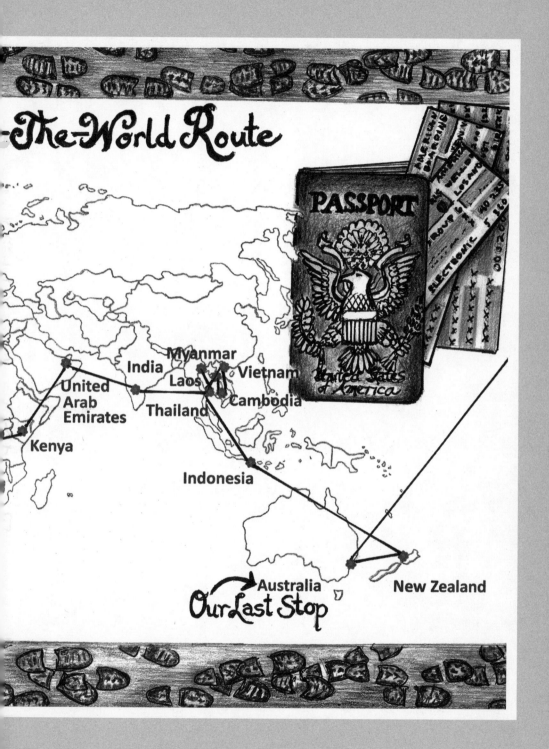

The Lost Girls

MAASAI VILLAGE OF ORONKAI, KENYA

W e weren't sure what we'd just heard or if there had been any sound at all, but the three of us felt a palpable shift in the atmosphere. One by one, our footsteps slowed to a halt. We stood frozen in the grassy clearing outside our hut, watching tiny knots of people push their way down the hillsides and into the valley below. Some were carrying staffs, and most were draped in brilliant swatches of scarlet, eggplant, cerise, and cerulean. The fabric pressed against their long limbs and billowed back out again, like wind filling dozens of spinnaker sails.

The three of us had encountered plenty of unusual scenes during the four weeks we'd been volunteering in rural southwestern Kenya—chickens riding shotgun in *matatu* vans, locusts for sale as snacks, children helping to birth calves during school recess—but we had yet to see anything as extraordinary as this. Brief snatches of words, almost like chanting, drifted through the fields all around us. As the sounds grew steadily louder, pulsing in a call-and-repeat rhythm, Emmanuel and his wife, Lily, our program coordinators, emerged from inside the hut and stood beside us.

They smiled when they saw our expressions and explained

what we were witnessing: the people streaming down the hillside were Maasai, a seminomadic East African tribe that was one of the most colorful—and certainly the most recognizable—in this part of the world. Many were friends and neighbors, but others had traveled long distances, some from days away, to reach our host family's farm.

Emmanuel and Lily, both members of the Maasai, had suggested that we come during this particular week in October, so our visit could coincide with a traditional ceremony performed on the crest of a hill near their home. We'd arrived as scheduled—but still hadn't had any idea what to expect.

"It's almost time," Lily said softly. "Come, let's get prepared."

She ushered us back inside the hut and showed us a small table covered with handmade jewelry. She selected three elaborate oval collars packed tightly with rows of turquoise, cobalt, and royal blue beads and gestured for us to put them on. As we helped one another fasten and secure the heavy pieces around our necks, the chanting outside grew even louder and was now punctuated by the sound of a beating drum. *Kung-ka-kung-ka-kung-ka*. It reverberated through the valley, and our pulses quickened to match the tempo.

"We are ready. Let's go," said Lily, motioning us to follow Emmanuel outside and along an incline that started at the edge of their property. We walked for several minutes, breathing hard as we pressed our way up the rocky backbone of the hill. As the thin path converged into a larger trail, we fell into step with several Maasai heading in the same direction we were.

Although we'd observed their migration from a distance, we weren't prepared for what we encountered after pushing through the last stand of trees. A massive group of men, women, and children, literally hundreds of locals, had gathered in a clearing at the top of the hill.

2

The women had tied sheets of pale yellow and beige fabric over deep sienna-colored shifts accessorized with beaded necklaces, bangle bracelets, and dangling earrings. They had encircled their slim waists with animal-hide belts studded with cowrie shells and adorned their heads with delicate tiaras made of copper, leather, and beading. Many of the men wore T-shirts and sports jerseys under the brightly hued clothes we'd spotted against the hillside earlier. They too wore jewelry—chokers, arm cuffs, earrings, and fur headdresses. The volume of the chattering around us increased until it reached a fever pitch, then, almost at once, dropped off entirely.

"Come now, the ceremony is about to begin," whispered Emmanuel, beckoning us to sit down.

Moments later, the tribesmen began the traditional *moran* warrior dance, leaping through the air in near-impossible feats of vertical prowess. Then, once the men's ritual ended, we watched the women move in to form a wide semicircle in the clearing.

As they began to sway and clap, slanted rays of sun lit up the beads in their jewelry and glinted off a young woman's copper headband. It was hard to tell for sure, but she looked to be in her late twenties, just about our age. Even though her face was smudged with ocher, a greasy red paint that coated her features like pancake makeup, her expression still revealed the connection she had with the other women.

For several minutes, they sang and clapped in unison, their voices folding over and into one another to become a single, powerful track. Grasping hands, they swung in a wide circle, their words growing urgent and more intense. Around and around they went, whooping and shrieking as they picked up speed. The mood was electric, the dance the most joyous form of expression. We were leaning forward on the blanket, absorbing the energy that swelled and sparked like a thundercloud, when suddenly three women broke from the formation and grabbed our hands.

We were all caught off guard (maybe the women meant to reach for someone else?), but there was no mistake about it: we'd been invited to join them. Accepting without a word—just a quick glance at one another—we allowed ourselves to be pulled into the swiftly moving orbit of the Maasai.

Of course we didn't know the steps or how to sing along, but it didn't matter. As we collectively spun like an out-of-control carnival ride, we did our best to swing our hips and move our feet like the other women. They watched from across the circle, throwing their heads back in fits of hysterical laughter at the artless antics of the foreign girls who looked clumsier (and dizzier) with every step.

Then, just as we thought the dance was winding down, the women began embracing us in a full-body, cheek-to-cheek hug. They repeated the love fest over and over again, one by one, until our cheeks and chins and foreheads were fully smudged with ocher. It wasn't until we pulled back and caught a glimpse of one another—the enormous necklaces, the beads, the red streaks running across our faces—that we figured out what every other person must have already known: We hadn't hiked up here to watch the ceremony as spectators. We had come to be initiated.

If we still weren't convinced, Lily delivered the final confirmation.

"You are Maasai now!" she shouted, her face glowing as the other women cheered. She was the last one to cross the circle and draw us into an embrace, making sure every inch of our faces was coated in red.

Between our burning lungs and this unexpected piece of news, none of us could speak. What's the right thing to say when you've been brought into the inner circle, literally, to join the ranks of spiritual, beautiful wanderers? The life we'd left behind in New York City—once all-consuming—now seemed like ancient history and as far away as a distant star.

As the three of us descended the hill later that afternoon, we walked in relative silence. Our initiation into the Maasai may have been purely ceremonial—a gift to us from Lily, Emmanuel, and their fellow tribespeople. But it reminded us how far we'd come since leaving our apartments, jobs, and loved ones behind in the United States to travel the globe.

When we'd first started plotting this adventure nearly two years earlier, the three of us—friends in our midtwenties—had shared the desire to take a giant step away from our own goal-oriented worlds to get a better sense of who we were—and what we really wanted from our lives. Up until then, we'd successfully hit the milestones that are supposed to give young women a sense of purpose: Moving away from Mom and Dad. Graduating from college. Getting our first jobs. Falling in love.

But as we rocketed toward the next major stage (the one involving mortgages, marriages, and 2.2 children), we all wondered: Were the paths that we were heading down the right ones for us—or were we simply staying the course because we thought we *should*? Was the road most frequently traveled the one that we wanted to follow?

Finding it difficult to gain perspective while living and working in New York City, we decided to take an unconventional detour: a 60,000-mile, round-the-world journey that would lead us across four continents and more than a dozen countries. Dubbing ourselves "The Lost Girls," a term describing both our own uncertainty about the future and an emotional state we felt represented many in our generation, we committed to spending one year of our late twenties wandering the globe. We

5

were searching for answers, but as we'd learn along the way, the ones you uncover are rarely those to the questions asked.

If we could transport ourselves back in time, we might tell our younger selves not to worry so much. Not to sweat the small stuff—or even the big stuff. We'd say that real life is the thing that happens when you're busy trying to map out your future. Then again, maybe we wouldn't tell them a thing. Those lessons might have made the last years of our twenties a little easier, but we wouldn't have traded our on-the-road initiation for the world.

✕

CHAPTER ONE

Jen

IGUAZÚ FALLS, ARGENTINA/BRAZIL

NEARLY TWO YEARS EARLIER

We were surrounded on all sides by an immense curtain of white water. The cascades heaved over a sheer cliff, carving jade green pools in the jungle floor of Iguazú National Park, and drowned out every sound save one: the pounding of our hiking boots as they tore across the metal viewing platform at the base of the falls.

Holly, our resident sprinter, led the charge toward the exit, with Amanda and me sliding right after her. As updrafts of mist swirled around our feet, we skidded across the final footbridge and shot up a steep staircase, our labored breathing and laughter echoing against the basalt rock walls. Slowing slightly to wipe the spray from my face, I glanced down at my watch. We had less than ten minutes to make it to the top, or we might be stranded in Brazil all night.

According to the ranger (who'd raced over seconds earlier to see why on earth the three crazy American girls were still casually snapping photos when the park was about to close), there was only one more shuttle bus leaving that evening. So unless we'd brought camping gear or a wad of extra cash to bribe the Brazilian border officials, we'd better be on it. Sure, it would've been helpful if our taxi driver had mentioned the one-hour time difference between the Argentinean and Brazilian sides of Iguazú (or Iguaçu) when he semi-illegally transported us across the border, but hey, where's the fun in that?

We probably should have taken this impending travel disaster a little more seriously. But considering that we'd all but signed over our firstborn kids to our bosses in order to take this little adventure in the first place, we weren't going to let a little thing like a potential immigration scandal bring us down.

In fact, our escape from New York City a week earlier had felt like nothing short of a prison break. When Amanda and I had first told our friends and coworkers that we were planning to take ten days off—in a row—in order to backpack around Argentina, we were met with some seriously arched eyebrows.

"Wow, I didn't even take more than a week off when I got married," one acquaintance remarked. "Better hope they don't fill your jobs before you get back."

Only Holly, another assistant editor who worked with Amanda at a women's magazine, seemed to share our enthusiastic attitude about escaping the freezing winter and the endless projects tethering us to our desks. Even though Holly and I had met just a few times and couldn't be sure that we'd get along for a single day on the road, let alone ten, she'd asked only two questions before anteing up the money for a ticket: "Which airline are we flying, and when do we leave?" For my part, I was thrilled to have a new coconspirator in my quest to find a more authentic "real world" than the one we were about to leave behind in Manhattan.

After moving to the city nearly four years earlier to take a job at a national television network, I had been dropped into a world of claustrophobic apartments, exorbitant rents, fourteen-hour workdays, mandatory media events, and gospel preachers predicting doomsday on the subways. I quickly learned that the city had spawned a new kind of Darwinian struggle: only the most career-driven and socially adaptable would survive. In order to cope with the pressure, people generally took one of two paths: the first lined with Xanax, therapists, and cigarettes, and the second with Bikram yoga, feng shui, and green tea.

My personal survival method? Escape. Even now, dripping with sweat and frantically racing to make it across country lines, I felt that familiar burst of exhilaration that flooded me every time I booked an international flight or added a new stamp to my passport.

And though it had been a challenge to get on the road in the first place, Holly, Amanda, and I had done our best to squeeze every ounce of life from our holiday. We'd arrived a week earlier in the "Big Apple" of South America, cosmopolitan Buenos Aires, and filled our time wandering its cobblestone alleys, savoring sumptuous *lomo* steak dinners, stuffing our bags with street market finds, and exhausting ourselves at late-night tango dancing sessions that lasted until the night sky was slivered with pink.

Although our love affair with the passionate culture and sultry vibe of B.A. had only just begun, the three of us were ready to drop even farther away from city life. It was time to head for the jungle. After a two-hour flight on LAN Peru, our small plane touched down in the frontier town of Puerto Iguazú and it was good-bye strappy tango sandals, hello hiking boots.

Glancing down at my own shoes, now filthy from the day's trek, I was amazed that I was still able to run, much less sprint up the final flight of stairs. As we finally broke out of the deep shade of the rain forest and onto the main road, we spotted the bus fifty yards ahead, packed to the brim with passengers. In a scene befitting a screwball silver screen comedy, the bus started to pull away at the exact moment we arrived. Holly, who by now

I'd learned ran marathons for fun, fired up her legs and dashed even faster, waving a tanned arm above her head as Amanda and I screamed for the bus to stop. Thank the jungle gods that we'd popped out into the open when we had, because the driver somehow noticed us in the rearview mirror and chugged to a stop. Gasping for breath and dripping wet, we stumbled aboard and were met by a busload of cheering tourists, all clapping for our frenetic victory. Collapsing into the only empty seats, Amanda, Holly, and I passed around the one bottle of water we had left between us, laughing and congratulating ourselves on yet another skin-of-our-teeth arrival.

As I chugged another gulp of water and caught my breath, I realized that I felt happier and more grounded than I had in months. Suddenly the thought of returning home in a few days sent a ripple of dread through my body. Unlike Amanda and Holly, who'd been desperate for a reprieve from their chaotic, cutthroat magazine jobs, I had recently scored an exciting new position as a marketing coordinator for a music television channel that I was eager to resume.

For once in my adult life, my career and living situation were actually on track, humming right along—but things with my relationship weren't going so smoothly. In fact, I was bracing myself for a potential train wreck.

After I had dated my boyfriend, Brian, for almost three years, the confidence to shout off the rooftops "Hallelujah! He's the One!" still eluded me. Though many empathetic souls reminded me that I was still young, a growing number of onlookers had begun to pounce on my uncertainty. "Shit or get off the pot," they'd say, invoking the single phrase I loathed more than any other. I mean, maybe I was just comfortable staying in a seated position longer than other people. Can't a girl simply enjoy the feel of cool porcelain without being judged?

While my romance with Brian hadn't followed the traditional cinematic structure—boy sees girl, they lock eyes, share a passionate embrace, and fall head over heels in love—it had grown out of something stronger: a true friendship. We'd met at a business lunch halfway through my "freshman year" in New York. Network television sales assistant meets advertising client—an industry cliché that always made us laugh. Soon we grew from casual acquaintances to after-work happy hour buddies to true confidants who organized late-afternoon photo shoots in Central Park, signed up for salsa lessons, and dined in cute garden cafés on Restaurant Row.

Before we knew it, we were a serious couple. And as the months turned into years, we never had a moment's pause about progressing naturally from one level to the next. Becoming Exclusive. Meeting the Parents. Planning Vacations. Discussing Living Together. I was one of the lucky ones, shattering the Manhattan urban myth that it was impossible to find a sweet, gainfully employed city guy who wasn't afraid to commit.

But within the past few months, we'd hit the proverbial relationship wall. We had no real reason to break up, but also no real catalyst moving us forward. I knew that Brian and I would have to face the question of our future eventually, but at twenty-six (for another precious few months, anyway), I was more than content to take the safe road—present bus ride excluded. As we neared the park exit, the driver slammed into a pothole, sending me and my wandering thoughts sliding off the bench and into the aisle.

Fortunately, the travel deities, it seemed, had decided to cut us yet another break: in the parking lot, we spotted the same snoring taxi driver who'd originally transported us across the border using a series of dusty back roads and convinced him to do the exact same thing in reverse. A few *por favor*s, 20 Argentine pesos (about $7), and we were on our way.

E ven after our mad dash through the jungle, none of us were quite ready to call it a night. By the time we'd reached our hotel—located within the national park on the Argentinean side—Holly had come up with a better alternative.

Her green eyes glinted, and a mischievous smile crossed her face. "Hey, so now that we've gained an hour of time back, do you guys want to hike over to Devil's Throat waterfall? When I spoke with the concierge this morning, he said it doesn't take long to get there and the view is the best one."

"I'm *definitely* down for that. Schmanders?" I asked, invoking Amanda's college nickname.

"Hey, why not?" she said, sweeping her blond curls off her neck and into a loose ponytail. "And at least we know we can't get stranded on this side!"

After smoothing on a fresh layer of sunblock (my fair skin tends to freckle and burn even in the light of sunset), I grabbed my day pack and we took off running down the trail.

Giddy from our day's adventure, Amanda, Holly, and I theatrically strutted across another set of Iguazú's elevated catwalks, following the signs to Garganta del Diablo. We passed over marshy wetland grasses and under verdant green canopies until we finally reached the park's main stage. Rather than staring at the thunderous, driving force of the water from below, this time we were perched high above the falls—at the same vantage point as the red-breasted toucans we'd seen darting through the rain forest. From this height, we could take in the full scope of the cascades rushing over the horseshoe cliff, thundering into a foggy abyss below, and enveloping us in a perfectly circular ring of rainbows.

"You know, I wouldn't have cared if we'd gotten stranded in Brazil," said Holly, stretching one of her lean legs along the railing. "I'd take this over opening mail any day of the week."

12

Amanda grimaced and plopped down next to me on the bench where I'd settled near the main lookout point. "Let's not mention work, please? I can't even think about the massive pile of papers and e-mails waiting to eat me alive when I get back."

"Oh, c'mon, Amanda. You know you'd rather be sitting at your desk working on that lifesaving article you're doing on . . . what is it?" I teased her, pulling a half-eaten granola bar out of my bag for emphasis. "The grooviest snack foods? The most artificially flavored?"

"The Skinniest New Snack Foods," she said miserably, grabbing the bar and acting as if she might toss it over the edge. "But I'd happily eat full-fat foods forever as long as I could do it here. I bet they don't even have a word for 'deadline' or 'anxiety attack' in Latin America."

"I'm with you," Holly said, coming over to sit next to us. "But at least we managed to escape for more than a week. That's way more than most people get away with. And even if we have to work until midnight every night for a month, it'll be worth it."

"Yeah, I can't believe we really pulled this off. Especially you, Hols. I mean, you hadn't even saved up for the trip like Jen and I did."

Holly shrugged and rolled her eyes playfully. "Well, I figured eating Luna bars for lunch every day and hiding flasks in my purse at happy hours was worth the sacrifice."

From what I'd learned about Holly already this week, I had a feeling she wasn't exaggerating about what she'd had to do in order to get on the road and travel. Though I'd done my fair share of scrimping since moving to New York, I'd thankfully never been in debt. I'd even managed to earmark a small portion of my modest television salary for overseas vacations. Holly, on the other hand, had never really had extra money to spare and had been picking up odd jobs—berry picker, cosmetics color analyst, lead paint poisoning tester, college dorm toilet scrubber, pizza delivery girl—since she was a kid in order to stay afloat with her expenses. Yet somehow she'd managed to visit nearly twice the number of the countries I had, because she'd either earned study-abroad scholarships or paid for the trips out of her own pocket. She prioritized adventure and discovery over stability and structure—yet another reason why Amanda and I were so excited she'd been able to join us at the last minute.

"Do we really have to go back? Can't we just set up camp and stay?" Amanda pleaded.

"Okay, fine, it's decided," I said, rising to my feet to face the girls. "We'll build a tree house right here and live like the Swiss Family Robinson."

"Yeah, and we could sneak into the hotel at night and steal leftovers from room service carts," Holly added.

Soon we all got caught up in the fantasy of transferring from the concrete jungle to a real one. Our skin would glow from pristine air quality; we'd have lean and chiseled bodies from 24/7 hiking; hot Brazilian men would magically appear and fall in love with us—all excellent reasons we tossed out for settling here.

"Well, I hadn't mentioned this to you yet, Hol, but Jen knows my plan. If I ever get promoted to associate editor, I'm gonna start socking away money, quit the magazine a year later, and take a few months off to travel," Amanda said, brightening at the thought. "I'd invited Jen to come with me—but how much fun would it be if you came, too? It'd be just like this week—only infinitely more awesome."

"Oh, man, I am totally gonna rat you out to your boss," Holly joked, uncrossing her legs and swinging them over the side of the bench. "Actually, I have a secret too. I've been interviewing for jobs, and one of the magazines already asked me for references, so I'll probably be gone before you are. If you do leave to travel . . . well, maybe I'll come for part of the time."

Despite what I'd learned about Holly, I was still shocked. "Are you serious? Would you actually come with us, Holly?"

"Would *you* really come with me?" Amanda said, now staring at me intently.

"Oh, please! You love your job more than life itself. You would *never* abandon it or New York," I said, tormenting her as only a true best friend could. "But I triple dog dare you to quit because it'd be nice if you graced us with your presence at social events again."

"Okay, so I'm not sure exactly when I would leave or for how long, but it makes me feel better to have an emergency escape route mapped out, just in case," Amanda shot back, grabbing her pack from the bench and walking over to the railing to get a better view of the sinking sun. "It's either move up or move on, right?"

Although I'd witnessed her frenetic race up the razor-sharp publishing ladder firsthand, I also knew that if Amanda Pressner committed to doing something, nothing would stand in her way—or woe to the innocent bystander who did. For starters, she was the only one out of five of my college friends who hadn't bailed on our postgrad Europe trip. She'd said she was moving to Manhattan afterward to work in entertainment, and she had, all by herself, with no help or nepotistic connections. When everyone had told her it was impossible to get an editorial position at a magazine without being published first, she'd given them the mental middle finger and done it anyway. So if Amanda said she was going to leave to take a trip in the future, I had no doubt that she would.

"You know what? Unless something drastically changes in my life by the time you're ready to leave, I'll nominate myself as your partner in crime," I announced.

As I spoke, I realized I was serious. For some reason, this particular trip to Argentina had intensified my itch to escape my New York reality more than ever. And if things didn't get better with Brian, I might feel the need to flee the city anyway.

From the safety of another continent, the idea of leaving everything familiar behind to live like nomads seemed almost possible. If all of our promotions and job transitions happened as planned, we'd have about eighteen months to save—and we could stretch out a trip budget for almost a year if we stuck to cheaper countries. With that much time, we could cross several continents and maybe pick up odd jobs along the way ("My friend made ten dollars a day picking fruit on a farm in Costa Rica," Holly tossed out) or volunteer with an organization in exchange for lodging ("I could secure some freelance assignments," Amanda added). And hopefully by then we'd be at a point in our professional lives where we could leave without totally committing career suicide.

"And we're all turning twenty-eight next year, which is the phase of our lives called Saturn Return," said Holly said, hastening to add, "It's an astrological thing—I used to edit the horoscope section for the magazine."

She explained that during the years between twenty-eight and thirty, the planet Saturn completes its cycle through your birth chart, which marks the end of youth and start of adulthood. And it brings with it monumental endings and new beginnings.

"So it'd be the perfect time to take a trip together," Holly said in a low, conspiratorial voice. "I say let's do it, ladies."

It wasn't the New Age talk that sent shivers up my spine. It was the Age part. The mention of our twenty-eighth birthdays stimulated a memory, an innocuous conversation I'd had with my mom about a year and a half earlier, which suddenly seemed epically relevant. The scene played out in my mind with eerie vividness . . .

My mom and I were sitting at a sidewalk table at my favorite neighborhood cantina, sipping frozen margaritas. In typical fashion, we gabbed for hours, covering all the usual subjects: my job, the extreme importance of maxing out my 401(k) contribution, how I couldn't afford to eat and would be homeless if I maxed out my 401(k) contribution, Dad's latest home improvement project, the dire consequences of not having renter's insurance, and of course, Me, Brian and The Future.

We'd been together barely sixteen months, and I'd already heard questions from people like "Is marriage on the horizon? Shouldn't you date other people if it isn't? You know it's safer to have kids in your twenties, right?" *Great! I'm already a bad mother, and I'm not even pregnant.*

As I voiced my frustrations about all of this pressure, my mom offered what, at the time, was a brilliant suggestion: "Maybe you'd feel better if you picked an age, any age you want. And make a pact that you'll just enjoy dating and not overthink anything until then."

Hmm, it would be a relief to let myself off the hook for a while. After all, still in my midtwenties, I was a mere babe by NYC standards. I could give uncertainty another few years, right? So I threw age twenty-eight out into the ether.

"That gives me plenty of time to relax and have fun. If Brian and I are still together then, we definitely should have things figured out. And if not, I'll have to do something really radical, like move to Colorado to become a ski instructor or join a rock band roadie movement or max out my 401(k) for the first time ever in my life," I teased.

"You're not funny," my mom replied with a laugh. "You should really put the full ten percent of your paycheck toward savings," she added, unable to resist.

Now, standing in the middle of an Argentinean rain forest, I couldn't shake the sense that the whole round-the-world trip idea had come up for a reason: the three of us winding up on vacation together; talking about the possibility of leaving to travel abroad *right after my twenty-eighth birthday*; remembering an impromptu pact I had made over Tex-Mex food. Considering the turbulent state of my love life and my overwhelming inability to make a decision, it was clear that I was nearing a critical fork in the road. Well, let's be honest: I'd set up camp there ages ago and was still sitting on my ass roasting marshmallows.

I'd secretly hoped a sign would appear to point me in the right direction, but I'd never expected it to be a trip around the world. It was an odd, inexplicable feeling deep in my gut, but everything seemed fated somehow, as if any path I'd chosen would've led me to this exact point. Maybe this was something I was meant to do.

Sitting there with Amanda and Holly at the top of a waterfall, in the middle of the jungle, I had a vision of what our life on the road together would be like. It was a lightning flash of the future waiting just an arm's length away, daring us to reach out and grab it.

Could I really spend an entire year traveling around the world with these girls?

As crazy as it seemed, I knew the answer was yes.

CHAPTER TWO

Amanda

Most "real" New Yorkers claim that you don't become one of them until you've lived in the city for at least ten years. Some say it takes a lifetime. According to the New York State Unified Court System, I'd managed to become a New Yorker in less than seven years, and it was time to show my appreciation by paying a visit to the courthouse.

For months, I'd been boomeranging jury notice slips back downtown, convinced that if I deferred enough times, the powers that be would give up on me altogether. But the government, as it turned out, was no sleazy day trader at happy hour who—eventually—took the hint. No matter how often I rejected the offer for a date, Uncle Sam wouldn't take no for an answer.

Our little courting ritual came to an end one Tuesday night in March. I arrived home to the cramped apartment Jen and I shared with our friend Beth and swept up the stack of mail threatening to slip-slide off our front table. There, wedged between a Vietnamese delivery menu and our latest cable bill, was a red-and-black envelope marked URGENT—FINAL NOTICE.

Ripping open the letter, I flung myself onto the futon and tried to figure out how I could possibly get out of going one more time. That's when I heard the key twisting in the lock. Jen didn't even get the chance to dump the three bags she was carrying on the ground before I pounced.

"There's just no way!" I railed, pacing the length of our ten-foot living room while Jen calmly hung up her pink wool coat with the patent leather trim. "I *can't* miss work right now. I'm already so overloaded that I'm starting to make really stupid mistakes. Misspelling words when I have to make changes on-screen. Our research chief pulled me aside today to remind me how to annotate copy."

"Ooh, that sucks. But I'm sure they know you're just busy. What'd you misspell?" she asked, shaking the snow out of her honey-colored hair.

"Safety. Can you believe that? I spelled it saf-tey, and the proofreader almost didn't catch it until it went to press. Claire was definitely *not* impressed with that one."

My new boss, Claire, a veteran women's magazine editor, had taken over the nutrition section after my previous supervisor, Kristen, had moved over to head the new sexual health department. Whereas Kristen had worked with me one-on-one to help me grow as a newbie writer and assigned me feature stories rather than busy work, Claire seemed to believe that assistants should pay their dues in messages taken and paperwork filed. To say that she and I hadn't exactly clicked professionally would be a major understatement. I'd always felt that if she could have replaced me instead of inheriting me, she wouldn't have hesitated a second.

"Well, I wouldn't freak out about jury duty too much. Every New Yorker has to do it at some point," said Jen, prying a micro-wave burrito from the back of the freezer. "You probably won't even get picked."

"Yeah, but what if I do? What if I get picked and they think I didn't try hard enough to get out of it and they decide to give the associate editor job to someone else?"

She looked at me in the amused way she does when I spiral from illogical into completely irrational. Which is often. "I promise—in the remote chance that you actually get chosen, there's no way they'd give the job to someone else. You've worked your ass off. And besides, it's not like they can forbid you to serve on a jury. So don't stress."

I sighed. Jen was probably right. In any case, I didn't appear to have much of a choice. As the notice implied, either I would serve my civic duty—or I could wind up serving time.

S itting in the courtroom a few weeks later, I tried to look as pathetic as possible. I'd made it a point to toss on sweats, leave my hair unwashed, and avoid makeup completely. Maybe the judge would think, "This girl can't even be bothered to use mascara—how can she possibly be qualified to sit on a jury?"

Glancing at the bored New Yorkers around me, I wondered who among us would get chosen to serve. I'd narrowly escaped the day before and hoped to shimmy through the cracks a second time. Every hour I sat here, trying to avoid attracting attention, was one more that I wasn't answering e-mails, which no doubt had already mutated and multiplied in my inbox like some resistant strain of flu virus. By now the pile of glossy proofs I'd yet to read had probably toppled and slid under my desk.

Maybe I shouldn't have gone to Argentina.

As that traitorous thought whined around my head, I tried to squash it senseless. What good was taking the trip of a lifetime if you were just going to regret it once you got home? Back in Iguazú, when we'd contemplated turning our dream vacation into a yearlong adventure, I'd been high on the idea of unplugging from my cell phone, my computer, and in fact, my entire life. But almost the second I'd dived back into my desk chair, reality had sledgehammered down. Somehow, during the ten days that I'd been away, I'd managed to fall at least a month behind on my assignments. Go away for a year? Yeah, right. By the third weekend spent shivering inside an empty office tower trying to get caught up, I understood why more experienced editors joked that it wasn't worth the hassle to take a vacation at all.

As winter faded and spring edged in, the pace at work never slacked. If anything, it grew even more intense. Ad sales were up, and we had more pages to write and assign. The hole I'd dug while in Argentina grew into a ditch, then a bottomless trench.

The same stress that had once motivated me to spring out of bed in the morning now chased me under the covers at night. I lay awake, heart racing and guts churning as I scribbled to-do lists in the back of my head. Stress became my chronic companion, an ugly, overcaffeinated little goblin that used my chest as a trampoline and my head as a boxing ring and laid off only when I was exhausted enough to pass out.

Despite advice from friends to set boundaries ("Tell your boss you can't take on any more work. Just walk out the door every day at 6 p.m., no matter what"), admitting I'd bitten off more than I could chew would be a huge mistake. I worked with five other ambitious assistants just as eager to prove themselves as I was. We all knew that to reach the coveted level of associate editor (and if you didn't want that, you might as well just get out now) we'd have to go way above and beyond our job descriptions, taking on any extra responsibilities we could convince the department heads to dish out.

The competition among the six of us was friendly but fierce. When the pressure got to be too intense we'd commiserate, but we still fought for assignments the way hyenas might scrap over felled antelope. Ironically, perhaps through the shared experience, the late nights, and the intensity of the situation, we forged a tight friendship, a bond built over blood, sweat, and take-out soy sauce.

Of those young women, Holly was always my closest confidante. Even though she had even more to do than the rest of us—she assisted three executives in addition to editing her own pages for the Happiness section—I'd never seen Holly break down or sob in the women's bathroom the way almost every other junior staffer had. She fielded the demands of the job with good humor and a can-do attitude (at least, when our bosses were around) but was never too busy to go on a caffeine run or join me in a gripe session. She even managed to break me out of the office a few times for yoga and Pilates classes, saying we'd end up being more productive mentally if we took care of ourselves physically.

When the to-do list got really long, both Holly and I would work late, taking breaks to vent over California rolls and fantasize about doing something on Friday nights other than partying at our desks. Running the editorial hamster wheel could be almost fun with Hol around—except that as soon as we got back from Argentina, she scored a job at a kinder, gentler women's magazine. I was thrilled for her (and, yes, slightly jealous) but mostly just perplexed when she started inviting me to hit the gym or designer sample sales at lunch. Had she already forgotten where she'd worked?

As the weeks ticked by, the anxiety I hid while at the office started to bubble over. I snapped at the deli guy if he accidentally put mayo on my sandwich or if someone cut me off going through a subway turnstile. I'd always been a tad feisty, but some days I felt as if I were one annoyance away from climbing the art installation in Union Square and opening fire on the skateboarders below.

Then, just before spring finally broke, two things happened: The magazine's sole associate editor spot, the position directly above mine, became vacant. And I was forced to leave the office to serve jury duty.

Despite my every intention to perjure myself, when the judge finally locked his eyes on mine and started asking questions, I heard the terrible, awful truth spilling out. I'd never been placed under arrest. I'd never been the victim of a hate crime. I'd never been stalked (unless you could count years of ex-boyfriend drama). And yes, I lived in Manhattan and had no immediate plans to leave the area.

It came as almost no surprise when, at a quarter to five, the court officer read my name off the list of selected jurors.

The judge assured the dozen of us that our case wouldn't last long, a week or so at most. Once we'd passed judgment on a relative stranger, we'd be free to go back to our regularly scheduled lives. Sounded easy enough.

As he spoke, it struck me that my new courthouse workday would be an unthinkably brief eight hours long—and for once I could actually leave the building for lunch. I couldn't remember the last time I had gone anywhere but the company cafeteria. Two years spent inhaling its greasy buffalo chicken wraps and oil-soaked pasta salads had caused me to gain fifteen pounds and a pretty substantial muffin top. Considering I was simultaneously instructing millions of women how to "Lose a dress size in 10 days!" and "Slim down in your sleep!" the irony hadn't escaped me. Nor, I figured, had my extra flab escaped the hawkeyed editors with whom I shared my office tower. As I headed out to grab a bite that first day, I wondered if jury duty might actually be a blessing in disguise.

Despite the incredible amount of carrying on I'd done beforehand, I was surprised to find that I actually loved serving on a jury. I slid from bed each morning on the third snooze rather than the tenth, dressed quickly (who'd care if I wore cargo pants and a hoodie?), and jammed out to my new iPod mini as I zipped downtown on the express subway line.

The trial, as it turned out, was nothing like those in *Ally McBeal* or *Boston Legal*, but I didn't care. Boredom was so unfamiliar a feeling that I actually welcomed it. During my hours in the jury box, my attention warbled in and out like an AM radio signal, my thoughts inevitably drifting back uptown.

As testimony played faintly in the background, I recalled how intense it felt, after years spent shifting between internships and jobs that weren't quite right, to figure out what I wanted to do with my life. The moment I finally hit upon that realization, I'd been almost manic about my quest to get into magazines. I'd interviewed for what felt like hundreds of positions before finally convincing my boss that, at twenty-five, I wasn't already too old and too experienced to take on the grunt work required of an editorial assistant (and make $24,000 a year while doing it).

It was just as my career began to get on track that my relationship with Baker—the first and only guy I'd ever fallen truly, deeply in love with—hit the skids. We'd had a passionate, tumultuous start, and over the course of three years, he and I had shredded ourselves apart so many times it was a wonder we had ever managed to stitch ourselves back together again. When we finally ended things after a roller coaster of a vacation in Mexico and a subsequent screaming match in the middle of Times Square, I think both he and I knew that this breakup had to be the last. He disappeared into the throng of pedestrians on 42nd Street that day, and I didn't talk to him again for months.

Still, I knew exactly where he was headed. Baker had been planning a multicountry backpacking trip in the years before we'd met and had grounded himself in Manhattan only long enough to give our blossoming relationship a fighting chance. Eventually, though, he'd grown restless, eager to move on.

25

"Let's get out of New York already," he'd urged. "Just hand in your notice, pack a bag, and let's go."

It was such a far-fetched plan—who abandons everything in her midtwenties to become a vagabond?—but a part of me ached to leave and see the world with him, to determine if the problems plaguing our relationship had everything to do with the extreme pressure of life in New York rather than some irreconcilable failure between the two of us.

I loved the possibility of adventure. I was still in love with him. But in the end, he couldn't commit to a future in the city and I couldn't bring myself to leave. So I let him go. After all that time, I didn't need a plane ticket or a stamp-riddled passport to know that he and I weren't meant to make certain journeys together.

Once Baker left, I wondered: How could I have ever considered leaving New York when I'd just gotten started?

The embers of my relationship still smoldering, I threw myself headlong into the new position I'd lobbied so hard to get. I couldn't work enough hours or take on enough tasks—no matter how mundane or unrelated to my career they might have been—to capture my attention and fill the void in my life. My higher-ups seemed delighted that their new nutrition assistant had little else to do besides spend her nights and weekends helping out at work.

Over time, the pain subsided, but my dedication to the magazine didn't. It occurred to me along the way that, unlike a relationship with a man, the more time and energy I poured into my job, the greater the satisfaction and reward I got out of it. It took only a year for me to get my first promotion (a subtle but important title change from editorial assistant to assistant editor), and when my boss broke the good news, she suggested it wouldn't be long before I got the next bump up—as long as I kept exceeding everyone's expectations.

The challenge had been proffered. So dedicated did I become to my job that I was willing to downgrade every other priority in order to put in more time at the office, to achieve that next level. Did I ever feel conflicted as I turned down trips to the beach with my girlfriends, guilty at blowing off night after night of friends' happy hours, or anxious over the fact that I hadn't left myself much time to go on dates with guys, let alone attempt a new relationship? Hardly a day went by that I didn't. But I'd gotten a later start than most. If I ever wanted to be viewed as something other than a mail-retrieving, phone-answering, yes-girl junior editor, I couldn't afford to slack off now. And if I got the promotion to associate and moved one more spot up the masthead, it really wouldn't matter what I'd given up to get there. I was still years away from my thirtieth birthday. There'd be plenty of time for family, friends, and new boyfriends then—right?

When I checked my messages on the last day of the trial, I had a voice mail from my executive editor, Helene, telling me that she wanted to discuss the associate spot as soon as I returned. Something in her voice threw me. I couldn't tell if she was being her typically reserved self or if something was wrong—but I couldn't wait until Monday to find out.

I forced myself to get through the closing arguments and the half-hour jury deliberation (unanimously not guilty! Now let's go!) without making it too obvious how much I wanted to run. Scrambling down the front steps of the courthouse, I dived down to the subway platform and slipped through the doors of the N train just before they slammed shut.

My body was shot through with adrenaline by the time I arrived at work. A few sidelong glances in the elevator reminded me that I hadn't dressed in uniform—I was wearing a pair of faded terry cloth pants and a long-sleeved tee—but I was too preoccupied to care that people were staring.

Rocketing past reception, I saw that my entire floor looked like a ghost town. Computer screens were on, proofs slung across desks—but no editors. I walked around until I spotted our office manager on the phone in her cubicle.

"Where is everybody?" I asked.

"Conference room," she mouthed, pointing down the hall.

The room was completely packed with both editorial staff and salespeople. I slipped in the back and shimmied in the direction of the other assistants. Our editor in chief, Beth, had just finished presenting the upcoming issue, something she did so the staff could get a sense of how the content in the whole magazine worked together. We'd had several of these presentations before, but never with champagne and chocolate-covered strawberries, which were reserved for baby and wedding showers and, occasionally, promotions.

Then it hit me. Were they going to announce the promotion? Now? I was suddenly mortified that I'd worn something so unkempt into a room full of fashion editors.

"Such an impressive issue, everyone. Thanks again for your hard work. I know you all have pages to attend to, places to be," said Beth. "But before you bolt out of here, I hope you'll join me in celebrating another piece of good news. Today I'm proud to announce the promotion of one of our hardworking assistants."

I glanced at Claire, who immediately looked away—and then I knew. There was no doubt in my mind that when Beth reached the end of her speech, it would not be my name that she announced. *Oh, my God, I have to get out of here.*

But there was simply no way I could escape without being noticed. There was no time. As everyone raised their glasses, Beth said how proud she was of Elizabeth Morton; no one would do a better job as the team's new associate editor. While everyone else sipped, I silently choked. I forced my throat not to close up and cut off my oxygen supply; I willed my eyes not to fill up with tears and commanded my body not to shake.

Mercifully, the meeting broke up, and at the earliest possible second, I made a beeline for the door. As I scurried away, miserable little hamster that I was, I felt a hand wrap around my upper arm and maneuver me down the hall to an office. It was my old boss, Kristen.

For once in my highly verbal life, I couldn't speak. I knew if I opened my mouth, torrents of tears and dammed-up emotions would come flooding out.

"I'm sorry, that was a terrible way to find out," she said. "Look, I know that Helene wanted to talk to you before you came in on Monday and heard it from someone else."

"But I don't get it, I just thought . . ." I managed to squeak. "Why?"

"Well, I think that Helene and Claire just have a few . . . concerns. I know they both wanted to talk to you sometime next week. We didn't think you'd be here today."

"Please, just tell me what's going on. I'd really just rather hear it from you so I can at least be prepared."

She sighed. "Well, it's not the end of the world. But it was a bit unprofessional that you never came in to work this past week. Everyone really feels that you should have taken care of your responsibilities and assignments, jury duty or not."

"You mean no one covered my section?" I was floored. "I was supposed to come in at night? After jury duty?"

She didn't say anything, but her silence confirmed it.

"I don't understand. Why didn't Claire just tell me that I needed to be here?" As the words left my mouth, I realized I already knew the answer. My bosses couldn't legally require me to come in after jury service—but a dedicated editor would have done it on her own.

29

"I think you should just meet with them," she said kindly. It was sinking in that things might be a lot worse for me than simply not being promoted.

An agonizing weekend and two weekdays passed, but the following Wednesday, I finally shut the sliding door to Helene's office and sunk into the chair next to Claire's. Helene, well known among our staff for being direct but fair, didn't waste precious seconds. "So, we want you to understand that you're not being let go—"

Let go?!

"—but in light of your recent performance, we're beginning to question whether you're really committed to your position at the magazine."

My head snapped left to get a read on Claire, who kept her eyes firmly forward.

"Claire has told me that since she's been your manager, you've been focusing on larger projects but neglecting your assistant duties. She says the newspapers don't get clipped daily, the mail hasn't been opened and distributed on time every morning. Is that correct?"

I knew it would be useless to explain that with the huge number of tasks on my plate—editing a monthly recipe section, writing features and front-of-book pages, running the internship program—sometimes phones didn't get answered on the first ring and I had to save clipping newspapers and opening boxes for the weekends.

I nodded, dejected.

"Well, okay then. What I have here is a list of the various areas where we"—she glanced over at Claire—"feel that your performance has been slipping. And you'll have one month to make improvements in these areas. If you can't, then we'll have to discuss whether or not this magazine is really the right place for you anymore."

Instantly I knew what was happening. I was being put on probation, the legal formality required before a company can show its undesirables the door. Here, when people were given a month to shape up, it was their cue to look for another job.

As Helene read slowly through the list, making comments after each point, I felt my body temperature start to rise along with her words. Fear ebbed away and was replaced with less polite emotions. She wrapped up her presentation and asked me if I had any questions or anything I'd like to say. You know, before the clock started ticking.

What *could* I say? That I really *was* a hard worker? That my mean new boss just didn't like me? That I couldn't possibly be on probation or lose this job, because the magazine was my whole life now? Please, please, pretty please don't fire me? The reins on my own future had been yanked from my grasp. There they were, dangling in front of me but just beyond reach. There was only one way I could think of to take them back—and so I did.

When I opened my mouth, instead of the Chernobyl-like explosion I feared, someone else's eerily collected words issued out: "Helene, I appreciate you letting me know about the areas where I could use improvement. Based on your feedback over the past two years, I really thought I'd been doing a good job, even exceeding your expectations. This is the first time that I'm hearing that I'm not."

I turned to my new boss, who still wouldn't look at me.

"Claire—I'm not sure why you didn't talk to me earlier. If I'd known that you wanted something done differently, I would have tried to fix it. But now I'm getting the feeling that it's already too late to make the changes that you want."

I dared myself to keep talking, knowing that if I stopped, I would never again be foolish enough to say what I did next.

"Helene, I've truly enjoyed working with this staff, and I've learned so much at this magazine. I don't think I need a whole month to get my act together. Please consider this conversation my two weeks' notice."

Ten minutes later, I was sitting at the Bryant Park sandwich kiosk, waiting for my friend and former coworker Stephanie, whom I had emergency-called on my flight from the building. By the time she got there, my face had already melted like sidewalk chalk after a downpour, streaks of charcoal, bronzer, and pastels rolling toward the gutters.

"*La-aaady*. What the heck happened to you?" Her jaw was agape as she approached. "You look like you got hit by a bus or something."

Indeed, I did feel as if I'd been pushed in front of an oncoming M15, but I wasn't surprised that she'd called my attention to it. Steph had never been the type to sugarcoat things, one of the main reasons I liked hanging out with her. Even now, as I hiccupped out the story of a pretty dismal few days, she gave me her unglazed opinion on the whole situation.

"So it sucks that you were put on probation instead of getting promoted. But seriously—what are you so upset about?" she asked.

"Well, for starters, I just lost my job."

"Hell, yeah, you did. But that's because you wanted to lose it."

I tried to correct her, but she cut me off.

"Come on," she said, in a familiar tone that indicated I was to cut the bullshit pronto. "You were the one who gave your notice. Tell me that you really wanted to stick around, that you were willing to do everything they were asking so you could keep your job."

"No, but I didn't want—" I dug a heel into the pavement.

"Look, I know that this seems like a really lousy situation right now, but give it a few weeks and you'll realize that it's so much better things worked out this way. That place was making you *miserable*. You're always working or stressed out that you should be working. I barely even see you anymore, and I sit four floors above you."

Ouch. She was right, but it still stung. I stared down at the black splotches of petrified gum polka-dotting the damp pavement, feeling a hot flush creep up my neck.

"But you know what's the best part about all of this?" she said. "You've been given this really cool, unexpected opportunity. This is your chance to cut the cord from work, to figure out something else to do with your life besides setting up base camp in your cubicle."

"You mean, like not get another job? What else am I supposed to do?"

"Anything—as long as it's different than what you've been doing every day for the past few years. Take some classes at the New School. Go on that big trip you've been talking about with Holly and Jen. E-mail editors and start freelancing. Haven't you told me that you want to break into travel writing?" She looked at me expectantly.

"Eventually, but there's no way I could do it now. You need to be, like, the next Bill Bryson to get an assignment from a major travel magazine. I'd have to get a lot more experience before I could even think of pitching a story to one of the glossies."

"And how are you going to get that experience if you're hanging out here?" Steph pressed. "You have to actually *leave* the island—and then you can write about the world."

Leave New York? The very thought threw me into a panic. I'd just lost my job; I didn't think I could handle losing my city, too.

"Regardless of what you decide to do from here, the hardest part is over. You may not have planned to leave, but you've outgrown your desk chair. It's so obvious; you're itching to challenge yourself, try new things. Don't you think?"

I was still too shaken to see the bigger picture. "I guess. Maybe."

"Don't talk craziness. Of course you are," she said, glancing down at the dial on her enormous watch. "Crap. I've got an interview that I've already rescheduled fifteen times. But don't worry. If you start to question whether you did the right thing, just ask yourself, 'Do I really need to work for a boss who wants me to improve my letter-opening skills?'"

It would have been kind of funny if it hadn't been so true. Steph gave me a quick squeeze and bolted across Sixth Avenue just before the light turned green. A fleet of taxis streaked across the intersection, and she was gone.

Unemployment felt like a spa getaway compared with my last two weeks at the magazine. Once I'd used the company FedEx number to ship my stuff three miles north to the Upper West Side (my final act of rebellion) and organized my files for the next assistant (to prove that I wasn't above it all), I found myself in workplace purgatory with no real responsibilities to call my own. Claire, who sat four feet from me, spoke to me only when vitally necessary. On my last day, she forced out a tight-lipped good-bye and slipped off without another word.

I knew I needed to put some kind of plan B into action. Common sense dictated that I update my résumé and scour career Web sites, but I found that I just couldn't bear the thought of interviewing for a job. The truth was, I felt completely unnerved by the possibility of landing another full-time staff position. If I accepted a job and failed to live up to expectations, the reason wouldn't be an insensitive boss or a miscommunication over jury duty—the problem would be me.

So I decided to blow off relative job security and guaranteed health insurance in order to give freelance writing a try, setting up shop with nothing more than my clunker of a laptop and some free business cards I scored from Vistaprint. I spent my wide-open days drafting e-mails to editors at other magazines to ask them if, by chance, they might have any small articles that needed to be written. I brainstormed ideas, wrote them up, and fired e-mails off into the ether. Several weeks went by without a single response or assignment, during which I started to become one with our futon. My roommates often returned home late at night to find me in the exact same position as they'd left me, eyes glazed over as I cradled the computer in my lap. Just as I was considering waitressing or temping or donating plasma—anything to avoid legitimate job hunting—I landed my first freelance assignment, a story for a kids' magazine on bizarre tales of heroism by family pets.

Shortly thereafter, a women's magazine editor asked me to write two pages on surprising ways your boyfriend could be making you sick (hint: friction is involved). Then a national newspaper assigned me a piece on how text messaging was transforming the face of dating and relationships. Within a few months, I'd secured enough work to keep me afloat and even put a chunk of cash away for a rainy day. I wasn't doing a ton of travel writing, but my freelance career had taken off.

So had my social life. For the previous two years, it had been on life support, barely breathing, but it made a quick turnaround once I left the office. For the first time since I could remember, I spent my free time catching up on friends' lives, rather than working through my bottomless to-do list. I accepted invitations to go to yoga classes and see movies. I arrived on time for happy hours instead of making excuses for missing them. I sharpened my pool skills, played darts, and rediscovered how to flirt. I went out on dates with inappropriate men, then commiserated with my girlfriends about the futility of finding a decent guy in Manhattan.

My days were laid back and calm, my nights intense and unpredictable. I stayed out far too late too often but no longer had trouble getting out of bed in the morning. I felt as if I'd moved to New York City all over again. But though I fully embraced this newfound freedom and felt more certain than ever that I'd made the right decision not to boomerang back into another job, I knew this couldn't be the endpoint of my transition. There had to be some other destination, some reason things had worked out exactly the way they had.

Again and again, I found that my thoughts turned to travel, the vagabonding bug I'd caught from Baker and the plans I'd made with Jen and Holly back in Argentina. I allowed myself to consider what would happen if our idea to backpack around the world—a concept that had seemed so ephemeral months earlier—ever solidified into reality. Exactly what would it take to set the wheels into motion? Could I really leave the life I'd created in New York to go backpacking like a college kid?

In theory, I guess I could. My lease expired in about a year. I didn't have a full-time job. Despite plenty of social activity, I'd yet to meet a guy I wanted to get serious with. I wasn't sure whether to feel thrilled or depressed that, at twenty-six, I didn't have a whole lot more tying me down than I had when I'd graduated.

Considering my commitment-free existence, I knew there would be few times in my life when it made more sense to travel. And I might have decided to do it on my own—or at least gone to Central America for a few months to hike through the rain forests, go to language school, and eat as many *frijoles negros* as my digestive system could handle—except that Jen and Holly sealed the deal for me.

The three of us had been meandering through the stalls at the 26th Street flea market, one of our favorite Saturday activities, when I asked them if they'd remotely consider making good on that wacky round-the-world idea we'd had at Iguazú Falls.

"Actually, I've been thinking about that a lot lately," Jen admitted.

"Me too," said Holly, looking up from a tray of garnet rings she'd been examining. "I was half kidding when I said I'd go, but for some reason, it doesn't really seem so far-fetched anymore. Would it really be so ridiculous to take a few months off before we all get tied down?"

"Not at all," said Jen as we strolled past a rack of vintage dresses. "For argument's sake, even if we started planning right now, we still wouldn't be able to get on the road until next summer. By then Brian and I will both be twenty-eight, and if we haven't determined our status at that point, I'm running away for sure."

"Oh, that's right . . . your age deadline." I said. "Look, you and Brian will figure things out. You'll have been together for nearly four years by then. I'm sure he hasn't been with you this long unless he figures you're marriage potential."

"That's the thing," she said softly, an odd note creeping into her voice. "What if I don't *want* to be marriage potential? If it doesn't work out and I'm single all over again—then what?"

Holly, always the first to find the silver lining in every situation, spoke up.

"Well, then, you *could* spend your time planning the biggest adventure of your life," she said, plopping a floppy hat with a massive brim on Jen's head. "I mean, what would you rather spend the money on—rubbery chicken cutlets for a hundred and fifty guests and a white wedding dress, or a round-the-world plane ticket?"

"Do I have to answer that now?" Jen laughed as she frisbeed the hat back at Holly. She placed it atop her own burgundy-streaked bob and flashed Jen a silly tilted-head grin.

"Well, maybe if we play our cards right, we can have the chicken cutlets *and* the world," I said, putting the hat back on the stand. "Just not in that order."

We shopped our way through the market and eventually emerged into the late-afternoon sunshine.

"Hey, guys," said Jen, walking between us. "About this trip. You know, I'm pretty sure I want to do it. Maybe not for a whole year, but I'd love to go back to South America. And maybe Kenya? You guys don't have to do it with me, but I've always wanted to volunteer there."

"Of course we'll do that with you!" Holly jumped in, her jade green eyes flashing. "I've always wanted to see Kenya too! And Tanzania. And Rwanda. Do you think we could go visit the gorillas while we're there?"

"Wait, are you being serious?" I asked, turning around so I could see the expression on both of my friends' faces. "Is this really an option? We're talking about a major life change here. As in quitting jobs. Leaving boyfriends. Living out of a backpack and sleeping in bunks and washing out your thongs in some grungy hostel sink. Not to mention staying together for months on end. Are we really ready to sign up for all of that?"

There was a long pause, and my heart started its downward descent. Hol and Jen glanced at each other, then back at me.

"Well, I'm totally serious," said Jen. "We've all traveled before and know what we're up against, underwear washing and all. And it's not like we're running away forever to, like, *live* with the gorillas or anything."

"All I know is, we'll never get another opportunity like this," said Holly. "I've backpacked on my own. I've done it with a boyfriend. I don't see how there's any way I could pass up the chance to travel with the two of you. I mean, if we don't decide to take a leap of faith and do it now, then when?"

"Well, if you're in," I said, almost afraid to believe what I was hearing—or saying. "So am I."

"Me too," said Jen, an irrepressible smile spreading across her features as she looked back and forth between Holly and me. "So I guess the only real question now is . . . when should we leave?"

CHAPTER THREE

Holly

Amanda was already waiting in the doorway of EJ's Luncheonette for Jen and me, shielding herself from the March winds that whipped between the buildings with enough force to push grown men backward.

"Holly!" she squealed, looking up from the celebrity gossip magazine she was reading and throwing her arms around me in a hug. Amanda has a way of making you feel like you're the most important person in the world simply by acting really, really excited to see you.

I loved that about her almost as much as I admired how she was so, well, ballsy. She was one of the only assistants who threw out her ideas in story meetings right along with women way higher up on the masthead, while I often kept mine to myself for fear of being shot down. She'd be the one to tell the guy who'd wedged a bar stool between us at happy hour that we weren't interested, while I'd fumble to make polite conversation.

Even though Amanda and I no longer shared an office, we saw each other more now than when we'd worked together, becoming closer friends who met every weekend for a yoga class or Sunday brunch.

As we dropped our arms, I asked, "So what do you think Jen's voice mail meant?"

Amanda's hazel-blue eyes clouded with worry. "Her message just said to come here for an emergency meeting about the trip. Oh, God, I think she changed her mind. Maybe we're not really going." My chest tightened. I hadn't even considered that.

It'd taken me a long time to get to the place where I'd felt I was really ready to pack up my life to explore the world. Soon I'd be moving from town to town and country to country, and the only home I'd know would be my backpack. If home is truly where the heart is, as the old saying goes, what did that mean for me? Is home a physical place, a familiar spot where you can stay in your PJs until noon and eat peanut butter straight from the jar? Or is it more of a feeling, like knowing where to find safety in an unpredictable world?

For the past four years, I'd considered New York my home. So in a way, home for me wasn't a specific address. The reason New York felt so right was that it was like a hundred countries squeezed into a single island. It was a land where Wall Street brokers bumped up against Mexican busboys on the subway; the scent of falafel mixed with dim sum in the East Village; and horse-drawn carriages shared the road with racing bikes in Central Park. I'd fallen in love with the energy in Manhattan. And then I'd fallen out of love with it. And then I'd fallen all over again. New York was like an addictive relationship—when it was good, it was really, really good. But when it was bad, it made me feel like I was on sensory overload, threatening to pull me under until I lost myself. Even the places I'd typically retreat to for solitude—parks that smelled of fresh-cut grass or the lumpy futon that took up my entire living room—felt crowded and confining. Sometimes I just needed more space.

When I'd first moved to Manhattan from Marcellus, New York, at the age of twenty-four, I'd accepted a position as an assis-

41

tant "happiness" editor at a national women's magazine. Though I'd always had an interest in psychology, I was suddenly required to research and write about self-fulfillment all day, every day. My job was to examine happiness and to ask, what exactly *is* happiness? Is it something you should allow to happen naturally, without thought, like breathing or your heartbeat? Or is it something you should search for, like a dream job or the love of your life?

So I spent eleven hours a day in a cubicle searching for those answers. I wrote stories like "Find Out What Drives You: Be Happier from 9 to 5" and "Boost Joy with a Gratitude Journal." Soon my favorite moments at the office were those spent brainstorming ideas on how to turn your aspirations into reality and reading the latest studies in psychology journals.

I'd stay at work long after the phones had stopped ringing and the lights had dimmed, rushing to meet deadlines for stories on five-minute stress busters. I'd research tricks for curbing emotional eating ("Take a bath!" or "Call a friend!"), neither of which I ever found time for myself. So I'd reach into my desk's food drawer to soothe myself with Snickers and caramel corn.

When I forgot what I was working so hard for, I tried to take the advice of the happiness experts I interviewed by thinking of all the reasons to be grateful. If I hadn't moved to New York, I'd never have been able to work in one of the world's largest publishing companies. I'd probably be filing boring office forms instead of getting paid to read the latest happiness literature (which I'd have done for free). Maybe I'd be reporting on a local fender bender, as I had when I'd interned for a small newspaper in college, rather than, say, interviewing women about what makes life meaningful or testing out guided meditation techniques on DVD.

I was learning even more than I had in school, writing stories that reached millions of women, expensing my lunches, and riding black Town Cars to parties paid for by the company.

Everything seemed right in my life, but a current of restlessness ran through my veins that nothing I did—from taking on extra writing assignments to occupy my mind to training for a marathon to push my body or going to a rooftop barbecue with friends to chill out—could extinguish.

The person who most understood my drive to find a deeper meaning in it all was Elan, my live-in boyfriend. Just breathing him in made me feel more relaxed—when I actually saw him, that is. As a graduate acting student, he was in an equally demanding program with a class schedule that constantly changed. The fact that we both clocked long hours in an effort to achieve our individual dreams also served as a kind of glue to hold our relationship together. Most significant others might feel neglected by a partner who channeled more time and energy into launching his or her career than advancing the relationship, but Elan and I saw it as a necessary sacrifice at that point in our lives.

Years earlier, I'd met him at a friend's birthday party in a smoky club in the West Village. I remember it was a Friday night; I'd worked till 8 p.m. and hadn't wanted to go out at all. My sister Sara, who lived with two of my college friends and me in a railroad apartment, had practically pulled me out by both hands because she thought I'd been spending too much time at the office. I glanced back at our lumpy futon as the door clicked shut behind us, wanting nothing more than to wear my favorite sweatpants and sink down into the couch eating popcorn. I hadn't expected to make it until midnight, let alone meet a love who would take my breath away. But New York does that. It can wear you down, and then—just when you feel like collapsing—it'll jolt you back with the best night of your life.

Magnetized by Elan's deep, soulful eyes and shock of anarchist curls, we ditched the friends we'd come with to spend hours huddled together in the corner of the dance floor. I remember our voices grew hoarse; we were spilling over ourselves to share our stories. I remember leaning in close to hear him above the music, catching the scent of his sweat in the humidity, and how it sent a charge through me that reached all the way to my toes.

When he called three days later (which seemed like an eternity to me then), we spent the entire following weekend together. We kissed as if we couldn't get enough on an empty bench in Central Park, sipped lattes at a sidewalk café in Little Italy, and lay on the roof of my Upper East Side apartment trying to find the brightest stars not eclipsed by the city lights. It took less than three weeks before he said he loved me. I felt the same way. It was instantaneous, a force I couldn't fight even if I'd wanted to. It felt as though we'd known each other before we even knew each other.

Three years had gone by so fast. We were still together and sharing an apartment in the hipster neighborhood of Williamsburg, Brooklyn. We'd go on long bike rides, stopping on a cobblestone street near the Manhattan Bridge at Jacques Torres, my favorite chocolate shop. We'd spend five hours on a Wednesday night spooning on the couch and watching *Lost* DVDs before I'd fall asleep in his arms. We'd pick tomatoes from the garden he grew on our patio to cook dinner on Sunday nights (which we'd divide into Tupperware containers to use for lunches during the week). We fought, too, over typical relationship issues, like his staying out late and not calling or one of us blowing off a date to work. Sometimes I wondered when we'd stop making our careers the thing we focused on the most and when our relationship would come first. Still, the mundane stuff, those little ordinary moments, seemed deeper with Elan next to me.

Have you told Elan about the trip yet?" Jen had asked a couple months before. I'd trekked into the city from Brooklyn one slushy afternoon to meet her at the Adventures in

Travel Expo at the Javits Center for yet another trip-planning expedition. Since getting promoted at another women's magazine, I had finally mastered the art of work-life balance. I was as in love with Elan as ever. But still I went.

"Of *course* I've told Elan!" I'd said in surprise—it hadn't occurred to me not to. But when I glimpsed Jen's crestfallen face, I'd hoped I hadn't been too insensitive. "Um, I mean, yeah, we've talked about it. Have you told Brian?"

"Not exactly," she said, nervously scratching her arm. It was the first time Jen and I had been alone without Amanda, who was out of town, and it felt as if we were on a first date. But instead of gauging whether we would upgrade from drinks to a full-fledged dinner, we were both weighing whether we could commit to talking, eating, and sleeping with this new person for 365 consecutive days.

"I've hinted that I may want to travel to South America this summer with you and Amanda," Jen continued. "But I haven't told Brian I'm actually going on the trip—yet. How did Elan take it?"

"Surprisingly well."

"Seriously? How'd you break it to him?"

Telling Elan about the trip hadn't been easy, of course. I'd brought it up one lazy Sunday morning when he was lying next to me in our bed, an arm thrown over his brown eyes to shield them against the light filtering in through the plastic blinds. All sharp angles and smooth skin like one of those Roman statues I'd studied in art history classes, his face still mesmerized me. I could look at it a million times, try to etch his features permanently into my mind, but then he'd turn and the shape of his nose or curve of his lips seemed to shift and I'd see him again as if for the first time. It was always like that with him: just when I thought I knew him, I'd suddenly glimpse him from a totally different vantage point.

I'd wanted to stay silent and keep my head buried in that safe haven on his shoulder. It was one of those beautifully simple moments where the way I wanted things to be and the way they actually were were one and the same. I felt the rise and fall of Elan's chest as he breathed rhythmically and heard the hissing of the radiator straining to heat the icy air that penetrated the thin walls of our apartment.

Mustering up the courage to tell him about my extended trip plans, I'd braced myself for the high probability of a breakup. Or, more likely, the knowledge that if he truly wanted me to stay, I would. But he didn't dump me; the two traits I admired most about Elan—his independence and open-mindedness—shone through. "It sounds like the opportunity of a lifetime. I think it could be one of the best things you could ever do," he'd said softly after a few torturous moments of silence, my hand tightly grasping his beneath the blanket. For a microsecond a doubt flashed through my mind: *If he really loved me, he wouldn't let me go.* Then it vanished just as quickly as it had come. Was I completely nuts? My boyfriend was actually *supporting* my big adventure, and here I was second-guessing his love.

"Hol, if two people are meant to be together, going after your dream is not going to change that," he'd said, putting his arm around my waist and pulling me closer. He'd said that someday he might accept a role that'd take him away. And there'd probably be many more times in life when one of us would want to chase a big goal. He stopped for a second as my body relaxed against his in relief. He rationalized that, in the end, it'd just make our relationship stronger because we'd really understand who we were and what we wanted to do.

I fell a little deeper for him then, completely grateful for granting me the opportunity to explore without taking back his love. In fact, we'd decided that my time on the road would be the perfect shot for him to go after his own dream by temporarily moving to L.A. to pursue his acting career. It felt as though everything made perfect sense.

As I tried to explain the winding path Elan and I had walked to come to that understanding, Jen was uncharacteristically mute. It made me realize that, until that moment, she hadn't let a millisecond of silence hang between us—not even pausing to breathe between sentences. I let it hang.

Finally she said, "Um, that's really highly evolved of him. I *know* Brian won't be that supportive." She hoisted her now-overflowing bag of brochures higher on her shoulder.

"How's it going for you two?" I asked, accepting a flyer from a tourist operator for safaris in Kenya.

"Honestly, we've been fighting so much the past few months I'm not even sure if we'll make it to the summer," she said, her blue eyes growing darker and her eyebrows drawing together in worry.

"Oh, Jen, I'm so sorry," I said, biting my lip. "Is it because of the trip?"

"It's just everything! I've been with this guy for over three years and love him to death, but how do you know when you find the person you're supposed to spend forever with? Everyone keeps asking me when he's going to propose!"

I was silent for a second myself, not really knowing what to say. Though I never lusted after the proverbial white dress and wedding bells, I could definitely relate to the pressure she was feeling. My own mother was questioning my motives after I had signed a second lease with Elan without the security of a ring on my finger. "Why would he step up to the plate when you're already giving him everything for free?" she'd asked. I'd told her that the rules of love and marriage had changed since her generation, and I was living my life as I wanted. Since I didn't know what to say to Jen, I said nothing and instead reached out to squeeze her shoulder to let her know I understood.

Somehow it didn't seem strange to launch right into such a personal topic with Jen, who wasn't one to hold back whatever she was feeling when she felt it. Before our vacation to Argentina last year, I'd seen Jen only a few times at group happy hours. She kept her golden brown hair blown out straight, usually wore at least one item in a shade of pink, and almost matched my height of 5 feet 4 inches (okay, 5 feet 3¾ inches) without her three-inch heels. But she also didn't seem like the typical girly girl: she laughed hard, spoke loud, and tended to voice the uncensored version of her thoughts. Since then I'd learned a bit more, like that Jen was a film addict with a flair for the dramatic herself. With her resonant voice and sweeping gestures, she struck me as a modern-day Katharine Hepburn. While Amanda was definitely ballsy, her quicksilver emotions gave her an air of vulnerability, while Jen's tendency toward total openness made her come across as almost fearless to me. So it also seemed fitting that she'd committed to such a big adventure.

"Come to India!" a woman with henna-stained hands and a scarlet sari beckoned, waving a brochure with an "Om" symbol.

"I *really* want to go to India!" I said to Jen excitedly.

"Have you ever been before?" she asked.

"Yeah, once in college during this study-abroad program called Semester at Sea. But I've only seen the southern part and really want to go to yoga school near the Himalayas."

And so the endless possibilities of the open road began weaving their way down almost every pathway in my mind as we continued walking through the labyrinth of exhibits. I listened to Jen tell me how she and Amanda had met in their freshman dorm and hit it off instantly, but it wasn't until departing on a postgrad backpacking trip through Europe that they had truly bonded. And after an incredible six-country tour in four weeks, they'd vowed to be travel partners for life.

Jen rattled off all the misadventures they'd shared—getting hopelessly lost on the outskirts of Venice, attacked by killer gnats on a bike ride in Bruges, stranded at a station in Antwerp after boarding the wrong Eurorail train, and caught pilfering hotel rolls and jam after breakfast hours by an irate Frenchman.

"I always said that we could never go to Thailand together or we'd likely get thrown in jail accidentally, like Claire Danes's and Kate Beckinsale's characters in *Brokedown Palace*—and even our friendship isn't worth that," Jen joked, dramatically flipping her hair.

I'd imagined what it would have been like if I'd met them back then on my own postcollege backpacking tour of Europe. Then my mind fast-forwarded to the three of us taking on the world, seeing wildebeest while hiking in the Serengeti or sitting next to monks in a Buddhist temple in Tibet.

As we walked, Jen and I collected brochures to plan our dream itinerary and took turns asking the country reps questions, such as what time of year was best to visit and whether the country required a visa for entry. Every booth we passed represented another new adventure we might actually get to experience on the road. My imagination started circling the globe at warp speed—Peru, the Seychelles, China! I wanted to see them all. As I was plotting how we might take a ship from South America to Antarctica, Jen placed a hand decorated with a dainty pink ring on my shoulder, and for the first time in our brief acquaintance she struck me as maternal. "Um, how 'bout we narrow it down just a bit. Is there anywhere you *don't* want to go?"

I smiled sheepishly. Okay, we were back into first-date territory, but I sensed we were in it for the long haul. When Jen and Amanda had first thrown out the idea to go on a yearlong trek around the globe, I knew they'd somehow change the way I saw the world, even if I didn't fully believe we'd all be crazy enough to actually circle it together. Even after telling Elan about the trip, I'd still feel torn about leaving a life of comfort and security for the great unknown. But as Jen and I roamed the expo hall vibrating with exotic music, food, and flags, I began to believe the journey could actually happen. It ignited the wanderlust that often simmered underneath my skin. There's a Buddhist saying that goes "Leap, and the net will appear." I didn't understand what the restlessness was that was driving me, but I was compelled to take the leap. I could only have faith that there would be a net to catch me if I fell.

N ow, seeing the worry in Amanda's eyes as the March wind whipped around us outside EJ's, I convinced myself in a matter of seconds that the trip wasn't going to happen and that it had all seemed way too good to be true. Then Amanda gazed past me, and I spun around to see Jen approaching, her eyes hidden behind dark sunglasses.

"You're backing out of the trip, aren't you?" Amanda wailed as soon as Jen got within earshot. Suddenly I was just as concerned about Amanda as I was about Jen because she was wringing her fingers in panic. Amanda could be like a kaleidoscope of emotions, shifting from excited to nervous to feisty in a single moment.

Jen let out a little laugh, but there wasn't any joy in it. "No, the total opposite, actually." She slid off her sunglasses, and I could see that her eyes were puffy and face was splotchy red. "Brian and I had a big fight. I told him about the trip, and he lost it," she said.

"I'm so sorry, Jen." I instinctively put my arm around her.

"What happened? What did he say?" Amanda asked, putting her arm around Jen's other side. Jen resignedly leaned into us but then straightened resolutely and motioned toward the restaurant entrance. "Let's grab a table so we can sit and talk."

As we pushed through the double glass doors and the door-bell clanged to announce our entrance, we were blasted with warm, cinnamon-scented air. Once inside the booth, I glanced at Jen. I noticed that her clothes were uncharacteristically wrinkled and imagined her slipping into them after grabbing them off Brian's floor in a hasty getaway. Her eyes had that pained, bloodshot look of someone who knew she was about to lose her best friend. I didn't want her to feel the inevitable emptiness that comes after a man—who has been the last person you've spoken to before falling asleep each night for years—has exited your life. Though I hadn't been there when she and Brian had first met, I sensed how much she cared for him.

I gripped the edge of the padded seat, preparing for Jen to start crying, but she surprised me. Rather than rehashing every minute detail like usual, she gave us the CliffsNotes version of her past twenty-four hours with Brian. After a sleepless night filled with tears and talking (and some shouting), they'd both decided to take things one day at a time and see how they felt after she traveled for the first two months. And until then, they weren't going to make any rash decisions.

"Taking it day by day is probably the best thing to do," I said, squeezing her hand and thinking that a gradual phaseout might be less painful than a quick break. Travel would give Jen and Brian both physical and emotional distance, and that might help them figure out what they really wanted.

Then I gave her the same advice I'd given myself many times: "You can always change your mind and come home if you decide that's best once you're on the road for a bit."

Amanda quickly broke in. "And it sounds trite, but if it's really meant to be with you and Brian, you'll figure something out. Even if you *do* stay on the trip the full year. He could come visit you. You could come back here a couple times if you had to. Or maybe you could meet somewhere halfway."

51

"Yeah, I think I just need to take my mind off it and get back to the trip planning," Jen said, her voice cracking slightly.

"Are you sure?" Amanda asked. "Do you really want to do this now?"

Jen nodded, so I reached for my laptop and sat it next to the mugs of coffee we'd already half downed. Then I pulled from my overflowing tote bag stacks of brochures we'd collected at the travel expo, pens, notebooks, and the Lonely Planet and Let's Go guidebooks.

"Think about it, this can be the year to live our dreams," I said enthusiastically. "Most people never get a chance like this in their entire life. Imagine all the things you want to do and places you want to see." I paused for a minute, chewing my lower lip as I thought. "I have an idea. Let's each make a sort of dream list, and then we can compare notes. Like for me, I really want to learn how to meditate in India. Write down whatever and don't censor yourself."

I stopped when I saw Jen and Amanda staring at me. *Do they think I'm crazy? Or just a hippie dreamer?*

But then Jen eased my self-consciousness with another one of her smiles. "I think that's a great idea," she said as Amanda nodded.

I tore three sheets of paper from my spiral notebook and handed them out with pens. Then we busied ourselves writing and dreaming so much we barely noticed when the waitress set pancakes dusted with powdered sugar and omelets framed with sausage links on our table. As our food grew cold, I finally looked up from my notes and asked, "So what have you got?"

Jen started with "I've always wanted to go on a safari in Kenya. And I absolutely want to do some kind of volunteer program there."

Amanda chimed in. "I want to practice my Spanish and to hike the Inca Trail in Peru."

They both turned to me. "You already know I want to study at an ashram in India. I've always wanted to see Angkor Wat in Cambodia and climb a glacier in New Zealand. And if I'm going around the world, I *have* to get certified to scuba dive." I paused to take a breath and realized they were both staring at me again. "I think we can fit it all in if we travel forever," I joked, and they laughed.

Until that day, the three of us had only fantasized about where we wanted to go. But with the weight of keeping a big secret from Brian off Jen's shoulders, it seemed the time was right to turn our dreams into action. So, in our favorite comfort food spot, we started constructing an itinerary. And that's how our crazy scheme began to take root in reality.

Over the next couple hours, we volleyed ideas about an exact route and the number of weeks we'd like to spend in each country and estimated how much money we'd need to save to cover everything from flights and vaccines to lodging and supplies. As I was the one with the least cash of the three of us, money had been my biggest concern (second only to leaving Elan). To make up for it, I'd been channeling the bigger paychecks I'd gotten from my promotion into a separate savings account. After all, I couldn't spend my raise if I didn't see it. Plus, I'd figured that trip or no trip, building a nest egg was a smart idea. And combined with taking on extra freelance assignments and skipping luxuries like eating out, I'd saved more money than I'd ever dreamed possible in the past eight months: almost $6,000. At that rate, I'd have $10,000 by the time we left.

The seemingly daunting task of coordinating such an extensive trip actually proved easier than we'd expected once we divided the duties by three. Throughout our planning session, our individual travel roles also began to take root. As the group dreamer, I threw out ideas about where to go and what to do. Amanda, the regulator, took charge of narrowing down the options. And Jen, the organizer, worked out the details. I was impressed with Jen's borderline obsession for charts and spreadsheets as I watched her type up timelines and use Excel spreadsheets to record estimated trip expenses so we'd have some concept of our budget.

The sparse selection of books we managed to find on round-the-world (or RTW) trips all warned against trying to plan too far in advance. And my philosophy was not to lock ourselves into a rigid itinerary because we couldn't possibly know what cool things we might discover along the way. So we decided to follow the guides and map out the year loosely but focus on only the first couple regions of the world to start.

When Amanda first threw out the idea of taking this trip, her sole motivation was to explore South America and experience Latin culture, so that was the logical place to begin. Not wanting to overextend ourselves, we chose the two countries we most wanted to visit, Peru and Brazil, and allotted two months' total for both. "So let's start by buying our plane tickets to South America," Amanda said, and Jen nodded.

I felt a surge of panic run through me. Once we bought these tickets, the trip would be 100 percent real and there would be no turning back. I'd actually be leaving my life as I knew it—and the man I loved—for an entire year. But I'd also be spending that time living a dream instead of sitting behind a desk. Plus, we'd talked about it so much that I couldn't back out now. "Okay, let's do it," I agreed, sounding far more sure than I felt.

Covertly pirating a stray Wi-Fi signal, we plunked down our credit cards and took the first of many anticipated financial plunges. For less than $400 each, we secured one-way flights to Lima, arbitrarily selecting a June departure on the cheapest date available.

Having a plan seemed to take Jen's mind off her troubles with Brian. She pleaded with us to take it one step further and charge the mandatory deposit to reserve spaces with an Inca trail operator. Maybe she needed a greater incentive to keep from backing out of the trip. Maybe she figured if she put her money where her mouth was, she'd be less likely to change her mind. Maybe that was the only way for all three of us to actually take the leap.

※

CHAPTER FOUR

Jen

LIMA AIRPORT/CUSCO, PERU

JUNE

S till . . . no . . . bag!" Holly exclaimed, a wide-eyed expression spreading across her flushed face. The baggage carousel spun in futility, tormenting us with a rotation of the same three deserted suitcases and mangled boxes tattooed with crimson THIS END UP and FRAGILE warnings.

"Okay, Corbett. Give us the play-by-play. What's happening?" Amanda said, her pocket-sized camcorder poised to capture every action and emotion of the long-awaited kickoff to our round-the-world trip.

So far we'd explored a dizzying array of international terminals, departure lounges, and overstuffed planes but had yet to set foot on foreign soil. No matter. We had 364 days of incredible adventure and never-ending thrills ahead of us. Assuming we ever got the hell out of Jorge Chávez International Airport, that is.

"Well, we just landed here in Lima and we already have a lost luggage crisis," Holly explained, hamming it up for our inaugural Peru video.

"I'm just curious, Holly. Why do you think *our* bags made it here and yours didn't?" Amanda inquired, feigning bewilderment.

"I already told you. I tried to get the vaccine out of my bag during our layover in Miami, but they wouldn't let me," Holly replied, referring to the final dose of typhoid prevention meds she'd meant to stash in her carry-on but had left in the side pocket of her checked bag.

"That's crazy. Why would the most savvy drug sniffers in America be suspicious of an unmarked vial of liquid packed in a thermos of ice?" I asked, throwing my arm over her shoulders to buffer my sarcasm. "Don't worry, though. I promise we'll get your bag back."

"Definitely, Hol. I'm on it," Amanda said, turning the camera on herself to sign off.

As Amanda marched over to the customer service counter, Holly and I plopped down on the dingy floor tiles, resting side by side against a row of abandoned skycap carts with weary grins spreading across our faces. After all the fantasizing and planning and whirlwind good-byes, the day we'd all been waiting for had finally arrived. We weren't going to let anything bring us down.

Sitting there with Holly, I could hardly fathom all that had transpired since the last time we had been in South America together. I'd returned from our Argentina vacation refreshed and full of hope, throwing myself headlong into my new job. Before long, my career was soaring high, but unfortunately, things with Brian had plummeted to an all-time low. Our minor squabbles were upgraded to knock-down, drag-out fights, and, more times than I care to remember, we'd hurled out angry threats about taking time apart or breaking up altogether. Neither of us was quite ready or willing to disband the safe and comfortable partnership we'd built together, so we'd eventually kiss and make up, fading our confrontations into the background for weeks on end.

Each time I'd believed that the answers would just *have* to reveal themselves over the course of the year, but as the months ticked by, it became painfully clear that no mythical relationship fairy was going to sprinkle magic dust over us. Suddenly, the round-the-world trip that Amanda, Holly, and I had fantasized about at Iguazú Falls felt like my salvation from a precarious and uncertain future. I'd been dating the same guy for nearly half a decade and still wasn't sure if "till death do us part" would ever roll off our tongues. Maybe some distance—from Brian, from New York City, from the status quo—was the only way to know for certain.

I longed to feel as inspired and alive as I had when I'd made the radical move to Manhattan with only two suitcases and a sliver of space on Amanda's living room floor. And since I never wanted to feel as if I'd given something up to get married and settle down, it was now or never to do something drastic. So from the second I'd told the girls I was in, I'd never had a moment's pause about committing to the trip.

It's not to say that the long road to departure hadn't been a bumpy one. But since boarding up my Manhattan life weeks ago—all that was left of my earthly possessions wedged in my parent's minivan—I'd felt only giddiness and enthusiastic anticipation for the journey to come. And though I figured pangs of fear or sorrow, even regret might rear their ugly heads eventually, right now I was happy to pretend that Amanda, Holly, and I were merely embarking on another extraordinary South American vacation. Luckily, Amanda returned with good news: Holly's bags were on the next flight from Miami and would be delivered to our hostel that night. With that, the three of us finally escaped the baggage area and headed toward our first of many customs lines.

After a perfunctory two-day sweep of Lima—our designated hub during our six-week Peruvian sampler—we found ourselves back at the airport. Travel weariness mostly alleviated and three backpacks tucked safely into the belly of a tiny local aircraft, Amanda, Holly, and I began the 350-mile journey to Cusco.

Perched among the clouds high in the Andes, the ancient "City of the Sun" was infinitely more breathtaking than we'd imagined. We reached the town center just as dawn began to wriggle its way through the frosted mountain peaks. Emerging from the dingy airport shuttle into the sun-soaked Plaza de Armas, we felt like Dorothy and Toto first discovering Technicolor. A vibrant kaleidoscope of emerald-painted fountains, freshly pruned flower gardens exploding with every color, lollipop peddlers, and rosy-cheeked "munchkins" swaddled in patchwork shawls twirled around us.

The Baroque-style Cusco Cathedral and historic Church of La Compañía de Jesús stood watch over the cobblestone square. Rainbow-striped flags soared above whitewashed buildings with sapphire and cobalt blue doorways. Shrunken grandmothers in traditional Quechua garb coaxed llamas into tourists' photos in exchange for a few soles. One thing was for sure: Cusco was certainly no place like home.

Eager to shed our forty-pound portable closets and do some exploring, we yanked out our *Let's Go Peru* to find directions to Loki hostel, a supposed backpackers' paradise I'd booked online weeks before. Following a crude street map, we slowly navigated the narrow brick roads until we reached a steep, crumbling staircase that stretched endlessly toward the crystal blue skyline. A staggering 11,000 feet (estimated) above sea level, Cusco's dramatically high elevation could send even the toughest Olympic athlete into a full-blown wheezing fit. Between the weight of our backpacks and the much thinner mountain air, Amanda, Holly, and I were short of breath before we'd barely broken in our new hiking shoes. Though we'd built in two weeks to acclimatize before attempting to brave the Inca Trail, at this point I now wasn't sure if that was enough time.

"Does anyone kinda feel like they want to die?" I sputtered. "I mean, it's been a couple weeks since I hit the gym, but this is ridiculous."

"Don't worry, it's not just you. I was running six miles a day before we left, and I can barely walk right now," Holly replied.

"Yeah, Jen, where is this place? Are we there yet? Are we there yet?" Amanda added.

Just then we heard a low rumble and crunching gravel behind us. We managed to waddle to safety just as a rusty taxicab sped past us and fishtailed to a screeching halt fifty feet up the hill. From the thick cloud of road dust emerged a youthful gang of gringos who effortlessly hoisted their packs from the trunk and disappeared through a hidden doorway.

"Ladies, I think we're on the right track," I said, a newfound burst of energy propelling me toward the finish line.

Though it's always a bit of a risk to book a hostel sight unseen, luckily for us, Loki was truly a high-mountain oasis, boasting a TV room, bar, and huge common area that provided the warm welcome and fireplace the girls and I needed for the bargain-basement price of $8.50 per person per night. It was too early to claim our bunks, so we stowed our bags in a secure closet and headed back down the hill in pursuit of one of the cozy cafés we'd spotted earlier in the plaza. Overwhelmed by the barrage of ticket touts and vendors pushing menus, we quickly settled on a quaint wooden lodge advertising a warm fireplace and prix fixe menus for 12 soles. We could hardly fathom that a $4 meal would be remotely satisfying, but for less than the cost of a Starbucks latte, we feasted on thick vegetable soup, *pollo a la plancha* (grilled chicken) with rice and French fries, and *frutas tropicales*.

Throughout the meal, we religiously sipped steamy mugs of *mate de coca*, local tea brewed with coca leaves and boiling water that our guidebook recommended as a natural herbal cure for altitude sickness. By the time the bill arrived, we felt surprisingly less dizzy and nauseated. At least, we did until Holly returned from the bathroom, passed off our shared roll of toilet paper and hand sanitizer, and announced that we were dealing with a "one-star" situation.

During our brief stint in Lima, we'd developed our own unique restroom-rating system, defining a rare "four-star" establishment as one with running water, toilet paper, soap, and paper towels. Unfortunately, one to two stars seemed to be the standard so far, so we added a couple important commandments: (1) Thou shalt not leave the hostel without something to wipe thy ass and cleanse thy fingers and (2) Thou shalt wait until meal's end to do thy business and/or refrain from announcing the star status so as not to spoil the appetite of anyone in the party.

With visions of food poisoning dancing in our heads, we returned to the chaotic land of Cusco to log some sightseeing before our Loki check-in time. Although we couldn't afford even one woolly mitten in the upscale retailers lining the plaza, there was no harm in playing tourist and window shopping. Craving an escape from the shockingly brisk Peruvian winter wind, we dipped into Werner & Ana, a cozy boutique filled with scarves, hats, and sweaters woven from the soft fur of Peru's ubiquitous alpaca, an adorable animal that could be the downy-soft love child of a llama and a sheep.

Determined to practice our Spanish, we bumbled through initial greetings and salutations with the petite store owner, Ana, and her friend Didie, a handsome local who looked to be in his midtwenties, before they switched to English entirely.

"So you have *las alas* for tonight, yes?" Didie asked.

"I'm sorry, *no comprendemos*. We don't understand," Amanda said, trying to make sense of the exchange.

"Each year there is a very big, very famous party at the Fallen Angel club in this evening. My friend is the owner and gave me extra passes to enter," he said, pulling red paper wristbands out of his pocket. "Here. You take three so you can go to the party."

"Oh, okay. *Muchas gracias*," Amanda replied, graciously accepting the scarlet strips and placing them in her pocket.

"But what was that you said, *las alas*?" I asked.

"Ahh, those are wings. You know, like an angel has," he said, making flapping motions with his arms. "Everyone must have some to get in, so you will need to buy or construct them."

Later, still laughing about the strange scene that had transpired, we breathlessly made our way back up the hill toward the hostel. Was this mysterious Fallen Angel party a real thing? If so, was it safe for us to attend? Stepping into Loki, we got our answers. Scattered across every available surface of the TV room were piles of panty hose, wire coat hangers, feathers, and glue sticks. In the few hours we'd been away, hordes of sleepy backpackers had come out of hibernation and were feverishly constructing what could only be interpreted as . . . *las alas*.

"Helloooo, Charlie's Angels," called a random voice from the doorway. "You must be new recruits here at Loki."

Simultaneously turning to locate the source of such unabashed cheesiness, the girls and I were met by a serious Don Juan–abee, fully equipped with mirrored aviator shades, a shrunken Hanes T-shirt, and what appeared to be a never-ending supply of hair gel.

"Yeah, we just checked in. And let me guess. You wanna play Charlie?" Amanda threw back.

"Oh, touché, girls, touché! I'm Anthony, but it'd be a lot cooler if you called me Charlie," he replied, his bleached teeth aglow against his overly bronzed complexion. "But seriously, welcome to Loki. It's a very happening place to be. I'm going on my fourth week here and just may never leave."

63

"Yeah, we all keep trying to get rid of the bloke, but he just won't take the hint!" a boyishly handsome Brit interjected, knocking Anthony out of the way. "But we told him he could come with us to get costumes for tonight. Wanna come too?"

After dumping our bags in our assigned dorm, Amanda, Holly, and I rejoined our new hostelmates and headed out the door. Cramming into a few passing cabs, we made a beeline to Cusco's piñata district, where it was rumored that shopkeepers had immense supplies of premade angel gear prepared for that night's festivities.

Along with Anthony and the Brit, James, we were joined by a friendly gaggle of guys and dolls from around the globe, including Stuart, a sarcastic and wildly flirtatious Irishman; Andrew, a pensive, soft-spoken German on summer break from university; Nate and William, two hilarious stoner dudes and rugby extraordinaires from Liverpool (whom I never could keep straight); and Lara, an excitable Portuguese model type who chattered on about the makeup and hair products she'd scored in town.

The group was surprised to discover that (a) we were American, not Canadian, as they'd speculated, (b) we had dared to venture beyond the standard Caribbean or European destinations, and (c) we'd taken an entire year off work to visit mostly third-world countries.

"Wow, guess for Americans that's a pretty big deal. Seems like your countrymen are a bit closed-minded about this sort of travel, yeah?" Nate said.

I wasn't sure if I should be flattered or offended, but before I had a chance to argue, Anthony belted from the front seat, "Hey, you know that I'm American too? From Queens, in fact, which makes us neighbors, ladies!"

"Oh, please don't hold that against us," I joked as Anthony grinned and made a dramatic dagger-through-the-heart motion.

Luckily, the taxi soon pulled to a stop on Avenida del Sol, where we began our hunt for ethereal accessories. After scoring enough heavenly couture to ensure our entry into the party, we returned to Loki to transform ourselves from hostel misfits to celestial city dwellers. Decked out in full regalia—sparkly gossamer wings, dramatically painted faces, and the one dress we each had brought along—Amanda, Holly, and I fluttered through the frosty night air. Joined by a winged cast of hundreds, we crossed Fallen Angel's gothic threshold and entered a netherworld of Heaven-, Hell-, and Purgatory-themed rooms in a designer venue that could've rivaled any back in the Manhattan.

Upon arrival, we were immediately swept into an underground brick lair bathed in crimson light and filled with a trippy assortment of heart-shaped leather couches, zebra-striped pillows, and wrought-iron candelabras. Winged porcelain pigs dangled from the ceiling above glass-topped bathtubs, which doubled as tables and aquariums filled with live angelfish. Neon cocktails in hand, we followed the crowd of locals, expats, and fellow backpackers through a maze of darkened hallways to the dance floor. A three-story aluminum Adonis stood watch as half-naked drag queens doused in glitter, feathers, and miles of theatrical kohl eyeliner playfully taunted the partygoers.

Forming a tight-knit circle, we danced for hours, taking breaks to refill our drinks or battle the endless lines for one of two avant-garde bathrooms: Evil, which was represented by a tangled mass of barbed wire, thorny roses, and pierced-heart brocades, and Good, which was coated floor-to-ceiling with shattered mirrors and bathed in an eerie powder blue light.

Returning to the dance floor after refilling my drink, I heard Holly shouting my name from above. Looking up, I saw her strutting her stuff onstage with a dozen drag queens. *Well, this is a surprise.* Although I'd gotten to know Holly a lot better during the months leading up to the trip, her boundless energy and free-spirited nature never ceased to impress me. If this night was any indication of how our on-the-road lives would be, I might never want to return home.

"C'mon, you crazy angels! Get up here and dance!" Holly shouted to Amanda and me.

Laughing hysterically, we locked hands with Holly and heaved ourselves onto the platform. Hopping, spinning, and twirling our way into the night, we returned to the hostel only after every feather had fallen off our celestial bodies.

An evil sun cackles overhead. Giant tumbleweeds of jagged metal and glass sweep across the barren wasteland. Brian appears riding an oversized saguaro, a mournful expression in his liquid eyes. Suddenly his face smears and melts across the cactus branch like a Salvador Dalí clock, forming a puddle of mirrors on the sand. I open my mouth to scream, but the words crumbled to dust as they pass through my parched lips.

Bang, bang, bang! Squawk! Bang! Squawk!

Wrenched back to reality by thunderous concrete drilling and a seemingly deranged rooster, my eyes shot open in a panic. For a moment, I had no idea where I was, until I spotted Holly across the room, sound asleep on the bottom bunk of our communal dorm room. Perched on the wooden ledge by my bed was a large bottle of water, a small plate with a butter knife, two rolls, and a side of jam, along with a note from Amanda: "Thought you might need this. Down the street using the Internet. Meet you in the Loki café at noon."

I pushed the note aside and pulled my scratchy wool blanket over my face. I didn't know if it was the rum punch hangover nipping angrily at my head or the haunting visions from my dream, but I suddenly ached to be back in New York in Brian's warm bed instead of fighting queasiness in this freezing cold dorm. It had been months since I'd broken the news to him about going on the trip, but the vivid details still came rushing back to me.

It was a typical Saturday morning in the city. Brian and I were nestled under his comforter, engaged in an intense game of rock/paper/scissors to determine whose turn it was to battle the winter chill for bagels and coffee. Even though he lost, I agreed to go with him. But only if we could stop by the pet store to visit my favorite Maltese puppy, a three-pound ball of fur that Brian dubbed the ultimate testosterone drainer. As always, he relented but reminded me that slobbery, ugly bulldogs were much funnier and insisted we also visit the dog park. "Okay, fine. But I'll need to borrow *my* favorite fleece to keep me warm," I countered, referring to Brian's softest sweatshirt.

Strolling along the East River holding fuzzy gloved hands and giggling at the ridiculous knit outfits owners forced on their pets, I'd felt a sudden flutter of sadness. While not all of our recent memories had been Norman Rockwell–worthy, I still couldn't bear the thought of losing Brian. If only I could've stopped time, locked the moment in a life-sized snow globe where the two of us would always be together, giddy and in love, kissing on a bench with glittery snowflakes swirling around us.

I'd *tried* to talk to him about the trip on several occasions, slipping it into conversations about summer plans or one of the endless talks about our future as a couple. But it'd always been easier for both of us to brush off the seemingly far-flung notion until it got closer to becoming a reality. It wasn't until Amanda and I checked off the "not renewing" box on our apartment lease agreement that it hit me: I was really going to do this. I could not in good conscience keep my plans from Brian any longer. The toughest conversation of my adult life needed to happen, and fast.

67

All that week, guilt and sorrow clung to me like the dark swirl of dirt and flies that perpetually trailed Pigpen in the Charlie Brown comic strip. The dread and despair mounted until finally I couldn't keep the truth bottled up any longer. Midway through dinner that night, I blurted out my decision to travel, casting my half-eaten egg roll back into its box in disgust as if it were somehow to blame for our impending pain and suffering.

Brian's face turned to stone, his cornflower blue eyes hardening to slivers of coal. Deliberately staring at a vague point across the room and not directly at me, he calmly and icily stated that he guessed we were over for good. My temporarily tough exterior withstood the piercing blow for about .003 of a second before it shattered into broken sobs and pitiful gulps. The damage was done. I'd smashed my fantasy snow globe to bits, forever casting the smiley Brian and Jen figurines into a depressing puddle of broken glass and counterfeit snowflakes.

Blame it on my overwhelming state of distress and shock, but my sorrow quickly morphed into frustration. Why did I always have to play the bad guy? How many years would Brian let this relationship drag on before *he* made a decision? Did he expect that our problems would miraculously solve themselves? Why did the entire weight of figuring "us" out always fall on my shoulders?

Before I knew it, we were head-to-head in an epic battle, with childish hissy fits, hysterical crying, screaming, and outright emotional breakdowns lasting well into the night. But despite all the logical reasons why we should've just ended things on the spot, somehow, by the time dawn broke, we'd negotiated a peace treaty, dictating in rather ambiguous terms that we'd stay together until I left for the trip, take the summer to reevaluate our relationship, and make a decision when I returned to New York between South America and Kenya.

"Oh, my God, Jen. What time is it? Where's Amanda?"

Holly groaned, pulling me back to my present state as a fallen postparty angel.

"She went to an Internet café, but she's going to meet us in . . . like . . . forty-five minutes," I said when my brain finally registered the numbers on my sports watch. "But look, she left us a minibreakfast," I added, willing myself to roll off my lumpy mattress.

Crossing the room with the water bottle and plate, I plopped down on the floor next to Holly's bed. As we gnawed on the crusty loaves, I recounted the details of my insane dream, a ritual I'd bestowed on Amanda every morning during our postcollege Europe trip. Holly nodded with polite interest, good-naturedly analyzing each scene from my subconscious. While there was not a doubt in my mind that taking this trip was the best thing for me, I still really missed Brian. I knew that Holly understood that on a personal level, and just having her there to listen to me was a surprisingly huge comfort. By the time we'd sopped up the last of the jam, I was ready to face a new day on the road.

As luck would have it, our arrival in Cusco had coincided with the frenetic conclusion of Inti Raymi, an age-old festival that paid tribute to the sun god—and in modern times made Mardi Gras look like a small-town homecoming parade. After meeting up with Amanda, the three of us joined the thousands of Peruvians and tourists from around the globe pouring into the Plaza de Armas, where an array of dance performances, colorful demonstrations, fireworks, and live music began at dawn and lasted well into the night.

Amanda, Holly, and I sat cross-legged on the stone steps of a church on the edge of the plaza, enveloped in a crowd of local families who happily made small talk with the American girls next to them. Mobile merchants shimmied through the tightly packed bodies, hawking cotton candy, postcards, and much-needed hot chocolate. Between the mystical aura of the city and

69

the warmth of its people, the girls and I were truly enchanted by Cusco. As we raised our flimsy cardboard cups of cocoa and toasted to a successful first few days on the road, I started to feel better about my separation from Brian. With Amanda to my left and Holly to my right, I was more certain than ever that I wouldn't have to walk the lonely road alone.

O ur first week at Loki felt like a freshman orientation in the Andes. We spent almost every day exploring Cusco with our new friends, cross-referencing travel guides to ensure that we wouldn't overlook a single historical site, crafts market, or restaurant. At night, after the warmth drained from the valley along with the sinking sun, we'd combat the cold by dancing to a live band at one of the town's gringolandia outposts like Mama Africa, Ukuku's Pub Cultural, and Mythology.

When exhaustion and the biting chill of a high-mountain Peruvian winter caught up with us, Amanda, Holly, and I would trek back to the hostel and pile on every stitch of quick-dry fabric we owned, plus a fleecy barrier of alpaca sweaters, hats, and gloves we'd snatched up at the Inca market. This was necessary to avoid getting frostbite in the meat locker of a dorm we shared with five random dudes, one of whom could awaken the entire room with the resonance and pungency of his epic-length farts.

But after we spent a week touring through religious monuments, taking hikes and horseback rides through nearby ruins, and going on day trips to the Sacred Valley, our Peruvian vacation started to lose its luster. Awakened yet again in the predawn hours by a bunkmate packing up his gear with all the delicacy of an angry hippo, the girls and I dragged ourselves to the breakfast room to grab some freeze-dried Nescafé, order a grilled cheese smashie (a fantastic creation involving a sandwich press and lots of butter), and discuss the current state of the union.

We were sitting around the table, silently making headway on our food, when Holly pointed out that we still had about 350 days left and, more immediately, the Inca Trail to climb. She figured we might feel better prepared for it if we checked ourselves into a nearby guesthouse, one that advertised private rooms, hot water—and no gaseous earthquakes rocking the top bunk at 3 a.m. Also, it wouldn't serve us to catch that nasty virus that was sneaking into the bunks at night and felling backpackers like wounded antelope—especially right before hiking the trail. Unfortunately, not long after transferring to Niños Hotel down the road, we discovered that we hadn't moved quite fast enough.

B ut we're supposed to start the hike tomorrow," I lamented to the doctor as I sat next to Amanda on her bed. She was burning up—and her high fever hadn't broken in days. "Do you think there's even a chance that she'll be healthy enough to go?"

"Well, I think injection will improve her within a few hours, maybe a day," said the doctor. "But I think maybe it is no good to do this hike."

He turned to glance at Holly, who was in the other bed, curled up in the fetal position. "She, maybe, can go. You have take this Cipro already?"

"Yeah, last night," Holly moaned from her bed.

"Then probably fine for tomorrow," he said. "I will inject medicine in your friend, and if she does not feel improved, she should stay here."

As the guy rustled around in the old-fashioned black doctor's bag sitting on the nightstand, Amanda tried to roll over to look at me. "What's happening?"

I sat down on the side of the bed and pulled Amanda's hair up over her head. "Don't worry, sweetie. We found a doctor and he's just gonna give you a little shot to make you feel better."

71

Her eyes suddenly grew enormous, and I almost smiled. Even in her late twenties, she was still afraid of needles.

"I'm gonna go out later to get some of the supplies he's recommended to make you and Holly feel better. She's got food poisoning or something, and he's not sure what you have. It's probably some bacterial infection. We don't know yet."

I stood up and moved across the room to make space for the doctor. Paper crumpled as he removed a syringe from its packaging.

Abject fear registered on Amanda's face. "Do want me to hold your hand?" Holly asked quietly from her bed.

"No, you're sick, too. I'll be okay," Amanda said. Ignoring her protest, Holly got up and walked over to Amanda, placing one hand on top of hers.

The man inched down the waistband of Amanda's pajama pants and swiped a path of alcohol against her right butt cheek. As Amanda scrunched her eyes shut, Holly squeezed her fingers to comfort her.

"That needle is new, right?" I asked the doctor, who paused to scowl at me.

"Of course, yes. Now relax muscles," he said to Amanda.

She flinched, and I held my breath until he withdrew the needle. When it was over, Holly retreated to her bed and crawled back under the covers.

The doctor gave me a few instructions, plus a list of liquids and medicines that I should buy to help my friends feel better. By the time I pulled the front door quietly shut behind me, both of them were fast asleep.

In the middle of the night—or actually, very early the next morning, I heard the sound of someone slowly getting up in the darkness and turning on the shower in the bathroom. I squeezed my watch and stared at the glowing green dial. Saturday, 4:51 a.m.

When Amanda emerged from the bathroom fifteen minutes later, both Holly and I were wide awake.

"How are you feeling, sickie?" I whispered. "Do you think we need to reschedule?"

All three of us knew the reality of the situation: there could be no rescheduling. Because of the intense restrictions on the number of hikers allowed on the Inca Trail each day, we had to go now—or wait until we traveled around the world next time.

Amanda took a deep breath. "Well, I know what my mom would say. Don't push yourself. You may feel better now, but you'll make yourself worse if you try to do too much. Let the girls go ahead."

I looked at Holly and gave her a sad half smile. Oh well. Even though Holly had started to feel better last night, there was no way that we'd hike the Inca Trail without Amanda—or push her to try to go with us. Even though we'd been planning this for several months, it was better to make sure everyone was healthy. We had a whole year ahead of us; surely there would be greater challenges to face, more Latin American mountains to climb.

Holly opened her mouth to say something, no doubt to try to make all of us feel better about the whole thing. That's when Amanda cut her off.

"But c'mon, when have you ever known me to play it safe— or listen to my mom, for that matter?" She grinned. "Better start packing, ladies—we're gonna be late."

73

❦

CHAPTER FIVE

Holly

INCA TRAIL, PERU

JULY

I was living out another one of my dreams: trekking through the Andes Mountains with my friends on a mission to see the sacred ruins of Machu Picchu (also known as the Lost City of the Incas). Ever since I'd studied Peru in high school history class, I'd wanted to go to that place where mysterious jungles kept stone temples under cover and Incas had worshiped the sun. I expected my first experience on the Inca Trail to be more mystical than commercial. But from the moment our tour bus arrived and our stiff hiking boots stepped down onto the trailhead, Quechua women enveloped us, pushing everything from wool hats to hiking sticks to candy bars into our chests, insisting that we needed them to survive the journey.

After we'd consulted our Peruvian tour guide, Reubén, about which essentials were *really* essential, we stocked up on hiking sticks, water bottle holders, alpaca socks, coca leaves, and yes, enough Snickers to feed an Incan army.

"Señora." A Quechua woman pulled on the sleeve of Amanda's quick-dry shirt.

"Gracias, no necesito algo más." *Thanks, I don't need anything else,* Amanda said in an attempt to wave her off.

"Pero, señora," the woman persisted, standing her ground at just five feet tall. But Amanda's gaze had already traveled far away to the Andes Mountains looming in front of us. Not to be deterred, the woman waved an object clenched tightly in her fist.

"Is that your money belt?" I asked, signaling for Amanda to come back down to reality.

Amanda immediately focused her eyes on the woman in the same instant she groped around under her shirt. The woman held out her hand to offer up the bundle of valuables, which must have slipped from its hiding place. Amanda took it from her outstretched hand with wide eyes, gave her a smile, then shuffled through her passport and the wad of tattered soles.

I studied the woman's sun-creased features and knew she probably made less money in an entire year than the amount Amanda had toted around her waist. I stood quietly watching as Amanda offered her a *propina* (tip), which the woman refused with a violent shake of her head. This must have been a real-life example of a concept called *ayni* I'd read about in a guidebook. It was the indigenous Quechuas' version of karma that held if you help your neighbor, they'll do the same for you someday. Amanda practically crushed her with a bear hug as an irrepressible grin spread across the woman's face.

Since the woman wouldn't take Amanda's money for payback, we bought another bag of coca leaves in the name of *ayni* before heading back toward our guide.

"Hey, everybuddy! I gadda question for you!" This exclamation, we soon learned, was Reubén's code to gather around for a group debriefing. With his aviator sunglasses, North Face pants, and sleek black baseball hat, the thirty-one-year-old looked better outfitted for a starring role in a *Bourne Identity* sequel than for his current job leading a pack of pilgrims.

Our group of a dozen formed a semicircle in front of Reubén as he pointed a walking stick at a painted trail map. "Okay, leesten up. You see that the Inca Trail es just one. If you stay on the path, et is eemposseeble to get lost." Jen, Amanda, and I looked at one another and smirked. Impossible? We'd already managed to take a wrong turn on our way back to Cusco after hiking the surrounding hills—despite the fact that a Cusqueño had insisted there was only one road leading into town. We were capable of pulling off the impossible.

Reubén then gestured to a bridge stretched over a churning river. "Do you remember the name of this reever that runs through the Sacred Valley of the Incas?"

Remember? I don't think I've ever even heard of it, I thought, wondering whether my high school geography classes had covered it and I'd forgotten. I wished I had read more of the guidebook.

"It's the Urubamba River," said Shannon, a twenty-eight-year-old Irishwoman with long legs and glossy black hair.

"You are one hundred percent corrrrect!" Reubén said. "Eggg-cellent!"

I was pretty amazed that Shannon seemed to have memorized every fact about the trail—so far, she'd had the answer to all of Reubén's trivia questions. Even with our unstructured schedule, I had never managed to get all the travel reading done that I'd hoped. Instead, I'd gotten sidetracked exploring Cusco's cobblestone streets during my daily run, or sifting through the rainbow-colored handicrafts at the markets, or staring at the fire in our hostel's common room and chatting with other travelers.

I caught Shannon's eye as Reubén wrapped up his impromptu lecture and offered her a friendly smile. On the bus ride over, I'd slid into an open seat beside her. As we'd watched the world melt into streaks of green beyond the window, we'd talked about how cool it was to be spending Tuesday morning heading toward the ancient Inca ruins instead of to an office. Quickly the conversation had deepened, and I'd learned she was part of a trio of late-twenty-something women who were essentially the Irish versions of ourselves. Bonded by a sense of exploration and at a crossroads in their careers, relationships, and life in general, they were traveling as a sort of time-out to think about which direction to head in next.

Finally the lecture was over, and it was time to begin the trek. The trail was a marathon-length twenty-six miles, and excitement for the journey pushed me across the bridge stretching over the river that marked the start. I hadn't gotten far before the sound of feet slapping quickly against the path made me turn to see who was approaching. I stepped aside for the porter wearing a yellow T-shirt, whose back was strapped with a blanketed hump of supplies approximately the size of his body. *"Gracias,"* he called out as he breezed past.

The porters were the men who made the trek possible by carrying up to sixty pounds of supplies on their backs—including tents, sleeping bags, and food. Most were indigenous Quechuas. Some looked barely eighteen years old, with barrel chests and knobby knees. Others appeared to be in their fifties or sixties, with deep lines etched into brown skin from a lifetime of exposure to sun and wind. Almost all had callused feet protected only by leather sandals. Despite their heavy loads, they managed to race ahead of us to set up camp and cook meals.

Reubén told me that many porters used to earn less than $5 a day, but the government had recently passed a law requiring companies to give them at least 42 soles, or about $15 a day. My heart went out to them, as I couldn't imagine that anyone could pay me enough to carry gas stoves, dishes, tents, and food for more than a dozen people on my back while trekking four days on what felt like an endless StairMaster session. Despite trying to acclimate myself to altitudes as high as 14,000 feet by running steps in Cusco all week, I was already panting from the weight of my six-pound day pack. Reubén must have heard me because he fell into step beside me and said, "Today is the easy day! It's just seven kilometers to Wayllabamba, and then we'll camp for the night."

"La Labamba?" I asked in confusion, my mind working to churn up something familiar to connect to. He chuckled, and I wondered if he ever tired of tourists asking him questions that must seem obvious to him. "No, Wah-lee-BAM-ba," he said slowly for emphasis, and I felt like a five-year-old asking her teacher "Why is the sky blue?" or "Why don't boys wear skirts?"

Still feeling like a grade school student, I walked beside him for almost an hour, soaking up his stories. What were the piles of coca leaves and corn placed along the sacred path? "They're *pago*, or offerings to Mother Earth. Giving to the gods—and others—helps to keep balance with the spirits, with nature, with your neighbors, and with yourself," Reubén said. He went on to explain that the Quechuans believed that connecting with the elements of nature—air, water, earth, and sun or light—would help bring them closer to the divine, or Pachakamaq. "The Incas also did things like covering drinking cups and stone walls with gold—it symbolized the light of the sun god," he said.

Reubén's stories sounded like fairy tales to me, as if the Incas had lived their lives by magic and energy and things unseen. But it was probably their way of finding order in a mysterious world. If I were to tell Incans that Christians do things like drink wine to symbolize their savior's blood, they might very well think that sounded like some kind of sorcery. I wasn't sure what I believed in as I hiked that trail, but I knew I was looking for something deeper, something solid, to hold on to. After all, weren't most religions a collection of stories and rituals, a way to make sense of the things we can't understand, of finding meaning in the chaos?

With a father born of a long line of Irishmen and a mother who traced her roots back to Italy and Poland, I'd had the standard Catholic upbringing that called for making the sacraments of First Communion and Confirmation. But even as a kid I'd wondered about religion—both about the church I was raised in and how other people worshiped. In fact, I'd pleaded with my mom to allow me to convert to Episcopalianism after going to church with my best friend's family and learning that this particular group of Christian rebels allowed women to be priests.

At thirteen years old, I could not wrap my head around why God would deny me the chance to lead a congregation simply because I was born without a penis. "What about equal opportunity? You always tell me that girls can be *anything*!" I'd said, but my mom had held fast to her traditions and wouldn't let me convert. "What would your grandparents think?" she'd asked. And so I'd honored my mother. I'd gone to religion classes after school for two years and fulfilled my required community service hours as a candy striper in a hospital in order to be confirmed by my parish in the Catholic Church.

I remember asking my teacher why the church would leave some groups out, such as women and gays. And she'd told me that that had come from people, not God. "The Catholic Church is an institution made up of humans who are imperfect. But God is perfect," she'd said.

Reubén and I turned to silence as my eyes flitted around the same natural world the Incas had found divinity in: tall grass strumming in the wind; the Urubamba River slicing through rock and dirt; sunlight filtering through gauzy clouds as if they were curtains for the heavens themselves. There were no sacred ruins to be seen that first day. There was only wilderness and the sounds of my breath and water rushing and feet striking against the earth.

After an easy hike, little more than three or four hours, we reached our first destination. Though Wayllabamba means "grassy plain" in Quechua, a better description might have been "free-range farm with a makeshift distillery." When we arrived, we found pigs, chickens, and goats clucking and braying at the intruders and the smattering of red tents our porters had constructed in a formerly uncluttered pasture. Surrounding the clearing was a little village.

When the government restored the Inca Trail, Quechuas who already lived there stayed. And while the animals might not have been happy to see us, the villagers made the most of the opportunity to make extra cash by selling treats to tourists. Consumerism had made its way even to the outskirts of the Lost City of the Incas: the makeshift wooden shacks flanking the path were stocked full of candy, Coca-Cola, and another beverage rumored to offer much more of a jolt than caffeine.

"*Quieres chicha?*" asked one red-faced man from the window of the wooden box where he'd set up shop.

"*No, gracias,*" I said firmly, remembering that Reubén had warned us about chicha, a potent corn-brewed alcohol fermented with saliva.

"*Solamente una Snickers, por favor,*" I said, and forked over a few soles to add yet another candy bar to the three already occupying space in my day pack.

Sure, part of travel's adventure is sampling exotic fare, but I opted for the safe route since I was still popping antibiotic Cipro pills like Tic Tacs. I really wanted to be brave like Jen and eat whatever landed on my plate. Deep down, I felt guilty over my utter lack of curiosity toward any beverage containing another person's spit as an ingredient, Peruvian delicacies such as guinea pig, and the meat of adorable, doe-eyed alpacas—but facilities on the trail were few and far between, and it was BYOTP (bring your own toilet paper). Some risks just weren't worth taking.

As we passed around the dishes at dinner, I piled my plate with enough rice and potatoes to feed a teenage boy going through a growth spurt. "Hol, are you feeling better?" Amanda paused momentarily between bites, glancing at my heaping servings.

After swallowing a mouthful of rice, I said, "I'm starting to feel like my old self now. How about you?"

"Whatever the doc gave me was like some miracle black-market drug—I actually feel better than before I was sick," Amanda said as she dug into a minimountain of potatoes.

The three of us polished off dinner, placed our dishes in the wash bin, and strapped on headlamps to cast a cone-shaped path of light toward our tents. It was only 8 p.m., but the exertion from breathing in the high altitude and all that walking made us want to collapse into our sleeping bags.

The temperature had dropped well below freezing, and the more body heat we could muster, the better. We could've slept in separate tents, but we laid out our sleeping bags—all three of them—inside a two-person tent and then pulled our alpaca hats farther over our ears. We stopped abruptly when we heard something brush against the tent. "What the hell was that?" I whispered, turning my headlamp in the direction of the noise. The intruder squealed as it hooved the thin plastic wall.

"Jesus, it's a pig!" Amanda exclaimed.

"Are we on the Inca Trail or Old MacDonald's farm?" Jen said, slapping the tent wall and yelling, "Get outta here—go away!" We heard grass rustling as the animal retreated, probably in search of our dinner scraps.

We were all wide awake now. "One time a bear clawed at my tent when my family was camping in the Adirondacks," I said, telling the girls the first of many random childhood stories on the road. "My dog, Corby, chased it up a tree to save me."

"Your dog chased a bear up a tree?" Jen asked. "And wait, your dog's name was *Corby*?"

"Yeah, what? I never told you that before?" I playfully feigned offense.

"Corby *Corbett*?" Jen giggled. "That's as silly as Amanda's white cat named Whyte Kat. I'm going to start calling you Corby."

"Fine then, *Baggy* Baggett."

"Wait, what about me?" Amanda chimed in.

"You can be *Pressy* Pressner," Jen exclaimed, and we laughed. I attributed our giddiness to the coca leaves we'd been chewing for the last few hours to ward off altitude sickness. (Disclaimer: Cocaine does indeed come from coca leaves, but, according to Reubén, it takes hundreds of pounds of leaves to create one kilogram of the drug. Any loopiness we may have felt while chewing the leaves was purely medicinal).

Once we'd caught our breath, Amanda reached into her day pack to pull out a foil space blanket—an emergency provision for hypothermia—and stretched it across the three of us for extra insulation. Trying to get closer for warmth, I was glad we had opted to sleep together. We were settled in head to toe: three women snuggled inside a two-person tent high in the Andes Mountains. Instead of the familiar electric glow of skyscrapers, we drifted off blanketed by a sky with a different kind of light: the same constellation that had once guided the Incas, the Southern Cross.

I lay there long after Jen and Amanda's breathing turned deep and even, next to them but alone with my thoughts. The flashing lights and honking horns gave New York City nights a sense of movement rather than stillness. I wasn't used to how deep the silence could feel when darkness clung to a mountainside. In the heavy quiet, my mind wandered to my older cousin

Adam, who'd unexpectedly died of heart failure two years earlier when he himself was just twenty-eight years old. I thought how our childhood selves, kids who had spent hours mixing the perfect mud pie or climbing the highest tree branch in the apple orchards behind my grandparents' house, would want me to be having this adventure beneath the Southern Cross. I wondered if life would seem more comforting if I believed, as the Incas had, that those stars could show me the way.

The next morning our porter, Ramón, was outside our door (well, our zippered tent flap) with coca tea before the sun's first rays penetrated the icy blackness. *"Buenos días, muchachas,"* he whispered with a singsongy cheerfulness that struck me as wildly inappropriate at that ungodly hour. The three of us huddled together, silently sipping our tea, reluctant to abandon the warmth of our down sleeping bags.

Once we'd gathered in the dining tent for a hefty breakfast of quinoa pancakes, eggs, and porridge, Reubén informed us that today was the hardest day: eight hours of steady climbing to the highest point of roughly 14,000 feet at Warmiwanusca, "Dead Woman's Pass." I was too worried about my own survival to ask Reubén how it had gotten its name.

Reubén commanded our attention with his now-familiar exclamation, "Hey, everybuddy! I gadda question for you!" Silence ensued in anticipation of Reubén's next bit of trivia. "Who remembers the name of the man who redeescovered the Lost Ceety of the Incas, Machu Picchu?"

I took a breath to speak as Shannon shouted out, "His name was Hiram Bingham! He was a professor at Yale who found the ruins in 1911 during an expedition."

"Muy, muy bien, Shannon," Reubén said. "Why Machu Picchu was built is a mystery. Some say it was the center of the In-

can Empire. Some say it was an ancient pilgrimage site thought to mark one end of the sun's path. As you walk along the trail, imagine yourself as an Inca making your own pilgrimage to this spiritual site."

I did believe my friends and I truly were on a pilgrimage, a search for what matters most. I wasn't sure if Jen and Amanda were as excited about being pilgrims as I was, but my life in New York, so lacking in spirituality, had left me hungry to feel more connected, either to a higher power or simply to the world around me. On my first big trip during undergrad on Semester at Sea, I had signed up for a world religion course to learn how people around the planet fill their lives with meaning—exploring Shinto shrines in Japan, Muslim mosques in Morocco, and Buddhist temples in Hong Kong. One of my most vivid memories is of the first day I walked Istanbul's cobblestone streets, holding my breath when I'd heard a powerful male voice chanting through the city's loudspeakers. Masses of men stopped, threw down mats, and collectively prayed toward Mecca in a sort of sacred time-out. The clouds above cast shadows over the scene below, proving the world was still turning even though I felt as if it'd momentarily stopped. Ever since, I'd longed to go back to places where holy rituals were such visible parts of daily life, the way it was for those men.

Contemplating the divine was proving to be a somewhat helpful distraction from the exertion of climbing a path sandwiched between boulders and a steep cliff—and from the knowledge that the distance between living and falling to a tragic death was about six inches.

"How long did you ladies say you were traveling for?" asked Shannon. She fell into step behind me, saving me from imagining one of us plummeting down the mountainside.

"We're on the road for a year," I said, suddenly sweating under the heat of the intense sun piercing through my fleece.

"This is our first country," Amanda called back from her place at the front of the line, with Jen a few steps behind her. I paused to peel off a layer of clothing, and the others took the opportunity to do the same. Shielding my eyes from the sun, I peered at people ahead on a peak, who resembled ants marching. The six of us women had formed a pack of our own on the trail, and that peak looked so high above us.

"How long have *you* been traveling?" Amanda asked.

Since leaving New York, the standard questions asked upon an initial meeting had changed from *Where do you work?* to *Where have you been?* and *How long are you traveling?* In fast-paced, success-driven New York, most people wanted to know whether a new acquaintance was, say, a Wall Street banker or a graphic designer. But on the travelers' circuit, the amount of time you've been on the road and number of countries you've visited pegged you as a causal vacationer, newbie vagabonder, or seasoned backpacker.

"We're doing six months through South America," Shannon answered. The others in her trio, Elizabeth and Molly, had fallen back behind us after resting for a little longer.

"It's so hard to find chunks of time to get away, especially if you have a boyfriend. Are you all single?" Jen asked.

"I've been dating my boyfriend for almost seven years," Shannon said after a brief pause.

"Holly and I have been with our boyfriends for more than three years," Jen shared, talking slowly to conserve her precious breath. "Shannon, do you think you'll end up marrying him?"

Shannon's walking stick made a steady thudding rhythm as she leveraged over the stones, and her breathing came out ragged between words. Maybe being in motion like that made it easier for us to open up so quickly because Shannon answered, "Everybody keeps asking me that question, but I never know how to answer because it's not really up to me." She sounded tired—both physically and emotionally. She revealed that her boyfriend was in medical school and that he kept postponing the marriage talk. Then she added, "I'm just not sure how long I'm supposed to wait." She pulled her dark hair into a long ponytail as she walked, and I noticed sweat beads clinging to her neck.

As I listened, it occurred to me that Elan and I had never really had a big marriage talk either, apart from a mention or two about the far-off future. Marriage hadn't been on our minds when we had met at twenty-three years of age (him) and twenty-five (myself). But the years had sped by as if on fast-forward, and I understood that the pressure to check off that adult milestone couldn't be avoided. I wondered if that pressure, mixed with his path as an actor, which would likely send him away too someday, would cause cracks in whatever that force is that holds a couple together. I hoped that it wouldn't. I hoped that, as clichéd as it sounded, love really would conquer all.

As I scanned the path for potential ankle twisters like tree roots and loose rocks, it struck me as funny that our group was on the Inca Trail discussing quarter-life crisis issues such as commitment (which apparently aren't confined to U.S. borders). After meeting the Irish girls, I was willing to bet that they were also struggling with the same questions we were: How long should I date a guy before getting married? Do I want to have kids? How can I make a living doing what I love?

Talking soon became too much effort as the climb grew steeper and the air thinner. That was just fine by me—I didn't want to think about the future anymore. Worrying about stuff like marriage and jobs and things that only *might* occur were just distractions from what was actually happening that very moment. We were almost at mile 12, and my mind was focused on the rhythm of the walking sticks clacking upon the uneven stones; the sweet smell of rotting leaves; the dull burn of my thighs as they repeatedly lifted my legs; the starbursts dancing before my eyes as sunlight filtered through my sunglasses; the salty taste of sweat when I ran my tongue over my dry lips.

I forced any thoughts about the rest of my life out of my head and was content to stare down, concentrating on the task of putting one foot in front of the other. I paused only periodically to replace the layers I'd removed earlier as the temperature dropped and wind slapped my cheeks. After about two hours of steep but steady climbing, I was so consumed with taking it one step at a time that I was startled by the cheers erupting from the mountaintop ahead.

That must be Dead Woman's Pass! I spied a rocky crest blanketed in clouds and nestled between two peaks. Bands of hikers yelled encouragement to those still on their way up. "You're almost here. Just a few more steps!"

Turning around, I saw specks of people below on what looked like a vertical path from my high vantage point. Natural endorphins must have flooded my body after hours of climbing because my thighs were suddenly completely numb. My lungs, however, weren't: My entire chest was burning from struggling to suck in as much precious oxygen as I could from the atmosphere up that high.

"Just a few more minutes, and we've made it halfway!" I called to Jen, who was walking steadily about five feet in front of me. Normally I'd have been up front, trying to push my body to the max by running toward the invisible finish line. But today I was willing myself to slow down and soak up the scene. I'd imagined what it would be like to walk this trail since high school. I wanted to hold on to the moment so it wouldn't disappear so quickly. Amanda had made it to the top just seconds earlier and wasted no time in pulling out the video camera. Though Jen had wanted to do the trip without stopping to document it, I was happy Amanda was making the effort to preserve our first big achievement together—especially because I never thought to stop and record the moment. I didn't want to forget the view from the top of our first mountain, where the sky itself looked so big it dwarfed even the snowcapped summits shooting up from valleys sprinkled with wildflowers.

Our third day, roughly twenty-four hours later and 5,000 feet below the hike's highest point, we reached the last campsite. It proved to be practically luxurious compared to the pasture-turned-distillery where we'd camped on our first night or our second night at the base of Dead Woman's Pass, where it got so cold ice crystals formed on our tent. Our group joined what seemed like hundreds of others in the lodge, where you could purchase showers by inserting coins into a metal timer. Though the bathrooms still lacked a few things I'd always considered essential (toilet paper, soap, a little bleach action), simply being able to rinse the grime from our matted, hat-head hair felt totally indulgent.

As we sat down for our last supper, it felt like the night before Christmas. The anticipation in the air was so thick that you could practically cup it in your hands. The next morning we'd start hiking around 4:30 a.m. to make it to our final destination, Machu Picchu, in time to see the sun's first rays illuminate the ruins.

We weren't waiting until tomorrow to celebrate, however. Reubén organized a tipping ceremony, and the porters stood in a semicircle directly across from our team of trekkers. The group of men with their callused, sandal-clad feet shyly shared their stories, and Reubén translated each into English for us. Reubén mentioned that Ramón had started this job when he was sixteen and that his fifty-four-year-old father, also working on this trek, was the oldest on the team. I'd noticed that Ramón was usually smiling. He smiled while shouldering a load as big as his body; he smiled while squatting over a pot cooking our dinner; he smiled while cheering on the tourists whose gear he carried. His life might not have been easy, but still he smiled.

Besides offering money, the trekkers also pooled together things to donate that we no longer needed, such as socks, T-shirts, and flashlights. Reubén assigned each donated item a number and wrote the numbers on scraps of paper to be plucked from his black cap. Each porter was invited to pick one, and they all clapped wildly when someone drew a number that corresponded to, say, an opened tube of antibiotic ointment. The porters' faces lit up, and they chanted, *"Gracias!"* as they clutched the bundle of castoffs.

Their enthusiasm over receiving unwashed clothing made my throat tighten. Far away from the glitz and grit of New York City, I thought that often the people who had the least in the way of material possessions seemed the happiest. The porters, who carried giant packs of other people's belongings, didn't appear to focus on what they lacked. Instead, they acted grateful for the small stuff that came their way—even used antibiotic ointment. And their eyes, though lined with creases and slightly weathered, looked to me to have more sparkle than any guy I'd seen walking down Wall Street in an Armani suit. I wished I had more to give than a measly bag of coca leaves, but living out of a backpack didn't leave much room for miscellaneous items.

On our last morning, breakfast wasn't the bountiful affair it had been on previous days. Instead, we quickly devoured cinnamon-sprinkled porridge by starlight, gathered our belongings, and then relied on our headlamps to guide us.

The earth quivered under the hundreds of feet tracing the path. We moved at warp speed through grassy fields and then forests with fan-shaped leaves that rustled in the wind. As the stars were gradually absorbed back into a brightening sky, it was a race against the sun.

We trekked the final few kilometers along the mountainside, slipped into a cloud forest, and then climbed about fifty steps to get our first view of Machu Picchu framed by the sun gate, or Intipunku. The Incas were genius architects, lining up the stone walls in this gate to match the angle of the summer and winter solstices. On those two days of the year, the sun was perfectly aligned to flood the gate's opening with a solid beam of light. As we approached, the light beckoned us forward.

Less than three hours after we'd started, our group sat crosslegged on a stone terrace to soak up the moment we'd trekked twenty-six miles to witness: The first rays peeked out from behind the sprawling ruins of Machu Picchu. As the sky morphed from pink to gold to periwinkle, the light pushed shadows across the stones, making them appear to be living, breathing beings.

The centuries-old city changed shape before our eyes, sunlight flowing like water through the labyrinth of rectangular passages, staircases, and buildings sitting on a flat plateau framed by a cloud-covered mountain peak. The ancient Incas didn't have wheels, so the sheer manpower it must have taken to construct such a monument was as impressive as the intricate architecture itself.

Despite the fact that Amanda and I had been sick just days before and we'd all spent the last few nights sleeping on rocky ground in the Andes, my friends' eyes shone brightly and their complexions glowed. The sun suddenly shifted higher in the sky, illuminating every stone in the ancient city.

"Can you believe people built this place by *hand*?" Shannon, always filled with facts, whispered beside me.

Though the ruins seemed to me like some sort of miracle, I wasn't contemplating the Incas' brilliant engineering as I watched the sun climb higher in the sky. I was thinking about my own journey to Machu Picchu and how it wouldn't have been the same if I'd done it alone. My thoughts flitted back over the past three days. The Quechuan woman who had returned Amanda's wallet at the start. How Reubén's voice had grown lower as he pointed out the offerings to the gods left along the trail. How Ramón's face had lit up during the porter-tipping ceremony.

I can't recall exactly how long I sat there, thinking that my teenage self never would've believed I'd have done this. It was long enough for the exhaustion from twenty-six miles of hiking to hit Jen and Amanda, who were leaning against each other and using their sunglasses to unsuccessfully hide eyes surrendering to sleep. Reubén jumped to his feet in front of them, signaling for us to gather around for another lecture. "Hey, everybuddy! I gadda question for you!"

Our pack of pilgrims dragged ourselves over as he continued, "You win a Snickers bar if you can tell me, what is the Quechua spiritual law of *ayni*?"

"It means reciprocity," I belted out, excited to finally be able to answer a trivia question. "Kind of like, give and you shall receive."

"Eggg-cellent!" he said, tossing me the chocolate.

My stomach grumbled, and I realized we hadn't eaten since the porridge hours before. Ready to rip open the wrapper and devour the chocolate, I suddenly stopped.

"Hey, Jen, Amanda, you hungry?" I asked, breaking the bar into three. Handing them each a piece, we ate in silence as we followed Reubén for a tour of the Sacred Plaza.

⁂

CHAPTER SIX

Jen

AMAZON JUNGLE, PERU
JULY

Floating down the Amazon River, Amanda, Holly, and I peered over the railing of the famous triple-decker *Amazon Queen*, eagerly scanning the depths for piranhas. It was rumored that these legendary underwater assassins were abundant in the area, but we'd yet to spot even one razor-sharp tooth beneath the surface.

"Hey, Hol, why don't you test the waters?" I cajoled, nudging her forward with my shoulder. "It's just a few fingers."

"Hah! I laugh at killer fish," she said, pushing me back. "I think Amanda should be the one to put her hand in . . . you know, since I had to sit by myself on the plane on the way here."

With a month of traveling already under our belts, Amanda, Holly, and I had settled into a comfortable sisterly relationship, teasing and tormenting each other as effortlessly as if we'd grown up in the same house. I still marveled at the fact that not only had all three of us committed to the trip but we'd actually grown closer—rather than wanting to throttle one another—after spending so much quality time together.

We'd packed in more adventures and bonding moments in the inaugural weeks of the trip than I'd been expecting from the entire year. So far, we'd hiked the Inca Trail, surfed down mountainous sand dunes in Huacachina, been rescued by a priest in a minivan in a Colca Canyon desert, visited the floating islands on Lake Titicaca, eaten alpaca in Cusco, very nearly been bucked off the backs of wild horses in the countryside outside Lima, and were now embarking on a five-day journey through the heart of the Amazon.

The sheer number of adrenaline-pumping activities we'd just experienced—and still had in store—had mostly overshadowed any homesickness on my part. Aside from one dramatic screaming and crying match with Brian in a very public Internet café in Arequipa (not my proudest tourist moment), we'd managed to shelve any serious relationship talks and decided to discuss the topic of "us" only after I left Brazil and returned to New York City for two weeks in August.

Until that day arrived, I intended to focus entirely on the trip and living in the moment. I pulled out my camera and started snapping pictures over the railing. Though there were no paint-smeared natives trolling the riverbanks, as we'd half expected, our leisurely cruise down the Amazon did provide a scenic overview of what was to come: emerald green rain forests, sleepy riverside villages, vast sherbet-colored sunsets, and an endless cacophony of monkey howls, parrot squawks, and cicadalike rhythms.

Upon arrival at our all-inclusive lodge (there really weren't many other sleeping options available to tourists in the Amazon), we were escorted to quaint, thatched-roof bungalows to freshen up before meeting Cliver, our local guide and 24/7 tourist-sitter during our stay. As we sipped syrupy ribbons of rum and fruit juice through curly bamboo straws, Cliver entertained us with jungle trivia, then rattled off a quick list of must-dos. Determined to pack in as many activities as we could physically handle, we crafted an itinerary that included every excursion from the lodge-sanctioned Amazon sampler menu—taking a rain forest night hike, darting through the treetops on shaky suspension bridges, making friends with wild monkeys, and fishing for piranhas.

Personally, I was so thrilled to have someone else take charge of our schedule that I almost didn't care what we did. As long as we were surrounded by nature, far from civilization and all the pesky Internet cafés I'd grown to loathe, I was a happy jungle camper.

"Hey, Cliver, I read that there's Wi-Fi here at the lodge. Is that true?" Amanda asked.

Without thinking, I rolled my eyes but quickly turned my head, hoping Amanda hadn't caught me doing it. Though I loved the tremendous reservoir of free time we'd just tapped into, it seemed she hadn't quite adjusted to the serious downshift in the pace and structure of our days. I didn't quite get it: though she'd been the one of us most determined to leave her high-stress job, she was also the one most determined to stay in touch with the world that we'd left behind. Every single person in our lives knew that we were overseas, but she still slipped off and checked her e-mail daily.

"Oh, sure, it's a tad compulsive, but now that we have so much time to just chill on the road, what's the harm in going online every once in a while? You know I'm addicted," she'd joke.

Blame it on the ancient IBMs or ultraslow dial-up connections, but soon the single hour she said she planned to spend in the Internet café turned into several. And once Amanda decided she wanted to pitch articles to editors back in New York, our daily itinerary was often shaped around her desire to do online research and be available between the hours of 9 a.m. and 5 p.m. Between Amanda's newfound ambition to become a travel writer and the monthly column Holly had been assigned to pen from the road, I found myself left to my own devices more often than I'd expected—or wanted. Just when I'd built up the nerve to share my frustrations with Amanda, she hit me with a piece of news that made me pause.

"Since girlfriend getaways are becoming a hot travel topic, I proposed a 'Girls' Guide to Cusco' to a former coworker of mine who is now working at a guidebook company. It'd be a kind of photo flip book of female-friendly places they could put online," she explained, her words tumbling out in a rush.

"Wow, that's an awesome idea," Holly said.

"Thanks. The editor really liked it too, and"—she paused, leaning forward with a conspiratorial grin—"this is where you guys come in. She wants you to write it with me."

"Wait, you mean you and Holly, right?" I said. "I've only ever written marketing proposals for work, which I doubt qualifies me to do this sort of piece."

"No, she wants you to do it, too. I told her all about our trip, and she thinks it would be more interesting coming from all three of us. If we do a good job, it could even turn into a regular online series. And of course we'd be getting paid for it," Amanda added hastily. "Not much, but enough to pay for a few nights' sleep a month."

I could tell Amanda expected me to be thrilled about the opportunity, but I was still on the fence about whether a group writing assignment was a good idea. After taking a few days to mull it over, I'd hesitantly agreed. I knew it was important to Amanda, so I didn't want to hold her back. Plus, as the keeper of our trip budget, I knew the extra cash would come in handy.

But when Cliver responded, "Yes, we do have the wireless Internet throughout all of the lodge," my heart sank a little.

While the group project was still hanging over our heads, the last thing I wanted to think about in the Amazon was working. This portion of our trip was exactly the type of wild, off-the-beaten-track experience that had prompted me to leave

New York in the first place. Maybe once we were installed in the jungle, Amanda would forget the Internet—at least for a little while.

For the first time in weeks, we awoke not to the sound of sledgehammers smashing concrete, car horns blaring, wild dogs barking, or roosters screeching, but rather to something we'd forgotten existed: silence.

Tugging at the cloth window panel, I took in the exotic spread of vine-wrapped trees, tropical flowers, and rainbow-painted macaws perched on a poolside gazebo. Well rested at last (and uncharacteristically cheery at such an early hour), I bounced out of bed to join the girls in getting dressed for our first great adventure. The morning hike would lead us to the Canopy Walkway, which Cliver dutifully pointed out was one of the longest treetop pathways in the world.

Pumped full of malaria meds, our water bottles topped to the brim and a tube of SPF 30 sunblock shoved into a side pocket of Holly's day pack, we felt amply prepared to plunge into the jungle and explore the steamy surroundings. After a winding trek down a palm-fringed trail, we arrived at the base of the first (of fourteen) narrow suspension bridges lashed together with steel cables and thick twine, and began the long ascent up the staircase. Our guidebook wasn't kidding when it said this experience wasn't for the faint of heart.

The narrow wooden boards were suspended more than a hundred feet in the air. They creaked and shuddered with every step, and we felt more like characters in an Indiana Jones film than a trio of wide-eyed tourists. Even though I could see the mesh netting installed underneath the bridges to keep crossers from plummeting to the jungle floor, traversing the planks with no harness required some seriously steely nerves—and all my concentration. On the first bridge, the girls and I moved at a snail's pace, literally learning the ropes as we went. But with each new crossing challenge, I got braver and faster until I was eventually navigating bridges without using my hands to steady me. Between our Cirque du Soleil–worthy stunts, Amanda, Holly, and I loitered on the treetop platforms, attempting to digitally capture the aerial view that only we—and an extended family of spider monkeys—were privy to.

When we finally stepped back onto terra firma, I slowly came down from the high of our "near-death" experience. Fortunately, Cliver had another adventure in store for us. He was taking us to see a local medicine man named Luis, a healing shaman who lived deep within the jungle.

An expert in rain forest remedies, Luis was the go-to guy when anything from a toothache to a cold to a deadly snakebite struck one of the local villagers. We arrived at his makeshift clinic—an open-air, dirt-floored pavilion—and settled down on wobbly wood stools, waiting for Luis to give what Cliver described as a "beeerrry special lecture on the plants that calm sickness and disease."

"And there is a special drink to, how do you say, uh, make you be in the sexy mood," Cliver added with a mischievous grin. "It does not taste good, but you are very happy afterward."

Before any of us could respond to that comment, a shrunken man with deeply carved wrinkles and a shock of wild gray hair appeared before us in the clinic. He set up camp behind a rickety workbench topped with empty glass vials, baskets filled with leaves, roots and herbs, and unmarked jars brimming with crimson- and toffee-colored liquids.

With Cliver translating Luis's native Quechua into understandable (though slightly suspect) English phrases, the girls and I learned how mimosa root could be used as a contraceptive, a tea made from *paico* plants killed intestinal parasites, and the scarlet sap from a dragon's-blood tree had the power to heal cuts and quell the itch of mosquito bites. But by far the most impressive information that Cliver shared was the fact that nearly a quarter of today's Western pharmaceuticals, including some cancer treatments, are derived from tropical rain forest plants. This discovery gave us a whole new level of respect for our surroundings and the importance of environmental preservation.

After the presentation wrapped up, Cliver introduced us to Luis, and we finally discovered the meaning of his cryptic statement about rain forest remedies that could put us in the mood. Taking a generous swig from a bottle of what looked like dirty lake water, Cliver explained that by soaking the bark of the *chuchuhuasi* tree in local sugarcane rum (*aguardiente* or "firewater"), the medicine man had created a powerful aphrodisiac. And since Cliver was going to visit his girlfriend later, he wanted to be prepared.

"Waaaay too much information, Cliver!" I remarked as he crossed his arms over his chest and gave us a slow, sly nod. "The effects are probably in your head anyway."

"What, you do not believe me?" he replied, not even attempting to suppress a wide grin. "Maybe you try it for yourself and prove me wrong?"

"Oh, yeah, Jen. Take a sip and see what happens," Holly baited, a clear retaliation for my unsportsmanlike conduct around her and the piranhas. "C'mon, I dare you!"

"I quadruple dog dare you," added Amanda, extracting the bottle from Cliver's hands and forcing it into mine. "If it works, it'll be a great story to tell your grandkids . . . or, well, maybe your future husband."

"If I drink this shit, I may not live long enough to get married and have kids, let alone grandkids," I said, taking a whiff of the pungent formula, then recoiling in pain as the fumes singed my sinuses.

"C'mon, Baggy, this is totally one of those daredevil stunts you *say* you're not afraid to do," Amanda said, not allowing me to back down.

"Throwing myself out of a plane is one thing. Drinking a potentially poisonous substance is quite another," I rebutted, but I was already raising the bottle to my lips. "Fine. I'll do it."

Before I could change my mind, I downed a huge gulp. After staring for a second in disbelief, Cliver, Amanda, and Holly responded with enthusiastic howls, drowning out my theatrical hisses and yelps. I'd never exactly sampled battery acid, but it couldn't taste much worse or burn more than this stuff.

As we bid the shaman farewell and left the medicine hut, Holly and Amanda pummeled me with obnoxious questions.

"Are you oddly attracted to that tree? Or maybe that spider?" Amanda asked the second we were out of Cliver's earshot.

"How 'bout that monkey up there . . . looking pretty sexy right about now, huh?" goaded Holly, poking me in the side.

I didn't admit it, but about twenty minutes later, a peculiar, tingly warmth began to spread throughout my body. Blame it on the swill's alcoholic potency or the voodoo power of suggestion, but whatever it was, by the time we returned to the lodge I was eager to hit the freezing cold showers.

A lthough Amanda, Holly, and I reveled in the athletic opportunities the Amazon provided, it was one of the cultural excursions that most piqued our interest. On our third day, Cliver took us to meet a group of Yagua Indians, an indigenous tribe best known for its expertise in blowgun hunting. Not only were we going to watch them shoot tiny darts thirty feet and hit an impossibly small target, but, according to Cliver, they were going to teach us how to do the exact same thing.

After a brisk hike in 100 percent humidity, we arrived panting and dripping with sweat at the entrance of the tiny village, home to the elusive *ribereños* (people of the river). What little breath I had left was immediately taken away by the sight of this strange new world. It took me a second to spot them at first, but peeking out through the doorways of darkened huts, weaving fabric silently in the shade, and resting under trees, were the most intriguing figures we'd yet to lay eyes on.

Petite in stature with striking sienna complexions and red paint smudged across their faces, the Yagua still seemed to live in an era before huge swathes of the Amazon had been deforested and the ever-encroaching gringo had brought commerce and "progress" to the region. The men donned intricate wigs and long skirts constructed of dried grasses, while the women wore red cloth wraps on their bottom half and dangling neck pieces that covered a small portion of their chests.

As he ushered us into a large hut flanked with bushy reeds, Cliver explained that the Yagua relied solely on rain forest plants for their wardrobes and created fabrics from the fibers of the *aguaje* palm and red dye (*achiote*) from the fruit of the *Bixa orellana* tree.

We sat on hand-carved benches and watched in awe as the Yagua elders formed a snug circle and began to sing and dance around the room, their upper bodies swaying and their hips popping from side to side as they walked. One by one the others followed suit, filling the air with soothing drum and flute melodies. In a low whisper, Cliver told us the tribe was performing a traditional dance that paid homage to the rain god and encouraged us to join in when the younger tribeswomen pulled us to our feet.

After several turns around the dirt floor with our new friends, we were led outside for our next challenge: mastering the art of the blowgun. Without a word, the chief pointed to a wooden post in the ground across a wide clearing. We observed as men loaded darts (small sticks with cottony fabric on one end) into the mouthpiece of long hollow tubes, took aim, and blew. Within seconds, the points landed squarely in the middle of the target. When the Yagua actually went out to hunt, they'd dip the darts in curare, a fast-acting natural poison that paralyzes their prey. But fortunately they skipped that step when tourists were present.

One after another, the girls and I hoisted the heavy tube onto our shoulders, shouted, "Ready, set, blow!," and fired. A light puff was enough to send our ammo whizzing through the air, and after only a few failed attempts, our shots finally pierced the post.

As we returned the blowguns to the elders and started our journey back, Holly asked Cliver whether it was really such a good idea for outsiders like us to be visiting the Yagua tribe. Though the three of us considered our interaction with the locals to be an amazing once-in-a-lifetime opportunity, we wondered whether our presence was actually benefiting the community—or rather contributed to the demise of the traditional culture.

Cliver explained the repercussions if we *didn't* bring our dollars into the Yagua village. "It is the honest truth, my friends, that the only way to keep locals from cutting down the rain forest for farmland or lumber is to show them they can make more money by protecting it," he said glancing upward at the canopy as he spoke. "If they can make a living sharing their way of life with tourists like you, then they have more incentive to preserve it."

We figured that there was another side to this story (some fellow travelers lamented that the local villagers were selling off their culture and turning their customs into a charade for visitors), but we also hoped there was some truth to what Cliver was telling us. I wanted to believe that the tribal masks, necklaces, and fertility dolls we'd just purchased as souvenirs would actually help preserve the locals' way of life and keep their traditions alive. But as with the future of the Amazon rain forest itself, only time would tell.

The next day, the three of us wanted to take a break from the prepackaged jungle activities, so we asked Cliver if there was a safe place nearby where we could walk around or sightsee on our own. Nothing formal or touristy, just a real place with real people.

"Of course, *princesas*," he replied. "There are still many places like that around here. I will take you."

Hopping into one of the lodge's motorboat taxis, we zipped a few miles upstream to the nearby village of Indiana. Originally founded as a Franciscan mission, Indiana had grown into a large river community with its own market, high school, and small hospital. It was midday, and the riverside dock buzzed with the activity of a typical port town. Sun-scorched fisherman hauled in their daily catch as women unloaded baskets of brightly colored vegetables and children crowded around candy carts. Aside from a few curious glances, no one really reacted as we disembarked from the boat, weaved through the bodies on the shore, and walked to the heart of town.

Since Indiana was about as threatening as a *Star Trek* convention, we decided to branch out on our own and give our guide a break from the unending task of answering all our questions. We agreed to meet back at the main square in about an hour, synchronized our sports watches, and parted ways.

After a month on the road, the girls and I were almost as in tune with one another's habits and favorite on-the-road pursuits as we were with our own. For example, I knew that Holly needed to go running daily and embark on frequent missions to the market. Amanda would get antsy if a few days went by without going online, writing, and blogging. As for me, well, I just wanted to get involved in any hedonistic pleasure that didn't require technology. Much of the time, our interests intersected, but we were totally fine with a two-to-one group split when they didn't. So before Holly opened her mouth, Amanda and I knew what was coming. "So, uh, guys, I think I'm gonna go for a quick jog and then maybe look around some of the little stands, okay?"

"That's totally cool, Corby. Jen and I will hike on our own and meet you back here by three p.m. Just don't get lost, okay?" Amanda said.

"Yeah, and be safe, Hol," I added, knowing full well that she could outsprint almost anyone. Not that she'd need to, but still.

As it turned out, Indiana was far more pastoral than most of the Amazonian landscape we'd seen so far. Rather than toucans and macaws darting through the canopy, we spotted scrawny barnyard roosters pecking the dirt in small clearings. Wild anteaters were nowhere to be seen, but there were plenty of cows grazing in pastureland. Taking our trek very seriously, Amanda and I tromped through mud puddles, scaled the barbed-wire fences that crisscrossed farms, and stared down a few restless bulls (though we squealed and ran if they made any sudden movements). Along the way, we practiced our Spanish with the swarm of kids who tagged along with us for much of the journey.

When we returned to our meeting point, we found Holly and Cliver chatting with three young guys on motorcycles. It turned out they were friends of Cliver's who'd offered to give us a driving tour of the area for only 10 soles, or $3 total.

"I'll totally pay a buck for a bike ride. You guys in?" I asked Amanda and Holly.

Within seconds, we were all clinging to our drivers' waists

with a deadly vise grip as they tore down bumpy dirt paths and over shaky narrow bridges. Once it was apparent that we weren't destined to become road kill, I relaxed a little. We rode for miles, zipping past simply constructed farmhouses, vast flower-speckled fields, and the occasional watering hole before screeching to a stop at a makeshift gas station. Giving the attendant a few soles for water bottles filled with a citrine liquid, our drivers topped off their tanks, made a U-turn, and began the return trip. By the time we arrived back in the center of town, dusk was falling. We were all breathless from the ride, but exhilarated.

"You enjoyed the tour, *princesas*?" Cliver asked as we screeched to a stop. "Now maybe it's time for cold Cusqueñas at my friend's bar?"

"Definitely. Love that plan," I replied.

"Hey, uh, Cliver, I kinda need to go back to the lodge," Amanda interjected, suddenly looking anxious. "Is there any way I can go but the girls can stay and hang out?"

"Well, with one boat, we should go together," he said, wiping his forehead with a bandana. "Is something troubling you?"

"Oh no, nothing is wrong at all. I just . . . I just have some writing to do and need to use the Internet before my editor back in the States leaves work for the night," she said hesitantly as she shifted from one foot to the other. "But I don't want to make Jen and Holly leave now."

"It's totally fine with me if we go back," Holly said, clearly trying to keep a potentially uncomfortable situation light and happy—as she always did. "I'm kinda tired anyway, and I should probably work on my next column."

"Really, guys? Right now?" I asked, bummed to leave just when things were getting started.

I knew it shouldn't have been a huge deal, but I couldn't understand why Amanda kept wanting to cut our experiences short to run off and work. It's not as if I couldn't hang with Holly or with the abundance of on-call backpackers at our hostels. But since I'd known Amanda, she'd been a full-steam-ahead, unstoppable career girl, taking on multiple internships in college and as many freelance assignments as she could handle in New York. Frankly, I'd been a little surprised when she'd suggested taking a full year off from her career in order to travel—and even more impressed that she'd actually gone through with it. But over these past few weeks, I'd been gathering that Amanda might not put the brakes on writing while we traveled and, in fact, might want to work every single day in the year ahead.

Although the selfish side of me just wanted her around, the best-friend side wanted to see her find happiness and fulfillment from other sources. But this was neither the time nor the place to get into that, so I stayed quiet. Halfway down the river, a wave of exhaustion suddenly hit me and I was actually relieved we were heading back. I couldn't wait to lounge at the lodge pool with a good book and frozen beverage in hand.

Then, as if on cue, Amanda asked, "So when I'm done with my e-mails, do you girls maybe want to work on the guidebook article?"

"Umm, let me think . . . no," I replied.

"Well, I mean, we promised to hand it in next week, so why not work on it now, when there's nothing else to do?" Amanda said.

"What do you *mean*, nothing to do?" I exclaimed, feeling the noose of agitation tightening without warning. "We're in the Amazon jungle. And probably the only time we ever will be."

"I know, but you could say that about the whole trip," Amanda replied. "You told me that you were okay with us taking the assignment, but you never actually want to *do* it."

"Yeah, I know, but this may be the only time ever in our lives that we don't have to work. Don't you think we should find other things we're passionate about or challenge ourselves in new ways?" I asked, my voice still calm but rising an octave.

"Yeah, I guess this is the time to let go of things that have been holding us back or try something that scares us," Holly added.

"You know, I'd even travel by myself for a few days, even though the idea totally freaks me out," I offered, trying to bring the conversation to a more productive place. I shied away from solo travel and being alone at all costs, so I hoped Amanda would understand that this would be a sacrifice for me.

"I really want to learn more about Hinduism and meditation, so maybe I really should sign up for that yoga teacher training program in India that I read about," Holly said, launching another peacekeeping mission.

Amanda was silent, so I blabbed on. "I mean, do you really want to work on the road? This might be the first and last time in your adult life that you have absolutely no responsibilities and nothing but time on your hands. You've already established yourself as a successful writer. So why not give that up for a few weeks and see what else you love? The trip would be more fun that way."

Amanda's head snapped in my direction, and she gave me what I can only describe as a death stare. "That's so unfair of you to ask, Jen. It'd be like me suggesting you give up your love for film."

"Oh, please. It's not at all the same thing," I said, stunned by the ferocity of her reaction. "Movies are a fun passion. Writing story pitches is work. I mean, c'mon. Try being an *under*achiever for once in your life."

That did it. I'd crossed the line.

The tension was heavy enough to sink our schooner. And considering that we were in piranha-infested waters, I needed to defuse the situation fast.

"You know what, just forget I said anything. It was stupid," I said, hopping out of the boat and onto the dock we'd reached just in the nick of time. "I'm going to take a quick nap. I'll meet you girls in the lobby later."

Amanda and I had been close friends for years but had rarely fought, so the whole incident was seriously awkward. On one hand, I knew it was childish of me to whine so much about, God forbid, having to adjust *my* travel schedule to accommodate my friend's journalistic career, but I hadn't quite been able to shake the mild resentment that I'd been baited by one trip, then given the old switcheroo once we were on the road. I wanted to just get over it and agree to disagree, already, but that was proving to be easier said than done.

We awoke the next day with a bit of a heavy heart, bummed that it was our last one in the Amazon. But we were quickly perked up by that morning's field trip to Monkey Island, home to eight different species of monkeys that are cared for and protected by a wildlife preservation project. Designed as the ultimate petting zoo, the island provides adventurous tourists with the chance to interact directly with its inhabitants (who are supposedly people-friendly).

As we crept through the rain forest en route to the site, we could hear their distinctive howls and shrieks radiating through the trees. Swinging from branches, running through the fields, and leaping across a huge platform were more wild animals than in Times Square at rush hour. Without an ounce of caution or concern, the girls and I sprinted toward the main platform like kids racing to get the best swing on the playground. Clearly accustomed to humans, the monkeys didn't even flinch. In fact, they crept toward us, hoping we had snacks to give them. The groundskeepers handed us soft white fruits that resembled bananas to feed to our new fuzzy friends and, of course, lure them closer for the ultimate photo op.

With our cameras at the ready, Amanda, Holly, and I took turns coaxing *los monos* into our arms. We were pleasantly surprised by how sweet they were. That is until, out of nowhere, one of the larger monkeys jumped onto Holly's head. Possibly mistaking her for food, the crazy little beast grabbed at her hair and nibbled on her shoulder. Holly shrieked and twirled around in circles, trying to throw him off.

Between fits of laughter, we went to Holly's aid, but as soon as we extracted her from his intense grip, he merely refocused his attention on another victim: me! I screamed as the cheeky little monkey scrambled up my arm and started gnawing on my hand. I wanted to get him off me as quickly as possible, but Amanda had another idea. "This is great stuff! Hold on so I can get it on camera!" she exclaimed.

"What? Are you crazy?" I managed to squeak out in between wrestling rounds with my furry opponent.

"Come on, Jen. Just a few more seconds, and I'll have the moment on tape. It'll be excellent fodder for our blog."

"Oh, well, if you put it that way! What's a limb in the name of art?" I shouted over the monkey's howls.

"C'mon, Jen, hold still so I can—" Amanda began. She'd gotten only halfway through her sentence when the mother of all monkeys swung down from the rafters and landed on her back.

She screamed, pitching away the video camera, which Holly thankfully caught before it could hit the ground. Instead of turning it off, she turned the lens back around to capture Amanda's battle with the beast.

"Ahh, Jen, come over here and help me!" Amanda shrieked, unable to get a good grip on the animal behind her.

I grinned, walking toward her slowly with a piece of fruit in my hand.

"I don't know, Amanda, I've been trying to pull the monkey off your back the entire trip. Are you sure you're ready for me to do it now?" I smirked, wondering if she understood that I was referring to work, not wildlife.

"Yes, yes, just come over here and help me!" she shrieked, half laughing, half whimpering.

Okay, so she didn't quite get it, but I moved behind her anyway and did my best to disengage her new furry friend. I'd hoped she'd see things from my perspective at some point, but if not, I'd still be just a few feet away, ready to lend her a hand.

❧

CHAPTER SEVEN

Amanda

LIMA, PERU

AUGUST

"Okay, you can open your eyes. But don't get too excited," Jen warned, placing a heavy blue bag in my outstretched hands.

"You made it! Happy twenty-eighth!" Holly sounded nearly as psyched as if it had been her own birthday. Seconds earlier, she and Jen had ordered me to keep my eyes closed—tight!—while they ran around putting the finishing touches on my present.

"Wow, guys. Um, you shouldn't have," I said, laughing, as I dug through the tissue and pulled out an electric pink, blue, and silver kiddie tiara with matching dangly earrings. "This is *just* what I wanted."

"We did have to spend a whole dollar at the party store, and it's a matching set, so make sure you keep those pieces together," said Jen, poking fun at my tendency to misplace important items, such as keys, phones, and now possibly plastic jewelry.

"That's not all! Keep looking," Holly said as she dropped down next to me on the bed.

Setting aside two small bottles of Inca Kola, the biohazardous yellow soda that tasted like bubble gum, I reached back in the bag to pluck out a pair of delicate black high heels.

I was genuinely thrilled. In my effort to be practical, to commit to the true "rugged adventurer" spirit of backpacking, I'd brought just three pairs of shoes with me: hiking sneakers, Tevas, and Reef sandals. Though I'd initially felt proud of my monk-like ability to unburden myself of material possessions (and secretly, that my backpack was the lightest of the three), I'd lost my ability to feel feminine along with the extra weight.

In direct opposition, Holly hadn't bought into some arbitrary perception of what a "real traveler" should take on a journey—and didn't believe in lightening up merely to save her spine. Every time we shifted locations, her strong runner's legs would buckle under the strain of the travel novels, packing guides, energy bars, moisturizers, and cosmetics that consumed every spare inch of space in her pack. Whenever Jen or I would ask why she'd brought so much, she'd grin and say, "Just because we're homeless doesn't mean we have to look like it, right?"

Her tongue-in-cheek response never failed to make me shake my head and smile—she was only half kidding. Though I'd worked with Holly for almost two years at the magazine, I'd only recently come to realize that she had a sly, screwball sense of humor—which of course meant that she fit in perfectly with Jen and me. Together, the three of us could laugh about our most bizarre travel situations and agreed that we were totally at our most hilarious when exhausted (which, considering the late-night/early-morning nature of our travel routine, was 99 percent of the time).

In my recent quest to learn how to defuse stress with humor—and humility—it was Holly who had become my guru. After watching her soften up everyone from the grouchiest government officials to obnoxious bunkmates (and usually get her way), I'd learned that far more can be accomplished by being calm and sincere than letting your temper get the best of you. I still had a long way to go before I'd be even half as laid-back as Hol, but somehow, it was just easier to roll with the punches whenever she was around. Other than Jen, I couldn't think of a single friend I'd rather have at my first-ever Southern Hemisphere birthday.

Once we determined that my glamorous new shoes did, in fact, fit, Jen told me to get dressed: she and Holly were taking me out to dinner to celebrate.

I unzipped my pack to survey the contents. There's one undisputable benefit of cramming your wardrobe into 3,500 cubic inches: You really can't burn through forty-five minutes trying on and rejecting outfits when you have only six to choose from.

Digging underneath the mud-encrusted pants and Deet-scented tops I'd worn in the jungle, I located the one nonutilitarian article of clothing I'd allowed myself to bring: a black cotton jersey dress with a V neckline and twisted Grecian-style straps. Unrolling it and shaking out the wrinkles, I laid the dress carefully out on the bottom bunk, placed the tiara and heels next to it, and awaited my turn for the shower.

I'd once read that the real nightlife in Lima centers almost exclusively around the process of dining and drinking, rather than partying in pubs and clubs. The city's young elite breaks bread at new restaurants as a way to see and be seen—why hide in the shadows when you can be on maximum display on the floor of some trendy new tapas bar? So far, no place we'd visited brought this idea to life more stylishly than T'anta.

From our table situated along the back wall of the restaurant, I could see that the place was crawling with Peru's hipster bohemians. The girls, slender-limbed and beautiful, wore almost no discernible makeup but sported shaggy crops streaked with champagne- and manila-colored highlights. They dressed for the unpredictable weather of the Peruvian coast, layering floppy woolen scarves and off-the-shoulder tops over asymmetrically hemmed dresses or jeans, and stood strategically under the heat lamps.

"Where'd you hear about this place?" I whispered to Jen after a waitress delivered our Pisco Sours. "And how'd you get us a reservation?"

She smiled cryptically. "Oh, never mind. I have my special connections."

The three of us had sipped our way through our first round of foamy green drinks when Holly excused herself to find the ladies' room. I immediately looked down into my bag to locate our shared roll of toilet paper, and when I looked up, a saucer-eyed Holly was slinking back into her chair.

"Uh, I'm not sure . . . I could be going crazy, but you don't think . . . over there, that could be? Well, maybe not. But I think the guy really looks like . . ."

"What? What are you talking about?" I said, leaning forward to have a look.

My gut clenched even before I could identify the guy I'd just spotted across the room. How could I have missed him before? He was the only person in Lima I actually knew—but had no desire to meet again.

"I think I just saw Carlos," she said, squeaking out the name a second too late.

Crap. I melted back into my seat, my brain racing through potential escape routes. It seemed there were none. We were seated at the back of the restaurant, so I'd have to walk right past him to get out. Could I just crouch under the table until he left?

"Carlos? Here? No way." Jen swiveled around to look behind her and snapped back again, clasping a hand over her mouth. "Oh, my God, it *is* him."

"Only you, Amanda," said Holly, shaking her head. "Lady, I swear, this kind of thing only happens to you."

Stealing another glance at Carlos, I groaned. She was right. Most women could visit a foreign country packed with 28 million people and manage to avoid bumping into the one man they'd blown off just a week before, but not me.

Over the last few years, I'd become something of an expert at crossing paths with guys I hoped never to see again, usually in claustrophobic spaces like elevators and ATM vestibules. Obnoxious dates I'd neglected to call back. Setups that never should have been set up. Ex-boyfriends I could have sworn had left the state years earlier. Holly always joked that I had some kind of weird karmic energy or power of attraction that forced me to reencounter guys from my past over and over again. "Either the universe is telling you that you still have something to learn from them," she'd say, "or else someone up there just gets sick pleasure out of watching you squirm."

Natural-born pragmatist that I am, I never believed that "the gods" had put a romantic hex on me. I just figured that bumping into boys of relationships past was simply a matter of geography. Living on an island not much bigger than a university campus, wasn't it only a matter of time before I ran into someone I no longer wanted to know? Of course, that theory could hardly explain why one of them was sitting less than twenty feet away from me in a restaurant I'd never been to before ten thousand miles from home.

I'd met Carlos exactly a week earlier during a brief layover in Lima before we went to the Amazon. Once we'd secured our Brazilian visas and packed our bags for the jungle, we went in search of Café del Mar, a restaurant and jazz club Anthony had raved about back in Cusco.

Everything about the place had been done on a dramatic scale, from its forty-foot ceilings to the massive wall stocked floor to rafters with top-shelf liquor. Warm amber backlight made the bottles glow and turned bartenders into swiftly moving silhouettes. We'd parked ourselves on a cut-velvet sofa and were just noticing how underdressed we were when a waiter skated over to deliver a message.

"*Perdóname, señoritas. Alguien quiere comprarles una botella de champaña. ¿Aceptan ustedes?*"

"I think he's saying . . . someone wants to send us a glass of champagne," Jen said.

"No way," said Holly, looking around. "Who?"

"*¿De quién? ¿Quién lo nos compra?*" Jen asked the waiter. "Who's buying it for us?"

"I bet you a hundred soles that it's from those two," said Holly, motioning to a couple of guys in button-down shirts lounging at the bar about ten feet away.

"*¿Champaña es de ellos?*" Jen asked the waiter, make a subtle gesture with her hand. He somehow interpreted the motion as his cue to take off and return to our table with not a glass but a bottle of bubbly. I'm sure we could have tried harder—or at least somewhat—to prevent him from popping the cork, but we rationalized: wasn't half the point of traveling to meet new people?

The waiter tipped the frothing liquid down the sides of three glasses, and within minutes the guys edged their way over, pausing at our table almost as if it had been an afterthought. Carlos and Daniel, as they introduced themselves in English, admitted that they'd been our secret benefactors and asked if they could join us.

"Don't worry," Carlos teased as we shifted over to make room. "We have another place to be tonight, so you won't have to put up with us for long."

With thick, wavy hair that fell just below his ears, deep brown eyes, and a voice that trailed off in a low, throaty growl, Carlos definitely struck me as the more intriguing of the two guys. And so when he opted to sit beside me on the sofa—leaving sandy blond Daniel to slide into the chair across the table—I didn't complain.

Setting down his glass with a light *plink*, he turned to face me directly. Back home, this would have been the moment when the first-encounter interview started—a casual yet carefully phrased interrogation where one person determines if the other has the right combo of desirable attributes (résumé, title, earning potential, family background, social circle, geographic location, and attractiveness) to warrant a prolonged conversation. It was a dating and mating ritual that had at first intimidated me—but I'd finally accepted as an occupational hazard of meeting new people in New York.

But Carlos didn't seem interested in my on-paper attributes. He wanted to know my opinion on a wide variety of topics, such as . . . Peruvian politics. And social issues. And current events. Had I been following the tight presidential race between candidates Alan García and Ollanta Humala? What did Americans think of Humala's connection to the Venezuelan dictator Hugo Chávez and Fidel Castro?

I confessed that I'd learned about the details of his country's election only last month, not mentioning that just a fraction of Americans could locate Peru on a map, let alone voice opinions on its leaders. I felt completely lost, as if I'd memorized the answers to an English test and had somehow been given the MCATs instead—in Spanish.

Fortunately, Carlos didn't call me out on my ignorance. He patiently walked me through the basics, giving me the kind of insight into his country—its political corruption, the agendas of its parties, and his personal connection to its violent history—I'd never find in a guidebook. Once we'd covered the tough stuff, I trotted out the big guns of my own, broaching a topic that I'd been hesitant to discuss with strangers in Peru.

"Of course, you can ask me anything," he offered, placing a hand on mine.

"Well, okay, here it is. Since I've been here, I've found toilet paper in maybe six of the bathrooms. I mean, what do people do when they have to go? Do they pack their own before they leave their houses? Or, uh . . . just finish up and go without?"

It took him a second to switch gears, but once it clicked, he turned an impressive shade of crimson. He tilted his head back and coughed heartily to cover his laughter.

"Oh, yes, I see your confusion. People in Peru, sometimes they bring this paper with them. Why, maybe do you need to use some right now?"

Now it was my turn to go red.

As Carlos excused himself from the table to get our bill, I turned toward the girls and realized that they were deep into a heavy conversation of their own.

"But I do not understand," Daniel was saying. "Why do you vote your president George Bush into office for another term? He makes many poor decisions, no?"

Oh, man. I bit my lip and listened as Jen tried to explain the difference between red and blue states. In the short time that we'd been away, we'd already had to defend our own voting record (if not the president himself) several times to travelers from around the world.

Carlos returned and saved us with a proposition. He and Daniel were attending the opening of a new nightclub in the city—would we like to join them? After some deliberation in the bathroom (one with toilet paper, thankfully), the girls and I accepted.

It was clear immediately upon arrival that these guys were no slouches on Lima's club circuit. Interlacing his fingers

117

through mine, Carlos led the three of us right past a massive line of girls clad in stretchy fabrics and guys wearing Gucci sunglasses fitted snugly over slicked-back hair. He sidled over to speak with one of the bouncers, then ushered us up a long flight of stairs. When we emerged, the five of us were standing on a small VIP balcony space perched directly over the main dance floor.

Below us, a sea of bodies gyrated to music pumped out of Escalade-sized speakers. High above, a DJ commanded the entire room, an evangelist spinning hard house tracks. Mylar strips in saturated shades hung from the pipes, swaying and shimmering in the updraft created by so much heat and movement.

Everybody in the club was getting tipsy—and no one more rapidly than Carlos and Daniel. Between dances with us they retreated to the bar to refill their drinks. In their absence, the girls and I discovered that this VIP area was stocked liberally with men—mostly sweaty, frantic, unattached men. We tried to deflect their attention, dancing with one another in a tightly locked ring, the signature formation of women at nightclubs the world over, but our dodge, draft, and rescue maneuvers didn't work nearly as well in Peru as they had at home. Despite our best efforts, we were soon surrounded.

"*¡Que jodienda! ¡Estoy sudando como un puerco!* It's hot in here, no?" Carlos returned and broke up the mob. The men scattered a few feet, biding their time until he turned his back again.

Carlos danced with all three of us for a few minutes before he turned his attention solely on me, grabbing my hand and pulling me into the crowd as some technopop version of "Hips Don't Lie" filled the air. For some reason, we couldn't seem to escape Shakira. We'd heard this song playing in every Internet café, Laundromat, hostel, bar, and nightclub from Lima to Lake Titicaca and back again.

As we danced, Carlos moved in closer, insistently pressing

my body against his. His shirt was soaked through with sweat, and the heavy scent of whiskey clouded around him. When his hands wandered lower, I backed up. He allowed that, then tugged me in again, locking his arms around my body so that it was impossible for me to get away.

Looking up at his face, I could see that he was smiling, but his eyes seemed dull and obscured. I felt as if I were dancing with an entirely different person from the one I'd come with. With no preamble, Carlos leaned in to press his lips against mine, his tongue aggressively darting in and swirling around my mouth. I reeled back forcefully, separating myself completely from his grasp.

"Hey, where did Daniel go?" I asked, searching for something to say as I resisted the temptation to dry my face with the back of my hand.

"I am not sure," he said, eyes narrowing. "You wanted him maybe to dance with you?"

"No, it's just that I, well . . . maybe we should go somewhere else."

He shrugged and took a step toward me, wrapping himself around my body once again. I definitely didn't like where things were headed but wasn't sure how to get out of the situation. I knew without looking at my watch that we'd reached the witching hour, that tricky time of night where blood alcohol levels spike and personalities unravel. Few good things could result from sticking around. Just as I was contemplating my options, Carlos's hand slid under the back of my shirt and he leaned in, tongue first this time, to go for another kiss.

"Hey, Carlos . . . actually, I think maybe . . . maybe we should just go home."

A slow, sly smile tugged across his features. He put his arm around me again, a firm hand on my back drawing me in toward his open mouth.

Amanda · Lima, Peru · August

I jerked away. "That's not what I mean, Carlos."

"What?" he asked, his brows furrowed. "What is wrong?"

"Nothing. Don't worry about it. I think I'm just going to grab the girls and head out. It was great meeting you. But it's time for us to go home. Alone."

"No . . . you're wanting to leave?" He shook his head and stared down at me, glassy-eyed. "Please do not go. I have been enjoying you so much. Want to know you even more. My parents, they are not home this weekend—we have the whole place, just for us."

"Wait . . . you still live with your parents?" I couldn't believe it. He had to be rounding thirty at this point.

He looked at me, his sweaty forehead furrowed, clearly baffled. "Yes, of course. The men, they all live with the parents until they get married. Come, I promise . . . no one is home. *Estamos solo.* We are alone."

I had no intention of going anywhere with Carlos. As I turned on one heel and stalked off to find the girls, he trailed after me, baffled by my behavior. Did I not have a good time? Why wouldn't I want to go home with him?

"But you're an *American*," he sputtered, as if that should explain everything. "I thought you are, how do you say—touch-and-go?"

"What? What does that even mean?" I spun around.

"You know—you touch," he said, making an explicitly sexual gesture with his hands. "And then you go. Right?"

My mouth dropped open and I took a breath, ready to tell him off, when another hand grabbed my wrist. It was Jen's. "Hey, babe, let's just leave. C'mon."

She pulled me in the direction of the stairs, and we descended with Carlos following in hot, if clumsy, pursuit. He caught up with us just outside the door and reached for my hand again.

"Please, can you take this?" Carlos slurred in a voice that

almost made me feel bad for him. "Just take this, and call me when you are here again in Lima."

I turned around and looked down at the card in his hand. Jen flagged a taxi as Holly stood next to me.

"Amanda, I am sorry if I say or do the wrong thing," he said. "I'm not meaning to upset you. I would like to see you again. I take you and your friends out when you return from the jungle. We go paragliding. Dinner. Anything. You will contact me?"

I didn't answer but let him press the card into my hand before I got into the cab.

Rolling down the window for air, I breathed out the compressed tension. What had just happened? I recapped the end of the night for Jen and Holly.

"I hate to chalk it up to this, but he was just being a guy," said Jen, trying to make light of things. "No matter where in the world we go, they're always gonna try, right?"

Maybe. I watched as the lights of the city streaked outside the window, feeling exhausted and disappointed at how things had turned out. I'd really liked the prenightclub Carlos. Why did he have to go and get all aggressive on me?

As we walked inside the front door of our hostel, I let Carlos's business card flutter down toward the trash can. I had no plans to ever connect with him again.

So how was it then, exactly a week later, I found myself pretending not to watch Carlos as he pushed his chair back and starting maneuvering his way in our direction?

"Oh, no . . . I think he's coming over. What should I do?" I looked down, addressing my empanadas. "What do I say?"

"Just act natural, it's all good," said Holly casually as she watched him below shaded lids. "He probably just saw us sitting here, and now he feels obligated to say something."

As Carlos walked the last few steps toward our table, he

pushed a lock of dark hair behind his ear and tugged down his sleeves. He looked—nervous.

"Hello, ladies. You are back from the jungle, I see." Carlos came around to my side of the table. "Nice crown, *reina*."

I'd forgotten that I'd tossed on the sparkly plastic tiara and matching earrings. My hand reflexively reached up to tug them off, but I stopped short.

"Oh, what . . . this? It was a present from my friends. I mean, I wouldn't normally wear something like this to go out, it's just that . . ." I could hear myself rambling. "Actually, today's my birthday."

"Yes, yes, I remember you saying about this last week. Happy birthday. Maybe you will go out to the clubs again tonight?" he asked.

"No. I'm pretty sure after last time, we're done with clubbing for a while." I hadn't meant for it to sound harsh, but the comment dropped with a thud.

"Ah, I see. Of course." Carlos swiftly shifted the subject and his attention to Jen and Holly. "So, tell me about your trip to the Amazon. Did you enjoy this part of the country?"

The girls politely chimed their agreement.

He returned his gaze to me. "And for you—what was your favorite part?"

My favorite part? I flashed through the video clips in my short-term memory, trying to pull up a single headlining event from our time in the Amazon. My mind drew a blank. All I could think of right now was Carlos's Jekyll-and-Hyde transformation at the nightclub and how I'd left him standing there on the curb.

Sensing that no response was forthcoming, Holly jumped in to save the floundering conversation, compensating with animated tales of shaky suspension bridges and killer tree frogs and rodents of unusual size. Jen helped pick up the slack, distracting

Carlos with pictures of the three of us feeding the monkeys and hanging off the back of motorcycles in Indiana. Pretty soon the three of them were laughing while I sat there, trying to reconcile the fact that this polite, sociable guy was the same one who'd offended my sensibilities so acutely the week before.

As Carlos grabbed the camera and scrolled through the images, I let my shoulders drop, just a little. All right, maybe he *had* just come over to be polite, to mitigate some of the weirdness from the other night—not, as I'd thought, to give me a hard time. Compared with uncomfortable reencounters I'd experienced in the past, things definitely could have been worse. Besides, any second now, he'd wrap things up, retreat back to his table, and then we'd . . .

"So, ladies," he said, putting the camera down. "I have told my friends over there all about the traveling American girls, and now they are very curious about you. Would you like to come over and meet them?"

Three pairs of eyes stared at me, and I fumbled for a nice way to decline.

"Oh, well, that's really nice, but we wouldn't want to interrupt your dinner . . ."

"No, no, we've already finished."

What could I say? "Okay . . . sure."

Abandoning our mostly empty plates, we followed Carlos. The chatter among his friends, a lively-looking crew of artists and designer types, slowly trickled off. They shifted in their chairs, and I was relieved to see that Daniel was not among the bunch.

"Ah, it is the Americans," announced a guy wearing a jacket that looked as if it were made of tapestry material. "You better watch out for that guy. He's trouble."

"Oh, we've already discovered that," I said, glancing over at Carlos.

123

"Hello, I am Anabella," said a dark-eyed brunette with retro Brooke Shields eyebrows. "It is so nice to meet you."

Holly extended her hand, but the girl ignored it, kissing both of her cheeks instead.

The process repeated itself around the table, embraces and kisses subbing for handshakes as we were introduced to the entire group.

"Come, you will sit next to me," said Anabella, pulling Holly away. "I need to hear *everything* about New York. I will be visiting in the fall."

Within minutes, both of my friends were absorbed into conversations—Holly with Anabella and Jen with a shaggy-haired guy sporting thick black hipster glasses—and Carlos and I found ourselves standing awkwardly at one end of the table, not quite facing each other.

"So you had a good time in Peru? I hope it won't be the last time you visit."

"Oh, no, it won't be. I'll definitely be coming back at some point." I avoided his eyes, watching as a waiter whisked the plates off the table, skillfully balancing the heavy load as he returned to the kitchen.

"When do you leave?"

"Tomorrow. We're heading to Rio next, then traveling through Brazil for a couple weeks."

"Good, good. Brazil is very nice. Just be careful if you go out in Rio. Those Brazilian boys, you know, they're even more persistent than the Peruvians."

I finally cracked a smile. "Really? That's hard to imagine."

We stood staring at the group for a minute before Carlos spoke again.

"Amanda," he started, turning slightly in my direction. "I don't mean to bring up a bad subject. But I know I upset you the other night and . . . I feel terrible about this. We had a good time at Café del Mar, no? But after we got to the club . . . I don't know what happened."

"Yeah, I'm not sure what happened, either," I responded, crossing my arms over my chest. "One minute, we were dancing and the next, we were . . . and then you tried to . . . well, it doesn't matter."

"No, it does matter. Tell me."

"I mean, we'd just met, like four hours earlier, and already you were pressuring me to go home with you. I mean, do you really believe what you said about American women? Being touch-and-go, I mean? Because I hope you know, we're not all like that." Of course, if he did, I couldn't entirely blame him. Several British and Aussie backpackers had confirmed that American women have developed a real *Girls Gone Wild* reputation overseas.

"No, no, Amanda . . . of course not. I should not have said that," he said, now facing me directly. "I wanted all week to call you, to say something, to apologize, but I did not know how to reach you. And now you are right here. This is kind of crazy, no?"

I shook my head. "Yeah, it's pretty crazy all right."

"Do you think maybe we were meant to see each other again?"

I thought about that but didn't answer. We spoke for several more minutes, untangling any remaining knots of weirdness between us. By the time he and his friends had paid their bill and were ready to take off, I actually found myself a little sorry to see him go.

"I'm really glad that we bumped into each other, *reina*," he said, giving me a light hug.

"You know, Carlos—I am too."

The girls and I said our good-byes to Carlos and his friends as they left the restaurant, then returned to our own table to rehash the events of the previous hour.

"So what were you guys *talking* about over there?" Holly pounced.

"You two looked like you were getting pretty cozy," Jen joked. "Maybe you're the touch-and-go type after all?"

Just as I was filling them in on everything that had happened, Anabella came streaking back through the front door and collapsed at our table. "Oh, this is very good! You are still here. Ah! My friends and I have all been talking and we have decided that you cannot celebrate your last night in Lima, or the big birthday, just at T'anta. Dinner is nice, but not special enough. If you agree, we would like to throw for you a party."

"A party? When?" asked Jen. "We're leaving tomorrow."

"No, you crazy girl. Right now, at my house," she said with a grin. "I will stay with you until you finish up, and then I will drive you. You never find the place otherwise."

The idea of an impromptu birthday party seemed outrageous (who did something like this for people they'd just met?), but once again I rationalized—wasn't meeting new people half the point of traveling?

Twenty minutes later, we were squeezed into Anabella's ultracompact car and winding our way up steep streets that cut through the hills east of the city. As we climbed, I could make out the silhouettes of homes built directly into the cliffs, glass-faced affairs that bore no resemblance to the concrete sprawl and decaying tenements we'd seen in other parts of the city. From the look of things, we'd just entered the Hollywood Hills of Lima.

Anabella's place, by comparison, was relatively modest. Her apartment comprised the top floor of a two-story building perched directly over the valley. When she ushered us inside a dimly lit room, all I could see was the view of city lights spilling down the hillside and blurring into a golden haze near the ocean.

The crew from the restaurant showed up right behind us, along with a few new people we'd yet to meet. Within minutes the counter of Ana's pass-through kitchen was loaded with wine, beer, liquor, and mixers. One thing was for sure: Our new friends certainly knew how to celebrate. They'd managed to throw a party together in a less than an hour.

"A toast to the Americans," Carlos said. "Especially the birthday girl."

"Yes, we are so pleased you are spending your last night in Lima with us," added Ana, raising her glass of wine. "*Salud!*"

"*Salud!*" Everyone clinked the glasses in their hands.

It could have been the abundance of alcohol or just that twenty-somethings of any nationality rarely need an excuse to party, but Holly, Jen, and I managed to integrate seamlessly into our new group of Peruvian friends. I took it as a good sign when Marcus, the guy in the tapestry jacket, snatched the tiara off of my head and placed it on his own.

"It is after midnight. Birthday is finished. Now I am the king of the party, no?"

"Oh, let me take your picture!" said Holly, digging through her bag to find her camera. But before she had a chance, one of the other guys grabbed the tiara and plopped it on his head. Then someone else tried it on for size. Pretty soon everyone got a crack at my crown, with Holly documenting everyone's fancy new look.

I took my glass of wine over to a chair near the window. I watched the girls break it down Latin-style for a few seconds, then turned my attention to the view outside.

Wow—how ridiculous was all of this? Just a few hours earlier, I'd been at an $8-a-night hostel with Jen and Holly, content to have a low-key dinner and a couple glasses of wine. Now the three of us were celebrating my birthday with a dozen strangers in a swanky apartment somewhere high above Lima. I knew that

127

Amanda · Lima, Peru · August

if I hadn't bumped into Carlos again, the three of us wouldn't be in this surreal situation. And had our entire interaction taken place in New York rather than South America, I probably wouldn't have given him another chance at all. It would have been all too easy to decline his invitation, to claim that some other plans precluded me from attending his friend's party.

But that's one of the unexpected peculiarities of traveling, especially for so long. I really *didn't* have any other plans. The only friends I had now were the ones hanging by my side 24/7. Without a jam-packed schedule or an extensive social network to hide within, I suddenly felt free to gamble on new possibilities. I glanced across the room, watching both of my friends laughing hysterically at Marcus's attempts to tango with Jen. For tonight at least, the risk had definitely been worth the reward.

128

✢

CHAPTER EIGHT

Jen

RIO DE JANEIRO, BRAZIL

AUGUST

Perched on plush candy-striped bar stools at the Copacabana Palace hotel, Amanda, Holly, and I sat pondering our probable future as Rio de Janeiro vagrants.

"Maybe we could sneak into the business center and sleep there tonight," Amanda suggested. "I got a look at the room when I was checking e-mail, and it has tons of comfy couches."

I smiled weakly at her joke. Amanda, who was currently working on an article about South American honeymoon destinations, had been the one to score us two free nights at the legendary beachfront property through her press contacts in the first place. The 400 thread count sheets, private bath butlers, and room service were almost enough to make me reconsider my position on working on the road. But now, after forty-eight hours of bliss, the clock had run out on the luxury portion of our getaway.

"Yeah, but even if we could do that, they know we're not guests here anymore. And they'll definitely be suspicious if we're still lurking around after happy hour." I sighed, wondering if we could shack on the white lounge chairs that lined the pool.

"All right, Jen, you stay here and keep looking for hostels

online while Holly and I scour the neighborhood for something we can remotely afford." Amanda stood abruptly and scooped her tote off the ground. "I swore I saw a place called Yellow Banana, or something like that, when the taxi dropped us off here."

"There's nothing remotely close to that name in the guidebook, but maybe we'll get lucky," Holly said just before grabbing the Lonely Planet guide and taking off through the lobby.

Before touching down in the birthplace of samba, caipirinhas, and bikinis so teeny that they required their own waxing technique, we'd been told by numerous travelers to limit our days in Rio and instead hightail it north to the country's most pristine beaches. Heeding their advice, we'd booked a flight to Salvador, Bahia, set to depart three days from now, and intended to visit as many of Rio's iconic sites as possible in the next seventy-two hours. Unfortunately, we'd already spent half a day just trying to find a place to sleep for the night. Apparently, every single guesthouse, hostel, and B & B in town had been booked solid for weeks. At this rate, we'd have to venture into the favelas—the Rio slums made infamous by the movie *City of God* for their violent gangs and appalling living conditions—to find a room.

I hoped we wouldn't have to resort to that, but as usual we were making plans on the fly, waiting until we arrived in a new city to secure lodging. It wasn't that we didn't try to think ahead. But during the course of our travels in Peru, we'd found that it was inconvenient—and often futile—to prebook accommodations. Half the time we'd change our minds and detour to another destination at the last minute. Other times we'd stumble upon a place that hadn't made the Lonely Planet pages but that we adored at first sight. Not to mention that walk-in clients could sometimes take advantage of cancellations, negotiate a better price, and, most important, see the rooms that are so often hyped in print—but may be horrifying in reality. This time we'd been lucky: thanks to Amanda, we'd been legit guests in one of the most luxurious and renowned hotels in the world—and the experience had more than lived up to the hype. Sadly, now it was back to our lives as backpacker ragamuffins.

An hour later, after my intensive search through sites like HostelBookers.com and Hostelworld.com had yielded nothing but scarlet letter Xs (indicating no vacancies), I slunk over to the concierge and asked if he could ring a few of the grimier but cheaper hotels in the local area to see if they had any vacancies. I wanted to crawl under the Persian rug as his white-gloved hand dialed the first number. Half a dozen rejections later, I was on the verge of drowning myself in a nearby gilded ice bucket.

Let's face it, Operation "Yellow Banana" might be our last shot, I thought, as I continued to search online without much hope. Nearly an hour later, the girls returned with the day's first piece of good news—the Mellow Yellow hostel would be happy to squeeze us in.

As it turned out, our new digs offered a side of paradise that didn't require crystal chandeliers, turndown chocolates, or room service. Mellow Yellow was the stuff of backpacker legend. Housed in a twisty, five-story loft space, the hostel boasted all the essential frat house trimmings: a full-sized bar and restaurant, pool hall, foosball table, beanbag lounge chairs, and a Jacuzzi. Not to mention a $10 all-you-could-eat-and-drink barbecue and enough debauchery on the part of its international inhabitants to create the ultimate MTV *The Real World: Rio de Janeiro*. Piling our bags in the corner, we headed to the upstairs lounge for dinner. Before long, we'd met loads of fellow "mellow yellowers" and were all planning which Rio hot spots to hit up after dinner.

Luckily, we were so exhausted from dancing all night at Casa Roja—a hip bar set in a pink Tudor-style house in the charm-

131

ing Bella Vista neighborhood—that the severe lack of personal space in our room (a double "converted" to a triple) barely fazed us. But this was quite possibly the last affordable space in Rio, so we beggars couldn't be choosers.

Aside from afternoon jogs to Ipanema Beach—where we sat on the sand people-watching and sipping water from coconuts—Amanda, Holly, and I had remained on self-imposed Copacabana luxury lockdown during our first couple days in Rio. With such limited time left to explore the Carnival Capital of the World, we forced ourselves to get up and out of bed as early as we could.

After refueling on açaí berry smoothies from our neighborhood juice bar, Amanda, Holly, and I spent hours perusing the sprawling Feira Hippie de Ipanema outdoor market for cheap sundresses and jewelry and chatting with local shopkeepers. Strolling the city streets—which felt safer than we'd expected—the girls and I stopped periodically to listen to a bossa nova sidewalk band, browse art galleries, and sample *bolinhos de chuva* (doughnut balls) and sugared popcorn from street vendors. Everything and everyone in Rio seemed to move with a blend of equal parts syrup and spice that captivated us the same way Buenos Aires had.

After snapping photos of the iconic Christ the Redeemer statue, perched with open arms on the peak of Corcovado Mountain, the girls and I took a gondola up the famous Sugarloaf Mountain. Settling at one of several tables at the top, we soaked in the 360-degree view of the city, and watched a local woman in a white lacy dress and head scarf dance barefoot through the crowd of tourists. As twilight painted streaks of navy and salmon across the sky, we made our way back down to the street level and hopped a taxi back to our hostel.

Later that night, Amanda, Holly, and I were splayed out on neon floor cushions in one of Mellow Yellow's relaxation rooms when our friend Morris from the night before popped in to ask us about our plans for later.

"I assume you ladies are hitting up the favela funk party, right?" he asked. "I mean, you gotta come, it's gonna be seriously wicked."

From the little we'd read about favelas in our guidebook, we couldn't imagine that the notorious Brazilian slums, which were occupied illegally and often controlled by drug lords, would be an appealing or remotely safe place to party. But apparently the times they were a-changin' in Rio. According to Morris, despite the often dangerous conditions, the favelas had become increasingly popular tourist destinations and "everyone who was anyone" went to the weekly raves. Still, we wondered if this was one of those After-School Special Moments we were supposed to "just say no" to. I mean, was it really safe to go traipsing into those formerly forbidden barrios?

But after we consulted with other backpackers and receiving the same story, our apprehensions were mostly squelched. Apparently, the favela leaders were welcoming visitors into their ghettos in record numbers. Organized tour companies had even jumped on the bandwagon, conducting daily excursions into several of the better-known "hoods," and were promoting the popular funk parties as 100 percent gringo-friendly events. I immediately conjured a vision of a Brazilian Don Corleone sitting on top of the hill ordering The Family to buzz us through the gates. I couldn't possibly pass up the chance to see this strange social phenomenon for myself, especially since Mellow Yellow had rented minivans to safely escort backpackers, en masse, to and from the party *and* was doling out bracelets for VIP access at the club for only $2.

After dashing downstairs to scribble our names on the

10 p.m. departure sheet (how dangerous could something with a sign-up sheet be, right?), we returned to our room to get ready for our big night on the shantytown. While Amanda and I swapped our cargo capri pants for wrinkled skirts and dabbed a bit of makeup on our faces, Holly sat on the bed with her laptop. At first I thought she was just waiting for us to finish our mini-transformations before starting hers, but a few minutes later she hesitantly said that she might not join us.

"We don't have to go if you don't want to, Hol. We'll just do something else," Amanda said.

"No, you and Jen should definitely go. I just really miss Elan, so I wanted to try to catch him on Skype and then maybe get some work done on my column," Holly replied. "Plus, I'm beyond tired from not sleeping much last night."

"I hear ya. I was totally exhausted too earlier today. But somehow I got my second wind," I said.

"And of course I can't let Jen have fun without me," Amanda added. "But we'll only go to the party if you're absolutely positive that you're okay to stay here alone."

"Oh, I don't know. It'll be hard, but I think I'll survive," Holly said, a look of relief washing over her face.

At this point in our travels, I knew that Holly needed a little more alone time than I did, and I assumed from her reaction that this was one of those occasions. Still, knowing how much Holly had left back in the States, I was always a little worried that she'd get too homesick and quit the trip. I would have understood, of course. But after spending practically every hour of the past two months with Holly by my side, I couldn't imagine continuing our round-the-world journey without her.

With her perpetually sunny disposition that could overcome even the most frustrating on-the-road situations, Holly had taught me to face setbacks with more grace and to try to let go of things I had no control over—especially painfully slow connections in Internet cafés and differing travel priorities. And whereas I had a tendency to want to go wherever the travel winds blew, with no set schedule or limitations, Holly always had a new mission and motivated us to get up and get going each day. Always seeking to challenge herself physically (often with an impromptu hike or bike ride), and to immerse herself in the more cultural and educational sides of travel, Holly inspired me to push the boundaries of my own abilities and understanding of the world.

"Okay, Corby. Try not to miss us too much, though," I replied.

"Impossible," she said, grinning widely, hoisting her laptop onto her legs, and settling back against the wall.

With just a small stash of reals and cameras tucked in our purses, Amanda and I joined a huge group of fellow hostelers—including a bunch of our new Irish/English/Aussie friends from the night before—and headed out of Mellow Yellow for our inaugural favela funk experience.

Thirty minutes later, we'd crossed the city limits and were beginning the slow ascent up a steep hillside. As we drove deeper into the shadows, dilapidated houses, local watering holes, and makeshift food huts began speckling the narrow dirt roads. Suddenly my imagination started to run away with me: What if rogue militia popped out of the bushes with machine guns? We could be taken hostage and sold into slavery. Were we the only group of backpackers foolish enough to come up here? What if this was a suicide mission?

Before we could ask if it was too late to turn back, we rounded a sharp bend in the road and caught up with an extensive caravan of cabs and combis. A massive crowd of club kids and bodyguard characters—decked out in tight spandex, gold chains, muscle shirts, and fluorescent Daisy Dukes—packed the streets, pushing their way toward a gigantic warehouse. Crude bundles of cable wire hung from the treetops, running in all directions, powering the venue and, it seemed, every structure in sight.

Hordes of tourists poured from the vans, and the favela funk masters let us pass without so much as batting an eye. Ushered through the waiting line like cattle, we were quickly swept up in the torrent of partygoers. Along with hundreds of locals, we flowed steadily down a black-lit hallway before spilling out into a football-field-sized arena. The tin walls pulsed with reggaeton bass beats. An immense crowd bounced and swayed in perfect rhythm. And sweat formed steam clouds in the un-air-conditioned space, where a clothing-optional rule was in full effect. Most of the men were sans shirt, and nine out of ten women preferred bikinis to party dresses—the tenth opting for a tube top and booty shorts. You could hardly blame them, though, considering the sweltering heat and severe lack of oxygen.

"This is insanity!" Amanda screamed. "I'm so glad we came!"

"Me too! Although we're seriously overdressed!"

Hand in hand as to not lose each other, we wound our way through the throng of revelers, showed our wristbands to the burly watchman at the VIP entrance, and ascended to the top floor. Amanda and I danced, sweated buckets in the 100-degree heat, rocked out our best moves (all four of them), and sipped cocktails between guzzles of water. It wasn't long before the guys in our group, who had all ditched their shirts by this point, insisted that all of the Mellow Yellow ladies accompany them in a salsa dance-off. Hours passed, until 4 a.m., when we realized our motor coaches were going to turn into pumpkins if we weren't outside to meet them in a few minutes.

Standing on the sidewalk outside the club, Amanda and I waited for our van while covertly playing fashion police with the outrageous characters that passed by.

"I'm so glad you came out tonight. I was worried you'd bail," I said.

"And miss all this? No way? Besides, my eighty-year-old self told me that if I'd stayed in, I'd totally regret missing tonight," she replied as a band of muscle-bound men walked by, smiled, and whistled before continuing down the shadowy road on foot.

Laughing, I recalled the first time Amanda had mentioned her mysterious eighty-year-old self. During one of our countless 3 a.m. conversations in our freshman dorm, she'd explained that whenever she'd had a tough time trying to figure out whether she should take a risk or not, she'd ask, "What would the blue-haired, sun-parched, granny-panty-wearing future version of myself advise me to do? Would she tell me to stay in and study or go out and meet a cute guy?"

I had immediately understood where she was coming from. I often justified my more impulsive choices with a similar rationale that "I'll sleep when I'm dead" or "Live every day like it is your last." I guessed that overachievers like us needed some excuse, however quirky it might be, to defy our own conventions and just have fun.

"Well, *my* eighty-year-old self would have advised me to not act so bitchy to my friend Amanda when she wanted to hit up an Internet café to research an article," I said.

"What are you talking about? No, you haven't," Amanda said with a wave of her hand, then added, "I mean, I know you get frustrated with my writing, but it's something I really want to do for myself. I guess I just don't understand why it annoys you."

"It's not really your writing. It's more of my own shit. You saw what a crazy freak I was the last few months before we left New York. I mean, seriously. What the hell was I thinking trying to study for the GMATs, work fourteen-hour days, *and* try to figure out the Brian thing? I really just needed a few weeks on the road to relax and unwind."

"What's going on with you and Brian, by the way?" Amanda asked gently.

"Oh, who knows. We e-mail back and forth and chat on Skype, but we mostly just make small talk and try to avoid the elephant in the room . . . or on the line . . . or whatever. But, God, it's just so sad most of the time. I can't stand it. I mean, there's really nothing left for us to hold on to, but it's, like, we just can't let go."

"I know. I can't imagine how hard it's been for you guys. It totally sucks, Jen. I'm sorry," she said with sincerity.

"It's fine. Really," I replied. "I mean, being on this trip with you and Hol makes things seem okay somehow. Even when we're in the shittiest of shit hostels or trapped on a ten-thousand-hour bus ride—I don't know, I just love it. It's like I finally found something bigger than myself to focus on. It sounds a little cheese-ola, but that's why I'm always pushing us to live in the moment and use this time to explore new sides of our personalities."

"You mean like becoming favela funk partygoers," she said, motioning to a group of drunk college-aged girls stumbling into their hostel's assigned vehicle. "Look, I totally get that. We *are* doing those things and it's awesome, but it can't be like that every single day," Amanda replied. "I don't know. You're holding on to Brian. I'm holding on to my career. Maybe we're not supposed to let go of everything all at once."

"Okay, fair enough. I guess it really is just me pinning too many hopes on this trip to help me to figure out my own life. Because I don't have a clue about anything at this point. Not my boyfriend. Or career. Or plans for the future. I know *nothing*," I moaned.

"Well, we *do* know this . . . that girl's tangerine leotard thing is so *not* cute," Amanda said, nodding her head in the direction of the club before turning her attention back to me. "So things are totally crazy for you right now. I get it. But Holly and I will be there in New York if you need us, and then we get to go to Kenya so you can live your dream."

"Thanks, Schmanders," I said just as our ride appeared. "I know everything will work out the way it's supposed to in the end."

"It definitely will. And just think, tomorrow we'll be in Salvador with ten full days to chill out on the beach."

"Hey, there you all are. What a night, huh, ladies?" our friend Morris said, throwing his arms around us and pulling us into the packed minivan.

"Hell yeah, it was," Amanda replied.

"And just think, we have ten more months of travel ahead of us," I said, leaning my cheek against the cool glass window as we sped down the bumpy incline, attempting to beat the sun back to Mellow Yellow.

139

Jen · Rio de Janeiro, Brazil · August

❉

CHAPTER NINE

Holly

SALVADOR, BRAZIL

AUGUST

I'd never seen anything like it, except maybe on TV when Olympic gymnasts performed floor exercises. Men had gathered to cartwheel around their opponents and scissor-kick over one another's heads. One shirtless guy swung his legs low behind him to dodge a blow and then did a half-dozen flips before landing on his feet. It happened so fast, I got dizzy just watching.

It was our first day in Salvador, Brazil's oldest city, formerly the country's main slave port and home to people who are a blend of African, European, and Native American blood. This genetic pool has blessed many locals with the bodies of lean, muscular dancers and skin as smooth as polished mahogany. I was as captivated by their natural beauty as I was by their skillful performance as a group of about a dozen guys took turns doing *capoeira*—a cross between martial arts and dancing—on the beach down the street from our guesthouse.

Toes buried in the sand, I closed my eyes and tipped my face up happily to soak up the heat from the Brazilian sun, which was so much more intense than the rays in New York. Moments earlier, Jen and Amanda had walked toward the water to watch the show and to buy coconut water for a buck apiece. Here, as in Rio, you could sip the sweet liquid directly from the coconut via a hole that's been sliced into one side and fitted with a bendy straw.

"Oi. De onde esta você?" I turned to find a petite woman with skin the color of honey and waist-length hair sprawled on a beach chair behind me.

"Lo siento, yo no hablo portugués. ¿Habla español o inglés?" I'm sorry, I don't speak Portuguese. Do you speak Spanish or English?

She giggled and turned to say something to another twenty-something woman wearing a white string bikini and a guy with hazel-green eyes, both planted beside her.

"Where . . . you from?" She tried again.

"New York. Are you from Salvador?" I asked her.

Rather than respond (maybe she didn't understand?), she gestured for me to join her and her friends. I glanced toward the water to see Jen and Amanda, who were now moving their legs back and forth in an arc while a guy swung his arms in front of his body, instructing them on the basics of capoeira.

Grabbing our day packs, I plopped myself in the sand next to the three Brazilians. The guy offered me a can of Skol, a popular beer, and I felt the fizzy liquid cool my throat as I took a gulp. Since we didn't speak the same language, we sat there smiling awkwardly at one another between sips, until they gave up on silence and began chattering with each other in Portuguese.

Once again, I was back to feeling like a toddler learning to speak for the first time. While in Peru, I'd picked up enough Spanish to carry on basic conversations, but all of mine were peppered with communication breakdowns. (My first week there, a Peruvian guy who offered to buy me a drink at a bar looked shocked when I tried to say I was embarrassed for mispronouncing his name. That's when Amanda laughed and said,

"Holly, you said *embarazada*, which means *pregnant*, not embarrassed!") I worried I'd make a similar misstep while trying out my Portuguese.

After several minutes spent in silence with me smiling stupidly at the group while they talked, the trio stood up and one of the women pulled me to my feet.

"Hey, Holly, where are you going?" Jen asked as she returned from the capoeira lesson to sprawl out on her towel.

"I don't know. But I think my new friends want to show me something. Can you watch our stuff?"

"Sure." Jen shimmied over to grab our bags, and I let the woman lead me away.

If I had been back in New York, I would never have allowed a stranger to drag me off to some unknown locale. But as she pointed to the end of the pier, where a crowd had formed, the mission seemed more like an adventure than a danger. I followed her out to the edge, joining her and the cluster of locals who sat with their legs dangling. Men, women, and kids were chatting wildly, laughing freely, and sipping drinks as they stared at the skyline. The sun looked like an oozing ball of lava, turning from yellow to orange to red as it sank into the ocean and lit the clouds above. The second it disappeared, the crowd erupted into cheers.

They came out here just to watch the sunset. I clapped with energy I didn't even know I had. When was the last time Elan and I had taken the time to watch the sun set over Manhattan? The cheering faded along with the sun, but the crowd lingered. Some talked excitedly, while others jumped into the water as the clouds clung to the last streaks of light. The two women and the guy I'd been hanging out with were taking turns diving off the pier like kids. Without stopping to think, I got to my feet, took a running start, and jumped off, too.

I pretended that my plunge into the Bay of All Saints had

the power to wash away any heaviness I felt from missing Elan. For a moment it was only me, the sky above, and the salt water swirling around me. I let myself sink deeper, briefly losing sense of which way was up and which way was down.

When I resurfaced, the first stars were faintly dusting the sky. I glanced over to see that my new friends had already climbed back onto the pier. The girl with the waist-length hair stood scanning the ocean and waved me in once I surfaced.

"It's okay, I can get up by myself," I said, floundering on the slippery ladder, the waves pounding at my back. She didn't understand me and wrapped her hand around my wrist. I braced myself against the wooden planks and let her help me out.

S *queak, slam, crash!* After hours of staring at the ceiling, counting backward from a hundred and imagining myself spooning with Elan, sleep had finally overtaken me. That is, until a drunken backpacker stumbled into the room, let the door slam behind her, and then missed a rung on the ladder leading to the bunk above mine. She fell to the floor in a messy heap.

"Are you okay?" I bolted upright, knocking my head on the bed above me. "Ouch!" I howled.

"I'm fine—no worries!" slurred the Australian girl.

She tried crawling into the bunk again, shaking the rickety frame as she collapsed onto the mattress. Within seconds bearlike snores reverberated through the room. I spent the next few hours tossing and turning, my runaway mind bouncing first from whether I'd saved enough to pay my student loans each month to missing my sister's birthday back home to how I could convince Jen and Amanda to change guesthouses. They still didn't seem to understand that an insomniac like me could not spend an entire year in noisy dorms.

Sleeping with strangers—or attempting to—was turning me

into a walking zombie. Although my friends and I had quietly disagreed about our hostel arrangements, I was beginning to worry that the real issue wasn't about sleeping at all but rather about wanting to spend our time on the road in very different ways. I didn't mind having a cocktail now and then, but after exploring the nightlife in Lima, dance clubs in Arequipa, and backpacker bars in Rio, I was starting to worry that my traveling companions wanted to turn our trip into a yearlong spring break. I cringed just thinking about Mellow Yellow in Rio, where I'd curled up on a mattress no thicker than a notebook in a closet-sized room that vibrated with drums and bass from the in-hostel bar just three feet away while the girls were out at the favela party until dawn. Jen and Amanda had been thrilled to stay at Mellow Yellow, but it'd been my idea of Hostel Hell.

Although we'd sworn at one point to share our expectations for on-the-road life *before* we actually got on the road, somehow we'd never gotten around to it back in New York. It wasn't until I spent every waking and sleeping minute with Jen and Amanda that I learned how they preferred to spend their daily lives—and night lives. I was scared that they'd merely traded partying in Manhattan for partying on the road, changing their surroundings but not their lifestyle.

Feeling as if I might be acting like a princess or a baby or both, I'd hesitantly tried to tell Jen and Amanda that I didn't want to stay in party dorms. Once they finally seemed to hear me, they'd looked at me with disappointment.

"Holly, we want to be around other backpackers. How are we supposed to meet people if we're stuck in some boring hotel?" Amanda had argued.

"Yeah," Jen had agreed. "Besides, dorms are cheaper and we have to stretch our money."

They definitely had a point about the money thing—communal rooms could cost as little as $5 each, while a private triple might cost $10 apiece—or more. The difference meant we could afford to stay on the road for twice as long. Did I need to loosen up? Wasn't traveling as a group all about compromise?

But finally, as the dawn's early light cast lines on my face through the blinds, I decided that enough was enough. I didn't want to squander my trip feeling hungover and exhausted. I wanted to feel healthy and free. As I stared up at the ceiling, its cracks amplified in the morning shadows, niggling thoughts morphed into full-blown fears. Had I thrown away a fulfilling career, left the man I loved, and sacrificed my idea of a home all to hang out in backpacker hostels?

Bleary-eyed but suddenly motivated, I climbed out of bed and started loading my quick-dry towel and other belongings into my backpack. My plan was to pack and then read in the common room until Amanda and Jen woke and I could tell them my next move.

"Holly, what are you *doing*?" Amanda whispered loudly, leaning her head out of the bottom bunk across the room.

I paused before answering, "I've got to find someplace quieter where I can sleep—I'm seriously exhausted."

"Wait, what?" Now it was Jen who bolted upright in the bunk above Amanda's. "You can't leave!"

I stopped for a second, surprised. It's not as if I was cheating on them by taking off with a new group of backpackers—I was just going to sleep in separate quarters. "You know I love you guys, but I've tried to tell you . . . I'm just not down with the wild party dorms. And I don't want you to change your trip for me. Believe me, it's nothing personal," I said, hoisting on my backpack.

"But it *is* personal, Holly. We're in this trip together. If you go, we have to come with you," Amanda said. She placed her bare feet on the wooden floor and fished around for her backpack.

And with that, my two traveling partners loaded their packs, checked out of the hostel with me, and headed for the Old Town section of Salvador.

It was a tense cab ride—I despise conflict and felt guilty for uprooting the girls. But I knew keeping silent wouldn't benefit the group in the long run. I tried to distract myself by paying extra close attention to the world streaking by outside the window. In the city's Old Town, cobblestone streets wound around seventeenth-century houses painted in shades of banana yellow and ocean blue. Hundreds of churches stood side by side with *terreiros*, holy places where worshipers merged the traditions of two religions: Portuguese Christianity and Afro-Brazilian Candomblé. As we passed by so much history, my outburst at the hostel suddenly seemed silly and insignificant compared to the journey I'd agreed take with Jen and Amanda. I had my two friends, and I was traveling the world. What the hell was my problem? I hoped we could find a way to merge my idea of the trip as more of a learning vacation with the girls' desire for partying and relaxing.

As we walked into Albergue das Laranjeiras Hostel, its dark wooden lobby fashioned like an old ship, I glanced around at the bustling café where travelers were lined up for a buffet breakfast that included yogurt, pastries, cheeses, and sliced mangoes. Instead of a bar, I spotted an open loft above where visitors lounged in hammocks and read guidebooks.

"Is this place okay with you?" I asked. To my relief, they both nodded.

When the man behind the counter said they had only one single and a few dorm spaces left, the girls told me to take my own room and they'd save money by sleeping in the dorms. After that, Amanda and Jen agreed that we'd always try to stay in triples if they were available.

I felt thankful. Money may not buy happiness, but in this

case, a few extra bucks could buy sanity. I laid out my sleeping bag in the narrow room, big enough to fit only a single bed but filled with silence, and happily burrowed inside in search of sleep.

B y the time Amanda and Jen came knocking at my door, it was nearly evening. I'd slept the entire day away— something I don't think I'd done since I was eight and had the chicken pox. It had taken only a little rest for me to feel calm again. Hoping things wouldn't be awkward between the three of us, I asked them to go for a walk. I was itching to explore a new part of town together.

As Amanda, Jen, and I lounged at a table on one of the cobblestoned streets branching off Largo do Pelourinho, I felt as if I'd stepped back in time. A fellow traveler had recommended we check out the pedestrian road lined with bars and restaurants to try *vatapá*, a yellow stew made with shrimp. Though the cuisine was delicious, it was definitely not diet-friendly: palm oil, coconut, and cashews were all staple ingredients. And to spice it up even more, many dishes came with red peppers so hot, they were guaranteed to make your nose break into a sweat.

We each ordered a different dish and then passed them around so we could sample more flavors. "Hey, I'm sorry about the whole hostel thing. I still feel bad for making us move," I said, holding out my plate like an olive branch.

"Holly, seriously, don't worry about it. We love our new place," Amanda said, spooning some rice onto her dish. "Jen and I just don't want you to quit the trip and go home. For a few minutes this morning, we were seriously worried you might!"

"I was never going to quit!" I said, again surprised that they'd thought I'd leave for good. "I guess I'm not the best at communicating, and so things just kind of built up in my head.

It wasn't just about the sleeping thing. I'm worried that all the trip is going to turn out to be is partying with backpackers," I said.

"Hol, that's *not* all it's been and not all the trip will be, I promise," Jen said. "Look, I know this might sound like an excuse, but being in really social places and going out a lot has kept me from worrying too much about Brian and what's going to happen when we get back to New York."

"And I think that we've just been trying a little too hard to re-create our postgrad trip through Europe," Amanda remarked. "Until now, that was the best month of my life."

"Definitely—we *have* been treating our South America portion a little like an extended vacation," Jen added.

"I know, and I don't want to ruin your good time," I said. "We *should* be having fun—that's the point." I went on to explain that I knew so many people who would have given their right arm to be without obligations like work and rent and romantic entanglements. "We owe it to ourselves to do more with this time. Sure, we could find a different pub to drink in every night, but what are we learning from that? How are we growing?" I finally was able to say flat out what'd really been bothering me: I wanted to push us beyond the lifestyle that felt most comfortable.

Jen put her hand on my shoulder, "Things are going to change after this leg of the trip, I'm sure of it. Soon we'll be volunteering in Kenya, where I'm pretty sure we won't have running water, let alone alcohol or backpacker bars. It's not going to be easy travel anymore."

"Yeah, and thank God for that!" said Amanda. "If we drink one more *ron y* Coca-Cola Light at happy hour, I think I may have to bail on the trip before Holly does. I'm officially done, as of now."

"Guys, I was *never* bailing!" I reminded them, laughing.

Then, to prove to the girls that I wasn't totally lame—and that they didn't need to stop enjoying themselves to appease me—I suggested we head to O Gravinho bar to sample *chopps*, Brazilian draft beer, and the country's famous sugarcane liquor, *cachaca*. They protested a little—but not too much.

As I took a sip of the *caipirinha* that my friends and I were sharing, my eyes met those of a guy wearing a straw fedora. His skin was paler than ours, and his long legs jutted out from underneath the table across from us. He sat with a Brazilian boy who was wearing a torn T-shirt and looked to be half his age.

"Where are you ladies from?" he called over to us. Jen, Amanda, and I paused for a moment before Amanda answered, "New York."

"No way, really? I'm from Brooklyn."

"Me too. I live in Williamsburg. Or I *did*," I said, unexpectedly delighted to have stumbled across someone from my neighborhood after almost two months on the road.

"This is Igo." He gestured to the boy, who was sitting silently beside him. "I'm Sam."

We all introduced ourselves, and, after asking if he could join us, we pulled the tables together. He turned to Igo and spoke in Portuguese.

"*Oi*, Igo," I said, grinning at the teen. He smiled shyly but said nothing. I turned to Sam. "How'd you guys meet?"

"He asked me for money, so I offered to buy him dinner if he practiced Portuguese with me." Just then, another boy approached the table and pulled on Igo's arm. Igo said something to Sam in Portuguese before rejoining the band of boys across the street.

"How'd you learn Portuguese?" I asked, impressed. Spanish and French were much more likely languages for Americans to speak.

"Have you heard of capoeira?" he asked, offering me a roasted cashew from the paper cone he was holding.

"I took one class at my gym back in New York," I said, popping a sweet and salty nut into my mouth. "But we saw guys doing the real deal yesterday on the beach."

Sam explained that the sport had been started when African slaves tried to disguise intertribal fighting from their masters by playing the drums. "You could say they turned it into a sort of dance," he said. "I got into training a few years ago in New York and started to pick up Portuguese during my classes."

Jen asked what Sam did. He told us that he had just taken the bar exam and figured he'd travel for a couple of months before getting a job as a lawyer.

"That's cool—and really unusual," said Amanda. "We've met tons of Israelis, Brits, and Australians—and a few American women. But we haven't come across many guys from the States who are taking long trips."

"Yeah, why do you think that is?" I asked, curious to get his take on the mysterious lack of American males on the road.

Sam took off his hat and ran a hand over his shaved head before responding, "I don't know. Maybe it's because we're taught that men should be providers. And taking time off to travel means time away from work and therefore making money. Maybe guys are afraid they'll look lazy if they take an extended vacation."

I'd never before thought about how reverse sexism and an ingrained sense of responsibility might discourage many guys from hitting the road. Mention famous American travelers, and my mind instantly went to male explorers such as Jack Kerouac, Bill Bryson, and Paul Theroux. But the reality is that most men probably reflect the image I have in my mind of my grandfather: a dedicated provider who spent more than thirty years working in a factory, who saw it his greatest duty to earn enough money to take his kids to the movies on Sundays and to help them pay for college. The only time he traveled abroad was to serve in the army in World War II, and he never wanted to travel again if he could avoid it.

My grandmother, on the other hand, said she would've loved to have traveled more, but she'd been far too busy raising four kids and waitressing at night. Now, if the popularity of "girl-friend getaway" trips is any indication, more American women are hitting the road than ever before. Maybe that's because women are no longer restricted to describing themselves first and foremost as homemakers, wives, and mothers. I wondered if that was a coincidence or if there was a direct connection between a woman's ability to forge almost any path she chooses and her desire to take the one that leads beyond U.S. borders in order to gain perspective on which direction is right for her.

In this situation, maybe guys really did have it tougher. None of our friends or coworkers had accused Jen, Amanda, or me of shirking our responsibilities as future breadwinners when we shared our travel plans. True, some New York friends had questioned whether we'd be stunting our career growth, and Amanda's mom had insisted that Amanda would never find The One if she was traveling to a different destination every week, but in general, the close friends in our lives had thrown major support behind our plan. Many had even said they would do the same thing if only they could find friends to travel with them.

I glanced at my friends and then back at Sam. Had the people in his life been as supportive of his journey? I was just about to ask when Sam ordered us another round and answered the unspoken question.

"I think I could only get away with traveling for this long because I'd just finished law school, and people understand you might need to take a break before starting a career," he said. "I also think some Americans tend to associate vacation with a week of sitting on a beach and travel with partying rather than exploration."

Considering the jam-packed schedule that most Americans keep, it makes sense that many of them might view vacations as opportunities to escape and unwind rather than explore. And that's if we actually sneak away during the two weeks we're allotted. Back home in the city, it was almost a bragging right to be overscheduled. Statements like "I'm just so busy I don't even have time to sleep," actually garner respect. I was impressed that Sam had created his own sabbatical of sorts.

Now he had a proposition for us. "I'm going to a capoeira class tomorrow at the Bimba school," Sam said. "Bimba was a *mestre*, or master, who helped make capoeira legal again in the 1930s. Do you want to come?"

"We'd love to!" I said, turning to consult Amanda and Jen. *That* was the kind of stuff I wanted to spend my year on the road doing. "What do you think?"

"Definitely!" they agreed.

152

S am became our adopted Lost Boy for the rest of our time in Salvador, accompanying us to capoeira classes that began with beating drums, chanting, and clapping. Because he knew about a lot of local events and could speak the language, he was able to show us a different side of the city than we'd normally have discovered on our own.

"Hey, do you ladies want to go to a soccer game tonight?" Sam asked as we walked out of the capoeira studio one morning, sweaty and sore from a week of training.

"I have to get some writing done," Amanda said. "But you go ahead."

Jen and I looked at each other and grinned. Jen had been a soccer player for most of her life, and the Brazilians seemed as passionate about *futebol* as they did about the annual collective party, Carnaval.

When we arrived at the local stadium later, firecrackers were exploding in the sky. "They shoot them off when someone scores a goal," Sam explained.

We bought another paper cone of those roasted cashews I found so addictive and a draft beer, all for only about a dollar, and Jen and I linked arms as we staked out a spot on the metal benches. Men made up most of the crowd, so we kind of stuck out. The masses were screaming, stomping their feet, and clapping their hands. Trying to blend in, I echoed the cheers of the guys in front of me, *"Porra!"* (pronounced *boo-ha!*).

The men turned around to stare at me with wide eyes and gaping mouths. Sam just laughed. "What?" I asked, thinking my accent must sound ridiculous.

"Holly, that literally means 'cum,'" he'd said. "You'll learn a lot of Portuguese at a *futebol* match, but most of it won't be for everyday conversation." My cheeks grew hot and Jen punched me in the arm, delighted I was making a fool of myself.

"I'm not at all *embarazada!*" I told her, and she laughed again. Just then, a swarm of armed guards carrying riot shields and firearms escorted the refs off the field. "It's halftime!" Sam said.

"They take their sports seriously," I noted.

"Things can get pretty violent if a fight breaks out—fans really defend their team," he said. "It's not a good idea to wear a local team's shirt to a match, but wearing a foreign one is guaranteed to start conversation."

I filed that tidbit of information away in my brain right next to "Never pull out cash in public" and "Don't drink the tap water."

My head was pulsing with the beat of the drums that'd kicked off before a whistle signaled the second half. The matches seemed to be as much of a musical event as a sporting event.

Sam waved a Brazilian flag he'd bought on the way in, and I let myself get lost in the crowd's thundering cheers.

It was our final night in Salvador, and our group of four spent it dancing to samba and listening to live music at a street festival. We were sandwiched among revelers as Brazilians grabbed our hands in another show of openness that made me feel at home so far away from my own. Some guy gave me his hat, and I twirled around to the music, melting into the crowd. Jen, Amanda, and I showed off our hip-swiveling maneuvers for one another before two Brazilian women laughed at us *gringas* and demonstrated moves that appeared to require the absence of any joints in one's lower body. Part of Bahians' beauty was in their genes, and I was beginning to think that a sense of rhythm was also inherited.

Bass vibrated through the cobblestone streets, and I felt almost as if I were absorbing the energy from so many people celebrating in that open space. As I danced with Jen, Amanda, and Sam, our clothes sticking to our bodies in the humidity, I knew then it wasn't partying itself that had been bothering me.

As I was learning from the locals, who seized every opportunity to have fun, dancing and drinking and partying were just some of the many ways to celebrate being alive. While I still didn't want *every* night of our trip to be that, I loved doing it when it made me feel more a part of the places we'd come so far to see. Once we got out of the backpacker bars, parties were a way to connect with the locals.

Spending less than two weeks in Salvador had made it easy to believe the poet who called it Terra da Alegria, or Land of Happiness. With a steady lineup of parties culminating in Carnaval, the city felt festive, like Christmas in the tropics, and the people seemed relaxed, as if the only place they had to be was right where they were at that moment.

Of course, our experience in Salvador came after the government prettified the Old Town to make it a UNESCO World Heritage Site. Before the government fixed it up, Pelourinho (which was supposedly home to the first slave market in the New World and actually means "whipping post" in Portuguese) had been awash in poverty, prostitution, and drugs. And the areas surrounding that section were still pretty broken down.

I thought of Igo and the other kids I'd seen begging on the streets. Then I thought of the woman who had taken my hand at the beach to show me the sunset. Maybe their warmth sprang less from happiness in the classic sense of elation or joy and more from their resiliency and a seemingly collective appreciation of the small things such as watching a sunset, drinking a cold beer on the beach, or dancing in the streets.

155

※

CHAPTER TEN

Amanda

NEW YORK CITY
AUGUST–SEPTEMBER

Few experiences have ever moved me as deeply, and with such consistency, as crossing back into Manhattan after a long stretch away. Even if I'm exhausted following a red-eye flight, or depressed to find dirty gray snowdrifts piled alongside the highway, something changes the moment I spot the skyline rising at the far end of the bridge. It's like a booster shoot of adrenaline, a surge that reminds me how lucky I am to live here and how I've managed to become a tiny but integral part of this iconic place.

But rather than the rush I'd expected, on this trip home, all I could feel was a lead balloon rolling around on the floor of my stomach. As Holly, Jen, and I shot between the silver trusses of the 59th Street Bridge in a cab with a broken air conditioner, it hit me: *You don't live here anymore.*

For the record, I hadn't wanted to come back here after Brazil. I knew that Jen and Holly wanted to spend some time with their boyfriends before we left on the next leg of the trip and that we had to pass through New York to make our connecting flight to Kenya. But though I could understand the logic, I couldn't come to terms with our return to town. Hadn't we just said good-bye to all of our friends? Made a clean break from the city?

I planned to spend the next two weeks hiding out at my friend Sarah's place. She and her husband, Pete, had just bought a brownstone in a yet-to-be-gentrified neighborhood in Brooklyn and had insisted that I spend my layover with them. No need to convince me, since, unlike the girls, I didn't have a boyfriend to shack with. It was Brooklyn or bust.

Our cab pulled to a jerky stop outside Sarah's office on Madison and 68th Street, and I slid out to retrieve my backpack from the trunk.

"So I'll see you guys next week, right?" I said, handing my friends some cab fare. After spending nine weeks glued to one another's sides, it felt bizarre to go in separate directions.

"Yeah, we'll catch up at the Indian consulate," said Jen. "Let's not wait until we get to Nairobi to get our visas."

I'd barely waved good-bye before the cab pulled away leaving me loitering in front of Oscar de la Renta. It felt weird. While my Teva sandal tan, bandana headband, and grungy, overstuffed pack put me right at home in the company of backpackers, I felt sloppy and glaringly out of place here in the swankiest part of the Upper East Side. And come to think of it, in the Manhattan fishbowl in general. Trying to avoid eye contact with a matron walking two Yorkshire terriers, I hauled my stuff to the nearest pay phone and called Sarah.

"Schmanders! You're here!" she shrieked. "Where are you? Don't move. I'm coming right down."

Within forty-five seconds, she'd flown down from her office and located me on the corner. "It's so good to see you!" she said, giving me a huge hug. "I figured you'd have this big ol' mama jamma bag, so I asked Pete if he could pick us up and drive us home."

"Perfect," I said, relieved to avoid the subway. "Wait . . . Pete's driving?"

"Oh, I didn't tell you? We bought a car!" Sarah beamed.

"Congrats, Sar! Sounds like you guys are really moving up in the world."

"Yeah, right. We're really living large." She made a face as she whirled her mermaid-length hair up into a messy twist. As usual, she had pulled together some funky-chic outfit that would seem over the top on me but looked amazing on her five-foot nine-inch supermodel frame.

"Yo! Ladies! Need a lift?" Pete pulled up to the curb across from us in a red Honda Civic hatchback.

"Hey, babe." Sarah opened the passenger side door and gave Pete a kiss. "Look who showed up at my office. Can we keep her? Can we?"

"Hmm, I'll have to think about that," he said, tossing my pack into the trunk. "So, what's up, Miss World Traveler? Hope you're hungry, because I've been smoking ribs for half the afternoon."

As I'd recently discovered, in addition to his job as a psychotherapist and devoted husband, Pete was also an award-winning barbecue champ. On summer weekends, he and Sarah hauled several grills and smokers up and down the East Coast, competing for prizes with their team, Notorious BBQ. I won't lie: part of the appeal of staying with my married friends was the prospect of their nightly gourmet dinners.

Pete wasn't kidding. As soon as he nudged open their front door twenty minutes later, the sweet, charred scent of caramelized meat hit my nose and sent my taste buds into mouth-watering overdrive. It was all I could do not to rip off the tinfoil covering the plates, grab a piece of pork, and tear into it like a wild animal.

"Why don't you get settled in, cleaned up, or whatever, and we'll put everything out for dinner," Sarah proposed. "It'll just be a few minutes."

Stashing my bags near the futon (already made up with sheets and pillows), I couldn't help but feel a bit like Pete and Sarah's grungy kid who'd just showed up from two months of summer camp. I even had a big bag full of stinky laundry.

Even though she was two years younger than I, Sarah had always been the more mature one in our relationship. Giving myself a little tour of her very grown-up, very couple-y new place, it struck me just how differently our lives had evolved since college.

While I'd spent my early years in the city jump-starting my career, falling for (and subsequently disentangling myself from) my first very serious boyfriend, whirling through a new roster of guys, and eventually abandoning city life to go traveling, Sarah had lived more deliberately. After college, she'd moved to Manhattan, become an interior designer at an Upper East Side firm, met the love of her life, had a gorgeous destination wedding in Puerto Rico, bought a brownstone in Brooklyn, and landscaped the backyard that I was now wandering through. Sarah's life seemed as immaculately, stylishly in order as a display window at Barney's, while mine still looked as scattered and disordered as a sale rack at T.J. Maxx.

It wasn't that I felt envious of her choices or wished I'd done things differently. If I'd gotten married in my midtwenties like Sarah, I certainly wouldn't be traveling the globe with two friends, on my way to Africa, India, and Southeast Asia. But sometimes, like right now, I wondered what it might be like to walk in my friend's Marc Jacobs flats, just for a day . . .

S omeone had tried to pull the front door shut as quietly as possible, but the click of metal snapped me awake. Sliding off the futon, I stumbled into the kitchen and found that Sarah had left a pot of coffee warming for me and a note next to it:

"AP—Home by eight or so. Help yourself to anything in fridge. BTW, we keep cigs in the freezer for guests, so feel free. Have a fun first day back in town!—Sar."

Funny. I hadn't smoked much since we'd been roommates during her first year in New York, but it was just like Sarah to remember my tastes (and bad habits).

So what now? Except for the spinning of the ceiling fan above the table, the room was completely quiet. I realized I'd be alone all day. It was the first time that had happened in months. I took a seat in one of the four empty chairs and plotted what to do with myself.

When we'd booked these tickets home, I'd decided against sending an e-mail to friends to let them know I'd be back. It felt disingenuous to tell everyone I'd be gone for an entire year just to roll back into town two months later. It would be better if I stayed out of sight and used these borrowed days to catch up on all the writing I hadn't done in South America.

While I'd been away, I'd filled almost an entire notebook with half-fleshed-out ideas for pitches but had been growing too self-conscious to spend the hours necessary to transform them into full-fledged articles. I knew Holly didn't care when I slipped off with the laptop stashed inside my day pack—she'd brought her own to write her *For Me* column—but I couldn't pretend that Jen was indifferent.

Jen and I had diffused some of the tension between us in Rio, but it was clear that we still had a serious difference of opinion over working on the road. For me, crafting stories was a creative outlet, another tool for interpreting the world around me, but Jen had emerged as a travel purist. She believed the best way to experience a country was to live, eat, breathe, and sleep entirely in the moment—no electronics necessary.

Getting up to pour myself a bowl of Kashi Good Friends cereal, I wondered if Jen and I would ever see eye to eye on this issue. Things between us had come to a head during our last week in Brazil, as the final editing deadline for our Web site article approached. It had taken us days longer to complete it than we'd expected, forcing us to spend afternoons hunkered over the laptop rather than exploring the islands off the coast of Bahia. After that, even I had to admit that taking on such a labor-intensive project while traveling might have been a mistake.

I knew Jen's suggestion to give up writing and assignments for a while made sense. Maybe I'd even have tried things her way if we had been on a two-week vacation. But we'd committed to this journey for an entire year, and I wasn't prepared to sever ties with the professional contacts I'd worked so hard to establish. Did I really need to disappear off the radar just so I could free up another hour or two each day for self-exploration? I couldn't understand setting aside my travel writing aspirations just when I begun having travels to write about.

Fired up and ready to get to work, I placed my cereal bowl and coffee mug next to Sarah's and Pete's in the sink and went over to my day pack to retrieve the laptop buried inside. I had a long, uninterrupted stretch of time in front of me, and I was determined to use it.

I'm not sure how things went so wrong, so quickly.

My first few days in Brooklyn were exactly what I needed. I reveled in the newfound autonomy. I got a ton of work accomplished—pitches written, e-mails answered, blogs posted—but the novelty of so much solitude wore thin pretty quickly.

On day three, I had trouble getting motivated. By day five, I'd grown distracted and restless. I constantly leapt up to pour more coffee. Or to make a snack. Or to wash the dishes (lest Pete and Sarah find me a bad houseguest). Instead of writing, I checked my e-mail obsessively. While I'd been hoping to get responses from editors, my only messages were "friend requests" for some Web site I'd never heard of, called Facebook.

When I'd started getting these messages several weeks earlier, I'd figured they were just spam and deleted them. Now, starving for distraction, I grabbed another cup of coffee, created a profile, and accepted the fifty or so requests I had waiting.

Within minutes, any plans I'd had to work that Friday were totally abandoned. I was dragged into a black hole of procrastination, devouring every scrap of information that my old friends from high school and college had posted on their home pages. I hadn't spoken with some of them since the day we'd graduated, but now I was eagerly learning every lurid detail of their adult lives.

The first pictures I saw were of my friend Celeste getting married on the steps of the Don Cesar Beach Resort, not far from where we'd grown up. Then the cute guy I'd sat next to in high school English holding his wife and their baby. My best friend from gymnastics as a kid—who now had a few kids herself.

Scrolling through the profiles, I was hit right and left with news of engagements and weddings and babies. I should have been happy for them, thrilled even. But sitting there in Pete and Sarah's empty living room, with the fan creaking and clicking overhead, I felt a kind of heaviness settling upon my chest.

Somehow, while I'd been distracted by other things—like getting on my feet in the city or inching up the magazine masthead—girls I'd once had slumber parties with had proceeded to grow up and settle down. I knew twenty-eight wasn't a shockingly young age to start a family, but because I live in Manhattan's bubble of eternal youth, it was easy to trick myself into thinking that I had years before marriage and kids would enter the picture. After all, if thirtysomething career women in New

York were still going out, sipping Cosmos, and dating a new guy every week, I still had plenty of time to get serious—right?

I clicked through several more profiles created by friends and colleagues in the city (who, thank God, were still single). By the time I'd worked through the list, there was still one person from my past whom I had to find, someone I'd been thinking about ever since we'd left for Lima back in June.

I wanted to know what had happened to Jason.

I'd started dating him about five months before the girls and I were scheduled to start our RTW trip. We'd both agreed in the beginning that it couldn't possibly turn into anything serious, but we both fell a little harder than either of us had expected to. He was the first guy I'd felt such a strong connection with since Baker.

In tears during our breakup, Jason promised to keep in touch and said that if we were both still available after I returned, we could try to pick up right where we'd left off. He'd sent me an e-mail shortly after we arrived at Loki hostel, which I took as a good sign. Maybe we *could* keep the door open for a relationship down the road.

We'd traded a few newsy e-mails since then, but something had definitely gone wrong after I'd sent a note saying that I'd be coming back through New York in August. That's when he'd just . . . evaporated. I couldn't figure out if he'd gotten busy or just missed my e-mail. So I'd sent him a second, ever-so-casual note on the day I'd arrived back in Brooklyn, asking him if he'd like to hang out.

Digital silence.

At first I'd been disappointed. Then pissed. I mean, we'd been in a relationship, and he'd been the first to reach out after I left—why was he stonewalling me now?

After checking his old MySpace page, it took me all of 1.3 seconds to figure out why I hadn't gotten a reply. There, right next to a new photo of Jason dressed in some ridiculous

163

sailor's outfit and faux mustache (which I seriously hoped was a costume), were the words: "Status: In a Relationship." A little more scrolling revealed several gushy messages from some new GF, a mousy brunette who looked as if she'd yet to graduate college. And they'd posted a handful of disgustingly cute photos together. In one he was posed behind her as she held a puppy in her arms. A goddamn puppy?!

I should have been prepared for the consequences of my online snooping, but I hadn't steeled myself for that broomstick-in-the-solar-plexus sensation. Forcing myself to stop rubbernecking the remains of my relationship, I mashed down the power button. The evidence that Jason had moved on tunneled out into an empty gray screen.

I felt like slapping myself. What was my problem? Jason had every right to date some new (significantly less cool) chick now that I'd checked out of his life. But the fact that he'd forgotten me so quickly stung like a second-degree burn.

I stalked into the kitchen and yanked open the freezer, pushing my way through the tinfoil tundra to find the one thing that could offer immediate relief. I located the box of cigarettes behind a shrink-wrapped slab of meat and yanked one out even before I'd walked outside. Wait. Matches. Phone. I found both and went into the backyard to light up.

"No way! He's already got a new girlfriend?" shrieked Holly as I sucked on the end of the American Spirit. "Wow, that man must really have been crazy about you."

"How in the world do you figure that?'

"Well, he clearly had to fill the void you left as quickly as possible."

Holly always had a truly impressive way of spinning the truth to make me feel better.

"Look, Amanda, he adored you—there's no question about that. But he knew you were leaving for an entire year. Most guys wouldn't have hung in there for as long as he did. Not unless they really cared."

"Even if that's the case, it didn't take him very long to get over it."

"Trust me, he's not over you. If he were, he'd have no problem grabbing a beer for old times' sake, now, would he?"

Thank God for Holly. She spent a half hour talking me off the ledge, refusing to let me descend into total depression. But it was only after she considered me stabilized and in no danger of causing harm to myself (other than chain-smoking, of course) that she released a bombshell of her own.

"So you remember my editor at *For Me*, Meghann, right? Well, she just called me about an hour ago, really upset."

"Oh wow, is everyone having a bad day? What happened?" I selected another thawed-out cigarette. I already felt nauseated, but lighting another one seemed like the right thing to do.

"Apparently, the magazine folded today. It's finished. They're not going to run any more issues after this one."

I stopped in my tracks and let the lighter fizzle out. "Wait . . . what? They're folding the magazine? What's going to happen to your column?"

"The column is done, too. I won't be getting more checks after my next one."

"God, Holly. Are you okay?" I raced back inside. "Do you want me to come over? I can leave right now. What's your subway stop again?"

"No, no, it's fine. Don't come over," she said firmly. "I'm already here with Elan, and we've been figuring things out since Meg called. It'll be fine."

"Holly. Are you sure? I can be there in ten minutes. It's no problem."

"Yeah. I'll be okay. I just don't know what to do about money, because that column was really my only source of income for the trip. I've only got about six thousand in the bank, and we haven't even bought our round-the-world tickets yet."

Holly was referring to the string of tickets that we'd secured through a San Francisco–based travel agency called AirTreks—international flights starting in Kenya, then connecting through India, Dubai, Southeast Asia, Bali, New Zealand, and Australia. The $2,200 price tag was a bargain—unless we couldn't actually come up with the money to pay it.

I could barely ask the next question. "Can you still come on the rest of the trip?"

"I don't know. Of course I *want* to come with you guys. But is it really smart to fly all the way to Africa without knowing if I can afford to fly back again?"

The answer was probably no, but I couldn't even imagine continuing at this point without Holly. The three of us were a team now, a force. There was just no way two of us could face the world without our third.

"Well no, but, Holly," I said, scrambling to think of a creative solution. "Whatever you do, don't decide to stay just yet. There has to be something else we can do to make money on the road. Could we work at one of the hostels? Pick fruit somewhere?" I joked that we could all sell our eggs to a fertility clinic for cash—I'd actually spoken with one traveler who'd done as much and pulled in about eight grand in the process.

My brain was racing on all cylinders, trying to calculate how much money I had left in the bank. I'd made some decent money while freelancing, and I had some savings I was using to fund my own travels. Could I afford to lend Holly the money for her round-the-world ticket? Would she accept?

"Holly, just promise me one thing. No matter what you ultimately decide to do, just say you'll still meet us next Monday to get the visa for India. You can always decide later not to come with us, but you should at least apply, just in case."

There was a long pause on the other end of the line.

"I'll come meet you guys," she said. "But I can't promise anything."

I didn't need her to. If she showed up, that would be enough. As soon as Holly and I said good-bye, I clicked the receiver to get a dial tone, then immediately called Jen.

A few days later, I found myself back across the East River, laptop bag slung across my body and pillow lines cross-hatched across my face. I'd opted to reenter the city a couple of hours early, hoping the quick pace and frenetic energy would kick-start me back into writing mode. Jen, Holly, and I weren't meeting at the consulate until 11 a.m., so the idea was to grab a cup of coffee and get cracking.

Standing with the restless mob at the coffee pickup counter, I felt my anxiety level rise. Man, I'd forgotten how hostile a Midtown Starbucks could be when people desperately needed a $5 attitude adjustment. The smell of stress percolating in the room was enough to make me appreciate the moments of relative calm and stillness the girls and I had experienced while sipping freeze-dried Nescafé in Latin American hostels.

In the back seating section, the air vibrated at an even higher anxiety level. People jammed elbows to get their laptops plugged in at the single four-man workstation, and others were hovering intently over two-tops, trying to command the space even before the current occupants had finished their coffee. The situation triggered my fight-or-flight response, and I just didn't have the energy right now to duke it out for a sticky table next to the bathroom.

Jostling past the business suits, wayward tourists, and posh media girls, I pushed my way outside into the milky September sunshine and felt a brush of chill against my skin. Fall was a whisper away. I prayed Holly wouldn't have to stick around New York to usher it in.

I managed to find an empty seat in a public atrium nearby, popped open the laptop, and willed myself to do something useful. Unless you could count draping myself across the futon, eating processed snacks from the corner bodega, and forcing Pete to give me free therapy sessions, I'd done absolutely nothing of value in the past few days.

Despite the high-octane Starbucks latte and my best intentions, I didn't fare much better in Manhattan. I procrastinated, sifting through the photos we'd taken during the first part of the trip, before giving up on working altogether. I decided to stroll a dozen blocks uptown to the consulate and wait for the girls.

I was surprised to find Jen already there, slumped against the porous stone face of the building as if she might keel over without its support. Her normally vibrant, amber blond hair hung limply around her face in strings, and behind her sunglasses, her expression looked flat, utterly deflated. As I stood next to her against the wall, I suspected that this had much bigger implications than Holly's pending status on the trip.

"Jenny." I searched her face, trying to figure out what was happening on the other side of her dark lenses. "What's going on? Are you all right?"

"Yeah, I'm fine." She sounded hollow. I could now see the streaks where tears had been hastily brushed aside.

"You sure?"

"Well, not exactly." She adjusted herself, pressing her shoulder into the wall and letting her bag drop to the sidewalk. "I just . . . I know that when we leave for Africa, things with Brian and me are over."

"Oh, Jen. I'm so sorry." I moved in to give her a hug.

"It's okay. I knew this was coming, but now that it's here . . . well, I'm just so sad."

"Well, you know you don't have to go," I said, trying to sound strong, convincing. "If you're having doubts, you could stay here, try to salvage things . . ."

In a flash, I envisioned Jen dashing across the city to reunite with Brian while I tried to navigate through Africa and India without either of my friends.

"No, that's the problem. I really don't have any doubts. I want to keep going—but that will mean it's totally over."

I was just trying to figure out what to say, whether or not to suggest that there might be hope for the two of them, when Holly came bounding down the block.

"Ladies, I made it on time! I made sure to leave twenty minutes early so I could . . ." Holly was instantly alarmed once she got up close. "Oh no, Jen. What's wrong?"

"I promise that I'll explain everything later, but right now I just don't feel like getting into it," she said softly as she slid the strap of her bag back onto her shoulder. "Can we just go inside?"

"Of course, yeah," said Holly, sounding stronger than the last time we'd talked. "We don't have to discuss anything right now. Let's just go in."

Despite our varying states of crisis, I felt a tremendous sense of relief to be with both girls again. We pushed open the heavy black door and went inside. The scene at the consulate made the Midtown Starbucks look as chill as a Buddhist monastery. People in every manner of dress were absolutely everywhere, crammed onto lines that appeared to go nowhere, sitting on the floor to fill out forms, shouting across the room with no concept of indoor voices. But even the chaos couldn't distract from the tightly wound American woman at the front of the line who was shrieking about some papers she'd faxed in but that had apparently been lost.

"Who is your supervisor? This is absolutely ridiculous! I

169

took the time to get those forms signed and notarized and faxed in. Where are they?"

We couldn't hear what the guy on the other side of the glass was saying, but he didn't look ruffled. He motioned for her to move aside, and a smallish Indian man approached, shoving his papers through the slot in the window. The woman started shouting again, whirling on the guy who'd dared cut her off before she was done.

The three of us gawked at the scene for a minute, then glanced at each other.

"Holy shit, you guys," said Jen, sounding both shell-shocked and thrilled. "Are we really doing this? Are we really going to India?"

The moment she posed the question, I could sense a shift in the mood between us. Jen wasn't just asking whether or not we were headed to India. She was asking if we were ready to commit ourselves to this journey all over again.

When we had first agreed to go around the world, the three of us had had no real concept of what it would be like to spend every single day, hour, and minute on the road with two other people. We'd never tried compromising on every single decision. We hadn't yet experienced the gravity of our choice to leave behind the people we loved.

Now, with South America behind us and the consequences of our actions as real and in your face as the shrieking woman before us, we were confronted with yet another decision: Could we commit to several more months of travel? Were we ready to leave New York City yet again in order to find something unknown and intangible on the road?

In that moment, the goals I'd been focused on all week seemed utterly trivial. The only thing I wanted now was to ensure that my best friends would continue on this adventure with me; that we'd see the world together, with no woman left behind.

I turned to Holly and shared what I'd been thinking from the moment I'd heard her column was going under.

"Look, I know you're probably going to think this is a crazy idea, but please just consider it. If you're willing to take it, I'd like"—I swallowed hard—"I'd like to lend you the money to buy your round-the-world ticket."

Holly's jade green eyes widened, and her mouth dropped open.

"Just think about it," I said. "You don't have to decide now. It's not going to be enough to cover your daily expenses, and you probably don't want to mix the whole friends and finances thing. But even if you take a year or two to pay me back, it's okay . . . "

"Amanda," she said softly. "You'd really do that for me?"

"Yeah, I would. I just know there's still so much you want to do. Like getting your yoga certification at an ashram. Learning to scuba dive. Bungee jumping in New Zealand."

"I never said I wanted to do that!"

"Oh, wait. You're right. That was Jen. But still, consider it. This trip won't be the same with just two of us. In fact, it probably wouldn't work at all without you. Jen and I have talked about this—we might actually kill each other if you weren't around."

"Yeah, it's true. You're the buffer," said Jen, smiling but still serious. "Three's always supposed to be a crowd, but in this case, it's really the perfect number. We all contribute something to the mix, balance out each other's good and bad traits. Like, Amanda's the motivator, I'm the planner—"

"And Holly, you're the peacemaker," I said. "What's more important than that?"

We all descended into a rare silence as we snaked our way up through the long, painstakingly slow line. Nearly an hour passed before we handed our paperwork over to the Indian guy behind the glass.

"How long you visit India?" he asked.

"About a month. A little less," Jen answered. He flipped through our passports and placed our forms inside of them.

"You come back four-thirty. Other line pick up."

The three of us walked outside and started heading in the direction of Central Park. Once inside the stone walls, we sat down on one of the unoccupied green benches. I pulled out the nearly empty box of cigarettes and started to light one.

"You're smoking?" Holly asked, staring at me. "I've never seen you smoke."

"I started again this week," I said, offering her the pack. "But I think I'm done."

"No, thanks. I'm quitting, too," she said. "They definitely don't let you smoke at the ashram, so I should probably get a head start by giving them up now."

I digested that comment for a couple seconds before turning to face Holly.

"What are you saying?" I asked, afraid to get my hopes up. "You're coming?"

"Well, did you really mean what you said in there? About lending me the money. Is that really an option?" Holly shifted her gaze from her shoes to my face.

"Of course I meant it. I really want to do this. I mean, you've already paid for the volunteer program in Kenya, and India's just a hop skip away from there. Besides, I can't think of a better investment than you, Corbett. So do me proud and say you'll accept."

I felt as if I were proposing, and in a way, I guess I was. If she said yes, we'd all be tied to one another, for better or worse, through the next nine months and eight countries. "Okay, sugar mama," she said. "Let's do it. I accept."

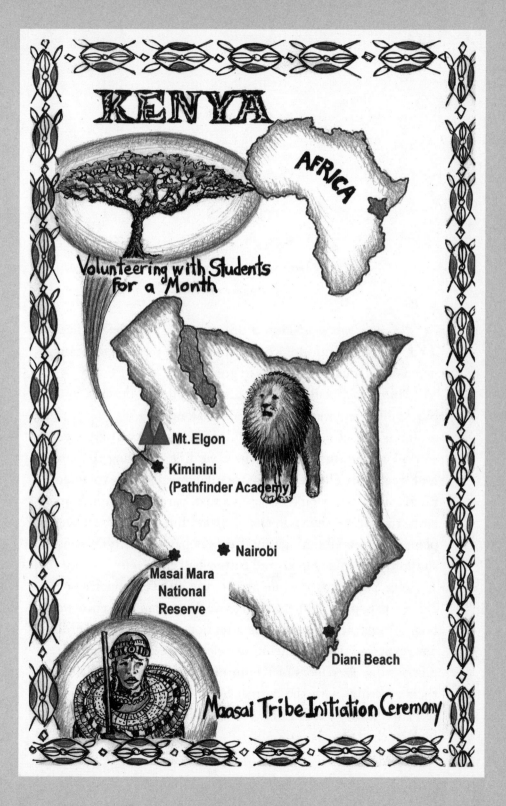

KENYA

AFRICA

Volunteering with Students
for a Month

Mt. Elgon

Kiminini
(Pathfinder Academy)

Nairobi

Masai Mara
National
Reserve

Diani Beach

Maasai Tribe Initiation Ceremony

·⅍·

CHAPTER ELEVEN

Jen

KIMININI, KENYA
SEPTEMBER

*M*zungu, *mzungu!* How-a are *you* . . . *mzungu*?" echoed across the sun-drenched farmland as barefoot kids scampered down mud-caked roads to greet us.

"*Msuri sana*," Amanda, Holly, and I replied in our best Swahili, smiling and waving as we walked along.

It was our second day in Kiminini, Kenya, and we were eager to explore the small village where we'd be spending the next four weeks. Back home in New York, I'd imagined our volunteer program location would be set in a vast, parched savanna similar to the variety shown in *Out of Africa*. But instead, we'd been plopped into a vibrant, pastoral canvas painted with immense sunflower-sprinkled fields and cotton-ball clouds.

Since a *mzungu*, or white person, was still very much a novelty in this part of the country, we knew our presence was bound to garner at least some attention. But we could hardly have expected the overwhelming welcome we received from the pint-sized ambassadors of Kiminini. Even when we replied to their greetings with the correct Swahili phrase, "*Msuri sana*" (very well), the brood trailing us burst into a fit of giggles and high-pitched squeals.

By the time we reached the edge of town—little more than a cluster of tin shacks and wooden stalls offering everything from used bicycle tires to ice cream cones–we'd acquired quite the entourage. These kids, who ranged from about three to eight years old, were dressed in a hand-me-down collection of smock dresses, pajama pants, khaki shorts, and cartoon T-shirts. At first our wide-eyed onlookers kept their distance, but eventually they grew bolder and started walking directly in our footsteps. When we'd turn around and pretend to run after them, they'd shriek and dash away, clearly thrilled at the prospect of being chased by three strange, but seemingly friendly, women. Before long, they started sneaking closer and touching us gently, egging us to play this new and exciting game over and over again. But it wasn't until we broke out our cameras that the real fun began.

We'd learned in South America that children would often get extraordinarily excited to see a photo of themselves—for many of those in rural or impoverished areas, it was for the very first time. And as I tilted my three-inch Olympus viewing screen down so the kids of Kiminini could see their own reflections, they had a similar reaction. Jumping up and down, they squealed with joy as if as I'd unlocked the doors to the world's largest candy shop. They formed a tight circle around me, leaping onto my back and pleading, "Again, mzungu, again!" At the same time, Amanda whipped out her camcorder to capture what she already knew would be a moment I'd want to relive long after leaving Kenya.

"So, Jen, does this experience fulfill all your *Flame Tree* fantasies?" she asked, mirroring the tone of a reporter interviewing a fresh-off-the-field Super Bowl champ.

"Well, I'm glad you asked that, Amanda," I replied, striking my best interviewee pose. I then launched into a speech about how unbelievably lucky I felt to be crouched in the dirt, surrounded by children, in a country I'd dreamed of visiting since I was still carrying a lunch box to school. Anyone who knew me well would have heard about *The Flame Trees of Thika*, a PBS miniseries I'd fallen in love with decades ago.

Unlike my friends' parents, mine had the crazy notion that cable television was an unnecessary luxury I could live without. Despite my constant begging and pleading to be "like all my friends," my Nickelodeon-fueled fantasies never came to fruition. Instead, I became the only kid in my neighborhood with an in-depth knowledge of the Saturday-night *Masterpiece Theatre* schedule.

One evening, my parents called me into the TV room to watch a new miniseries called *The Flame Trees of Thika*. Naturally I was skeptical. I could barely pronounce the title, let alone get excited about some nature program about a burning forest. That all changed after the first scene when I realized that the show was actually about a little girl my age—score one for Mom and Dad!

Based on the true story of Elspeth Huxley, whose parents left England in 1913 to start a coffee farm in Kenya, *The Flame Trees of Thika* was my first introduction to life in East Africa. By the end of the first episode, I was already intrigued by the mysterious culture of Kenya's indigenous people, the exotic animals that roamed freely across the plains, and the country's breathtaking natural beauty. I longed to be just like Elspeth: to mingle with the native Kikuyu tribe, to explore the vast expanses of wheat-colored savanna, and to have my very own white pony. Aside from slumber parties and soccer practice, each new episode was the highlight of my week. That was, until the sad day when the series ended.

Sobbing uncontrollably to the rolling of the credits, I was consoled only by my mom's insistence that she was certain PBS would rerun the series and I'd be reunited with *The Flame Trees of Thika* again in the near future. But no matter how many hours I logged rewatching my coveted VHS copy in the years to come, the viewing experience never replaced my desire to see Africa for myself. And now, after almost two decades of planning the pilgrimage in my head, I'd finally made it.

By the time we'd arrived in Kenya, my expectations couldn't have been higher. A wave of nervousness had washed over me as our plane approached the Jomo Kenyatta International Airport in Nairobi just a few short days earlier. I could only hope the experience would be all that I'd imagined.

After a brief two-night stint in the country's capital (which, fortunately for us, didn't live up to its "Nairobbery" nickname), Amanda, Holly, and I were escorted to the bus station by our on-ground volunteer coordinators.

After extensive online research and personal inquiries, we'd committed to a one-month program with Village Volunteers, a Seattle-based nonprofit that partnered with rural towns across Kenya. Since all three of us were interested in youth education, the company's founder, Shana Greene, recommended that we work with the Common Ground Program, a grassroots NGO (nongovernmental organization) that housed a primary school serving hundreds of children, many of whom were orphans or had lost at least one parent to illness or disease.

We'd been warned that the eight-hour journey toward Mount Elgon in the western part of the country would be a tad bumpy. In reality, our vehicle bounced and crashed over the rain-gutted roads like a mechanical bull on warp speed, forcing its riders to hold on for dear life—and us to change into sports bras at the first opportunity. The ride may have been jarring, but no amount of head-to-ceiling bumps and bruises could knock me off my cloud. Hoping Amanda and Holly wouldn't notice, I set my iPod to play Toto's "Africa" on repeat and gazed dreamily out the window.

While almost a century had passed since Elspeth Huxley had lived here, Kenya's most distinctive features had stood the test of time. Delicate acacia trees, masquerading as wispy umbrellas, rose majestically from silky cornfields. Ginger red roads streaked the landscape, winding in endless pursuit of the horizon. And a family of zebras held court around a crystal watering hole that reflected the sapphire sky.

Eventually, sporadic signs of civilization punctuated the vast wilderness. Men emerged from ditches carrying hammers and machetes, while women balancing large bundles on their heads returned from the market. As we crashed and banged through one of the isolated roadside towns, my attention was diverted to a grassy ledge jutting out from the hillside. On it was a tiny boy, maybe three or four years old, sitting alone swinging his legs and singing to himself. When he caught sight of our bus, his face lit up like a jack-o'-lantern, and it seemed as if his doe eyes locked directly onto mine. In an instant, he leapt to his bare feet, jumping up and down and waving furiously.

I sat frozen in place, blinking rapidly to ensure the boy wasn't a product of my *Flame Trees* fantasy. But he kept staring and smiling and fluttering his arms in the air. I grinned from ear to ear and waved back, which propelled him to run along the ridge, giggling and chasing the bus from above until it drove too fast for him to keep up.

I turned to tell Amanda and Holly what had happened, but they were sprawled across the brittle plastic seats, trying to catch a catnap between jostles. I smiled, recalling one of my favorite scenes from *Stand by Me*, in which the main character has a sentimental encounter with a deer by the train tracks that he doesn't share with anyone until he writes his novel. In that moment, a tear slipped down my dusty cheek, and I decided to keep my encounter with the boy to myself.

As our bus continued down the lonely dirt road, the image of the boy stayed with me and I couldn't help but interpret his presence as a sign. Starting that day, I would be living out a dream I'd been harboring for twenty years, and I knew without a doubt that I was finally on the right track.

I t was approaching nightfall by the time we reached the grounds of Pathfinder Academy. Even in the dim light, there was no denying that we'd landed squarely in farm country. The school, built of cinder blocks and tin, sat to the left of the main gate. Down on the right, I spotted a traditional mud house and two round huts with thatched roofs. A menagerie of cows, chickens, and stray dogs wandered the sludgy lawn, replacing the giraffes, elephants, and gazelles we'd romantically envisioned.

Joshua Machinga, our volunteer leader, waited proudly outside, greeting us with an enthusiastic *karibu* (welcome). He introduced us to his five children, Sandra, Tracy, John, Cindy, and Shana, who ranged from two to thirteen years old, and his wife, Mama Sandra, a bright-eyed, full-figured woman with a youthful complexion and a high, ringing belly laugh that echoed across the entire farm. Joshua ushered us into his family's modest two-room house for a meet-and-greet tea party, only here the china saucers had been replaced by small tin cups and lightbulbs swapped out for old-fashioned kerosene lanterns. Once we were seated on a long bumpy sofa covered with crocheted lace, I noticed that the walls and floor were made of some kind of hardened earth. It wasn't until days later that I learned they were actually made from cow dung and a fresh layer was spread on every few weeks to keep things, uh, well . . . fresh.

Jen • Kiminini, Kenya • September

Sitting shoulder to shoulder, Amanda, Holly and I made small talk with three naturopathic medical students from Bastyr University near Seattle who'd been working at various Village Volunteer sites across Kenya. According to them, Common Ground was one of the most modern and prosperous programs, and Joshua's family was considered to be fairly well off by local standards—a sobering thought given that there was no running water and very limited electricity. Before I could ask the volunteers more about the poverty that lay beyond the barbed-wire fence surrounding the property, a petite brunette burst into the room. She wore a T-shirt that read THIS IS WHAT AN ENVIRON-MENTALIST LOOKS LIKE, and her green paisley wrap skirt was streaked with flour.

"Oh! You must be the New Yorkers. I'm Irene, one of the other volunteers. I've really been looking forward to meeting you guys!" she exclaimed with a grin, placing a covered dish on the table. She dusted her palms on her skirt before reaching over to offer each of us a handshake. "I've been helping the cooks make chapati bread, so I hope it tastes all right."

Within a matter of minutes, we learned that Irene was an undergrad at Yale but was taking a semester off to travel and pursue philanthropic endeavors. Already she'd constructed a so-lar dehydrator so that Joshua's family could dry fruit for longer storage and was spearheading a tree-planting project the fol-lowing day.

"I'll introduce you to Emmanuel, who organizes the sustain-able farming projects, so maybe you can help too," she offered.

Still slightly disoriented, I breathed a sigh of relief at having so many friendly faces to greet us. Hopefully Irene could show us the ropes and help make Amanda and Holly feel more com-fortable. Because although they'd fully supported my dream to volunteer in Kenya, I couldn't help but feel responsible for their happiness here. This was a pretty huge leap from even the grittiest of conditions we'd faced in South America, so I could only cross my fingers and hope I hadn't gotten us in over our heads.

Just then, one of Joshua's eldest daughters came in to set the table, followed by three men carrying bubbling cast-iron cauldrons. Joshua and Mama Sandra settled in nearby chairs, cranked up the kerosene lamps, and shared what was on that evening's menu: stewed chicken with tomatoes, lentils, potatoes, two kinds of beans, flatbread, and an overflowing bowl of mangoes.

As children of the "We Are the World" generation, the girls and I had envisioned the food in Africa as being rationed out by the spoonful, so we'd strategically stuffed energy bars in every crevice of our backpacks for this part of the trip. But what lay before us was a veritable feast. We could only hope that everyone on the farm enjoyed the same generous portions and that this meal wasn't being served just for our benefit.

Once everything had been laid out, Joshua cleared his throat and turned in our direction. "So, to our new volunteers, Jenni-fa, A-men-da, and Howly, we welcome you to Common Ground and to Pathfinder Academy. After the meal, the fourteen girls who are boarders here will arrive to provide you with entertainment. They have won many district awards for their performances in the areas of singing, dance, for poems, and also for scholastics," he said, his shoulders set back with obvious pride. "So I hope that you will enjoy it."

Shortly after we finished eating, I heard light footsteps and giggles from outside. The calico fabric curtain covering the doorway was pushed open slowly, allowing excitable whispers and "Shhs" to float across the threshold. Peeking shyly at us, fourteen little women filed in two at a time and formed a circle around the room. Suddenly the boarders erupted into song, clapping and swaying their hips in a choreographed rhythm. Most of the lyrics were in Swahili until they pointed to Irene, who shouted her own name. After that, every tenth word or so was "Irene," like the Kenyan version of the "name game" ("Irene, Bean, Mo Mean, Banana Fanna, Fo Fean").

Soon we were all twisting our hips, shaking our booties, and repeating the lines as best we could. I waited for my cue and then yelled "Jennifer!" at the top of my lungs. That made the girls giggle, and one called out, "Ooh, like Jenni-fa Lopez!" Once they shouted my name another nine times, the group moved on to Amanda and Holly.

The festivities continued for another half hour before Joshua released his charges back to their dorm to get ready for bed. The girls approached us one by one to shake our hands before dashing out the door. After only a few hours at Pathfinder, there was no doubt in my mind that I was going to love getting to know them.

"That was amazing. Thank you, Joshua," Holly said. "The boarders were so brave to sing in front of us. Will we get to spend time with them tomorrow?"

"Yes, that is certain. After their classes end around three o'clock in the afta-noon," he replied. "But now we need to determine where each of you will sleep for the evening. There is one space with Irene in the volunteer hut, then there's another room here in the house for two more."

Since it'd been my idea to come here, I figured it was only fair to let Amanda and Holly stay together, so I offered to bunk with Irene. Entering the cement hut, I was surprised to discover that it had working overhead lights and a linoleum-tiled floor. There were two windows, a small table, and a couple folding chairs. In the center of the room sat two twin beds with oversized mosquito nets that hung from the ceiling and floated above the mattresses. A few creepy-crawlies were scaling the walls, but hopefully they'd stay put. All in all, it was pretty much like camping—only with a stray cow or two moseying by outside.

"So, that blanket should be enough but there are extras on that shelf if you need them," Irene said, explaining that the weather in this part of Kenya was a lot cooler than she'd expected. Selecting a book from a huge pile, she settled under her own woolly throw.

Although a thin layer of dust still clung to my face and bare arms from the open-window bus ride, I was too worn out to care. In less than a minute, I'd swapped my dirty clothes for slightly cleaner pajamas and cocooned myself in my silk sleep sack.

"I can't believe it's only eight thirty p.m. It feels so much later," I said with a yawn.

"I know. I rarely go to bed after ten p.m. here," Irene said. "Especially since Elijah, that's one of Joshua's workers, wakes us up at six a.m. for our showers. So do you think you'll want to go first tomorrow?"

"Oh, well, I don't know. I kinda assumed showers weren't an option," I remarked.

"Well, it's more of a sponge bath, but it's really a very effective system. One of the cooks puts out two buckets of water, one boiling and one tepid. Plus a third that's empty, so you can mix your own hot-to-cold ratio to take into the stall. You probably didn't notice it in the dark, but it's the one to the left of the toilet," she added.

As we'd discovered upon arrival, the "toilet" she was referring to was actually a shed with a crude hole cut into the ground—and quite the social venue for families of flies and gnats. After hours of riding with no potty breaks, our bladders had been bursting, and the girls and I were squirming around like kindergartners, desperate to go almost anywhere—even in a scary outhouse that added a whole new level of negative stars to our rating system. I shuddered at the thought of trying to do any, er, *extended* business in there, but I figured we'd cross that daunting bridge when we came to it.

183

"Gotcha, okay. Well, why don't you go first, that way if I screw up the bucket system, your shower won't be ruined," I said, still a bit unclear how it all worked (and admittedly not a fan of early mornings).

"Sure thing. But I'm confident a savvy New Yorker like you can figure it out," she joked, setting her book down and flipping onto her side to face me. "It must be so exciting to live there. Do you love it?"

Pulling up the extra blanket I'd grabbed from the shelf, I told her about working in television, the late nights and crazy parties, Sunday brunches on the Upper West Side, and other silly details of a typical week in the city. In turn, she enlightened me about her experiences as a Yalie, the coed naked parties at secret, off-campus locations, her passion for environmental studies, and the gorgeous new guy she was dating and currently missing like crazy.

"So do you have a boyfriend?" she asked, propping her head on her hand.

AAaa . . . BOoooYyy . . . FRIEeeeNnnDdd. The letters wafted across the room in ultraslow motion, smothering my face like the psychedelic caterpillar's smoke rings in *Alice in Wonderland*. A *boyfriend*. I'd desperately been trying to avoid thinking about that word—and Brian—since we'd gotten onto the plane, but now that Irene had said it, even my "curiouser and curiouser" new Kenyan reality couldn't stop me from reliving the heartbreaking one I'd just left in New York.

I could hardly believe that less than a week earlier, I'd been sitting on the floor of Brian's studio, sobbing hysterically into a plate of chicken pad Thai, struggling to face the inevitable demise of our relationship. Though a breakup had clearly been on the horizon since I first announced my plans to travel, somehow the months had slipped carelessly through our fingers like a worn-down sliver of soap.

I'm sure most people thought we were nuts for dragging things out as long as we had. But in my mind the reason was simple: Brian and I just weren't a cold-turkey kind of couple. We needed the emotional equivalent of, say, the patch or Nicorette gum. We had apartments only an M86 bus ride apart, and Central Park never proved a powerful enough barrier to keep us apart for any significant length of time. Even after the worst fights, we easily succumbed to temptation, sprinting back to the source for just one last fix, "we swear."

Maybe it had been unfair of me to run away. But the only way I could think of to finally end this relationship was to literally put oceans and continents between us. My justification: If we were meant to be together, we'd find a way back to each other. If not, then at least Brian could have custody of New York for a while and we'd both have our space to grieve.

The logical side of my brain could accept that rationale until all the easy distractions—the happy hours, Yankees games, dinners out, lazy hours in bed—came to an end. It was my last night in town, and that far-off future moment we'd been dreading and avoiding for so long was staring us down. It was finally time to face reality.

I kept my eyes glued to the greasy takeout containers while Brian's ultimatum hung in the air like an ominous rain cloud. "If you can't promise me you'll come home after Kenya or at least after India, then we're over," he said quietly. While I was tucked safely away with Brian in "our" apartment, my fingers wrapped tightly around his, the round-the-world trip temporarily melted away. For one brief moment, I thought, Just stay. Stay here cuddled up with the man you love and never leave.

The old me would have broken the tension with a witty one-liner like "C'mon, sweetie, I'll throw in half a spring roll and raise you a dumpling if you fold." He'd pretend to be mad for a second but would quickly start laughing. Then we'd both snug-

185

gle together on the couch and forget the silly argument had ever happened. But I couldn't joke my way out of this.

It took every ounce of strength I had to say the words that needed to be said. "I'm so sorry, Brian. I just can't quit the trip. I need to see it through to the end." And then that was it. We were really over. I was going to lose him. Not for a few days, not for a few months, but probably forever. By the next day, I'd be on another plane with Holly and Amanda, preparing to face the world again. Only this time there wouldn't be a boyfriend waiting for me when I got home.

Although I'd shed plenty of tears that day in New York—hysterically sobbing my way down Second Avenue the entire morning before departure—somehow my grief just didn't feel appropriate here in Kenya. One of the main reasons I'd wanted to volunteer in the first place was to transfer some of the focus off myself and channel that energy toward someone else in need. If there was one time that my own struggles could—and should—take a backseat, it was now.

So, very simply, I told Irene that I'd dated the same guy for the past few years but it just hadn't worked out. I could tell that she sensed there was more to the story, but since we were still getting to know each other, she didn't press the issue. Instead, she gave me a friendly half smile, maybe to let me know that she understood. Grateful, I smiled back at her, then rolled over and finally succumbed to exhaustion.

While unexpected early-morning construction wasn't a factor at Common Ground, evil roosters swooped in to continue our wake-up curse, piercing the air with their persistent squawks at 5 a.m. I buried my head under my pillow, snatching morsels of sleep until it was my turn to take a bucket bath. Somehow I bumbled through the three-bucket process and managed to scrub a surprising amount of dirt off my body. By the time I emerged from the shower shed to face the rising sun, all the volunteers, including Amanda and Holly, were already seated in the living room.

As we dined on another surprisingly huge meal of omelets, fresh mangoes, bread with jam and peanut butter, and popcorn, of all things, our conversation quickly turned to our volunteer applications. We'd each filled out a detailed questionnaire about which areas we were most interested in—with child care and youth theater topping my list—and were eager to see how everything worked.

After breakfast Joshua took us on a brief walking tour to help us get acquainted with the grounds, which included the Pathfinder Academy school and several fields used to grow the food that we were eating at each meal. Reaching the main entrance at the far side of the farm, we were almost swept away by a flood of children that poured through the gates.

Dressed in faded navy and lavender uniforms, some two sizes too big for them, the knee-high super troopers marched proudly toward their classrooms, shouting, "Good morning, Headmaster," when they spotted Joshua. The tiniest of the group, a boy no older than four or five, ran over to get a closer look at us. To my surprise, he dropped his small bag and reached up for a hug. I couldn't resist. I got down on one knee and hugged him back.

"Joshua, do you think that we'll be able to work with some of the students, like maybe teach classes or do after-school programs?" Amanda asked. "How can we help while we're here?"

The students already had full-time instructors, Joshua explained, but several of the boarders still needed sponsors who could assist with the cost of their school tuition, uniforms, and meals. He wondered if maybe we knew some people back in the States who could help. "It does not matter how much—any amount great or small would be very useful," he added.

"Well, we'd be happy to ask our friends and family for financial support and raise awareness for your program," Holly said.

"I have acquired many more boarders this past year, so that is much appreciated," said Joshua.

"We'd love to learn more about them. Do you think we could sit down and talk with the girls later today?" I asked.

Joshua agreed, then gave us a bit of background to explain why and how they'd ended up at Pathfinder in the first place. He said most of the girls boarded here because they lived a great walking distance away and had been attacked on their way to or from school. In most cases, it was a crime of opportunity, an attempted rape by drunken idlers on the side of the road. Some girls had managed to escape, while others were not as fortunate. "It happens a lot of the time," Joshua said. "But sadly, there is nothing that can be done."

Sorrow and disgust churned in my throat, dropping like a lead weight into the pit of my stomach. What did he mean, nothing can be done? We could teach these girls to fight back. Get them some sort of alarm key chain to blow the eardrums out of those bastards. Or we could organize a self-defense program!

From the incensed and horrified looks on Amanda and Holly's faces, I knew all three of us were on the same page, if not thinking the exact same thing. I was just about to share my sentiments when Joshua added, "Yes, it is very sad for these girls, but that is the way it is here in Kenya." He explained that the government didn't do much to stop rape—and most of the time, neither did local citizens. The most effective thing he could do, he said, was to keep the students out of harm's way so that this didn't happen to them again.

"It is very good for the girls to have volunteers like you here as role models. To show them what can be accomplished if they stay in school and study hard," he said, leading us back to the main house. It sounded as if this wasn't the first time he'd explained the issue to female volunteers.

Raised to believe that a woman had a right to protect her body at any and all costs, we instinctively wanted to push the envelope and advocate a radical new way of thinking to keep the boarders from harm in the future. But one of the main reasons that the Village Volunteers organization was so effective at its mission was that it developed programs with local sensibilities in mind rather than trying to force-fit Western ideals. So, for the time being, we bit our tongues. Our best course of action, it seemed, was to observe, learn, and simply be available to Joshua and the boarders.

Since Holly and Amanda had been assigned a tiny room in the big house until the Bastyr students left in a few days, they spent their after-meal hours hanging out with Irene and me in our hut. Sprawled out diagonally across the two beds, the four of us fell into our own little worlds—Irene and I pored over books, Holly caught up on journal entries, and Amanda uploaded our latest crop of photos onto the computer. As groups of boarders passed by our open door, they smiled and waved but continued on their way. As the evening progressed, the more outgoing girls popped in to say hello or ask what we were doing. Irene reintroduced us to each girl as they entered. There were Naomi, Nancy, Esther, Calvin, and Joshua's eldest, Sandra, a thirteen-year-old girl, who made the others feel less self-conscious about coming inside.

189

The moment they spotted the computer, any shyness they harbored instantly dissolved. "What is it that you ah doing, Miss, umm . . . ?"

"Amanda," Irene offered.

"Miss A-men-da," Naomi repeated. "Will you please instruct us on how to use this?"

"Of course, come over here and I'll show you some pictures."

"Pic-chores?" Nancy asked. "Ahh, yes, photo-graphs. I see," she said, smiling and moving closer to see the screen.

Although Joshua had mentioned that almost all of the boarders could speak Swahili and English, I was amazed at how proficient they were at both languages. Not to mention how dedicated they were to doing their schoolwork and learning new things. They told us all about the subjects they were studying and then peppered us with questions about the books and electronics that filled our room.

"Have you girls ever seen a movie?" I asked, remembering our bootleg library of DVDs from Peru.

"Yes. Yes, we have. A volunteer that stayed here before you. He had a movie with him," Naomi explained. "I do not rememba what he called it, but it was very good."

I scanned our selection for the few PG-rated titles and popped in *Mona Lisa Smile*. Our audience was over the moon. Six boarders piled onto the beds that we'd pushed together and were mesmerized by the scenes of girls only slightly older than them running around on a school campus covered in snow.

As we sat and watched, the girls chatted animatedly, and before we knew it, a slumber party of sorts had ensued. Sandra drifted to sleep, Calvin and Holly distributed lollipops, and Naomi played with Amanda's hair, which prompted Esther and Nancy to follow suit on mine. They grabbed a handful of strands and began twisting them into braids.

"Your hair is very funny, Miss Jenni-fa. It does not stay in the place that we put it," Nancy said, giggling. "Maybe you have a rubba-band we could use?"

"Yes. I know. It is funny," I replied with a sleepy laugh, my eyes half closed from the relaxing head massage. "Holly, will you grab a few ponytail holders from my stash over there, please?"

"No, you silly mzungu. Get them yourself," she said, but as always, helped me out.

"Silly mzungu," Nancy repeated. "That is very funny too, Miss Holly."

"You know, when I first got here and heard the word *mzungu*, I wasn't sure if I should be offended or not," Irene interjected, looking up from the storybook she was reading to Shana, Joshua's two-year-old, who'd toddled in after the boarders.

"But it's not meant in a derogatory way at all," she continued. "In fact, I learned that it originally meant 'one who travels around,' referring to the European traders who came in the 1800s. *Mzungu* just became synonymous with 'white person' because of the color of their skin."

"Impressive, Irene. You certainly did your research," Amanda said.

"Actually, Emmanuel explained it to me. But he was much funnier. He said that even though there were a lot of European settlers, they all looked alike to the locals. So even if different people passed by, they'd think it was the exact same person they saw before, just wandering around in a circle because they were lost."

"Someone who wanders around because they are lost, huh?" I remarked, throwing sidelong glances at Amanda and Holly.

Oh, yeah. We were mzungus for sure.

191

꙳

CHAPTER TWELVE

Amanda

KIMININI, KENYA

SEPTEMBER

S unlight had barely pierced the curtains on our sixth morning at Pathfinder when I felt a housecat pounce onto the bed at my feet. It trampled over the blanket, using my thighs as a scratching post as it stalked upward toward my head. Clinging greedily to sleep, I flopped an arm outside the fabric and tried to push the cat onto the floor. But instead of meeting a soft coat of fur, my hand connected with a downy body at the same time a frantic *flack flack flack* filled the air.

"Ahhhh! Get it off of me! Get it off!" I screamed, hurling the blankets and a cyclone of tawny white feathers across the room. The chicken beat its wings furiously and let out a few pissed-off squawks before scrambling out the door.

Next to me, Holly groaned and adjusted her eye mask before rolling over again, determined to squeeze in another few hours of sleep.

"Oh, c'mon, you can't be that upset," Irene said later at breakfast, laughing as she used a Swiss Army knife to pare away the skin of a mango. "Besides, you're the ones sleeping in her nest, not the other way around. She laid an egg in there every day till you guys came."

"Are you saying Joshua doesn't care if a chicken uses the second bedroom as a coop?"

"Well, no. The family doesn't mind it at all. In fact, they probably wouldn't like it if she couldn't get in there to do her business, so don't lock her out."

"But it's taking our blankets and clothes and making a nest out of them," groaned Holly, who finally realized I hadn't been sleep-talking or hallucinating at 6 a.m.. "Why doesn't it just stay outside with all of the other animals?"

"Well, she's a pretty smart chicken," said Irene. "She's figured out how to open the door and close it again behind her."

"Kind of like a *Jurassic Park* velociraptor!" added Jen, always able to find a movie reference to match the situation. I scowled in her general direction.

"What?" she asked, making a show of cracking a hard-boiled egg against the side of the table and peeling it slowly. "Don't be in such a *fowl* mood."

My scowl morphed into a mini-death-stare. She grinned back at me.

I spread a gooey layer of jam onto a thick slice of bread (after this morning's episode, I vowed to become a full-fledged vegan) and wondered whether refusing to share my bed with a barnyard animal officially qualified me as a spoiled city brat.

The three of us had expected that volunteering in Kenya would require some serious lifestyle changes, and so far, I thought, we'd all adapted pretty well. This week, we'd learned how to shower by dumping soapy cupfuls of water over our heads, honed our squat-aim-fire method in the little wooden outhouse, and developed a subtle technique for plucking out any critters that had accidentally gotten cooked into our stew at lunch (at our candlelit dinners, we just crossed our fingers and hoped for the best). In fact, other than my barnyard squabble, none of the physical challenges of life at Common Ground had fazed

193

me as much as I'd thought they might. Instead, what had really thrown me for a loop was the lack of a clear-cut purpose—or even a vague idea of what we should be doing during our time here.

Maybe we'd read one too many articles on Alternative Spring Breaks and Habitat for Humanity, but Jen, Holly, and I had figured that after reporting for duty in Kenya, an on-site coordinator would put us right to work constructing homes, digging wells, distributing supplies—anything to improve the quality of life of the local community. It had been Jen's dream to volunteer in Kenya, but in the days leading up to our arrival, Holly and I had felt almost as eager as she did to put in several hours of hard work each day and to fall into bed every night feeling exhausted, sore—and fulfilled.

But things hadn't worked out as we'd imagined. Upon getting here, we learned there were no orientation sessions, group leaders, or volunteer guidelines to follow. Once Joshua had introduced us to Mama Sandra and the fourteen boarders, he'd left the three of us to our own devices. We'd figured the work would be doled out soon enough, so we'd spent the unstructured time getting acclimated, using the days to walk around the farm or to explore Kiminini. Every evening, after playing *kati*, a form of dodgeball, with the boarders, we'd pull ourselves away to get cleaned up and head in to dinner. That's when one of us would find the right moment to repeat the question we'd been asking Joshua, in various forms, since we'd arrived: "Is there anything we can do to help?"

At that he would shrug and tell us that our presence alone was making a positive impact. And maybe he'd have something for us tomorrow.

Jen and Holly were as perplexed as I was by this response. We'd come all this way to rural western Kenya to volunteer—and there was really *nothing* for us to do?

Part of the reason we'd decided to sign up with Village Volunteers, rather than a larger, glossier nonprofit, was that we'd been assured that nearly the entire monthly program fee would be transferred into the hands of the people who needed it most. Lower overhead and administrative costs translated to less waste, but, as we were learning, it also meant that there was no budget for an on-site coordinator to guide new volunteers. Joshua technically fulfilled that role, but he was pretty busy overseeing a school, operating a farm, running an NGO, and being a father to his five kids.

Trying to figure out if we were doing something wrong, Jen busted out her neatly organized Village Volunteers file and scanned the pages. She found a section that we'd either overlooked or hadn't quite taken so literally and read it to us.

"The Volunteer Program isn't designed to provide a highly structured schedule that guarantees eight hours of work each day. Volunteers who have the most fulfilling experiences are ones who are highly self-motivated and require limited direction. They understand that the pace of life is significantly slower than what they may be used to at home, and that 'making a difference' may be as simple as making a child smile."

Irene, who'd been reading Jeffrey Sachs's *The End of Poverty*, put down her paperback long enough to reiterate the message: If we wanted to make a positive impact here, we couldn't wait for Joshua, Shana, or anyone else to invent a project for us. We had to figure out what talents we'd brought to the table and find a way to put them to use. Her assessment was logical, matter-of-fact—and easier said than done.

I quickly realized that most of the idiosyncratic abilities I'd honed as a working professional—turning groaner puns into snappy headlines or instantly recalling the number of fat grams in any given food—had zero practical application in my new environment. In fact, none of us really had an ideal skill set to be a volunteer. Unlike the Bastyr students, we weren't trained to administer vaccinations or medications to the families who would wait hours or even days for treatment at the on-site medical clinic. And even if we'd earned our official TEFL certificates (a requirement for teaching English as a foreign language)—which we hadn't—the Pathfinder school already had a staff of young Kenyan women doing the job.

Even my attempts to help out in the kitchen, while appreciated by the cook, Peter, didn't exactly go over that well with the other volunteers. The chapati flatbread I'd tried to make—clearly the most dummy-proof of all kitchen tasks—still cooked up to the consistency of unleavened Play-Doh. The girls tried to be polite as they sucked glutinous goo off the roof of their mouths, but their expressions said it all.

That morning over breakfast with the girls, I wondered if I might be more of a liability to the volunteer program than an asset. Maybe I should quit now, while I was already behind?

"Don't do that," said Irene. "Look—you're a journalist. Maybe you could just write a couple stories about Village Volunteers while you're here. Raising awareness for the program would be one of the most important things you could do."

It was a perfectly reasonable suggestion, and actually something I'd already considered, but not such a great breakfast topic. I glanced at Jen and saw her eyes widen, as if she'd accidentally gulped down something she'd meant to pick out of her bowl. I shoved a huge wad of bread into my mouth and didn't respond.

Because we'd yet to identify a real objective or routine here, I'd already started retreating into familiar habits—and that meant spending more and more time in front of the laptop. I'd even commuted with Joshua into Kitale a couple times to visit a cramped, overheated room housing a few old computers outfitted with dial-up connections. It was probably ridiculous to make an hour-long journey just to check e-mail, but there didn't seem to be a viable alternative. If I let too much time pass before getting back to my editors, they'd move on and find another writer to do the job.

Fortunately, we were all rescued from the awkward pause by the return of a visitor from early that morning. It took me a second to identify the snowy-colored blur that darted under the fabric covering the front door, but Holly was quicker on the uptake.

"Oh no! Out! *Out!*" she shrieked, chasing the chicken as it streaked toward our room. A chorus of squawks and an angry flurry of feathers made the bird's intentions clear. In the end, it was Holly who bolted out rear end first and retreated to the couch for safety.

A few minutes later, the bird strutted out of the room, taking her sweet time as she crossed the dung-coated floor and returned back to the yard. Jumping up, we all ran over and stuck our heads inside the door frame. There, just as Irene had predicted, was one large, creamy white egg—sitting right on top of Holly's pillow.

197

A s we spent more time with the girls at Pathfinder, what surprised me most was how much they acted like typical schoolkids back in the States—they cracked jokes, whispered secrets, played pranks, and gave one another a hard time. According to Joshua, most of the girls had lost at least one parent to malaria, AIDS, or poor medical care, and all had been removed from their homes to live here. Considering these challenging circumstances, it was remarkable that most of them were as outgoing and seemed as well adjusted as they did. They'd even formed little cliques and filled the archetypical roles that I still remembered from junior high school. In this group, pretty Calvin was the alpha female whose posse of friends followed her every move, hung on her every word. Naomi, the petite, fleet-footed jock, was the one you definitely wanted on your side whenever someone broke out the ball for kati. Also in the group: the chatty one (Constance), the big sister (Sandra), the clown (Tracey), and the troublemaker (Diana).

But it was Barbara, awkward, gangly-limbed Barbara, who unwillingly played the role of the outsider. She was taller than the others with a physical condition that made her limp, and so painfully shy that the other girls rarely invited her to join them in games of tag or beauty parlor or even slowed down so she wouldn't be the last in the line for dinner.

To help everyone get to know one another better and encourage some of the shyer girls to participate, we invented a game called "My Favorite Things." This involved sitting in a circle and taking turns sharing the things that we liked, such as meals, games, and school. As Holly explained this to the boarders, a few of them looked confused.

"But, Miss Holly, I don't undah-stand," said Alice, who was dressed today in the same daffodil yellow taffeta dress that she'd worn since we'd arrived. "What is this word—fay-voh-ritt?"

It hadn't even occurred to us that in order to have a favorite of anything, you had to have choice: what you wanted to eat, what to do, where to go. The word hadn't been taught in their English classes, so we asked if they knew what the word "best" meant.

"For example, is yellow your *best* color or is it blue?" explained Holly. "Red or green?"

The girls nodded to show they understood, so we took turns going around the circle.

"Okay, Nancy, what is your best activity?" Jen asked the boarder who wore a pink calico smock dress, one of the girls in Calvin's clique. "What do you like to do after school?"

"My best act-tee-vity is to . . . wash the plates."

Jen smiled. "Oh, that's good, but we mean . . . what do you like to do for fun time? Once you're done with school, when you're playing with your friends?"

"Yes, I see," said Nancy, looking confused. "I like to . . . clean the silverware?"

I thought she didn't understand the question, but almost every boarder gave a similar answer: *Polish the silverware. Sweep the floor. Carry water. Feed the chickens.* The girls' "best foods" included corn, rice, beans, and chapati bread. Not a single mention of candy or snacks, even though the treats were available less than a kilometer down the road in Kiminini.

Changing the game, we asked the girls what they wanted to be when they grew up. Several said they wanted to become farmers, nurses, or nuns, but some had grander plans.

"I would like to be a secretary in Nairobi. Or a police officer!" shouted Diana, jumping up and crossing her arms like a tough female cop.

"If I could go to school in the United States," said Alice, sounding dreamy about the possibility, "I would attend university and become a doctor."

"Yes, yes, that is my wish as well," responded Constance, nodding vigorously. "But I would prefer to be a surgeon. This is possible in America!"

At the mention of this mystical, faraway never-never land, the tone of the conversation changed. Suddenly, several decided that they needed to come visit us after leaving Pathfinder, and they wanted us to tell them all about the United States.

What was it like to live in America? Did everyone dress as funny as we did? What did the movie stars and rappers look like in real life? Were we very good friends with Madonna and Beyoncé?

"So you guys like American music, huh?" I asked. "Just a sec . . . I'll be right back."

199

I tore off in the direction of the volunteer hut, returning a couple minutes later with my pink iPod and new minispeaker, an impulse purchase I'd made on my last day in New York.

Creating a short playlist of top dance tracks, I cranked up the volume. The speaker coughed up only a few decibels of music, but that was more than enough. The boarders, upon hearing the opening strains of "Crazy in Love," bolted up from their cross-legged positions and started rocking out.

It was joyous, unbridled pandemonium. They jumped, spun around, and waved their arms wildly to the beats of J-Lo, Jay-Z, and Christina Aguilera. The four of us were pulled into the mix by eager little hands, and we grooved together on the lawn between their dorm and the cookhouse. Noticing that something was amiss, Mama Sandra came down from the house. I was hugely relieved when, instead of making us stop, she erupted into peals of high-pitched laughter. At least we knew that we weren't corrupting the girls with inappropriate music.

Just to be a ham, I tossed in a little freestyle hip-hop choreography.

"Miss Amanda, stop! Please demonstrate this again!" shouted Naomi. "You can show me this dancing, and then I will copy it."

Of all of the borders, Naomi was definitely the most eager to learn. Jen and I had agreed that under other circumstances, she almost certainly would have been an athlete of some kind—a track star, a soccer player, or maybe even a little gymnast.

I repeated a version of what I'd just done, and Naomi echoed the moves, performing them almost exactly as I had. Pretty soon everyone wanted in on the action. Even Barbara came over to join the group, and Irene walked her slowly through the steps I was doing.

By the time my playlist ran out, fireflies were lighting up the dusk. At the boarders' behest, I clicked repeat and we started all over again.

"Okay, guys, I think that Mama Sandra wants everyone to come to dinner," I heard Holly say. It was almost pitch-black outside.

The boarders retreated, but only after we promised to do it again tomorrow. And the next day. And the one after that. Our nightly dance classes had officially begun.

A couple days later, the four of us were holed up in Jen and Irene's hut reading when there was a knock at the door.

"*Karibu!*" said Irene, using Swahili to instruct the person to enter.

There was a pause, and then Naomi cracked the door, peering inside. "Miss Amanda? You ah ready to come down now? Many students, they ah waiting."

It was 5:45 p.m., fifteen minutes before dance class started, but Naomi looked worried that we wouldn't show. I'd assumed that the novelty of listening to the same songs and repeating similar steps might wear off, but if anything, the boarders had become more dedicated day after day. We'd moved our lessons into a classroom at Pathfinder, one of the few buildings wired for electricity. That way we could continue dancing after night fell.

Naomi waited for the four of us to put on our shoes, then led the way toward the schoolroom. She'd been right; nearly all of the boarders had already gathered. Barbara and Sandra were scraping the heavy wooden tables and chairs into a clump at the very back, while the younger girls waited.

"*Habari*, ladies, thanks for showing up early," I said, glancing around. "You've made it look like a real dance studio in here. Are you ready to get started?"

As they chorused their replies, I took my iPod out of my bag and set it on the blackboard. Even before I turned around, I knew exactly what I'd hear next.

"Shah-kee-rah! Shah-KEE-rah!" the girls shrieked, no less pumped to hear "Hips Don't Lie" emanating from the tinny speaker than if they'd been watching the singer live at Madison Square Garden. I'd played the track at least eight hundred times, but they never tired of it.

"Not yet, girls," I said, putting on my instructor hat. "What comes before that, at the beginning of dance class?"

"The warm-up!" shouted Naomi, thrilled to know the answer.

"That's right. Okay, let's get started. Everyone stand with your feet hip distance apart, swing your arms up over your head, and take a deep breath in," I said, guiding everyone through a series of gentle stretches and low-impact movements. "Now let it out slowly . . . good . . . and let's repeat that again."

This warm-up—something I'd done a handful of times with the boarders—was an abridged version of one I'd done hundreds of times as a kid. When I was five, my mom had enrolled my sister and me in gymnastics, the perfect activity for two girls with enough pent-up energy to demolish her perfectly tended home.

We'd both excelled at the sport, so after we were old enough, Mom had moved us both to Houston to train under Bela Karolyi, coach to the gold-medal Olympians Nadia Comaneci and Mary Lou Retton. I thrived under the intense pressure, but when a back injury forced me out of competition, I didn't want to give up the sport altogether.

I still can't believe that at fourteen, younger than some of these boarders were now, I was hired by a local gym to teach classes. I was responsible for three sessions per day, every day, after school. My students not only listened to me, they actually looked *up* to me, something that blew my mind at the time. I continued coaching gymnastics through high school and part of college but decided to stop midway through my sophomore year, right around the time that it dawned on me that pretty soon, I'd be entering the "real world" and I should probably start preparing for it.

While many of my friends at Florida State were partying or chilling out on the beach, I went to the university career center to research internships. Spring break of sophomore year, I skipped a trip to Cancún with my sorority sisters and flew to New York, where I managed to talk my way into a summer internship at Miramax Films. After eight weeks of watching rough cuts of movies, clipping articles out of *Variety*, and spotting celebs at the office, I knew I had to do two things after graduation: move to New York and get a job in entertainment.

Almost as soon as I crossed the stage and collected my diploma, that's exactly what I did. By the time I got hired in the city, I'd long since stricken "gymnastics instructor" from my résumé. My passion for working with kids had been neatly wrapped up and packed away along with my high school scrapbooks and old ballet shoes. In fact, I'd buried that side of myself so well that years later, when Irene had given us her whole "talents and abilities" speech, it hadn't even occurred to me that I'd once been a coach and mentor to dozens of little girls. It wasn't until my fellow volunteers and I began spending several hours every day with the boarders that I remembered the other job I'd once been pretty good at and started to think that I might have something to offer the Common Ground program after all.

During tonight's class, I wanted to try something a little different. After hitting REPEAT on Shakira for the eight hundred and first time, I stopped the iPod and made an announcement.

"All right, everyone, line up in the corner of the room and watch me. Don't move your feet yet, just look with your eyes," I called out as the girls immediately moved to follow what I was doing. I explained that instead of me showing them the moves,

I wanted each one of *them* to take turns teaching the class. Jaws dropped, and they looked totally freaked out.

"It's just like follow the leader," I said. "Everyone will start here in the corner, and one person will walk across the floor, doing whatever steps they want. It can be anything. Heavy clumps like an elephant. Lunges from side to side. Skipping on your tippy-toes. Then everyone else copies those exact same steps until we call out the next person to lead."

Once Jen, Irene, and I demonstrated, the girls caught on quickly. I started the music, and the girls laughed hysterically as I went first, popping my head in and out in a version of the chicken strut. Naomi was up next, and she did a jazzy little walk, crossing one foot over the other and bouncing her shoulders. Then Diana went, followed by Nancy and Barbara, who got into the spirit of things, tossing in funky moves that impressed the other girls.

One by one, every student got her chance to lead. Any self-consciousness they had over being the center of attention dissolved after the first round. By their second pass, they totally had the hang of it.

The momentum and energy in the room started to build, and at some point it was impossible to tell who was the leader and who was following behind. We were moving in a big circle now, teachers and students, kicking up a chalky cloud of dust as we blew around the room like an incoming storm. The girls were shrieking and laughing, completely caught up in the moment.

It didn't seem to matter that you could no longer hear the music coming from the tiny speaker or that the electricity flickered, plunging the room into semidarkness for a few seconds at a time. Utterly empowered, the girls seemed to be creating their own music and light. Whatever had happened to them before coming to Pathfinder and whatever would come next didn't seem to matter now. In that moment, they could let down their guard, let go—and just be little girls.

We danced like this for I don't know how long, moving in a frenzy until we were all sweaty and exhausted enough to collapse into a heap. Lifting my head to look around the room, I caught eyes with Naomi, who was completely out of breath.

She flashed me a grin, and I sent one back. I knew there was probably some teacher rule against having a favorite kid, but sue me. She definitely qualified as my "best" student.

"We ah. Doing this. Again tomorrow?" she asked, as if I might suddenly renege.

I pretended to consider the question for a while before answering.

"See ya here at six."

O ver the next several days, Jen, Holly, Irene, and I witnessed some remarkable changes within "our" girls. Many had been shy when we'd first met them, and they'd lacked a sense of cohesiveness within their ranks. But eventually, one by one, they all started to open up, to become more confident. Within the framework of the dance classes, they took risks and, for the most part, supported one another's efforts—no matter who led and who followed.

Of course, they still teased the hell out of one another. But it seemed pretty good-natured, a way of bonding rather than tearing one another down.

The four of us—who'd all become initiated as dance teachers by now—wanted to keep the progress going after we left, to leave behind something more lasting than a few routines. We put our heads together to brainstorm, but in the end, it was Jen's idea to write a play.

It might have been a lot faster to poach a script like *Alice in*

Wonderland or *Cinderella* from the Web, but we quickly ruled out that option. What would the boarders really learn from a fairy tale of a country girl transformed by magic into a princess?

Rather than adopting someone else's story, we decided to write our own original script, one featuring a powerful heroine. We wanted to show the girls that they possessed the strength to rise above adversity and make powerful changes in their world—no pretty dress or fairy godmother required. With the help of Shana Greene and a little online research, we discovered that few women in Kenya—or indeed anywhere—embodied the spirit of self-empowerment more than Wangari Maathai.

Known as the "Tree Mother of Africa," Maathai was responsible for launching the Green Belt Movement, a massive grassroots effort to help women conserve the environment and improve their quality of life by planting trees. Her organization has assisted women in planting more than 40 million of them on their farms and school and church compounds, efforts that have reversed some of the deforestation threatening Kenya's future.

What we loved about Maathai wasn't just her groundbreaking environmental efforts but that she fought hard for what she believed in. Despite being arrested several times for her political beliefs (she was an advocate of multiparty elections and women's rights) and being beaten by the police for her attempts to protect the environment, Maathai never abandoned her convictions. It was only after decades of fighting that Maathai was finally vindicated. In 2002 she was elected to Kenya's parliament by an incredible 98 percent majority, and in 2004 she became the first African woman to win a Nobel Peace Prize.

We hoped this would be the kind of role model that would strike a chord with the boarders, a real-life superwoman they could feel proud of, if not eventually emulate. After Shana sent us several documents with background information on Maathai, the four of us spent nights after the dance classes taking turns writing our opus. Although we thought it might be tough to break down the biography into an engaging, kid-friendly script, Maathai's life was filled with both dramatic and tender moments that made for a pretty cool story with more than enough parts for all the boarders.

After a week of writing, we had our full-length play, *A Tree Grows in Kenya* (or at least one copy of it), but we'd struck out with Kitale's copy machines. None seemed capable of printing off more than a page a time, making copying the script a daunting task. Irene and Jen volunteered to hang out in the stuffy stationery shop and take turns copying and sorting eighteen scripts by hand.

"No sense in all four of us just hanging out here, watching the toner dry," Jen said. "Why don't you and Hol go head to the grocery store or the Internet café or whatever and we'll meet you at the matatu depot around four thirty?"

"Really?" I asked. "That would be amazing. Are you sure? I really have like, six things that I need to send out, and as long as we're in town, it would be—"

"Just don't get sidetracked," she warned me. "We can't leave any later than about four forty-five if we're gonna make it back on time for the auditions."

"Of course, no problem. I'll see you at the matatu stop near the Hypermart in about a half hour." I said, already rushing to grab my bag and make a dash to the café.

"Amanda."

I stopped.

"Seriously, we're already running tight on time. I know you've got stuff to do, but we've been promising the girls for days that we'll get started right at six."

"No, totally. I understand. If for some reason something comes up, I'll take the very next matatu right after you. I'll be like, a half hour behind you . . . forty-five minutes at most."

I turned back to confirm that she was okay with that and saw her features cloud over, just for a second. Then, as quickly as it had come, the emotion blew itself out.

She sighed and tossed me the computer flash drive.

"Hey . . . thanks," I said, pausing on my way out.

Jen didn't respond. She turned back to the pile of papers and started sorting.

The sky had already turned navy blue and was fading to black by the time I took the *boda boda* bicycle taxi the last mile or so to Common Ground. I'd left my watch back at the volunteer hut, so I couldn't tell exactly how late I was. But I knew no matter what the Indiglo dial might have read, the news wouldn't have been good.

As Jen had no doubt predicted, I'd taken far longer in town than I'd promised—at least a good hour longer, or maybe even more. I felt terrible about it. The girls had probably waited as long as they could for me before finally hopping on a matatu back to the farm.

Ugh. I knew I should have gotten finished faster, should have made it back on time. These auditions tonight were among the most important things we'd planned during our time at Pathfinder Academy, and I was missing them.

But going over it again in my head, I figured it wasn't really my fault. How could I have known that after all of this time with so few assignments, I'd get an e-mail from a magazine editor saying she'd loved my idea for "Traditional Healing Remedies from Around the World"? Or that the only way she could assign it to me was if I sent her additional examples and potential experts by the next day? Upon reading that, I'd scrambled to throw a memo together with some ideas but had been working too fast to remember to save my document. When the power cut out, as it almost always did, I'd lost half my work. By the time I repeated the process and hit "Send" on my e-mail, I knew my friends were long gone. I guess I just didn't process how much time had flown by until I walked outside and saw that dusk had already fallen.

It had taken me ten minutes (and triple the normal fare) to convince the *boda boda* driver to take me to Pathfinder in the semidarkness, but I'd finally made it. Heart pounding and breathing way too fast, I practically sprinted past the guard at the entrance of the farm and into the compound.

From outside, in the darkness, it was easy for me to see inside the well-lit classroom. The girls were clutching the scripts that Jen and Irene had printed, and a few were standing in the middle of the room taking turns running the lines.

I tried to be as inconspicuous as possible as I slipped inside, to silence my heavy breathing, but everybody still stopped what they were doing and stared. Then Irene gently called their attention back to the scripts, and they kept going. Despite my mortification, some small part of me felt thrilled at hearing the boarders read the words that we'd written for them.

"Miss Amanda! You are okay? You are safe now," whispered Naomi, clearly worried, coming to sit next to me as I slid into a chair behind one of the wooden desks. "We were thinking you would not come. I believe we are close to finishing for the evening."

Finishing? They couldn't be done already. Glancing up at the clock above the blackboard, a cold flush rinsed down my body: 7:42. Oh, my God, I'd basically missed it all—plus made the girls worry by staying out after dark.

I kept quiet all through dinner, just listening as Jen, Holly, and Irene discussed how the auditions had gone and which boarder would be right for what role.

After we'd cleared our plates and walked outside, I pulled Jen aside.

"Hey, got a second?" I asked tenuously. I knew Jen well enough to sense that she was upset.

"Sure . . . what's up?"

We stood outside in the semidarkness, holding the kerosene lanterns we took to the huts with us every night. I could hear the quiet rustling of the cattle that grazed in the pasture directly behind our volunteer huts. In the beginning, it had been a little disconcerting living in such close proximity to livestock, but now the animals' presence—the soft footfalls, the deep lowing—was slightly comforting.

The words tumbled out in a rush. "Jen I don't even know where to begin. I know you reminded me what time the auditions started. I can't believe that I screwed up. I'm so sorry to you, to Irene, to Holly—"

"Hey, you don't have to be sorry to us at all." Her voice was stiff as she shifted her weight from one foot to the other. The lantern light threw long shadows across her face, making her expression all but unreadable. "I mean, it would have been great for the boarders if you'd been there, but realistically, you don't need four people to hold auditions for fourteen girls. We handled it okay by ourselves."

"I know, but I really, really wanted to be there, to watch the girls read for the parts." I brushed away the whirl of the insects drawn in by the glowing lamp in my hand.

"Really? No offense, Amanda," she said evenly, "but I don't think you did."

That made my head jerk up.

I took a step closer to Jen, held the light higher. "Of course I did. It's just that something unavoidable came up, an editor had some questions for me that I had to answer right then and there, something that couldn't wait another three days."

"I'm sure it was important. It's always important. But realistically, you made a choice tonight. It was either that pressing work thing, whatever it was, or the auditions we've been preparing to do with the girls all week. And one was just more important than the other."

I tried to think of a response, to find some way to show Jen that the boarders meant more to me than some stupid e-mail, but I couldn't. I *had* chosen some nameless, faceless editor who might see fit to assign me a story over fourteen boarders whom I'd spent every single day with since coming to Common Ground. I'd promised the girls I'd show up, that I'd be there on time, and they'd trusted me. It wasn't good enough that Jen, Irene, and Holly had covered for me. I'd been the only one of the four of us to completely flake out.

Now, not only had I prioritized the little girls who'd come to trust me below my work demands—I'd disappointed my best friend. I didn't need to see her face in the darkness to be sure of that.

I could hear Holly freaking out and slapping at things under her mosquito net just before she turned on her headlamp and ripped the netted nylon away from her body.

"Hey . . . you awake?" she whispered loudly as I snapped my headlamp on in response. Awake? I was lit up like a lightning rod. I felt like some kind of tweaked-out junkie who thought that she had roaches crawling all over her entire body. Except the difference was, the bugs that Holly and I both imagined were darting beneath our sheets were very, very real.

The Bastyr students had vacated this hut that morning, so Hol and I had finally been able to move in and get our own beds in a private, chicken-free room. Unfortunately, it sounded as if we had some new visitors. The second the lights went off, I could hear the pitter-patter of little roach feet scampering nearby. Down the walls. At my feet. Near my head.

I dashed over to the wall and flicked on the overhead light. Holly shrieked, a true bloodcurdler, as she bashed the headboard with a rolled-up magazine. "Oh, my God, they're everywhere! We can't sleep like this! What are we going to do?"

I couldn't comprehend how, since three people had slept in this room directly before us, no one had noticed that our wooden bed frames were infested with roaches. When a full can of Doom bug spray failed to kill every last creepy crawly, we tried to be brave, to endure the *mendes* (cockroaches) that the boarders had seemed shocked we were afraid of. "We do not fear them. They will not harm you," Naomi always said to me. But tonight, as Holly and I levitated above our mattresses and attempted not to scream loud enough to bring Joshua and Mama Sandra running, I decided that a little fear was probably healthy.

"C'mon, we're going over to Jen and Irene's," I said, shaking out my sweatshirt for good measure and tossing it on.

"I was praying you'd say that!" Holly said, hustling to get her shoes on.

We knocked lightly and pushed our way into the other hut. The girls were reading placidly in their noncontaminated beds.

"Let me just come over and take a look," Jen said. "If it's really so bad, you guys can just stay here for tonight. We'll figure something out."

"I'll go with you," I said.

Jen put on her headlamp before walking outside. "Are the headboards really infested?"

"Yeah, it's pretty awful," I said, relieved that Jen and I were talking about something other than computers or e-mails or missed auditions. Even if it was about the bugs in my bed.

"Doesn't this remind you of that time in Belize?" said Jen. "With the dive-bombing roaches?"

"Oh yeah, totally!" I laughed. Belize had been the first vacation Jen and I had taken together after getting "real jobs" in New York. We'd spent a chunk of cash on a jungle lodge in the Cayo District and been booked inside a thatched-roof hut with a tree branch resting on top. Which would have been fine, except the tree branch happened to have a roach nest inside. No matter how fast we'd killed them, more bugs had wriggled through the thatch and dropped on the floor. Then, as if our panic incited theirs, the roaches had started *flying* directly at our heads. We'd run outside onto the porch and screamed for a good five minutes before a guard went to the main house and woke the owner's wife.

"I mean, this is the *jungle*, ladies. We've got living things here," she'd said, pissed that we'd interrupted her beauty sleep to come down and see what the fuss was about. She'd barely finished her sentence before the mother of all roaches landed in her hair, sending her into paroxysms of terror. The last thing I remember is standing outside watching the woman thrashing a few bugs before finally coming back out and switching our room.

Now Jen stared at our bed frames—alive and shimmering with roach bodies—and said the one thing that made me abandon the room for good.

"Wow . . . they're probably in your mattresses too."

Shit. I hadn't thought of that.

"Okay, you're sleeping in our room. The beds are a little bigger than a twin, so we could probably line up head to toe. It's not ideal, but you absolutely can't sleep in here."

"Are you sure? I mean, would that be a huge imposition?"

"An imposition?" She stopped short and shined her headlamp directly in my face. "You're ridiculous, you know that?"

We walked back inside her hut and laughed. Holly hadn't been worried about imposing. She'd already curled up underneath Jen's covers, put on her eye mask, and lowered the mosquito net.

"So, um, Irene, I would never ask if the cockroach situation weren't really bad over there, but is it okay if I share—"

"Don't sweat it." Irene pulled up her mosquito net. "I promise, this wouldn't even broach the territory of weird or too personal back at Yale."

Once we were as cozy as we could get with our feet in each other's faces, Jen snapped out the light, and we finally got some sleep.

214

✲

CHAPTER THIRTEEN

Holly

KIMININI, KENYA

SEPTEMBER

T he woman stretched out her bony hand, and her knuckles were rigid and knobby, like knots on an old oak tree. I wrapped my hand around hers, and my skin glowed white against the blackness of hers. It was the first time I'd ever touched a person with AIDS. Well, at least that I knew of. I thought I'd feel scared, but standing there with her hand in mine, I wasn't.

"*Habari,*" I said. She smiled back, revealing a gap in her mouth where her two front teeth used to be. Then she put her arm around me to lead the way inside the small home with a corrugated metal roof.

There were twelve women crammed in the main room. Some of them had scarves tied around their heads, some wore beaded necklaces, and all were draped in long skirts that covered their ankles. There wasn't any furniture apart from a low table and five empty wooden chairs. The women stopped speaking when Jen, Amanda, Irene, and I tucked our heads to duck through the doorway. "*Habari!*" they called in unison.

"*Msuri sana!*" The four of us gave the now-automatic response, standing so close to one another that our shoulders were touching. The women just stared back at us expectantly.

"Are we supposed to say something?" I whispered to Jen after a few seconds of awkward silence. Before she could answer, the first plump woman I'd seen yet in Kenya besides curvy Mama Sandra strutted over and grabbed Amanda's hand.

"Thank you for coming to visit the Masaba widows' group. My name is Rose, and I'm the secretary." We each introduced ourselves, and Rose asked, "Did Joshua tell you of our purpose?"

"He said you're a support group for women who've lost their husbands and that you've started businesses using micro-finance," Irene announced for our watchful audience. We could always count on Irene to take charge—I'd had yet to see anything intimidate her, not even killing a chicken for our dinner. "If I can't kill a chicken, then I shouldn't eat meat," she'd declared as a flurry of feathers whizzed by us in the cooking hut. Like Amanda, I'd become a vegetarian in the weeks we'd been living so close to our food.

Indeed, Joshua had explained that many of the widows had lost their husbands to AIDS, and many had also become HIV-positive themselves. Common Ground and Village Volunteers helped come up with small loans for the women so they could start their own businesses to support themselves and maybe even send their kids to school.

"Let us eat first, and then we'll show you the kiosk," Rose said, gesturing for us to sit in the rickety chairs. Some of the women had set up small stands in front of their homes to sell staples such as rice, salt, and eggs to their neighbors. Three of the women disappeared behind a back door, and I spied a black pot set over an open fire before the door slammed closed again. The women returned minutes later, holding a pile of plates, silverware, and ceramic bowls heaping with ugali, kale, and beans.

"I had no idea they were going to cook for us," Jen whispered.

"Yeah, Joshua hadn't mentioned that," Amanda agreed. At this point, we were used to going with the flow. Joshua had taken us on what we referred to as "field trips," proudly showing off his many projects in the surrounding villages. This often called for stops at farms where he'd taught a family how to increase the amount of food they grew so they could feed themselves rather than have to rely on food from the markets. As soon as the farmers saw Joshua approaching, they'd stop their work and wave wildly. "Come, sit in my house," they'd offer. And then Joshua and the four of us women would crouch on the edges of tattered chairs, or on the floor if there wasn't enough seating, as our hosts stood before us. If there wasn't a man around, there was sometimes a grave dug at the edge of the yard where he now rested. Sometimes they'd ask us if we'd like tea, but usually they didn't have food or drink to offer. That's why eating lunch with the widows' group was so unexpected. We felt honored, and a little embarrassed about all the fuss.

Seated in the wooden chairs next to Rose, we spooned piles of beans and kale on top of the starchy ugali. The rest of the women ate standing, talking in small groups while Rose filled us in on their names and stories. "That's Mary. She has twelve children. Her husband died of AIDS last year, and so did his other wife."

I'd heard that Kenyan men sometimes had more than one wife, but I'd never met a man who was married to more than one woman at the same time.

"He had two wives. And when a woman's husband dies, she loses everything. Her husband's family can take her home, her cows, and even her children."

"Seriously?" squeaked Amanda, echoing my astonishment.

"Yes, and when your husband dies, his brother can inherit you." That's another way HIV spreads, because a woman whose husband has died from the disease might be infected too and can pass it to his brother. That's why the widows' group was so important: it educated members about the disease and also helped them combine their money so they had better buying and negotiating power. It gave them more freedom. I thought about how different my life would have been if I had been born here in Kitale instead of upstate New York.

Rose paused to take a spoonful of ugali. Then she turned to me. "How many children do you have?"

"None," I said.

Her eyes widened, startled. "How old are you?"

"Twenty-eight."

"Not even one, sistah? Not a single one?" she prodded.

"Um, not that I know of," I said, trying to make light of the fact that I surely ranked at the bottom of the totem pole by Kenyan standards, where the more children you have, the higher your social status. In fact, it's tradition that women change their names entirely when they deliver their first baby, adopting that of their child. For example, Joshua's wife is called "Mama Sandra," after her eldest daughter. At first I felt a little funny calling another grown woman "Mama," but I quickly learned it's a sign of respect.

"How many children do you have?" Amanda asked Rose.

"Only six," she replied.

"And how old are you?" Jen chimed in.

"Twenty-seven," said Rose.

Rose asked Jen, Amanda, and Irene how many children they had, and each shook her head to indicate she didn't have any. Rose clapped her hands over her mouth, trying to keep from cracking up. "Not a single baby between all of you?" Her amused expression turned stricken.

"Don't worry, Rose. We're going to have babies just as soon as we return to America," I said, hoping my pledge would relieve her concern. The other three girls animatedly nodded their heads in agreement.

O n another field trip to a medical clinic a few days later, we met Sister Freda, as the locals called her out of respect. Leading Jen, Amanda, Irene, and me through her farm, she freed avocados from their branches with a flick of her wrist. Sister Freda was dressed in a white nurse's uniform, and a silver cross dangled next to a stethoscope around her neck. Her face, the color of ebony, didn't have many lines, so she looked as if she were in her early forties. I later learned that she was actually in her late fifties. She'd finished her work for the day, which called for treating the sick from surrounding villages who couldn't afford to go to the hospital in Kitale. If she didn't help them, many would probably die.

Joshua had insisted we stop by and meet Sister Freda. Although we were still doing dance classes and play rehearsals with the boarders every night, Joshua also wanted us to spend our days learning about a few of the other organizations Common Ground had partnered with, such as the widows' group and this clinic.

Eager to explore the world outside Pathfinder's gates, the girls and I flagged a *boda boda* and rode sidesaddle in our skirts. Our drivers dropped us at the matatu stand, which was really just a dusty street corner where a crowd of locals waited for the next van to arrive. We crammed in beside villagers clutching babies or chickens (or both) in their laps. The van eventually slowed down just enough so we could hop out, and we plodded along a red road crisscrossed by rivers of mud and bordered by cornfields.

About two miles down, we spotted a wooden sign that read: SISTER FREDA'S MEDICAL CLINIC. Rounding the bend, we converged into a clearing filled with a mass of people. "Oh, my God," I said under my breath. *Are all of these people waiting to see a doctor?*

A line snaking around a whitewashed building teemed with skeletal men, rag-clad women holding hollow-eyed babies on their hips, and children with bloated stomachs, a telltale sign of malnourishment. The afflicted spilled from the front door, streamed around the sidewalk, and flooded the muddy road. Their pain stretched in front of us, wrapping all around until it was raw and real. I'd watched the faces of the porters on the Inca Trail light up after receiving open tubes of antibiotic ointment during the porter-tipping ceremony and Igo, the kid begging on the streets in Brazil, grin as if it were Christmas when Sam had bought him dinner at that sidewalk café. But now, for the first time on the trip, I saw poverty on a larger scale. Joshua's house may have lacked electricity and running water, but still, he and his family had food. The boarders had school uniforms and a bed to sleep in. I suddenly understood that staying on Joshua's farm was like living in a protected bubble. We'd been sheltered from the hunger and disease that were the reality for some rural Kenyans.

When we arrived, Sister Freda came outside to greet us, pausing along the way to pat the back of a waiting child or place a hand on an old man's forehead. When she got to us, she ignored our outstretched hands and pulled us in for a hug. Despite the overwhelming need around her, she radiated calm and peace.

"God bless you for coming!" she said before gesturing us to follow her for a tour of the compound.

"We don't want to take you away from your patients," Amanda said, echoing my worry.

"I have doctors volunteering today who will be taking care of them," she said, and so we followed her lead.

The shock started to melt, and I felt weirdly detached, as if my emotions had temporarily gone missing. Back home, pain meant a very different thing to me. I might've used the word "hurting" to describe a friend who'd gotten fired and was worried about making the rent. I might have called myself "devastated" after finding out a boyfriend had cheated on me. I might have felt life just couldn't get any worse for the homeless man begging on the subway steps. But the thought "Will my neighbor die today?" or "Will *I* die today?" didn't cross my mind the way it might have for someone waiting in line at Sister Freda's clinic.

To cope, I put on my reporter hat and started firing off questions. "How much funding does it take to run the clinic—does the government help?" I asked Sister Freda while we walked in the farm behind the building.

"I don't really understand your question," she paused, twisting free another avocado before continuing, "I don't receive money from the government, but I do raise some of what I need by growing crops on this farm." She sold coffee, maize, bananas, avocados, pears, kale, and local vegetables such as *dodo* and *sutcher sucker* at a local market to earn income. The farm also helped her save on the cost of medications, since she harvested plants she could use in traditional remedies.

"But the government has to help you a little, right?" I asked, incredulous. A small farm couldn't possibly pull in enough cash to run a healing center that treated hundreds of people.

She laughed at the question and explained no, but she channeled all the money from a few paying patients to buy meds and to help cover doctors' wages. She also said a few churches back in the States helped support her work.

"Truthfully, most of my patients are poor and can't afford a single Kenyan shilling," she added. She'd watched men die of AIDS, leaving behind wives and children to live in makeshift shacks and forage for firewood and food in the slums outside Kitale. She believed it was just as much her responsibility to

221

help those who couldn't help themselves as it was anyone else's. "*Someone* has to save them. Why shouldn't it be me?"

I kept asking questions and learned that Sister Freda hadn't been in a much better position than many of her neighbors. Like many rural women in Kenya, her family had married her off when she was barely fifteen years old to a man she didn't know. By the time she was nineteen years old, she'd already had four children. But her husband had had lots of affairs, which had put her at risk for contracting HIV. Sister Freda was brave enough to actually file for divorce and cut ties with her husband, even though many Kenyan women wouldn't because they depended on men for financial support. Only in Kenya financial support typically didn't mean a house with a white picket fence but a hut with a cow-dung-coated floor to call home and chapatis to feed the kids.

Still, Sister Freda left her husband and didn't ask him for help but was able to go to nursing school because her parents and sister took her in and watched her kids. Then she worked her way up at a private hospital in Kitale, caring mostly for wealthy patients. She'd accomplished something I took for granted as an American: she was able to earn a living as a woman on her own, without a husband.

Still, Sister Freda wanted to do more to help. She couldn't wipe away the images tattooed into her mind of the poor crawling to the hospital each day but unable to reach it, some dying along the roadside. Rather than just shake her head over how wrong the situation was, she raised money to open a mobile clinic to bring treatment to those who couldn't travel to the hospital, let alone afford payment. After ten years, her mobile healing center had expanded into the full-blown hospital we were walking through, thanks to donations, her personal savings, and funding from Richard—her longtime friend and second husband. She had even started a feeding program for the hundreds of poor children, and created a separate wing at the clinic for orphans who'd been literally abandoned on her doorstep. As her center grew, she left her coveted hospital position in Kitale, and some of her former coworkers from the hospital in Kitale even volunteered their services.

Sister Freda was the closest person I'd ever encountered to a living Mother Teresa, and I couldn't hold back questions about how she'd done so much. As I spoke, she just clutched the cross around her neck, and I realized she'd never thought she was working alone. "It's a miracle. When I'm deep in trouble with no medicine and a dying patient, I pray for help from the Lord and He answers, maybe by sending someone to pay an overdue bill or a visitor to give a donation," she explained. "God is always here and listening to our prayers."

In a land where AIDS has been called an epidemic, where many people can't afford to eat, where girls are often married before their sixteenth birthdays and have little chance at a higher education, maybe the only way to keep going is to wrap yourself in faith. I watched Sister Freda, smiling in spite of witnessing so much suffering. She was living proof of how something as intangible as faith—in God for listening to her prayers, in herself for having the courage to divorce her husband and find a job, and in the goodness of other people for donating their time and money—can provide the power to make a real difference. Sister Freda carried her faith beyond the wooden walls of her Sunday church services, sharing it with the people forgotten on the roadside. She filled me with hope.

A toddler with a crop of rebellious braids and Cabbage Patch Kid features waddled into the dark room that served as the orphans' nursery. There were seven adults crammed inside the roughly four-by-eight-foot space, with Sister Freda, another nurse, and the den mother named Agnes standing next to Jen, Amanda, and Irene near the doorway. I was perched on the edge of a narrow bed taking notes as Sister Freda told the story of how the orphanage had begun.

When I glanced up, the child locked her charcoal eyes on mine. Then she bolted past Sister Freda, Agnes, and everyone else in the room to fling herself onto my legs, burying her head in the folds of my skirt.

"Hey there," I said, pulling her into my lap. She was wearing a striped shirt two sizes too big under a jean dress practically shredded into strips. She wrapped her little arms around my neck and stared into my eyes.

Sister Freda laughed in delight as Agnes stood guard. "I've never seen Esther approach a stranger like that!" said Sister Freda. But she didn't feel like a stranger to me. As I held her little hand in mine, I had the most peculiar feeling we'd already met. It wasn't logical, but that sensation of recognition was practically tangible. The professional reporter mask I'd been hiding behind slipped off the second that the child and I touched.

When I heard how Esther had found her way to Sister Freda's, I felt as if I couldn't breathe. A woman who might have been her grandmother, or maybe just another villager, had dropped Esther at the clinic when she was eight months old. Her mother was "deranged," Sister Freda explained, and she'd drowned Esther's older sister in a tub before disappearing into the bush.

By the time Esther got to Sister Freda, she was malnourished and had a near-deadly case of malaria. She was also deformed—her legs stuck straight above her head from her having been bound to her mother's back for days on end. The villager handed her to Sister Freda with the parting words "If you can save her, save her. But if it's not possible, it's all right."

"We gave her malaria medication and healthy food," Sister

Freda told us. "The nurses and I worked with her for over nine months to train her legs to come down and taught her how to walk. She mostly hopped around at first." But to Sister Freda, "saving" Esther didn't mean just providing her with food and medical care. She also blanketed her with love and offered her an education. I knew that if Sister Freda hadn't stepped in, Esther could have died.

When Sister Freda headed for the door to signal that it was time for a tour of the medical facilities, I trailed behind Jen and Amanda, reluctantly handing Esther to Agnes. I was surprised when I felt Esther's little body stiffen and when she sank her fingers into my hair, fighting to hold on to me as tears rolled down her face. "She doesn't want you to leave. You can bring her with you on the tour," Sister Freda encouraged. "You like children, don't you?"

"Yes," I said softly. I'd always been drawn to kids, the way they can turn exploring even a dirt pile into an adventure, their ability to forget about everything else but whatever they are doing at the moment, and their tendency to say exactly what they feel when they feel it. I'd always known without a doubt that I wanted kids of my own. But I'd never before held a child who had already endured so much in her short lifetime. She was a survivor, and she was only three years old.

Our group trekked into the clinic with its bare walls and concrete floors. Hordes of people, from infants to those who looked as if they'd already lived three lifetimes, waited patiently in a hallway that was so narrow you could touch both walls with outstretched arms. They sat on wooden benches or leaned against the wall. Older children held little ones in their arms while younger brothers and sisters formed circles around them. They were sick, they were tired, and still they waited. Many had no money; Sister Freda's clinic was their only hope.

I waded through the crowd with Esther on my hip, and she waved at the patients like a goodwill ambassador as we brushed past. Sister Freda proudly cracked the doors to show us where surgeries were done on operating tables that looked more like lounge chairs. There was also a closet-sized room lined with shelves that served as the pharmacy, but the shelves were only half filled with bottles and syringes. An assistant wearing a white jacket was busy taking inventory of the drugs in a spiral notebook. It was a task that wouldn't take long.

"What kind of medicine do you need?" Jen asked. Unlike Amanda and me, who broke into a sweat around blood and needles, Jen felt completely at ease in hospitals. Both of her parents had nursing degrees, so she'd grown up exposed to medical lingo, and was as intrigued by hospitals as she was by airports and amusement parks. It had all made perfect sense once I'd discovered Jen loved being surrounded by tons of people—she rarely if ever wanted to sleep in a room alone on the trip or hang out solo in a coffee shop like I did.

Sister Freda's eyes shined at Jen's question, and she said they desperately needed saline solution and malaria medication. Jen promised to pick up supplies from a pharmacy in Kitale. Then Amanda turned to me with a huge grin. "Esther's fast asleep," she whispered, brushing her fingers across the child's plump cheeks. Despite the commotion happening all around, Esther had closed her eyes and was snoring into my neck. Too consumed with taking in the tour, I hadn't even noticed the pins and needles running down my arm from supporting her for the past hour. She definitely wasn't underfed anymore and, in fact, felt as solid as a brick.

"Come, let us go to the house and have food," Sister Freda invited as we shook the staff's hands good-bye and walked across the spiky grass to a cottage painted white. A cat swatted at our feet as soon as we swung open the door.

"Hey, little guy," Amanda purred as she reached down to scratch behind its ears. Esther was awake now, running her fingers through the ends of my ponytail and humming quietly. Sister Freda said I should probably return her to Agnes to be with the other children before we ate. But when I set her down, she started wailing. Her cries felt like icicles inside my chest. I tensed up, torn about what to do next. Agnes seemed on edge. She instructed me to walk away, saying that Esther would be okay, so I turned toward Sister Freda's cottage, Esther's cries fading with each step.

I thought about how frustrated Agnes must feel, nursing an abandoned kid back to health, only to have to console her after a Westerner who'd shown her a few hours of attention left to return to her comfortable life.

I'd never realized how many opportunities I'd been given simply because I'd been born an American. I'd learned that even going for my daily runs was a privilege, particularly after seeing how much attention a woman jogging attracted. When I'd sprint over red roads weaving through fields of sunflowers, the men would yell at me in astonishment, "Sistah, where are you going? Where on earth are you trying to go?" Groups of children chased after me like American kids might chase after the ice cream truck, and the little girls would ask, "Why are you training, sistah?" their pounding feet catapulting speckles of mud up their bare legs.

"To beat the boys!" I'd say and laugh. They shrieked and howled at the thought of a woman beating a man, and soon I had a following that rivaled Lance Armstrong's.

It was a comment from Joshua, though, that really hit home. "My daughters are worth as much as my cows," he'd stated matter-of-factly one day as we walked to a neighboring farm. "My daughters will get married and then leave to live with their husbands. It is my son who will stay to help with the farm and start a family." And that was just the way things worked.

Holly · Kiminini, Kenya · September

Still, Joshua lavished encouragement both on his daughters and on the girls he'd taken under his protection. One night after finishing a meal of chapatis and beans in his living room, he'd called for the boarders. The girls filed in, still wearing their school uniforms because they were the only clothes they owned apart from their Sunday dresses.

Joshua then plunged into what we'd soon learned was his standard motivational speech, telling the girls that the way to succeed was to study hard and stay away from boys. He looked hard at each girl individually as he spoke. When his eyes met Naomi's, she said, "We shall not fail," her brown eyes sparkling in the light cast from the kerosene lamp.

Joshua was definitely a godsend to these girls: not only did he take care of his own family and farm, he also granted kids who otherwise wouldn't have had a shot to get an education. He was a living example for the children he stewarded that one person could make a difference.

After the girls left, Amanda mentioned what a talented dancer she thought Naomi was. "That girl is in trouble," said Joshua.

"What do you mean?" Amanda asked, surprised.

"She's pretty, and it's the pretty ones that will be married young. Others, like Barbara, will be able to stay in school and get their education," he explained. "The pretty girls don't go far. Only an ugly woman could become president!"

Unfortunately, not all girls had a choice about whether they got to go to school or not. Some lived too far away to walk safely, while many couldn't afford books and uniforms. Others had to work their family's farm or take care of parents who might be sick from, say, malaria or HIV.

Besides getting married young, another all-too-real option for some girls was prostitution. Because they usually didn't get the chance to go to school or have a family to take care of them, female orphans were likely to have few other options apart from marrying early or selling sex to survive. All of this flashed through my head as I listened to Esther's cries fading in the distance.

As I cracked open the door to Sister Freda's cottage, Jen and Amanda were setting the table. I'd just grabbed some plates to help distract myself from the tightening in my chest when Jen turned to me and said, "I really want to get medical supplies in town and bring them back here."

"I'll go with you whenever you want!" I said, jumping at the chance to see Esther again. I glanced out the window to the yard where I'd held Esther just moments before, now empty.

A few days later, a little body slammed into me from out of nowhere and a pair of arms wrapped themselves around my legs, almost toppling me. I regained my balance and turned around to see Esther grinning up at me with outstretched arms. I laughed, lifted her up, and swung her toward the sky.

"So we meet again," I said as I hugged her to my chest.

Agnes came running across the yard in pursuit of the child who'd escaped from the playground as soon as she spotted me entering Sister Freda's gates.

"She remembers you!" Agnes said, surprised.

"Hi, Agnes," I greeted her, bouncing Esther on my hip. Jen stood next to me with the bags of the supplies she'd promised for Sister Freda. After spending the afternoon in Kitale to get the medicine and run errands, Irene and Amanda had hopped a matatu back to Pathfinder Academy. I'd stuck with Jen to ride to Sister Freda's for the special delivery.

Simply being in Sister Freda's presence both energized me and made me feel at peace. And I hadn't stopped thinking about Esther since we'd met. I thought about her before I fell asleep.

229

I thought about her when I woke up. I thought about her as I watched the boarders rehearse the play we'd written.

"We wanted to drop off these supplies to Sister Freda," Jen announced.

"She's in the clinic. I'll take you to her." Agnes led us past villagers waiting for care, Esther still attached to my hip and twisting the garnet studs I always wore in my ears. The line outside the clinic was much shorter today.

Sister Freda was bent over a table, giving a shot to a boy not much older than three who sat without flinching. A grin spread across her face when she saw us standing in her doorway. "You came back!" she said, delighted. "And you found Esther," she added, waving to the child in my arms.

"Esther found her first," Agnes said, recounting how she'd raced right over to me.

Jen held up the supplies, the bags heavy and dangling from her outstretched arms.

Sister Freda thanked her saying, "God has answered our prayers again!" and then instructed a nurse to take the goods to the "pharmacy." On the matatu ride over, Jen had told me that the meds cost about a tenth of what they would back in the United States.

I thought about how most Kenyans wouldn't be able to pay for prescriptions at American prices—most couldn't even afford them at Kenyan prices. The sad fact was that many Americans couldn't afford prescriptions either, despite living in one of the wealthiest nations in the world.

"Come, let me give you something in return," Sister Freda said, leading us to her garden. Esther cooed into my neck as her little body bounced with each of my steps across the uneven ground. I noticed she had mud on her jean dress and, breathing her in, that she smelled like sunshine, grass, and dirt.

"Sister Freda?" I said. "There's something I wanted to ask

you. It's about Esther." Jen was trailing behind us, chatting with one of the nurses.

"Yes?" she said, looking at me expectantly.

"I'd like to sponsor Esther, to help out with whatever the costs are for her food, clothing, and education."

She stopped midstride and wrapped me in a heart-stopping hug. Embarrassed, I felt my cheeks turn the color of pomegranate. My small gesture wasn't a sacrifice. Sister Freda had quit her well-paying hospital job to spend her savings—and her life—healing the sick and poor. Sister Freda and Joshua were real-life heroes. They were the people who remained on the ground day after day, working to heal, to educate, and to save their neighbors. They'd given me something I didn't even know I needed: the faith that one person could absolutely make a difference.

Still, it's easy to get overwhelmed when faced with so much poverty, to turn away altogether. Sure, I'd seen the Christian Children's Fund infomercials with Sally Struthers stating otherwise, pleading for viewers to just save one child. But now that I'd held Esther's living, breathing, warm little body in my arms, I couldn't simply change the channel. I *could* do something.

Six months from now, I'd probably return home to my safe bed, far away from Sister Freda's clinic. Until then, one tiny thing I could do was share some money and leave Esther in Sister Freda's—and God's—hands. By vowing to myself to support her education until she graduated, I prayed that Esther wouldn't have to marry young or turn to prostitution in order to survive. After finding Esther, I hoped that touching the life of just one person was enough—or at least a start.

As Jen and I left the farm, our arms were piled high with avocados, a gift from Sister Freda's farm. Crossing over the threshold of the clinic's gates, I wondered if I'd ever go back to that place and if I'd ever see Esther again.

✳

CHAPTER FOURTEEN

Jen

KIMININI, KENYA

OCTOBER

E lbow deep in bubbles, I sat cross-legged on the lawn, hand-washing an elephant-print skirt. "Mama Sandra, look how many buckets I have! Aren't you proud of me?"

She popped her head out from behind a wet sheet on the clothesline and howled with laughter. "Ah, yah, Miss Jen-nifa. You are Kenyan woman now," she said, before cracking up again.

Since our arrival at Pathfinder, Amanda, Holly, and I had done and said countless things that made Mama Sandra chuckle. But the first time I attempted to do laundry, I swore she almost popped a blood vessel from laughing so hard.

Since I had no more clean underwear (or emergency bikini bottoms) left in my backpack and my skirts were so stiff from dust and grime they could've doubled as an ironing board, Jen's Laundromat opened for business halfway through our month-long stay. I'd seen Mama Sandra and the boarders cleaning their clothes outside on countless occasions, so I understood the general process. Pull up some water from the well, grab an empty bucket and detergent, plop down on the grass, and scrub away. No problem.

During an afternoon break, I'd set up shop on a vacant patch of grass and selected the first item from my pile, one of many Champion quick-dry thongs. I daintily dunked it into a bucket of soapy water, gently rubbed the fabric together for a few minutes, then rinsed it in a second bucket of clean water, stood up, draped it over the clothesline, and repeated the process with the next pair. Before long, I heard faint snickers wafting across the yard. I looked up. Naomi and Nancy were looking at me strangely and giggling.

"Hello, my gorgeous girls. What's happening?" I asked, grinning in their direction.

"Miss Jenni-fa, what is that you are washing, and where are your other buckets?" Naomi asked.

"Umm, it's my underwear," I said, which only led to more giggling and questions, like "Why are they so small?" and "How do they fit on you?" and "Do Amanda and Holly have the same kind?"

I deflected their hilarious (and acutely savvy) inquiries as best I could, but the damage was done. I was now an official target for laundry scrutiny. As I swished a skirt through the suds, Mama Sandra approached, observed for a few seconds, and then doubled over in laughter.

"Jenni-fa, let me do that for you," she said, grabbing a dirty garment off the ground.

"No way, Mama Sandra. You do way too much around here to help Joshua and the girls. We're supposed to make *your* life easier, not the other way around."

"Yes, but you will never get these cleaned this way. You will be here all the way through the night," she added with another laugh.

Try as I might to convince her that I really could wash my own clothes, she wouldn't take no for an answer, calling in the troops to bring more buckets—apparently anything less than four was unacceptable. Before I knew it, Mama Sandra and her helpers were rigorously scrubbing, plunging, and twisting my "unmentionables" along an assembly line of plastic pails, as methodically and gracefully as a choreographed ballet.

Mouth agape, I immediately scanned the farm for a tree or cow to hide behind. Luckily, my mortification was short-lived. After I offered up the magic words "My Kenyan experience would be far more rewarding if I learned to do laundry the way you do," Mama Sandra gave in. Reviewing the proper procedure one more time, she allowed me to reclaim my clothes, but eyed me like a hawk every scrub of the way.

Maybe I was delirious from squatting in the hot sun for so long, but after washing side by side with Mama Sandra for the next hour, I thought I saw nods of approval from neighbors and other passersby. My laundry skills were finally up to the strictest local standards; everything from here on out would be a drop in the bucket. Or in this case, many buckets.

234

Now, crouched in the same spot two weeks later, a more highly evolved laundress, I couldn't believe our time at Common Ground was almost over. Since my inaugural underwear wash, we'd witnessed the birth of a calf (which Joshua had named HAJI after Holly, Amanda, Jen, and Irene), planted hundreds of baby saplings in the garden, perfected our chapati-rolling technique, and held Dr. Seuss readings in Pathfinder classes.

But by far our most rewarding experience and contribution was our *A Tree Grows in Kenya* play project, during which we had witnessed even the shyest boarders bloom into brave and talented actresses. Timid Barbara had chucked the "slow and steady wins the race" fable right out the classroom window, sprinting out of her shell and into the spotlight. Whereas some girls merely memorized and recited their lines, Barbara cloaked herself in the President Moi character, delivering emotions and mannerisms that broadened the script's horizon. Like proud parents, Amanda, Holly, Irene, and I pushed back tears, cheering and clapping along with the rest of the cast.

With each play practice and evening danceathon, we'd grown closer and more connected to our little women. Our hut soon became a dedicated space for them to escape and unwind from their rigorous class and chores schedule, providing a friendly forum to express their preteen sensibilities. Whether it was a DVD screening or a homework tutoring session, our time with the boarders turned out to be the greatest reward we'd received as volunteers. Although we'd been a bit skeptical at first, as the Village Volunteer site suggested, it seemed that our presence alone had made a positive impact on them. And as a final token of our appreciation, we'd planned to make goodie bags for the girls and cook a special dinner for them and the entire staff.

Since it was now the morning before our departure, it was a race against the clock to get everything done in time. We had to hightail it to Kitale, blitz the grocery store, beat the daily afternoon thunderstorm back, and prepare the food—all before nightfall.

The last of my laundry washed and Holly back from her morning run, we grabbed Amanda and Irene and the countdown officially began. Now black belt masters of the matatu schedule, we made it to our favorite Kitale supermarket in record time. Grabbing a jumbo cart, we reviewed the list of ingredients we'd need to make our surprise meal. Though there was an ocean between us and Taco Bell, the generous supply of avocados we'd received from Sister Freda made our mission clear: to introduce our Pathfinder family to the joys of guacamole and Tex-Mex cuisine.

Given our limited grocery selection, the girls and I had devised a strategy: thinly rolled chapatis would double as tortillas, kidney beans and rice would serve as burrito filling, tomatoes,

235

onions, avocados, chili sauce, and limes in various combinations could make both guacamole and salsa. We even planned to create dessert using banana slices with ground cinnamon and sugar, cooked over the fire until it was golden and bubbly.

For the boarders' gifts, we wanted a mix of fun and practical items, so we grabbed everything from hair ties, lollipops, plastic bracelets, and modeling clay to colored pencils, crayons, and small sets of silverware. The four of us blasted through the aisles in less than a half hour and made it back to Pathfinder just as classes were dismissed. Knowing the boarders would be occupied in study hall for at least another hour, we spread their treats on our beds to sort and separate. After wrapping each girl's gift in pink cellophane paper and securing it with white ribbon, we tucked all fourteen bags out of sight and set out to commandeer the kitchen.

Soon after our arrival at Common Ground, we had noticed that the staff would disappear for hours on end into dark, smoke-filled huts, which we learned were the food prep and cooking areas. With only a wood-burning fire and steel cauldrons full of well water at their disposal, they'd have to work tirelessly all day long just to get lunch and dinner on the table for everyone. Knowing that, we couldn't in good conscience have our meals served to us on a (tin) platter without pitching in to help.

While we'd each eventually mastered the art of rolling dough and slicing mangoes, we'd never attempted to cook an entire meal until now. Neither Mama Sandra nor the chefs were fazed in the slightest by our inexperience. But the menu we'd suggested . . . well, now, that threw them for a loop. From the looks on their faces, you'd think we were speaking pig Latin as we explained why we were mashing up the avocados and adding spices to the mixture.

"Just wait, Mama Sandra. You are going to love guacamole," Amanda said as she chopped and blended the ingredients.

"Yeah, and Amanda's recipe is the best too. She makes it all the time back home. Although the amount she has in that bowl contains about twenty dollars worth of avocados, if you can believe it," I added, which was the biggest shock of all to her, as an avocado could be purchased at the Kiminini produce stand for about ten cents.

"Jen, chapati cockroach alert," Holly interjected, glancing down at my workstation.

"Oh, thanks," I said, brushing a few wandering critters off the table near the dough I was rolling. They hit the dirt and skittered back to the wall to reunite with their relatives. I scanned the plywood table with my headlamp to make sure the roach coast was clear, then went back to the task at hand.

Not too long before, such an incident would've sparked a fit of spastic convulsions and shrieks and sent us bolting for the nearest exit. It's not that I was suddenly thrilled to have the planet's only plausible nuclear fallout survivors crawling across my hands or swan diving into my meals. But since cockroaches were as much a part of the landscape as mud or grass, our bug-induced breakdowns started to seem foolish. Sure, Amanda and Holly had continued sleeping head to toe with Irene and me to avoid the bugs in their assigned beds. But when every kitchen wall and most available surfaces teemed with troops of cockroaches on 24/7 patrol, a few stowaways in the food weren't the end of the world.

Although the boarders normally ate dinner in their dorms, our Tex-Mex experiment required a different course of action. Setting up a buffet in the food prep area, we constructed a sample burrito so they could see how it was done. After that we asked them to proceed down the line, while we took individual orders and heaped food onto their plates like lunch ladies. Moving outside, we all sat on plastic chairs to eat. Like students nervously waiting for the results of our final exams, Amanda,

237

Holly, Irene, and I watched with bated breath as everyone dug in. Would they like our meal? Would Mama Sandra think our avocado concoction was gross?

Soon our worries were squelched as even the most apprehensive boarders were smiling and scooping spoonfuls of food into their mouths. Mama Sandra practically fell out of her chair when she tasted her first bite of guacamole, and the cooks were already helping themselves to second portions.

"So do you like it, Miss Naomi?" Amanda asked, giving the little girl a hug. "We did not fail?"

"No, you did not fail. We very much like all of this that you have prepared. Thank you, Miss Amanda."

After the last of the guacamole had been scraped from the bowl and the burrito station broken down, we all headed up to the main house to say our final good-byes before bedtime. In preparation for our departure, Joshua had coordinated another special performance so we could see our girls in action one last time.

Opening with the name game, which by now we knew by heart, we twirled around the room together, a symphony of little voices sewn onto our own. When the boarders showed off moves from Amanda's dance routine, we laughed. When they recited poems we'd helped them write, we cheered. And when they grinned for our cameras, we grinned too. But when they opened their gift bags, we cried. Not just because it finalized our good-bye but because out of all the items we'd included, it was the spoons, knives, and forks they held most dear. Not the whimsical trinkets. Not the candy. But basic utensils. Eyes sparkling, the girls clutched the silverware to their chests and thanked us for their very first sets.

Since our arrival at Pathfinder, we had constantly been amazed by how courageous and cheerful the girls were even though they had so little, but I had never anticipated how dif-

238

ficult it would be to leave them. Hiding my tears in the shadows of the kerosene lamps, I watched them smile and squeal over their goodies, honored to have been in the presence of these remarkable young women even for a brief while.

Back in Manhattan, the personal problems that had once plagued my life had seemed all-consuming. Yes, in theory, I'd known that compared to most people in the world, I was pretty well off. But in reality, I'd had no idea how extraordinarily lucky I was. It's not that I would never again stress out about my career or get annoyed at a friend or shed tears over a relationship. In fact, I could almost guarantee that I would. But if those were the worst of my woes, I was blessed and could no longer turn a blind eye to those less fortunate around the world or back home. And even though our time as volunteers was almost up, I vowed to take those lessons with me.

Glancing over at an equally emotional Amanda and Holly, I was hit by an overwhelming sense of pride and gratitude to have them by my side. Without hesitation or complaint, they'd wholeheartedly adopted my lifelong dream to visit Kenya as their own, encouraging me to turn it into a reality. And not only did they go along with my desire to work with children in a poorer, rural part of the country, but they'd flourished as mentors themselves, which made the experience so much more meaningful and beautiful than I ever could have imagined.

As we bid tearful farewells to Joshua, Mama Sandra, Irene, and all the boarders the next morning, Amanda, Holly, and I promised to stay in touch and to continue our efforts to find sponsors for the girls. Our backpacks loaded into a van bound for the Maasai village of Oronkai, we waved furiously out the window until Pathfinder faded from view.

239

%

CHAPTER FIFTEEN

Holly

NORTHERN INDIA
OCTOBER

I wanted to close my eyes to avoid seeing the accident, but my lids felt glued open. The jeep in front of us swerved to avoid hitting a cow that seemed to think a highway teeming with rickshaws, motorbikes, and cars was a fine spot for an afternoon nap. Cows are considered sacred in India and often roam free. The frenzied scene morphed into slow motion as I watched the jeep crash into a man, woman, and baby all perched atop a motorbike.

The crash catapulted the mother and child, who'd been riding on the back, off the bike. Rather than using her arms to break her fall, the woman instinctively wrapped them around the baby swaddled to her chest. She did a somersault before landing flat on her back on the pavement.

Almost as soon as the woman's body touched down, she miraculously sprang up, peeling away the layers of fabric used to bind the infant to her chest so that she could inspect it for harm. The baby seemed to be unscathed. The man, however, didn't fare so well. The bike lay on its side with the wheels still spinning, and his legs were pinned underneath the smoking metal.

Traffic halted, the cow wandered away, irritated that her

nap had been disturbed, and I grasped the door handle to jump out.

"Stay inside! It's dangerous," ordered Sunil, the driver and guide for our Golden Triangle tour, which covered Delhi, Agra, and Jaipur. His black eyebrows resembled two fuzzy caterpillars and twitched uncontrollably, making him look like an Indian version of Groucho Marx.

"Dangerous? But the accident is over," Amanda said, and Jen nodded in agreement, ready to spring out of the car to see what we could do to help. Not that we had any idea of *what* to do exactly—we didn't have a cell phone to call for assistance, and, even if we did, we didn't know the Indian equivalent of 911.

"Don't get out," Sunil repeated firmly. "The driver of the jeep will now be beaten."

Having Sunil as a tour guide was kind of like viewing India through the reflection in a fun house mirror: we had no way of knowing which explanations of his native culture were real and which were distortions. We were pretty sure the majority of Sunil's caveats —from warning us that women shouldn't wander alone after dark due to the high risk of rape to banning us from eating at hotels because owners often poisoned guests so they'd stay longer—were exaggerations.

Suddenly dozens of men materialized to form an angry roadside mob. They'd abandoned nearby wooden shacks, food carts, or their vehicles to ball up their fists and bang on the perpetrator's jeep door. At the same time, a smaller crowd surrounded the injured family, lifting the motorbike to free the man pinned underneath.

The vigilantes kept on coming. If the hodgepodge of vehicles fighting for space on the roadway struck me as anarchy just moments before, the swelling mob and haphazardly abandoned bikes charged the air with utter lawlessness. The men succeeded in opening the driver's door and pulling him from the vehicle even as he tried to clutch the steering wheel like a lifeline.

I strained my eyes to see what was happening, and Amanda quickly started her video recorder to capture the drama. "We just witnessed our first traffic accident in India and—" *SLAM!* A man's fist pounded on the window near her face, blocking the lens.

"Maybe you should put the camera away," Jen said as another fist slammed into the thin glass, rocking the car. My own hands gripped Jen's arm, fear freezing my heart and confusion clouding my brain. I had no previous experience with traffic accidents in India and no idea of what was going to happen. Not knowing made the scene seem all the scarier.

Beep! BEEEEEP! Sunil honked the horn like a man possessed, trying to inch the car forward despite being blocked by a crowd. He honked louder and hit the gas. The noise made the men disperse slightly so Sunil could drive around them. He sped away, leaving behind the acrid scent of burning rubber.

Since our car lacked working seat belts, the three of us could only grab the "Oh shit!" handles for dear life. We watched Sunil steer between trucks headed straight for us as well as the occasional cow idling on the highway—not one of them cognizant of the concept of separate lanes.

When we finally regained control of our vocal cords—hoping the same could be said of Sunil's grasp on the steering wheel— we asked why anyone would leave the scene of an accident.

"If you hit people, you drive away fast. If you don't, the men will beat you in payment. You only have five seconds in India," he said. "If you don't drive away fast, people will hit your head until you must go to the hospital."

That sounded like a tall tale to me. "You mean you're *supposed* to hit and run?" I asked.

"Yes! If you're too slow, the crowd will beat you," he explained.

243

I didn't believe for a second that a driver responsible for a crash would hit the gas in order to escape roadside vigilantes. In any event, logic dictated that the police would both arrest the driver and protect him from the angry mob in question. Jen, Amanda, and I exchanged more skeptical looks.

"Will the driver be beaten to death?" I asked, deciding to play along with Sunil to see how far he'd take this.

He gave me a look in the rearview mirror that illustrated that he thought me extremely uncivilized. "No, he just has a lot of blood. And he has to pay in cash at the hospital for the family's medical bills and broken bike."

"But what if he doesn't have the cash?" Amanda asked.

"Then they keep his jeep as payment and he has to take a bus home."

Too incredulous to respond, I watched the world turn into a blur outside the car window. It rolled by in waves of women wearing jewel-toned saris and puffs of curry-laced smoke from cooking fires near the roadside. Families piled atop single motorbikes like some kind of circus act. India made me feel more alive, with competing sights, scents, and sounds putting me on sensory overload until I felt hyperaware. The country was more different from my own than any I'd ever visited before. It struck me in everything I saw: small stuff like eating masala dosas instead of pancakes and bacon for breakfast, and big things like seeing a society built on the caste system, in which people are born into certain roles, so totally different from the Declaration of Independence's notion that "all men are created equal"—even if the idea wasn't always practiced in reality back home.

In India, the caste system lives on—despite being outlawed—in traditions such as arranged marriages. Parents searching for a match for their child typically look for someone from the same caste, barring other deal breakers such as age, height, and education. Sunil's parents, for example, had arranged his marriage to a woman who, like him, was a member of the highest caste, known as Brahmins.

When I first learned about arranged marriage while on Semester at Sea, I was just twenty-one and idealistic, and the idea struck me as painfully unromantic. But after listening to countless girlfriends in New York stress about dating, I could see how having someone else make the decision for you might be a relief. Plus, arranged marriages actually last longer—love marriages in America are more likely to end in divorce than Indian marriages. Of course, the lower divorce rate could stem more from women's rights than from matrimonial bliss. Since Indian women seem to depend on their husbands for social and economic standing more than their American counterparts do, maybe divorce wasn't such a feasible option.

Curiosity now got the best of me, and I asked Sunil about his own upcoming wedding. Sunil was twenty-eight, the same age as us, and his bride was twenty-five. He'd invited the three of us to the wedding happening that spring in the Himalayas, but by then we'd already be in Southeast Asia.

As he explained that his wedding celebration would last four days and would have two dozen costume changes, Jen's eyes widened in fascination. Jen loves dressing up and going to black-tie affairs and weddings, so the idea of extending festivities for days rather than merely hours must have sent her brain into fantasy overload. However, it was much harder for the three of us to stomach the idea that Sunil would have to wait for the wedding to see his bride-to-be in person for the first time. That gave a whole new meaning to "saving it for marriage."

"So do you think arranged or love marriages are better?" I asked.

"Both are good, but an arranged marriage is much more successful." He said he'd had a love relationship once in college, but his parents had made him break it off.

"If I defied my parents and married her for love, I would inherit nothing." Sunil thought love marriages were more apt to fall apart because there's too much pressure that comes with being estranged from your family and cut off from your inheritance.

"What do women do who don't want to get married?" Amanda asked, and I laughed. Generally the one of us with the most spunk, Amanda never thought you had to do something just because everyone else was doing it. Sunil gave us yet another glance in the rearview mirror that suggested he thought we were uncivilized—or maybe just plain crazy.

When we'd arrived in Delhi a few days earlier, it had been like landing on another planet. Nothing was ordinary to us, and we were thrilled to be in a place that felt so, well, foreign. Venturing outside our dingy, $12-a-night hotel, we'd stepped right into a chaotic side alley clogged with rickshaws, women frying cumin-laced rice in pans near the roadside, and half-naked children scrubbing themselves down with soap in the gutter. Packs of kids grabbed at our skirts, trying to sell us everything from postcards to bracelets to gum. The air smelled like curry, car exhaust, and jasmine from the garlands women sold on the streets, and tinny, warbled lyrics sung by invisible Bollywood stars ricocheted down from radios perched in open windows. It was both awesome and disorienting.

We quickly learned that three white women wandering around without male escorts attracted much more attention in India than anywhere we had visited so far. We'd been in Delhi barely a day, and already numerous men had "accidentally" bumped into our breasts as we strolled along the congested sidewalks. And soon we'd traded in one type of adventure for another.

We'd walked into a tourist office to grab a few maps to help us get our bearings and walked out with Sunil, who had strong-armed us into an all-inclusive tour. Though this was not our usual traveling style, we were all bewildered by our newest surroundings. It was a relief to let a guide choose which temples to visit and hotels to book.

With Sunil in the driver's seat, our first destination was arguably one of the greatest monuments to love of all time: the Taj Mahal. None of us had been to the Taj before, and, like a lot of tourists, we didn't want to leave India without seeing the legendary site. Besides, with Elan on the other side of the world, it'd been a while since I'd experienced any romance, and I was eager to witness that famous testament of one man's undying devotion to his beloved.

The story goes that Shah Jahan had the marble tomb built after his favorite wife died (apparently he had others) so that a symbol of their love would last forever. He supposedly fell for her at first sight, and she gave him fourteen children. (If that's not a reason to love your wife, I don't know what is.) Set on the banks of the Yamuna River, the Taj took some twenty thousand workers more than seventeen years to finish.

Driving through Agra on the way to the Taj was like sifting through dirt to get to the buried treasure—the city was filthy and poverty-ridden. The air was filled with both burning brush and body odor. Monkeys and dogs marked their territory atop piles of trash, and men shat on the roadside. The Taj was the diamond in the rough, and to help protect its delicate marble from pollution such as car exhaust, vehicles had to park far away from the site.

As soon as the three of us left the safety of Sunil's car (well, safe now that it wasn't in motion), we were surrounded by more suffering than I'd seen even in the line of sick patients waiting outside Sister Freda's clinic. On our walk to the Taj, barefoot

247

toddlers with rags falling off their bony bodies put fingers to their mouths, gesturing for food. A guy dragged himself down the dusty path, carrying what appeared to be his own leg in his hands. Children grabbed at our clothes and bags, begging us to buy their postcards.

My first instinct was to move closer to Amanda and Jen and to block out the suffering, because I was scared and uncomfortable. But Esther and Sister Freda's faces were with me now. Having had the chance to talk to them, to get to know them a little, had blotted out my instinct to run away, and I wished I knew how to do it again here, even as a tourist. Was it possible to move beyond seeing those in front of me as beggars before I saw them as people just like myself?

I forced myself to slow down, to make eye contact with a girl, probably about five years old, clutching a handful of postcards. When she held them out to me hopefully, I stopped and asked her for her name. "Padma," she said. I crouched down to sift through her collection of images of that famous mausoleum at different times of the day, pretending to consider each one carefully. Then I selected three and handed her some rupees. She yelled, "Thank you!" as she laced her fingers around mine to shake my hand. I smiled at her as I stood, and suddenly there was a frenzied mass of kids pressing up against me from every side and thrusting postcards and gum into my face. This time I pushed past, jogging to catch up with Jen and Amanda. I looked back to see the kids all circling around Padma.

Falling into step beside Jen and Amanda, we joined the long line of pilgrims—Indians, Europeans, and Asians—that radiated out from the sandstone gateway. Both barefooted children and men dressed in crisp white shirts grabbed at those in line, offering tour-guide services.

We crossed the threshold of the gates inscribed with words from the Koran, a legacy left by the Muslim rulers known as

Mughals. Once inside, we were greeted by immaculate open space, acres of manicured lawn, and gardens exploding in full bloom; the sandstone mausoleum that housed the queen's body was reflected serenely in a rectangular pool. Each building looked symmetrical, a mirror image of the other.

We continually snapped our cameras to capture the play of light caused by the setting sun as the sandstone shifted from lotus white to buttercup yellow to marigold orange. Then a shadow fell over my lens, and I looked up to see a group of Indian tourists standing in front of us.

"Can we have a picture, madam?" asked an Indian Ashton Kutcher in aviator sunglasses.

"Of course," I replied, reaching for his camera. But he pulled the camera away, handed it to his friend, and gestured for Jen and Amanda to come closer.

"I think he wants a picture of *us*," said Amanda, surprised. We stood awkwardly next to the guy, who casually threw his arm around my shoulders. His friend clicked the shutter and thanked us. Not knowing what to say, we flashed him a smile before walking away.

"That was strange," said Jen.

The same thing happened at least half a dozen more times. Parents wanted a shot of us holding their charcoal-eyelined infant, groups of teenage girls with bindis fanned around us to pose with the reflecting pool in the backdrop, a family of six arranged themselves next to us according to height.

"Now I know what it feels like to be a D-list celebrity," Amanda joked. When we asked Sunil why so many Indians wanted pictures with us, he gave a vague explanation that getting shots with Westerners at famous landmarks was a prized souvenir they could show their friends, sort of like a status symbol. Funny, we felt the same way about having our pictures taken next to them.

Sunil eventually played the role of bodyguard, denying any more photo requests. "We will never finish this tour if you keep stopping for pictures!" he scolded, as if we were his kids instead of clients.

T he woman in a red sari bent over to remove her shoes, and the part in her hair was a matching shade of blood red. Much like Westerners wearing wedding rings, some Indian women apply a vermilion paste to symbolize that they're married. I smiled shyly at her and glanced down at my own $2 rubber sandals, slipping them off my feet, as was customary before entering a temple.

Jen and Amanda slid out of their black flip-flops. They were both dressed in ankle-length skirts purchased in the labyrinth of shops lining the streets of Delhi. The three of us stood on the threshold of the lotus-flower-shaped sanctuary called the Baha'i House of Worship, adjusting our shawls to make sure our shoulders were covered.

The silence inside was thick as we followed the woman's lead to sit on a cool marble bench. I can't say how long we stayed there in that airy space, savoring the stillness that wrapped around us after so many days being immersed in honking horns, Bollywood beats, and vocal vendors.

Sunil had taken us to the temple after I bombarded him with questions about the difference between the Hindu deities I'd seen the last time I was in India, such as Ganesh with his elephant head and Shiva with his necklace of snakes. I'd been drawn to the country's hodgepodge of temples, mosques, shrines, and churches and felt like I'd stepped into an otherworldly, spiritual mecca whenever I spotted a sign of everyday devotion, such as fruit placed inside a household shrine or a street stall overflowing with flower garlands for prayer offerings.

Seeing those connections to a higher power all throughout India had made me want to cling to it like a safety blanket the first time I'd visited. The way many Indians practice little acts of faith in the middle of, say, going to the market reminded me that just being alive is sacred in and of itself. As I experienced more of how people everywhere found comfort in faith, moments stuck in my mind like a collage: the knickknacks left by the porters on the Inca Trail as offerings to the gods; Sister Freda clutching the cross around her neck; my own grandmother, fingering the rosary she always took with her to Mass.

Echoing the message of Gandhi, Sunil refused to be pinned down to any one religion. "I am Hindi, Muslim, and Buddhist—God is found in all beliefs," he said. So it was fitting that he took us to the Baha'i House of Worship, which welcomes all regardless of what religion they align with. Most Indians are Hindus, and Hinduism's umbrella of different deities struck me as one big rainbow of gods and goddesses that each represented a different wavelength of a single universal Being. Hindus believe God is everywhere and have lived next to the Christians, Muslims, Buddhists, Sikhs, Jains, and Jews of the subcontinent for centuries.

Once we'd risen to our feet and tiptoed back outside, the white petal-shaped temple suddenly reminded me of Disney's Epcot Center. We scanned the central walkway for a food cart. Beads of sweat broke out on my nose as the sun beat down on our heads. "Ice cream would be really good now!" I said, knowing we were more apt to encounter savory treats such as *bhaja* (vegetable fritters) and *vadai* (spicy doughnuts).

"That guy is selling mangoes on sticks!" Jen pointed toward a cart stationed near the parking lot, and we practically skipped down the concrete path. Amanda handed the vendor a few rupees, which reminded me of colorful Monopoly money except that each note was stamped with Gandhi's face. The vendor

251

handed back three mangoes on a stick, and as we hunted for a spot to sit and enjoy them, we dodged others touting bracelets or curried cashews.

By this point, we'd developed a highly effective strategy for escaping the clutches of aggressive vendors. After reading that guides often scored commissions for delivering tourists to shops, we weren't shocked when Sunil pulled up to a street lined with stores so we could "meet his friends." Knowing it was part of the tour-guide/client transaction, we politely sat through demonstrations on how to make mosaics and silk saris before being draped in fabrics and jewels in not-so-subtle sales pitches.

That didn't mean we had to buy anything, however. The girls and I tried many unsuccessful attempts to deter them with put-offs. Amanda's "These shirts just aren't my style" was met with "No *problem*, madam! We can sew whatever style you like!" *Damn!* "Unfortunately, I don't have any more room in my backpack," Jen said, trying another angle. "That is why we offer international shipping at cheap price for you, madam!" the expert salesman shot back. Thwarted again!

Through trial and error, I'd finally discovered the one excuse that actually worked: "This fluorescent orange sari is, um, stunning, but I'll have to ask my husband before I can buy anything." That stopped the vendors' onslaught instantly, and they responded only by pressing a business card firmly into my hand and ordering me to bring my husband back.

But the same novelty I found so exciting also kept me feeling like a child learning how to act in the world. Even the most mundane interactions were grounds for a communication breakdown: at first I thought Indians wobbling their head from side to side were shaking it no when they actually meant yes. And sitting next to a man in a rickshaw quickly turned into a version of musical chairs as he moved to the other side to take a seat further away, then repeated the process again when Amanda hopped in beside him. Apparently, it's too intimate for an un-married woman to sit so close to a man.

So I was happy to take a little rest and simply sit cross-legged in some spongy grass near the temple, sucking sweet juice from the mangoes.

"Excuse me, madam?" I squinted up through the midday sun to see the woman in the red sari standing above us, this time with a man at her side. "Could we get a photograph?"

"Of course!" I said, holding out my hand for her camera. She quickly offered it to the man before plopping down beside us. There I went again, forgetting my social skills.

Amanda retrieved her Olympus from the tiny fabric purse she'd haggled for earlier that day, and jumped up. "Can you get one with ours too?"

253

✻

CHAPTER SIXTEEN

Jen

SOUTHERN INDIA/SHRADDHA ASHRAM

NOVEMBER

D on't move," I instructed, as a band of cockroaches scurried across the train car wall, straight toward Amanda's head. She sat rooted in place on the sticky seat cushion, squeezing her eyes shut and bracing for my attack.

Clutching our *Lonely Planet: Southern India*, I moved in for the kill. In one fluid kung fu motion, I propelled the book past Amanda's face, adding more carcasses to our growing collection. At the same time, Holly leapt up and splattered a few culprits en route to our stash of assorted snacks, while Amanda pulled a flip-flop from her own foot to pick off newcomers streaming in from the windowsill.

By this point in the trip, the girls and I had grown fairly accustomed to third-world conditions, learning to tolerate a vast assortment of creepy crawlies and less-than-desirable accommodations. But nothing could have prepared us for this, our first overnight train ride through the sun-scorched subcontinent of India.

We'd arrived in Bangalore a few days earlier, and, for the first time since leaving New York City, we were racing to meet a deadline. Our assignment: we had less than twenty-four hours to get Holly to Trivandrum for the first day of her monthlong yoga teacher training program.

With nearly five hundred miles of ground to cover, we'd planned to hop a domestic flight to save time, but after hearing news reports that terrorists were targeting southern Indian airports, we'd decided that riding the rails would be safer. Not to mention an infinitely cheaper and more authentic way to travel. If only we'd known that the 6526 Bangalore-Kanyakumari Express was not only competing for the Guinness World Record as the slowest express train in the world but was also in serious need of an exterminator.

Since we'd booked our passage at the last minute, all the first- and second-class tickets had been sold out, so we had to settle for the third-class sleeper car. For ten bucks, we figured the compartment wouldn't have air-conditioning, but we didn't count on the complimentary army of cockroaches. No sooner had we slid into our assigned seats than a river of six-legged critters poured down the walls and over the benches.

"I feel like we're playing that game they used to have at Chuck E. Cheese's. You know? The one where you bash the fuzzy purple moles that pop out of their holes?" I said, wildly scanning the area, ready to pounce at the first sign of movement.

"Umm, thanks for tarnishing the image of one of my favorite childhood pastimes," Holly joked, inspecting our coveted food bag for stowaways. "Uh, this is seriously gross."

"It's our cockroach curse. They've followed us from Kenya, I swear," Amanda said, shrieking and wildly shaking out her curls to eliminate the chance of hangers-on. "And yet again, it seems like we're the only ones on this train who are concerned about sleeping with a million bugs."

Many times in India, Amanda, Holly, and I had felt like a three-ring circus, constantly on display to amuse and bewilder the locals. This train ride proved no different. As floods of extended families spilled on board, they'd stop dead in their tracks in front of our bench seats, mouths agape at the sight of three white women in mass hysterics over a few tiny insects.

Unable to repress our cockroach-slaying instincts, we ignored the obvious stares—at least at first. But eventually, embarrassment and the sheer exhaustion from jumping up and down every two seconds forced us into silent submission. If we were going to survive the remainder of the claustrophobic seventeen-hour journey, we'd have to sit down, remain calm, and pretend that we hadn't stepped into an episode of *Fear Factor: India*.

For once the utter lack of personal space in this part of the world worked to our advantage. As hundreds of passengers wedged themselves into every available square inch of the locomotive—unhinging foldaway beds from the walls to stockpile bundles of fabric, oversized trunks, and picnic baskets—our unwelcome bug mates scattered for cover. Our skin no longer crawling (at least not as much), we hunkered down in our booths, falling into rhythm with the train as it rattled along the tracks.

As night fell, Holly settled into one of the coffinlike sleep compartments, face mask and earplugs firmly in place. Along with the majority of other passengers, she soon dozed off, leaving Amanda and me to indulge our night-owl tendencies. Headlamps at the ready, we holed up across from one another on bottom bunks to savor reading the rare glossy magazines we'd managed to pilfer from a guesthouse lobby.

"Hey, listen to this," I whispered. "Dear *Marie Claire India*: I have been in an arranged marriage for almost five years and while I respect my husband, I greatly dislike having sex with him. Most nights, I feel physically ill when we have intercourse. I have considered leaving him, but this would destroy my family. Is there anything I can do to learn to like sex with my husband more?"

"Wow, does it really say that?" Amanda asked, pulling the

page down to look. "That's terrible. She must feel so trapped. I guess that sort of puts our petty troubles with men in perspective. At the very least we get to have a physical connection before we walk down the aisle."

"True. Although statistically I think arranged marriages work out more often than love matches, so maybe we're no better off in some ways. Hey, you should totally pitch a story about that. It could be something like 'Dating Around the World: Would you have better luck in someone else's country?'"

"Good call, but no thanks," Amanda replied with an odd seriousness to her tone.

"Oh, c'mon. It's an awesome idea. I mean, I would totally read that article," I whispered between the vociferous snores and guttural coughs that filled the car.

"While I don't dispute its awesomeness"—she paused and took a breath—"I meant that I've decided that I'm not going to pitch stories anymore."

"What do you mean?" I asked, brushing an imaginary bug off my neck.

"I've actually been planning to talk to you about this. I think I'm finally ready to shelve the idea of being an international journalist. At least for a little while anyway."

"Okay, am I on *Candid Camera* or something?" I said, hoping to joke my way out of another potentially tense conversation.

"No, I'm serious. I've been thinking a lot about this over the past few days, and I'm just not sure it's the right thing for me to do anymore. I mean, I've sent out dozens of idea memos and query letters and pitches. And spent about a jillion hours holed up in Internet cafés. For what? None of my editors are even getting back to me anymore, so lately I've felt like it's all been for nothing," she replied, sifting through the pile of magazines in front of her.

"Look, I really shouldn't have snapped at you the way I did

257

that day at Pathfinder," I said, thinking back to the argument we'd had in Kenya. "At least you have something you want to accomplish, unlike me. I'm just running away from real life altogether. I mean, who am I to tell you what's best?"

"I know, but I honestly think it *would* be best for me to give up working for a while and just try to enjoy traveling without some sort of mission or purpose attached. Seriously, for the next couple weeks, I've decided: we're doing the trip *your* way."

Scanning Amanda's face with the beam of my headlamp, I could see that she genuinely meant what she was saying. As much as I hadn't wanted to guilt her into abandoning her on-the-road career goals, I couldn't help but feel relieved. I knew that a week later, we were going to part ways with Holly and travel as a duo for nearly a month, and I didn't want to have any unresolved tension between us.

"All right, you win," I said, holding up one of my hands in surrender. "And hey, you never know. You might love backpacker life so much, you'll want to give up working for the rest of the trip."

"Don't push it, Baggett," she replied, throwing me a mock-evil scowl.

"Never." I grinned before turning my attention back to the joys and woes of other women that danced across the moonlit pages of *Marie Claire India*.

C hai, chai, chai . . . coffee, coffee, coffee, chai, chai," ricocheted off the metal walls, piercing my seemingly ephemeral slumber.

I cracked one eye open and peered out of my protective silk sleep sack to see what on earth was making such a racket. A rail-thin man, draped in white linen from headdress to toe, maneuvered a pushcart with a tall silver kettle and plastic cups through the cramped corridor. Every few feet he'd pause to swap a steaming libation for 5 rupees (about 10 cents), all the while projecting the same nasally sales pitch into the muggy, cardamom-scented air.

Across the aisle, I spotted a fresh-faced Holly cheerfully making conversation with a family of eight. She glanced over at me and grinned.

"So do you know if chai is available on this train?" I asked sarcastically, groaning as I stripped the sweat-soaked fabric from the top half of my body.

"You're awake—finally! You and Amanda have been dead to the world for hours. I was starting to get worried."

"We didn't go to bed until nearly three in the morning. What time is it now?"

"I think almost ten a.m., but I'm not sure. My watch is still on Kenya time. How many hours are we ahead now?"

"I don't know. Three? Four? What time do we get to Trivandrum?"

"Not till two p.m.," she said.

"Well in that case, I'm going back to bed," I replied, fumbling through my daypack-turned-pillow to locate my iPod.

"What? No way. You have to keep me company," Holly protested.

"Sorry, can't hear you," I replied sweetly before cramming my earbuds in and rolling over.

I was just on the verge of drifting off when I felt a hand on my back. Startled, I flew up and hit my head on the bunk above me. A little girl with a mop of raven curls and an armful of sparkly pink bangles jumped back and giggled. Cajoling her baby brother to join her, the two tag-teamed me, pulling at the cord running into my ears. Oh well, it's too hot and noisy to sleep anyway, I thought, sitting up.

"You want to listen?" I asked, pulling out my right earbud and holding it out to them.

259

Awestruck by the realization that music could flow out of such a tiny machine, they squealed and leaned in, pressing their heads against each other. At first they were content to share the speaker, but before long, sibling rivalry reared its ugly head and an all-out tug-of-war ensued. Across the aisle, mom, dad, grandparents, and cousins sat chuckling at their feisty brood's attempts to play with the Westerner's toy.

I'm sure any child psychologist would have scolded me for indulging their bad behavior, but rather than risk destroying my main form of on-the-road entertainment, I decided it was easier to surrender it, giving them each one earbud to listen to. With the delinquent little duo tucked safely in the corner of the bench, quietly jamming to *Monster Ballads, Volume 2*, I felt free to roam about the cabin with Amanda, who was finally awake.

As we slowly edged our way down the aisles, we were swept up in a montage of strange and exotic scenes. Men sporting polyester bell-bottoms and disco jackets from the *Saturday Night Fever* era smoked hand-rolled cigarettes in the vestibules between cars. Mothers cloaked in Day-Glo saris pressed chunks of buttery naan into outstretched hands. Babies with kohl-smudged eyes howled in time with the screeching brakes.

Although I would've gladly accepted a space in first class, I doubted it would have been even a tenth as interesting as the third-class end of the train. And as much as I hadn't relished bunking with cockroaches (or cared to repeat the act), I felt a twinge of pride: we'd toughed it out, done as the locals had, and earned ourselves one very important backpacker merit badge in the process.

Maybe it was the soft rays of sunlight casting warm shadows on the walls or the absence of any obvious bugs, but our compartment felt considerably more inviting during the day. Finding a seat near an open window, I settled in for the remainder of the journey. As the train drifted through Kerala, the glossy photos I'd seen of the picturesque region boasting vast mangrove forests, golden sand beaches, jade green backwaters, and fields of coconut trees materialized before my eyes. The cleanest and best-educated state in India (literacy rates top 90 percent here), Kerala is a renowned tourist destination and one we were eager to explore.

Three hours (and one dead iPod battery) later, our train finally arrived in Trivandrum. Tucked among verdant hillsides at the southern tip of the country, the state's capital city—reputed to be a hub of art, literature, and politics—was the jumping-off point for our Kerala tour. Our first stop: the Shraddha Ashram, one of the subcontinent's innumerable spiritual centers, which, according to its Web site, was an easy sixty-minute drive from the station.

Staggering through the thick crowd of tourists, food vendors, and ticket touts, we emerged from the train station into the chaotic city streets. Heaving our packs onto our shoulders, we began the sluggish swim through a sea of residents, shopkeepers, stray dogs, auto-rickshaws, and taxi drivers waiting to pounce on us. In less than a minute, sweat poured from our foreheads, down our bodies to our filthy toes. An excitable young man, assuring us that he knew the way to "the very sacred, very special Shraddha place," squished our stuff into the trunk of his cab and we set off down a bumpy dirt path—hopefully toward enlightenment.

Prior to planning our trip, I didn't really know much at all about ashrams, let alone considered living in one. But with all the enthusiasm of a spartan cheerleader, Holly had educated us on the bountiful physical and spiritual benefits that the yoga/meditation center provided. While the rigorous thirty-day teacher training program Holly signed up for sounded like a form of cruel and unusual punishment to Amanda and me, we were inspired enough to commit to a more moderate-sounding weeklong vacation package. Why not, right? Where else could we mingle with serpentine cerulean Gods? This was India— land of powerful Hindu deities, birthplace of yoga, religious epicenter of the world (plus, a little exercise and healthy eating couldn't hurt before we headed north to the beaches in Goa to pursue more earthly pleasures).

After a surprisingly accurate hourlong journey, we rumbled up a gravel slope to the entrance of Shraddha. All the noise and congestion of the city had fallen far behind us, replaced by a peaceful, sprawling paradise of lush green forests and tropical flowers. Set above a sparkling lake in the foothills of the western Ghats, the ashram certainly afforded its devotees some pretty spectacular views. Although, as we soon learned, smoking, alcohol, drugs, meat, fish, eggs, garlic, onions, cell phones, sleeveless shirts, and public displays of affection (to name a few) were all strictly prohibited on the premises, so I figured the actual premises had to make up for that somehow.

As we followed the palm-fringed path in pursuit of the check-in area, a deep "Om" echoed through the treetops like the ominous hum of a battle horn. But rather than an angry militia, we were met by hundreds of serene yogis in drawstring pants and baggy T-shirts who floated up the hill toward an open-air pavilion.

We arrived at the front desk, and an impish blond waved us over to the end of the counter, where she stood guard over stacks of colored folders. She explained that the students had just finished their second *asana* (yoga) class of the day and were headed to dinner. Once we finished filling out the mandatory paperwork, we were welcome to join the group or just chill out until evening *satsung* (silent meditation and chanting).

After quickly scribbling our signatures on dozens of forms, we headed to our assigned dorm to set up camp with our Shraddha-issued sheets, pillowcases, and mosquito nets. While

Holly busied herself with the massive teacher-training manual, Amanda and I reviewed the daily schedule:

    5:30 a.m.: Wake-up bell

    6 a.m.–7:30 a.m.: Satsung

    7:30 a.m.: Tea time

    8 a.m.–10 a.m.: Asana class

    10 a.m.: Brunch

    11 a.m.–12:30 p.m.: Karma yoga/selfless service

    1:30 p.m.: Tea time

    2 p.m.–3:30 p.m.: Lecture

    4 p.m.–6 p.m.: Asana class

    6 p.m.–7 p.m.: Dinner

    8 p.m.–9:30 p.m.: Satsung

    10:20 p.m.: Lights out

Despite all the rebellious thoughts swimming through my mind ("There's no way in hell I'm getting up that early! Are two satsung sessions really necessary? Lecture, smecture!"), I was intrigued by ashram culture and genuinely excited about the yoga, brunch, dinner, and tea sections of the itinerary. And thanks to the über-cheap price tag of $11 per day for all meals, classes, and lodging, Amanda and I would shave enough money off our weekly budget to splurge on a scuba dive outing in Goa.

While I suspected that conforming to such a chaste existence might prove challenging, the first couple days were surprisingly carefree and rewarding. Sure, my foot fell asleep during morning meditation, sending me into an epileptic tailspin, and I was shushed by goody-goody students for disregarding the SILENCE signs during the meals, but I'd held my own in the more advanced of the two yoga classes, almost enjoyed the vegetarian slop, and memorized a few lines from the "Shri Ganesha" chant. Yes, I was well on my way to achieving transcendence.

263

*Y*ou can check out anytime you like, but you can never leave! The line from the Eagles song echoed through my head as the gangly, bug-eyed Indian blocked the exit gate, refusing to let Amanda and me pass. Even though the sun had already burned off the early-morning mist, I could feel a Hotel California–twisted haze settle over the sacred grounds. Somehow, an innocent attempt to swap our satsung for a DIY nature hike had landed us in the middle of a hostage crisis.

"You can't stop us from leaving," Amanda sputtered in disbelief. "We're just going to walk out!"

"No, no, you must be needing a pass from Swami, permission and then to go," the bewildered guard replied in fractured "Hindlish"—rapid-fire Hindu with English-sounding words tossed in.

"Yeah, well, the swami is kind of tied up at the moment leading satsung," Amanda replied tersely. "And we'd like to go now."

"Oh, Christ, it's barely sunrise and I already need a drink," I muttered under my breath. At this rate, I was beginning to think a few mimosas might help me reach nirvana faster than chanting and headstands ever could. But now I'd never get to test that theory, as it seemed Amanda and I were trapped here forever, or at least until we were reincarnated as dung beetles and could scurry under the fence undetected. Damn! If only I'd bothered to read the epic list of Shraddha rules, I would have noticed that my personal freedom was in direct violation of its strict moral code.

"If you leave, it must go forever. And you must to pay," the guard shouted, maniacally bobbling his head and shaking his nightstick at us in disgust.

"Are you saying you're going to kick us out for trying to take a walk?" Amanda asked.

karma plate. Before a swarm of angry locusts could attack, I sprinted up the stairway to the dank and dingy communal student barracks and collapsed onto my cot.

To an innocent bystander, my behavior might have appeared a little erratic. Okay, maybe a lot erratic. But it didn't take a guru (or a shrink) to figure out that my intense overreaction sprang from a much deeper place. After only a few days of spiritual training, even I was enlightened enough to realize that the true source of my emotional outburst was not the shrunken Indian man blocking the ashram exit but rather a taller American one back home.

Less than twelve hours earlier, I'd made a quick trip to the Internet hut near the ashram check-in desk and found an e-mail from Brian waiting in my inbox. While our exchanges had been understandably strained, we'd still been making an effort to keep in touch, periodically checking in, and trying to come to terms with our breakup as best as we could from such a long distance. Although hearing from him caused my heart to seize and my stomach to sink down to my knees, I was more than willing to endure the pain if it meant getting to keep him in my life in some capacity. But his latest message made it clear that he didn't feel the same way.

In the kindest way possible, he explained that it was too difficult for him to continue any communication with me and asked for some time—without e-mail messages or calls—to get over everything. At the time, I'd simply logged out and pretended the e-mail didn't exist. It's not that I was in total denial. I'd seen the writing on the wall for quite some time, but I'd hoped that it was scribbled in disappearing ink. And that after a couple months apart, Brian would feel different about everything and that maybe someday we could even go back to being friends.

Sprawled across the creaky ashram cot, I felt reality hit me. I had lost my best friend, probably forever, and there was abso-

"You very bad womens! You go!" our captor spewe
ing us speechless.

Ordinarily, a comment like that would have rolled
my backpack-toughened shoulders. After all, this ov
ashram guard was far from the toughest adversary w
on the road. But as our minor dispute with him escal
a full-scale Bollywood battle scene, an overwhelming
anger and panic began to brew deep within my gut. I h
here to relax, clear my head, and tap into my inner har
something like that), not to be reprimanded by some sta
ber with a clipboard holding me prisoner against my w

All of a sudden, I couldn't breathe. The cement wall
to close in around me, the neck of my sports top tighte
a noose and the guard's face twisted and distorted like
in a fun house mirror. Despite having lived for half a d
a city where residents regularly popped Paxil and Xan
their postwork martinis, I'd never personally experie
bona fide anxiety attack. But in the heat of this bizarre m
I was beginning to unravel.

"This is absolutely ridiculous!" I wailed, my shrill voic
tically sending a ripple across the placid lake. "We're just
to take a freakin' walk by the water, to connect with natu
find some *peace*, for crying out loud! You can't keep us lo
this crazy place! I will not put up with it anymore!" I sh
Turning my back on the astonished gatekeeper, I imme
fled the scene, my arms flailing like those of a petulant c
the midst of a tantrum.

As I cut across the meticulously pruned lawn, my
seized and spasmed as freshly formed tears threatened to
I heard Amanda calling after me, but I refused to stop. I
bled blindly through the Serenity Garden, inadvertently
ing down a few Shiva and Krishna statues in my path. Pe
another blasphemous deed to heap onto my overflowing

lutely nothing I could do about it. Maybe the ashram guard was right. Maybe I *was* a bad woman. I had convinced myself that it would be easier on Brian if we stayed together until I left on the trip, but I could see now how selfish that choice had really been. In an effort to delay the pain of separation, I'd strung Brian along and maybe hurt him more than I would have if I'd just made a clean break the moment I knew I was leaving NYC. And worst of all, I was the one who got to move on—experiencing new things, meeting new people every single day of my adventure—while he was the one left behind to pick up the pieces.

Suddenly I felt sick. For the past two months, I'd successfully repressed any breakup-related emotions, pretending that if I wasn't back in New York, none of it was actually real. Now, as I sat alone in the Shraddha dorm, a hollow sensation settled in the base of my stomach like a sticky mass of pulp at the bottom of a freshly carved pumpkin. I could run away to the farthest recesses of the globe, but I could never really escape my problems. All the irrational fears I thought I'd gotten over suddenly came flooding back: What if I never found anyone I loved more than Brian? By the time I got back from the trip I'd be twenty-nine. What if that was too old to start my dating career? What if I never found The One or got married and had kids? What if I wound up an old lady surrounded by cats and other scary things, like doilies and dusty knickknacks?

Of course I remembered having had a similar reaction when things had ended for good with my first serious boyfriend, Rick, but back then, I'd been a naive twenty-two, not a practically over-the-hill twenty-eight. And at the time I'd been living at home in Maryland with a huge support system of friends and family. If I'd been back in the States right now, my girlfriends would have organized an emergency intervention session: sappy chick flicks, an overstuffed box of Puffs, and a full pan of extra-fudgy brownies (the real deal too, not the bullshit low-fat kind).

267

Or I would call one of my best guy friends, and he'd be at my door in a second, ready to cuddle on the couch with a funny movie or to take me out dancing until 3 a.m.

But here at the ashram, all I had was a pamphlet on Proper Breathing and Ayurvedic Massage, a lumpy mattress, and a few raisins for dessert—if I was lucky. Just as I was slipping further into my self-created pit of despair, an unexpected voice pulled me back.

"You're cutting meditation class too, huh?" asked the friendly girl who slept on the cot around the corner from mine. I'd chatted with her a few times in the twenty minutes they gave us between evening chanting sessions and mandatory lights out, but I couldn't for the life of me remember her name. "I'm Laura, by the way," she said, saving me from asking her again.

"I'm Jen. And yes, I too am a Shraddha slacker," I replied, extracting myself from the cot.

We both laughed, and Laura admitted that she was mainly there for the yoga. I could believe it. With a six-pack that could rival Gwen Stefani's, she appeared to take her practice very seriously.

"Have you been doing yoga for a while?" I asked, contemplating the insane amount of crunches and cardio I'd need to add to my workout repertoire to get even a single ab of steel like hers.

She sat down across from me. "For almost seven years, actually. I got into it right after my divorce, and it seriously brought me back from the dead. Now I have my own studio in L.A., which, ironically, my ex-husband has been running for me while I've been touring Southeast Asia and India," she added, pulling on a baggy T-shirt, a requirement for our morning yoga session.

"Wow, are you serious? The fact that you have your own business *and* are on good terms with your ex is pretty impressive," I said, rummaging through my bag to locate my sports watch.

"Yeah, well, it took a *long* time for us to make peace with one another, but eventually we realized we were much better off as friends. Lucky for me, I was only twenty-seven when we split, so I had plenty of time to start over." I mentally did the calculation, and my brain did a double take. I'd assumed Laura couldn't have been much older than I was, but in fact she was thirty-four. If that was the effect yoga had on the aging process, I might change my mind and move into the ashram for good.

"And really, all of my most delicious love affairs have been in my thirties," she added.

"Really? That's comforting to hear. I'm twenty-eight and recently single for the first time in four years and I kinda freaked out about it just now," I confessed, oddly comfortable chatting with this relative stranger about my personal crisis. "Not because it wasn't the right thing to do, but it's hard to say good-bye to a boyfriend no matter what the circumstances."

"I totally understand. I know how devastating breakups are, but it does get easier. And on the bright side, you don't have to deal with divorce lawyers," Laura replied. "But you really are in a great place right now. I'm so envious that you're starting this phase of your life because it's the best. You can travel for a couple years, date whoever you want along the way, and still have plenty of time to get married when you get back. Or not at all if you're smart," she added with a wink.

Clang, clang, clang, the postmeditation bell sounded, signaling the half-hour tea break.

"Ooh, I better get going before the flock descends. But I'll see you in asana class," Laura said.

"Definitely. And thanks for the pep talk," I replied.

As I watched Laura head down the hall to the communal bathroom, I wondered if maybe she'd been dropped in my path

269

for a purpose. It's not as if I was already drinking the ashram Kool-Aid or anything, but our meeting just seemed like too much of a coincidence. Maybe I *had* done something right in a previous life after all?

Just then Amanda poked her head around the gauzy fabric "wall" that separated our bunks. "You okay?" she asked.

"You know what? I actually am," I said. "I just had a temporary freak-out about a bunch of stuff. The guard was just the icing on my stress cake, but I'm feeling a lot better now."

"Only you, Jenny B," Amanda replied, laughing and plopping down next to me. "I'm glad to hear you're okay. But just in case, I brought you a little surprise," she said, reaching into her pants pocket. "Ta da!" In her hand were two mini Kit Kat bars from the stash of chocolate we'd secretly purchased for Holly.

While being forced to remain inside the walls of Shraddha had triggered my emotional free fall, in a paradoxical twist, it was the ashram that helped get me back on my feet again (and my head too, if you count the vertical posture I finally mastered). It's not as if my sorrow and panic miraculously disappeared. But surrounded by hundreds of people, all seeking stillness of mind and mental peace, I eventually started to absorb that energy.

As soon as I got out of my own head a little, I discovered that I wasn't the only one wrestling with inner demons. Many of the students were facing a personal or professional crisis of some kind. A handful admitted to borderline abuse of booze, pills, or powders. In sadder cases, a few were grieving the loss of a loved one. But no matter what their reason, most considered Shraddha an ideal place to gain clarity or seek refuge.

Although swamis in cotton robes subbed in for men in white coats, in some ways, ashram culture wasn't a far stretch from a drug rehab or mental health center. Which, in a way, made it that much more appealing to me. A strange admission, I know, but books and films about substance abuse facilities or psychiatric hospitals—stories like *28 Days*, *A Million Little Pieces*, *One Flew Over the Cuckoo's Nest*, and *Girl, Interrupted*—have always fueled one of my escape fantasies. It's the one where I selfishly fall apart for once in my overachieving, always-put-together life, run far away from society and all its pressures, and just chill out and heal with the other patients. A product of my hyperactive imagination? Of course. But since arriving at the ashram, I had begun to wonder if maybe this trip around the world wasn't my own subconscious version of therapy.

As the week at Shraddha passed, something interesting happened: I actually began to let go. Let go of my regrets about the past. Let go of all the fears about my future. Let go of trying to figure out exactly who I was or who I was supposed to be. Maybe it was the constant surge of endorphins or the absence of liver-corrupting substances in my bloodstream or the mandatory hours of silence, but as the days floated by, a calmer and happier version of me pushed its way to the surface.

It was a slow and subtle evolution. But as my legs wobbled up into their very first half-locust pose, I felt an exhilarating sense of control over my body. On another occasion, I was sitting cross-legged on the lakeside yoga platform, eyes closed and hands in the chin mudra pose, and I could suddenly quiet my mind for ten whole minutes. But the most valuable and meaningful ability I gained at the ashram was to send a prayer out to the universe each day that Brian would find happiness and romance in his life.

When Rick had professed the same desire for me right after he broke things off, I'd been too devastated to comprehend the magnitude of what that meant. But as the wounds healed and we reconnected as friends, I realized how blessed I was to have had someone in my life who loved me enough to let me go. And I could only hope that, someday, Brian would understand that too. Because I did love him with all my heart and knew we both needed to take our own time to heal and move forward. That's what I was going to do for myself and what I'd always wish for Brian. Because we both deserved love in our lives—wherever and whenever we would find it again.

CHAPTER SEVENTEEN

菜

Holly

INDIA/SHRADDHA ASHRAM
NOVEMBER

It was still dark as I fell into step with the two hundred other students trudging down the path to the open-air prayer hall for morning satsung. With everyone wearing the mandatory teacher-training uniform—yellow T-shirts to symbolize learning and white pants to indicate purity—we formed into a homogeneous yogi mass.

The humid tropical air clung to my skin like a sari. Greenery was everywhere: palm leaves reached to the sky like fingers, and tufts of grass tickled our feet over our flip-flops. We climbed the steps, silently slipping out of our shoes at the top, and ambled through one of the dozen or so arches leading into the prayer hall.

The scent of lemon oil assaulted my nose as I fell into a cross-legged position on the stone floor. We slathered on this natural mosquito repellent religiously, but it didn't seem to deter the bloodsuckers in the least, especially when we were stuck in a shoulder stand or other posture where we couldn't easily swat them. The head swami wore his trademark orange wrap skirt and a T-shirt that covered his protruding stomach. He sat in the lotus position on a stage decorated with pictures of Shraddha's founding gurus. The framed photos were draped with garlands of orange flowers, and a smattering of burning candles provided the only points of light. Staring at the swami expectantly through the early-morning darkness, I listened as he began a guided meditation that sounded almost familiar after seven days inside the ashram.

"Close your eyes . . . Inhaaale deeply, exhaaale completely . . . Concentrate on either your third eye—the area in between your eyebrows—or your heart center . . . Watch your thoughts as if you were an outside observer . . . Let them pass by as your mind starts to quiet . . . Now try repeating a mantra with each exhalation to give your mind a place to rest . . . If you don't have a mantra, use the universal mantra, Om." A deep stillness washed through the prayer hall.

Even after a week of enforced discipline, trying to "quiet my mind" as the swami had instructed was leaving me more frantic than peaceful. In fact, I felt physically ill. It took only five minutes of sitting cross-legged for sweat to trickle between my shoulder blades, my right foot to fall asleep, and pain to crawl up my spine. With nothing to distract me, my restless mind went into overdrive.

Dad would probably have my head examined if he knew I volunteered to sit on the floor every day for an entire month and listen to a man wearing a skirt.

Just breathe in, breathe out . . .

Maybe I'm being selfish spending money to meditate instead of immediately helping Esther.

I WILL quiet my mind. My mind is now quiet. . . .

Being here kind of feels like boot camp. But I bet even at boot camp they feed you first thing.

Oh Lord, Holly. Shut up!

I wonder what we're having for breakfast. If the food is so healthy, why is the swami so fat?

My internal chatter was just that—pointless noise. And I seemed to have lost the volume control. I hadn't expected an ashram to be a spiritual happy hour, but I'd imagined it to be a sacred space where I could kick off a daily meditation and yoga routine. Besides a crazed morning subway commute, a lunch inhaled at my desk, and squeezing in a gym class, I didn't have many meaningful rituals in New York City, let alone one to connect me to something greater than myself. But my romantic expectations of ashram life did not exactly match reality—it felt more like I was at battle with myself. Rather than evolving, I felt I was regressing.

I'd first fallen into yoga when I was training for the New York City marathon a few years back. I'd read that yoga's deep stretches would help soothe my sore muscles and speed recovery after long runs. For me, yoga was more about stretching and lengthening muscles than the spiritual stuff that went along with it. Well, at least at first.

Eventually, though, I fell in love with the relaxation period at the end of each class. After an hour spent twisting my limbs into impossible-looking positions, balancing on one leg, and expanding my lungs with deep belly breathing, finally being able to sprawl out on a mat left my muscles buzzing and my mind blissfully silent. I wanted to be able to invoke that silence at will. I wanted to find a solid center in an ever-changing world, a place of peace I would know how to return to when sadness or fear threatened to knock me off balance.

I'd known that the ashram experience would involve entire days where the only things I'd have to do would be to sit in silence, listen to lectures on how to connect with the divine, and practice headstands—which didn't seem so tough after sharing my bed with cockroaches in Kenya. Though I'd understood that it'd be no trip to the spa, I'd thought it'd be invigorating—like plunging into an icy cold pool and then wrapping myself in a warm towel. The big shock, however, was just how much my body and mind were rebelling. I wasn't just uncomfortable, I was miserable. So after a week, instead of beginning each day in peaceful silence, I sat waiting impatiently for the moment meditation would end and the swami would interrupt my internal ramblings by chanting in Sanskrit to Ganesh, the elephant-headed god believed to help remove obstacles on our spiritual path. "*Jaya Ganesha, Jaya Ganesha, Jaya Ganesha Pahimam . . .*"

Even then, my knees ached from sitting cross-legged, and attempting to sing in a language I could hardly pronounce—let alone understand—got old fast. Self-conscious, I'd pretend to participate by silently moving my lips.

I wasn't the only one having a tough time. I noticed that many of the other students had circles under their eyes that matched my own, and they couldn't seem to keep from squirming during meditation either. Sitting on the other side of me was Chloe, a Pilates instructor and badass dancer from Brooklyn with baby blue eyes and endlessly long legs. She'd walked right up to me the very first day while I was sitting on a stone ledge outside the prayer hall during teatime. "I heard you were from Williamsburg, too," she said, plopping down next to me. I know I should have been focusing on life at the ashram, but in a land so unfamiliar, it was comforting to reminisce about running in McCarren Park or hearing bands at Union Pool. Then the bell rang to signal the five-minute grace period between lectures, and we were engulfed in a sea of students not wanting to be marked late.

"Do you kinda feel like we're in a cult?" Chloe had whispered. "Seriously, think about it: They're making us sleep-deprived and hungry so we'll break down. And they keep us so busy so we don't have much time to talk to each other." I *had* worried I'd landed myself in some kind of Indian cult with the militant schedule and guard stationed at the gate. Chloe's admission kept me from thinking I was all alone.

Now I glanced over to see Chloe drawing a block calendar in her notebook. A few years younger than me, she looked girlish with her lanky body, choppy brown hair, and freckles sprinkled across the bridge of her nose. I watched as she carefully placed an *X* over each day we'd passed inside the ashram. "How many days do we have left?" I whispered.

"Twenty-one," she said dejectedly. Another student turned around to give us a stern look, signaling us to start chanting or keep quiet. I could have sworn his eyes were a devilish red, but I attributed it to an overactive imagination—or sleep deprivation.

Straightening my back, I tried to focus instead on the spiritual talk that had just begun. According to Swami, the biggest obstacle on students' spiritual path is a preconceived notion of what yoga *should* be. "Yoga is more than just physical postures—it's about attaining unity of body, mind, and spirit through self-discipline," he told us. We could master self-discipline by practicing the "five points of yoga": proper exercise (the physical yoga postures, such as the tree pose); proper breathing (aka pranayama—controlling your breath helps you better control your mind); proper relaxation (such as lying in savasana, or the corpse pose, at the end of class); proper diet (unprocessed vegetarian food); and positive thinking and meditation. Okay, the message sounded easy enough to digest: ditch my expectations, and rein in my appetites. Learn to control my body in order to learn to control my mind. I knew what I had to do, so why did actually doing it seem like such a challenge?

At long last satsung ended, and we were given a "snack"—a small cup of tea and five grapes or a spoonful of banana chips—before a two-hour yoga class. My stomach rumbled in protest as we practiced downward dogs. I fell asleep during final relaxation, dreaming of eggs and bacon.

Another bell startled me awake, finally signaling that it was time to head to the open-air dining room for breakfast, five hours after we'd first woken up. I was walking with Chloe and Marta, a Polish woman my own age who looked like a china doll with her wide-set blue eyes and high cheekbones.

"Hey, Hooooolly! *Om shanti!*" I turned, hearing the unmistakable giggles of Jen and Amanda. A wave of relief washed over me.

"Hi, guys," I said, waving good-bye to my new friends Chloe and Marta, and heading to the stone ledge where my old friends sat waiting for me. "You skipped morning meditation again. Sinners!"

"We totally slept in. We're just lowly yogi vacationers, so it's not like anyone is taking our attendance," Amanda said happily. She was referring to the fact that teacher trainees were assigned a number and required to check in.

I grabbed their hands, pulling them down the hill toward the dining hall. "Come on, I'm starving!" A sign posted demanded diners "Eat in silence," but first a few hundred people chanted out the same two words, "Hare" and "Krishna," at the top of their lungs. We began both of our two daily meals with that chant, also known as the "Great Mantra," as an act of devotion and to help purify our hearts and minds before we nourished our bodies.

We found three empty spots on a bamboo mat running the length of the dining hall's stone floor. Each spot was set with a plate laid in front of it. Just as we sat, the group chanted "Om" and fell silent, as if someone had unplugged an enormous sound system. The only sound was tin clanking on tin as a yogi on kitchen duty heaped our metal plates with rice.

"What's the first thing you're going to eat when you're out of the ashram?" I whispered to Jen, sounding to myself like a convict about to get out on bail. It was the girls' last day of their weeklong yogi vacation. Though it was, of course, my choice to stay at the ashram, I was a little envious that tomorrow they'd be drinking beers on the beach.

"Silence, pleeeease! Pleeeease eeeat in si-lence!" bellowed the kitchen master, a guy named Vera, wearing wide-legged pants with a silver beard and the soulful eyes of some kind of Indian sage.

Glancing at Jen from the corner of my eye, I didn't think it was my imagination that she looked a bit more, well, calm. Her skin glowed a little brighter, and her mouth had softened somehow. The teacher-training program left us zero free time, so I hadn't been able to find out what had happened after Brian e-mailed her. Had she written him back? Was she okay with everything?

The girl talk would have to wait. Another guy ladled thin lentil stew over my plate and tossed me two chapatis. Before trying it, I'd thought the simple vegetarian food might be bland, but it was actually delicious. Every morsel was unprocessed, and it'd been so long since I'd eaten only foods without additives that I'd forgotten what "fresh" tasted like. After only a week at the ashram, I felt lighter. And Jen wasn't the only one whose skin glowed: I'd noticed my own complexion was clearer and brighter. Eliminating meat, preservatives, and caffeine made me look as if a lightbulb had been turned on beneath my skin.

Then I caught the eye of a woman with straggly blond hair sitting across from me and quickly looked down. Her eyes were puffy, oozy, a deep shade of crimson. Just looking at them made my own eyes burn. Figuring it must be a bad case of pinkeye, I gathered my dishes and went to rinse them at the outdoor sink, extra-careful to scrub my hands.

"I have to report for my karma yoga now. I guess I'll see you both at your last supper tonight," I said reluctantly to Jen and Amanda before heading to the dorms to fulfill my "selfless service." My teacher-training manual said, "Service purifies the

279

mind and makes us realize the Oneness of all." Every yogi was given a duty to help keep us humble, remind us to spend time daily giving back, and carry us closer to God. I thought back to what I'd learned in Sunday school, and remembered a verse in the Bible that said: "The Son of Man did not come to be served, but to serve." Some people were assigned to serve food, some to rake leaves, and some to take attendance.

My selfless service was cleaning toilets. I'd thought my days of scrubbing toilets other than my own had ended in college, after I'd finished a job as a housekeeper in the dorms. But here I was, a decade later and on the other side of the world, back down on my knees brushing a porcelain bowl. Only this time, I was giving thanks that there was actually a bowl to scrub—it was better than having to wash the cement floor surrounding a hole in the ground buzzing with horseflies like the kind I'd used in Kenya. And I was grateful for something I'd never thought to be thankful for before, running water, so I could fill my bucket in the sink rather than having to walk all the way to the river. I'm not sure if toilet cleaning was purifying for my mind (or any other part of me, for that matter), but it proved that, though complaining about getting stuck with a task worthy of *Dirty Jobs* might have been easy to do, it wouldn't make the task go any faster.

After an hour of selfless service came a lecture on the Bhagavad Gita, followed by a rare hour of free time (to do our homework), an hour-and-a-half lecture on the philosophy of yoga, another two-hour yoga class, dinner, and another satsung (meditation-chanting-lecture) before lights-out at 10:20 p.m.

Since sitting still was turning out to be more of a challenge than I'd ever imagined, I was itching for my one constant: running. Being in motion always made it easier for me to clear my mind, the steady pace pounding my awareness out of my head and back into my body. Besides, the swamis had said that a strong body led to a strong mind. Though I felt guilty running here because it probably fit less with hatha yoga's philosophy of easy stretching and more with what our training manual defined as "rajasic, or violent movements that increase adrenaline and stimulate the mind," technically it wasn't an act of rebellion.

Eager to make use of my "free" hour, I threw on a T-shirt and long pants despite the 100 percent humidity to avoid offending the locals with my bare knees, and made my way toward the gates. A guard blocked my path and stared at me skeptically. "Madame, please show your pass."

"I'm sorry, my pass?" I said, confused.

"You need pass from reception." He gestured toward the brick building to his left, bobbing his head side to side. Not wanting to waste a second, I marched up the steps of the building to request written permission from the Indian woman behind the counter.

"Why do you need to leave?" she asked.

"Um, I'd like to go for a walk, please," I said, fudging the truth a bit. I knew from running in South America and Africa that the locals did not see it as a ladylike activity—or maybe anything that purposefully burned calories wasn't a pastime of choice in places where so many suffered from food shortages.

"You better carry a big stick," warned a female voice with a distinctly American accent. I spun around to see Chloe.

"A stick? But why?" I asked. She explained that rabid dogs were rampant in the villages and said she'd heard stories of them tearing into students when they went outside.

"She's right—and I wouldn't go by yourself if I were you," said Marta, who'd walked in with her. Though Chloe and I had instantly shared our personal stories, much the way Shannon and I had on the Inca Trail, Marta's past had remained more of a mystery to me. So I was surprised to learn that this wasn't her first time at the ashram: she'd visited last fall. She'd been part of a group of hundreds of students doing a walking meditation when a dog had sneaked up behind her, sunk its teeth into her calf, and darted away. Marta had had to hightail it to a local hospital for rabies shots.

"Oh, my God! Why did you come back?" I asked after she lifted the leg of her white pants to show me a jagged scar on her otherwise perfect leg.

"Because I believe I still have a lesson to learn. And that's why I'm here—to learn," said Marta. Her and Chloe's friendship was one of opposites: Chloe was an ashram rebel who called bullshit whenever the swami said our egos threatened to sabotage our spiritual paths ("It's not my ego that's making me want to eat instead of meditate. It's those four hours of yoga I did yesterday!"). Marta, on the other hand, was the embodiment of a devotee, never missing class and spending our only day off sprawled in the grass studying the Bhagavad Gita.

I couldn't decide if Marta's return trip was brave or foolhardy. Still, her story reminded me to keep my mind open to absorbing the ashram's lessons (which I hoped included more than just "how to fight off rabid animals").

"Thanks for the advice, but I think I'll take my chances—and a stick!" I said, foolhardy myself. Then I accepted the index-card-sized piece of paper from the Indian woman across the counter and hurried back to the exit.

The truth was, I'd grown accustomed to naysayers worldwide offering all kinds of reasons why I should skip my daily jog. I'd heard every excuse, from male predators to reckless drivers to rockfalls. I pegged their concern as coming more from fear than reality, just as I did my parents' warnings that I'd be a victim of a terrorist attack by straying so far beyond U.S. borders. If I believed them, almost every place in the world was too dangerous to walk around. But I'd found that one of my favorite ways to explore was on foot. I met more locals, came across unexpected gardens, witnessed dozens of impromptu football games, and discovered other moments of daily life that I never would have had the opportunity to see had I quit jogging. I felt isolated from the rest of India inside those ashram gates. And so far, I'd never run into trouble.

After handing my pass to the guard, I flew down the stone steps dotted with heaps of moss and stopped at the bottom to select the sturdiest branch I could find on the forest floor. Leaving the ashram, I thought of the story I'd heard of Siddhartha and wondered what he must have felt when escaping from the royal palace to see how the rest of the world lived. With my iPod in one hand and a stick in the other, I was off.

It was a tropical wonderland, except that there were mountains and lakes instead of beaches and oceans. The dusty earth at the side of the road was speckled with sunlight and shadows from the palm trees that formed a ceiling overhead. The ashram was set on a hill across from a lake and a few miles away from the closest village. The road encircled the lake and led down the hill toward a dam, where small shacks clustered together. I glanced toward the shore. Women in red and yellow saris were scrubbing laundry and laying garments across the flat gray rocks to dry. The hot, moist air filled my lungs. It smelled like moss, cow dung, and burning leaves. I felt my cheeks flush from both my blood pumping and the strength of the sun.

I cruised down the hill and past a school. Children playing with a bouncy ball inside a gated yard stopped and screamed, "Hellooo!" I grinned and waved as my feet pounded the earth and propelled me forward. I crossed a bridge high above the dam and entered a forest on the other side that felt cool and clean. The path was littered with knee-high ferns. I kept moving forward on the dirt road until I came upon the hodgepodge of wooden shacks painted in shades of brown and peacock blue that I'd noticed during the ride to the ashram.

283

Open-air stores sold bananas and cola in glass bottles. Men raised axes to chop wood in front of their homes. Children in bare feet with dirt-smudged faces squealed and ran in circles when they saw me. Women carrying buckets of water on their heads stopped midstep to stare as I met their eyes and smiled, droplets of sweat periodically blinding me.

Completely caught up in exploring village life outside the ashram walls, I almost didn't see the dog running toward me from the roadside. His fur was matted with mud and his fangs were bared, frothy white saliva dripping from his jaws. All that blood running through my veins flooded with adrenaline, and my survival instinct took over.

"Stay back!" I shouted, my voice sounding a few octaves lower than normal and gravelly to my own ears. Oh, man. What had I gotten myself into?

I began waving the stick in front of me like some kind of machete, willing him to keep his distance and too scared to think about how ridiculous I must have appeared. Why did I ever think a measly stick would be any kind of defense against a rabid animal? My move could go down in some kind of Lonely Planet list called "The Stupidest Things to Do When Traveling."

The dog hesitated momentarily before snapping at the stick with his teeth. I slammed the branch on the ground with all the strength I could summon. He cowered, but not for long.

I should have listened to Marta and stayed put. I'd probably have to go to the hospital for rabies shots. As much as I loved running, it was definitely not worth dying for. When the canine advanced upon me again, a man with skin like copper and a black mustache halted his motorbike, picked up a rock, and hurled it at the dog's head. The beast let out a howl as the rock struck his skull with a thud. Passersby had gathered across the street to watch how the scene would unfold, much more interested in the foreigner's debacle than in their chores. Picking up another rock and winding up his arm, the man yelled something I couldn't understand with such force that the dog retreated slightly.

Visibly shaking, I backed away from the mutt, keeping my face toward the animal and the stick in front of me in case the beast made any sudden moves.

"Thank you for saving me!" I said to the man, who was still staring intently at the dog hovering by the roadside. As terrified as I was, it was a moment that filled me with hope. Like the Peruvian priest who had rescued us in the desert in Colca Canyon, it was one of many encounters that reminded me that the world is filled with guardian angels.

He offered a smile. "It's okay to go now," he said, bobbing his head in that now-familiar weeble-wobble way. He was probably in his late twenties, and looked both curious as to why I'd ventured this far into the village and maybe even apologetic for the dog's attempts to attack. I gingerly moved forward just as the dog crouched low to the ground as if he might pounce, teeth once again bared. Even my savior looked unnerved.

"He knows you are different. I think maybe it better you go that way," he said, pointing toward the direction from which I'd come. He didn't need to tell me twice. Thanking him once again, I walked backward down the road for a good quarter mile. Then I turned and sprinted with everything I had toward the ashram, praying that karma was on my side . . . but still gripping my stick the whole way back for protection.

Amanda and Jen sat next to me on my spartan twin bed inside the dorm. Their stuffed backpacks leaned against the wall beside us, an unwelcome reminder that they'd soon be gone, leaving me to navigate the ashram alone.

"Aww, guys, this is the best present ever!" I joked, clutching the bag of contraband chocolate to my chest, practically on a sugar high from simply smelling the sweet stuff.

"We knew you couldn't survive a whole month without dessert," Amanda said, squeezing my shoulders. I was quickly learning that sometimes it's life's little pleasures that can cheer you up the most—and the lack thereof can make each day feel practically torturous.

"You sure you want to stay here, Hol? You could come to Goa with us and just chill on the beach," Jen offered. I wondered what it would be like to go almost a month without the two extensions of myself known as Jen and Amanda. It was the first time we'd be separated during the trip. And though I'd never thought about *not* staying at yoga school just because my friends would rather be at the beach, the fact that I felt so lost without them showed me just how close we'd become. We'd taken care of one another through food poisoning. We'd slept head to toe. We were the first people we talked to in the morning and the last before we fell asleep at night.

I'd told Jen and Amanda about the afternoon's dog incident, and I knew they were worried. But I also knew that, God willing, there'd be many more times to relax on the beach during the trip and that now was not that time for me. Rather, I needed to commit myself to staying and learning. Though to learning what exactly, I still wasn't sure.

"That sounds like heaven right now, but the ashram's Web site clearly states, 'No refunds,'" I said, declining Jen's offer.

"That's probably because anybody in their right mind would ask for their money back," Amanda joked.

I could see from Jen and Amanda's eyes that they were hesitant to leave me behind in this land of elephant-headed deities, swamis spewing lessons of karma, and rabid dogs. But I could also tell, from how they were already leaning toward the exit, that they were aching to break out of yoga camp. "Well, we'd better get outta here before we catch whatever funky foreign bug is going around. Stay away from the sickies, Hol!" Jen teased.

It had turned out that the blonde I'd seen with the swollen, devilish red eyes in the dining hall didn't actually have pinkeye but a supervirus so contagious that almost a third of the students had already caught it. It was painful just to look at, so the infected hid behind sunglasses while everyone else avoided them like the plague. Our teachers didn't seem too surprised by the outbreak. In fact, they'd said that getting sick was normal: all this healthy living purged toxins in the process of purifying our bodies. The swamis said it was typical to feel bad while our bodies eliminated years of accumulated poisons before we felt better. Just to be safe, I'd already stocked up on rosewater eye drops from the on-site ayurvedic clinic, which were supposed to ward off infection but burned like hell.

"I'll be totally fine. What's three more weeks out of my entire life?" I said, my throat unexpectedly closing up. What was the matter with me? I alone had made the choice to come to yoga school. Wasn't *I* the one who'd wanted less partying and more exploration? Wasn't *I* the one who'd preferred learning to relaxation?

The chiming of the bells serendipitously filled the awkward silence. Vowing to toughen up, I quickly hugged Jen and Amanda good-bye. Then I solemnly walked away with the valid-sounding excuse that I didn't want to be marked late for afternoon lecture. The truth was, I just couldn't stand there and watch them walk away first.

❀

CHAPTER EIGHTEEN

Amanda

GOA, INDIA

NOVEMBER

My legs were burning and my bladder nearly bursting by the time I'd sprinted through the streets of Trivandrum and bounded up the steps of the train station. Just knowing that I'd failed to procure a single piece of toilet tissue, napkin, or paper of any kind only amplified the fear that I might actually wet my pants before making it to a bathroom. Jen and I had used up our emergency stash of scratchy one-ply back at the ashram, and in our haste to say good-bye to Holly, we'd forgotten to replenish the coffers.

Pushing through the mob of Indian travelers clustered in groups on the platform, I found my way back to the hard wooden bench where I'd left Jen babysitting our packs minutes earlier. She was gone—and so were the bags. Scanning the length of the station (even at five feet four, I could still see over most heads here), I tried to stay calm. She had to be here somewhere. She wouldn't have gotten on the train to Goa without me—right?

Climbing onto the bench to get a better look (a move that drew serious stares from the people shuffling past), I heard the unmistakable ring of Jen's voice coming through a grate high above my head, on the far side of the wall. Hopping down, I found the door marked LADIES WAITING LOUNGE and pushed my way through.

Within the claustrophobic, ammonia-scented room, a dozen Indian women and their children were chattering and making animated gestures at the spectacle taking place in the adjoining bathroom. Inside, a plump Indian lady spilling out of her blue sari was guiding—or rather strong-arming—a bewildered-looking white girl into a tiny bathroom stall. Jen protested as the woman shoved a hose-and-nozzle contraption into her right hand. The sprayer was similar to the kind attached to most kitchen sinks, but this one was built into the wall near a squat toilet and was clearly meant to wash something other than dishes.

"Amanda! You're back!" Jen looked visibly relieved as she spotted me. "Pass me the TP before I get a demonstration on how to use this thing."

I was just confessing that I'd failed at my one and only shopping objective when the woman wrapped her hand around Jen's and squeezed the nozzle, forcing a stream of water out of the hose and against the tiled wall behind her. Jen jumped, and the spectators in the bathroom giggled at her reaction.

I might have laughed too, except that I had more urgent matters to attend to. Dashing into the stall next to Jen's, I slammed the door and assumed the all-too-familiar position: feet astride the basin, pants gripped firmly in hand (so as not to drag on the floor), legs locked in a seated position. Not the most relaxing way to go, but better now than in a rocking, cockroach-infested train car.

"So, I'm gathering that we don't have any toilet paper?" Jen called from her side of the wall. She paused and asked quietly, "Are you gonna use that sprayer thing?"

I considered the hose to my right and the alternative. I

picked up the sprayer and held it out in front of me. Was there any chance in hell this process could be sanitary? Did it matter at this point?

"I will if you will!" I called back, screwing my eyes shut as I shot myself with a stream of water. Oh! Huh. It was lukewarm. Kind of . . . refreshing, actually. I squeezed the sprayer a couple more times for good measure, then shook my lower half like a puppy drying off after running through a sprinkler.

When Jen and I met outside our respective stalls, we giggled like little kids who'd just learned to use the big-girl bathrooms. The seats of our thin cotton yoga pants were both soaked with water.

"This why you must wear sari," said the woman, motioning to her electric blue outfit and then our backsides. "Make dry more fast."

Jen thanked her for the advice. We snatched up our packs and bolted for the train just before it could chug out of the station without us.

We arrived in Goa on the morning of Thanksgiving Day, a holiday that seemed incongruous to me now. We were eight thousand miles and ten time zones away from home. Normally during the holiday season, I'd be at my aunt's place in Peekskill, New York, helping my family devour a twenty-pound bird and two dozen accompanying side dishes before passing out with the group in front of a football game or the perennial James Bond marathon on Spike TV. Now, as Jen and I bumped along in a rickshaw from the train station to the coast, it was the scent of sandalwood and eucalyptus, not roasting turkey and pumpkin pie, that wafted past our faces on salty gusts of air.

"Hey, did you know that Western hippies used Goa as a hideout back in the sixties?" asked Jen, glancing up from *Lonely*

Planet: Southern India. "To make enough cash to hang around, they sold off their guitars and jeans and stuff, which is how the big flea market in Anjuna got started. Could we check it out on Wednesday?"

"Hmm, let me consult my schedule," I said, scrolling through an imaginary calendar. "I'm pretty busy . . . but wait. I just had some last-minute cancellations, so I'm totally free from right now till, oh, next June. Shall I pencil you in?"

Jen pretended to slug me with the guidebook.

"Hey, watch it. You washed that thing after the cockroach train, right?" I said, shifting around to avoid it. "No more squashed bug parts?"

"Of course. I scrubbed it down with bleach," Jen said, grinning as she taunted me. "Here, why don't you get a closer look?"

As she wiggled the book dangerously close to my face, I felt relieved rather than grossed out. Finally, Jen and I were starting to act like the dorks we'd been in college. Back then, we could utterly amuse ourselves just by racing carts through the aisles of a twenty-four-hour Wal-Mart or by dressing up as a premelt-down Britney Spears (circa "Slave 4 U") and acting out her latest music videos. I guess I'd taken it for granted that our crazy alter egos—Schmanders and Jen-Ba—would rear their heads on this trip, that just the act of leaving New York would reset the tenor of our whole friendship. We used to be silly and wacky. We'd always said that if we'd met as little kids in the sandbox instead of on the first day of college, we would have conquered the playground together. How odd, then, now that we'd decided to conquer the great big real world together, we'd been at odds over the very grown-up issue of *work*.

Leaving the ashram, I was relieved not to be returning to pitches and e-mails. On some level, I'd always understood and even respected where Jen had been coming from about writing on the road. What better time would there be to put our pencils down and experience the world with no distractions? But it wasn't until I'd missed the auditions with the girls at Pathfinder, and remembered the cut of disappointment when an adult let you down, that I really understood the lesson that Jen had been trying to teach me. Working constantly wasn't just driving a wedge between the two of us, it was keeping me from totally immersing myself in the places I was visiting and forging connections with the people I met. What if I returned home just to realize that while I'd been busy becoming a travel writer, I'd actually missed the point of traveling?

When I'd first told Jen I was taking time off from working, I'd imagined that it would be tough to break myself of the compulsion. But once I'd committed to powering down the laptop, going dark was far easier than I'd ever dreamed. It was only after we arrived at Shraddha that I realized my flaw in timing: just as I'd given myself permission to become a free spirit like Holly, I'd entered the one situation where total discipline was required. Now, on the road again, I found myself chomping at the bit, ready to live totally in the present without worrying about my past or my future.

According to the long line of pleasure seekers who'd visited before us, there's no better place to experience the non-spiritual side of India than Goa. While Goa is technically the name of the country's smallest state, most backpackers use the word to refer to the series of choose-your-own-adventure beach villages strung along the coastline. Each town has its own series of quirks and eccentricities, and offers a specific vice to match the vibe.

Judging by the scenery rolling outside the window of our rickshaw, Jen and I had just entered Summer of Love territory—

or the Indian approximation of it. Squat bamboo buildings lining the dusty streets were washed in psychedelic pastels; women hawked broomstick skirts, patchouli incense, and wooden prayer beads from behind rickety tables; tree-house cafés beckoned passersby with chalkboard advertisements for everything from garlic naan to falafel wraps to barbecue chicken pizza.

"Where are we meeting Sarah again?" Jen asked.

"Some place called Magdalena's Guesthouse," I said, double-checking a note scribbled in the margin of my journal. "She said she'd get there right after lunch."

Sarah, one of the few friends from home we'd end up connecting with on the road, was a savvy, outgoing journalism student I'd advised during my final months at the magazine. She and I had met during her internship and stayed in touch even after she'd returned to school and I'd made my ungraceful departure from the job. Then a couple months after her graduation—just as Jen, Holly, and I were launching the second leg of our trip—Sarah had e-mailed to say that she'd accepted a position as an HIV educator for an NGO in Mumbai. Would we, by any chance, be heading to India during our travels? Once we realized that our paths would overlap, Sarah and I had immediately scheduled a reunion in a location we were both dying to check out: Goa.

When the driver dumped Jen, me, and our dusty yoga mats by the front entrance of Magdalena's, I wasn't sure we'd come to the right place. The cluster of unpainted concrete buildings was guarded unconvincingly by a pack of malnourished dogs. Clotheslines strung across the yard were straining under the weight of still-sopping laundry.

Crunching up the gravel driveway, I was relieved to turn a corner and spot Sarah sitting on a porch, sipping a Kingfisher beer alongside a pair of scruffy-looking guys.

"Oh my goooooooiiiiid!!" Sarah was almost a blur as she

293

streaked across the yard and threw her arms around both of us. "You guys made it! I'm so glad that you're here!"

"Merry Turkey Day, lady!" I said, grinning at her enthusiasm. I'd yet to experience Sarah on any other channel besides high-octane, super-unleaded outgoing.

"So, you're gonna *love* our room," she said, grabbing our daypacks and leading us back toward the porch where she'd been sitting. "I'm not really sure, but I think Norman Bates might have actually checked me into the room earlier."

"Oh, jeez. That bad?" asked Jen.

"Well, we've got one exposed bulb, a few gross mattresses, and that's about it. Oh, and I'm not sure if the door actually locks. But if you hate it, we can totally find somewhere else to stay, no problem."

"Don't take off yet," said one of the guys, a lanky British backpacker in board shorts. He braced his tanned feet against the railing. "You won't find a better deal on the beach."

"Yeah, you can't really argue with three quid a night," added his buddy, a sandy-haired guy in a sweaty gray Quicksilver T-shirt. "Besides, you've got us right next door to look out for you, which I reckon sweetens the deal."

Sarah shook her head and introduced us. "Amanda and Jen, this is Cliff and Stephen—our extremely modest new neighbors."

Stephen, the guy in the gray shirt, held out a pair of beers as a welcome offering, and we ditched our bags in order to accept them. Within the first few sips, we learned that the guys were taking an extended vacation from their finance jobs in London. They both had a full six weeks off—with pay.

"Really? Why did you choose to stay *here* then?" I blurted without thinking.

Cliff didn't take offense and said that they preferred über-cheap hostels to pricey upscale accommodations. "How could we bump into cool travelers like you girls if we're stuffed away in some swank hotel suite?"

If I'd had any doubt about whether I'd choose a four-star room over a dilapidated, potentially rodent-infested guesthouse, one look inside our bathroom settled the debate. We were just contemplating who'd brave the mildewed shower first when Stephen knocked to let us know that he and Cliff were headed to the beach. Any interest in joining? The three of us were sporting more than twenty-four hours' worth of travel grime, and, considering the alternative, a dunk in the surf seemed an ideal way to come clean.

Vagator Beach bore little resemblance to the ones we'd visited in Rio, sugary strips that doubled as catwalks for Brazil's most beautiful bodies. Here the scene was anything but showy. Stands of shaggy palms hemmed a fat, croissant-shaped slice of burnished sand. Arcs of colorful beach umbrellas shaded lounge chairs in front of thatch-roofed cafés. Waiters delivered slender glasses filled with mango lassis and rum punches to tourists. It was a pretty idyllic scene, except for one thing: smack in the middle of everything, a group of fat sun worshipers had beached their large brown bodies across a prime section of the sand, utterly indifferent to the people maneuvering around them.

"They're actually considered sacred here," whispered Sarah as we tiptoed past. "No one would even think of trying to kick them off."

It was the happiest, most satisfied-looking herd of cows I'd ever seen.

As soon as we edged around the holy mooers, women carrying baskets heavy with fruit and girls laden with fabrics, garlands, and jewelry pressed into us, chattering urgent sales pitches as they moved and jingled.

"Please, miss, you very beautiful, but more beautiful with

scarf! Or maybe you try bracelet? Or necklace? No have to buy now. Just try. Free to try."

We didn't say anything, but my heart lurched. Many of these girls were even younger than the ones at Pathfinder. What was the right thing to do here? Step around them, treat them as if they were invisible—or hand over a few rupees and create an incentive for the girls to keep selling?

"Aye, miss, maybe one-a these fine skirts for ya? Right good, they are." I couldn't help myself—I stopped in my tracks as I heard the line delivered in a perfect British Cockney accent. Turning around, I saw that it came from a spindly-limbed teenage girl. She held up an armload of tie-dyed fabric twisted into ropes. "Beautiful skirt for beautiful lady?"

I shook my head, but she didn't break her stride and followed me across the beach. When the other women peeled away, off to find more pliable targets, she stuck around and followed our group to a café set up under a perky green-and-white awning. I wasn't going to buy anything from her, but figured it couldn't hurt to get her something to eat.

Rebecca, as she introduced herself, seemed thrilled to be the center of attention and chattered on about her life as one of Goa's beach girls. She explained that since her parents had passed away a year earlier, she'd been selling trinkets and clothes on Vagator to support her little brother and sister, to raise enough money to feed them and send them to school. It was tough going out every day and asking people to buy things, but at least the holiday season was approaching: that meant more customers and more sales.

"Do you ever get harassed by the people on the beach?" Sarah asked. "Are you ever afraid to walk home after dark?"

"Sometimes. That's why me and the other selling ladies, we team up and walk home together. One time a man tried to touch me, and I stood right up and told him to bugger off!" she shrieked, reenacting the scenario.

I wasn't sure whether the story about her parents was true or not, but I definitely believed one thing: Rebecca was quite the little fighter. I hoped that her instincts would somehow keep her safe from the danger she faced daily by approaching random strangers on the beach. I could imagine how easy it would be for someone to snatch her up, carry her away. I wondered if anyone would go looking for a missing fifteen-year-old.

As she finished her food, I looked through my purse to see if I had enough change left to buy one of the bracelets she was selling, but she waved me off.

"If you don't got the money today, no worries."

"Will you be here tomorrow?" I asked, pressing a few rupees into her hand anyway.

"Sure, I'm gonna be here tomorrow, and tomorrow after that. You see me, and then you buy skirt, bracelet, whatever you like. Just remember me. Remember Rebecca."

Our newly formed crew of five decided to celebrate our American, Indian (and British) Thanksgiving in the exact same spot we'd eaten lunch. Between rounds of tropical fruit cocktails and semideep conversations (discussions such as the need to enforce child labor laws in India and the ever-popular topic of the lack of mandatory vacation time in America), midday transitioned into languid afternoon. The five of us took turns cooling down by running into the surf, commandeering the trampoline that had been set up in front of the restaurant for little kids, and walking along the hard-packed sand to an old fort at the end of the beach. We started a game of volleyball, a sport I've always been terrible at, but today, the sweatier and sandier I got, the more liberated I felt (and better I played!). I couldn't have chosen a better week to immerse myself into the world of the vagabond backpacker.

"Hey, Jen, I think you might have been right about something," I confessed as we walked back to our table with Sarah and collapsed into the chairs. "This is *definitely* more fun than hanging out in some smelly old Internet café."

"Really? Are you sure? I mean, I saw a few on the main road into town," she teased. "You could still squeeze in a couple hours of work before you go to bed."

"Screw it. I'm over it," I said, suddenly possessive of my newfound free time.

"Okay, ladies, where are we going out tonight?" asked Cliff as he and Stephen returned from the beach. "What's the plan?"

Stephen explained that on any given night in Goa, you could party at one of dozens of bars, lounges, and nightclubs—and over the past couple of weeks, the guys had explored them all. They'd smoked hookahs in the back room at Tito's, gotten bottle service at Shore Bar, raved to trance anthems at Paradiso, and gone skinny-dipping with a cast of hundreds in the swimming pool at Club Cubana. The pool wasn't open tonight, but the guys offered to take us somewhere even better to check out the Goan underground culture. We all agreed to let them lead the way and headed back to shower and change before our big night out.

After a couple of hours of barhopping, I was ready to raise the stakes and go dancing, but was shocked when both Jen and Sarah begged off.

"Are you guys kidding?" I was stricken. "You don't want to stay out?"

"Well, yeah, we do, but maybe not tonight." said Jen. "I mean, we've been drinking all afternoon and . . . I think Sarah and I are just wiped out."

"Tomorrow we'll be rock stars, I promise," said Sarah.

I was disappointed, but I knew there was no sense in pushing them. Cliff, Stephen, and I put the girls in a rickshaw and headed to the next location.

About an hour later, we approached the entrance of Paradiso, a massive multitiered nightclub built into the limestone cliffs perched above the Arabian Sea. Slipping past the velvet rope, we walked under a darkened passageway cut through the rock and emerged into an outdoor section bathed in lantern light.

At our feet, local women had covered nearly every inch of ground with thistle mats. Most were arranging candy and mints for sale or brewing small pots of chai on miniature burners. Clubgoers wearing thin cotton shirts, loose pants, and colorful sundresses were spread out on the mats, lounging on their elbows, smoking hand-rolled cigarettes, and sipping cocktails from little plastic cups. The unmistakable, pervasive aroma of hash mixed with sweet tobacco hung like incense over the crowd.

The club was aboveground, but the dense saltiness of the air, the exposed rock walls, and the swath of darkness gave it the feel of an enormous grotto. The skittering electronic beats of Goa trance swelled and reverberated through the cavernous space, and the revelers moved to the waves of sound like an enormous jellyfish. Watching from the fringes, I felt energy firing through my muscles and out my fingertips. We worked our way into a crush of bodies, moving for what seemed like forever to a song that had no beginning or end.

"So, here's what I'm thinking . . ." Stephen shouted over the music as he surveyed the crowd. "I'm not really sure if I can handle this place tonight if all we're doing is drinking, you know?"

Cliff nodded in agreement, wiping his forehead against a T-shirt sleeve to clear the sweat. "Totally, man. It's a full-on rave in here."

"Well, if you guys are down, a friend of mine thinks that she can get us something a little stronger." Stephen looked directly at me. "You know what I mean, right?"

Yes, I knew what he meant. Thanks to Jen's Lonely Planet

research, I'd learned that drugs were as easy to come by in Goa as cups of chai and that travelers down them just as casually. I hadn't specifically planned to delve into that side of the local culture, but I didn't want to stand in the way either. I shrugged in response to the question, which the guys took to mean that I was down with whatever.

We walked back upstairs to the area where the chai ladies sat on their mats, and Stephen introduced me to Anna, a skinny German chick with steel-wool dreadlocks, chewed-up finger-nails, and a raggedy cotton skirt that clung to her bony hips.

"Hey. This is my boyfriend, Jack," she said, motioning toward the first beefy Indian guy I'd seen. "He's gonna come with us."

"Come with us? Come with us where?" I asked as we started moving toward the exit. "Where are we going?"

"Not far," said Anna breezily. "Just gotta make a stop to visit my guy."

I grabbed Cliff's forearm and sent him a "what's the deal?" expression.

"I know where we're going," he assured me, grabbing my hand. "It's okay."

Anna led our group out the front doors of Paradiso, past the electric lights, and up a road that gradually narrowed into a dirt path. Walking away from the beach, we entered a section of Goa where I was sure backpackers weren't meant to tread. In the watery light of the moon, I could just make out the outlines of tiny shelters, roughly constructed shacks made from wood, cardboard, and corrugated tin. It was some kind of shantytown village tucked away among the trees. What were we doing here?

Up ahead, without fear or hesitation, Anna was shoving back the plastic tarps and gauzy thin fabric that covered the door-ways, hissing the name of some guy called Devraj. I could hear muffled sounds and voices inside the shacks, but Anna ignored them. She was a woman on a mission. I willed myself not to freak out, convinced that her raspy voice would act as a bullhorn beckoning local police looking to make an easy bust.

To my relief, Anna finally found the guy she'd been looking for. Together, the five of us ducked our heads and crossed the threshold of a sagging hovel, entering a room lined with emaciated men draped across one another like a litter of abandoned kittens. As we made our presence known, they stirred, rubbing their sleepy eyes and staring at us like the weird white specters we were. The air here was as dense and humid as the inside of a dishwasher and laced with the musky, spicy aroma of too many bodies pressed up against one another.

Devraj, a shrunken man with a tangled gray beard and hollow eyes, wasted no time getting down to business. "You want red pill or blue pill?"

He knelt down before us, holding out the options in gnarled hands thick with calluses, an ersatz Morpheus in my increasingly bizarre Indian-*Matrix* world.

Cliff paid $5 apiece for a couple of the red pills (which Anna had assured us would be "mellow" and "pure") and gave one to me. For a second, I was convinced this had all been an elaborate setup. Any second now, the cops would step out of the darkness and haul the idiot Westerners (or maybe just me?) off to prison to rot.

I stared sharply as Anna and Jack, then Cliff and Stephen casually tossed back their pills and chased them with a single bottle of beer passed among them. Okay, so we weren't getting arrested, but still . . . did I want to do this? I could have backed out—pretended to take the pill, dropped it on the ground, handed it off to the dirty German girl, and just run back toward the ocean, but I stared at the pill, torn between fear and fascination. What would happen, exactly, if I just stopped thinking so hard about everything and took it?

"I think maybe you better do half that thing." Anna paused long enough to drag off the cigarette she and Jack were sharing. "That shit is pretty strong."

I glanced down at the red pill in my hand, then back at her. Gouging my thumbnail into the butterfly stamp in the top, I watched as it split cleanly along the wings. I sat there, contemplating the halves, trying to figure out which of the two was the smaller one. Willing my brain to divorce itself from all rational thought, I grabbed the bottle of beer from Jack's outstretched hand and allowed myself to get sucked down the rabbit hole.

Anna had not lied—the stuff we'd taken mellowed me out completely. The next few hours passed in a warm, incandescent haze. Once back at Paradiso, our group leased a parcel of straw mat real estate from one of the chai ladies. As the first waves of sensation hit, I looked up at the Indian woman's face and swore I could feel her disapproval. She poured the milky brew into tin cups, and I watched intently as the liquid landed smoothly in the bottom. Nobody drank.

As the club filled, people came to join us, friends of Anna's, strangers who wanted sweets, randoms seeking a place to chill. We talked with our new friends, conversations about extremely important issues, none of which I can remember now. I gazed across the endless landscape of the concrete floor, carpets affixed like patches across its bald face, and wondered what the other groups of people were talking about at that moment. What were they thinking? I wanted to find out, absolutely needed to know what was being discussed, but I was superglued to my spot, alternating between incredible swells of warmth and feelings of being sucked into the floor.

Minutes or hours later, I didn't know, I looked around, glancing at all of the strange faces. I recognized nobody. Where were the dreadlocks? Where were the other new friends I'd just met? How could they all be gone? My watch read 3:08 a.m.

Streaks of reality started to pierce the fog. Cliff and Stephen had already gone home—they'd tried to take me along, but I'd told them I wanted to stay. I couldn't find Anna and Jack, and even if I could, then what? Arrange a ride with my drug dealers? It was the middle of the night, and I had no idea how to get back. Then I remembered the rickshaws parked in front of the club.

I walked outside, in the direction of the drivers, and was almost instantly mobbed. Men were tugging at my clothes, snatching at my body, loudly demanding, pulling, and insisting that I get inside their vehicle. I could hear myself shriek as I reeled backward toward the entrance.

Almost at once, things turned completely lucid, and I immediately regretted that I'd stayed alone at some nightclub on a beach in India until after 3 a.m. without a safe way to get back. I had no cell phone, no number for our guesthouse, no way to get in touch with anyone who could rescue me. I returned to the club, frantically searching the floors for a face I recognized.

Several desperate minutes passed as I lurched between bodies. In a crowd filled with young people, I was hopelessly alone. I started questioning groups of girls—"Are you leaving soon? What town are you going to?"—aware that I must sound psychotic. Most shrugged or ignored me altogether. Then, from the corner of my eye, I spotted a guy I'd been chatting with for a few hazy minutes on one of the straw mats. He was in the middle of a conversation, but I interrupted anyway.

"So, hey. Hi. Remember me? I was wondering if I could talk you into coming home with me tonight?" I asked, racing through the words. "No . . . not like come home in *that* way, I just mean . . . look, I've lost my friends and I can't take a rickshaw back alone. Could you do me a huge favor and ride with me back to Vagator?"

He shrugged. His hostel was a few streets away, and he wasn't ready to take off.

"Look, I'll give you every rupee I have left in my bag if you'll just ride back with me. I promise. Everything I have after I pay the cab fare."

He looked about as enthusiastic as a guy facing a vasectomy. It took several minutes and a visual confirmation of the cash—worth about $20—but I somehow dragged him outside and together we plunged into the hornet's nest of rickshaw drivers. With a guy at my side the transaction and ride home passed without incident.

As I slid out of my seat and onto the ground, the club guy got out behind me.

"Oh, yeah! Here's the money. Thanks for riding with me," I said, shoving the crumpled bills in his hands. He took it but didn't make a move to leave.

"Well, I figured now that I'm here, maybe I should come in with you?" he asked.

I didn't even respond. Spinning around, I sprinted inside the front gate of Magdalena's, past the dogs sprawled out on the driveway, and straight to my room (which, thankfully, my friends hadn't figured out how to lock). Once inside, I shoved the door closed and collapsed next to Sarah in bed. Without bothering to change out of my party clothes, I slipped under the sheet and pulled the grungy top cover up around my shoulders.

It was a warm night, but I was shaking.

T he hangover I had the next day couldn't quite compete with the one I'd had senior year of college (the night I learned that chugging Jägermeister and Goldschläger shots straight from the bottle is a recipe for alcohol poisoning), but it was definitely in the top five.

I was so mortified to be passed out, stinking like a distillery, that I dragged my ass to the beach with Sarah and Jen. Lying on a chair with a towel draped over my head, I felt a little better but apologized to Sarah over and over again. I'd once been her supervisor at the magazine, and now I was a quivering, nauseated mess who'd screwed up royally the night before. Had I totally let her down?

"Of *course* not," she insisted. "First of all, let's get one thing straight. We are way, way past the intern-boss thing. We're just really good friends now, you know that—right?"

I tried to nod my agreement.

"And second of all—and this you may not realize—you *deserve* to have a good time. You really do. Just remember that everyone goes a little nuts at some point, and considering how your night went, you must have been overdue for a serious bender."

"I can vouch for that," added Jen.

"Thanks, Sar," I said, grateful that she was trying to make me feel better. "I just feel bad that I'm such a wreck. I guess I'm not the same buttoned-up girl you used to know."

"And seriously, thank God for that. You know, I always thought you were a pretty cool chick and I totally respected you as a mentor, but yesterday—it was like hanging out with a different person than I knew back in New York."

"Is that a bad thing?" I asked, and Sarah laughed.

"No way! Now it's like you've finally given yourself permission to just let go," she said. "Trust me—that's a good thing."

I smiled underneath the terry cloth and felt something bump up against my chair.

"Aye, it's my America girls! How ya going today?" I recognized the voice as Rebecca's. I was suddenly mortified all over again, especially when she lifted the edge of my towel and smiled when she saw my expression.

305

"Ooooh . . . rough night?" she asked in a way that made me want to laugh and cringe at the same time. No fifteen-year-old girl should understand the meaning of that phrase.

Jen jumped in and explained that I'd eaten some bad chicken tandoori and wasn't feeling well, which Rebecca seemed to accept.

"Well, I won't be botherin' ya long, just wanted to say 'ello . . . and oh, I made something for you."

I squinted upward and saw that she was holding out a little fabric bracelet, the kind with the knots that I used to make by the dozens as a kid. This one was done in a chevron pattern of scarlet red, orange, and white. One again, she waved me off when I tried to reach for my cloth bag, saying that she'd made it for me as a token for lunch the day before. I thanked her back a few times, clutching the friendship bracelet as she dashed away from our chairs, sprinting like a kid on her way to recess. I watched as she disappeared down the slope of the beach, off to sell more trinkets to tourists, now feeling more awed than anything else. My new buddy Rebecca had a harder job—and a tougher life—than any young girl should have to endure, but she still ran, laughing as though she didn't have a care in the world.

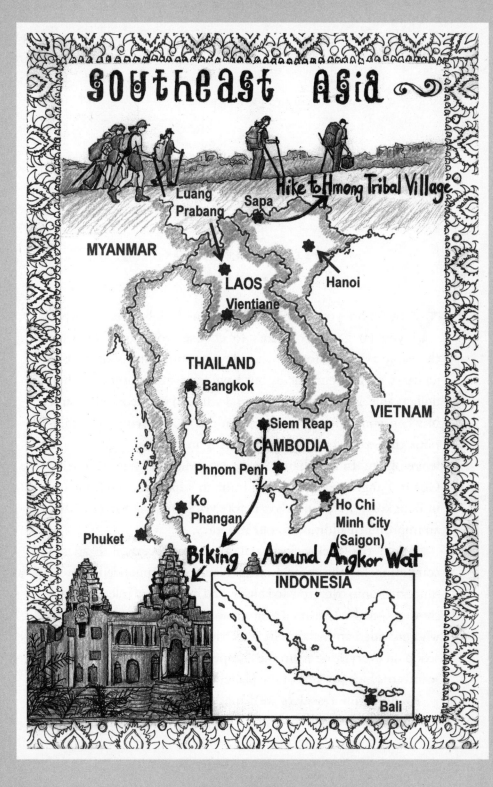

CHAPTER NINETEEN

Jen

VIENTIANE, LAOS

DECEMBER

You know you're an overly seasoned globe trekker when you (a) have six outfits to choose from, but you wear the same two, (b) forget what day or even what month it is, (c) carry several currencies but have long since forgotten their dollar value, and (d) have to remind yourself what country you're in when you wake up in the morning. Considering our ambitious time zone crossings, this last item was our biggest challenge of late. In less than a week, Amanda and I had gone from Goa to Bangalore, flown from India to Thailand, and hung out in Bangkok for a couple days before voyaging eastward to Laos, an impromptu addition to our itinerary.

While the backpacker trail guaranteed certain hassles—competing for the same Lonely Planet–recommended hostels, squeezing onto overcrowded buses, and learning to tolerate frosty showers—it also bestowed a hip crowd of international vagabonds who provided an instant circle of friends and gave us the inside scoop on everything from the cheapest meals to common tourist scams to which pockets of the planet were most worth exploring.

Many fellow travelers we'd met in India had also explored Southeast Asia, so Amanda and I peppered them with questions about must-see sites and how to best divide our time in that region. Many were quick to tout the southern Thai islands, Cambodia's Angkor Wat, and Halong Bay in northern Vietnam, but the one location that rolled most enthusiastically off everyone's tongues was Laos. And it was far from a "it's a cool place if you can fit it in" or "I had fun there, but you could skip it" reaction. Anyone who'd spent even a modicum of time in Laos professed their undying love and devotion and suggested we immediately run, not walk, to the closest border.

Despite a steady influx of tourists in recent years, Laos was still a fairly untapped travel resource and represented a chance to legitimately fall off the beaten track. As one of only five lingering Communist states—along with China, Vietnam, Cuba, and North Korea—Laos had been open to foreign visitors only since the mid-1990s. So although Amanda and I had less than two weeks before we had to meet our friend Beth in Phuket, we were determined to squeeze in a field trip to Laos, starting with the country's capital, Vientiane.

Armed with spare passport photos for our visa application, a secondhand *Lonely Planet: Southeast Asia on a Shoestring*, and a wad of Thai baht to exchange, Amanda and I hopped an overnight train bound for Nong Khai on the northern border of Thailand. Fortunately, the Thai rail system was as delightfully quiet and orderly as the Indian one had been chaotic. Exhausted from our whirlwind cross-continent jaunt, the second our heads hit the plastic bunk pillows, we were down for the count and peacefully remained that way for nearly ten hours.

With promises of crumbling French mansions, bougainvillea-shaded sidewalks, ancient Buddhist monasteries, and steaming noodle stalls awaiting us in Vientiane, Amanda and I were as keyed up as little kids at Disney World as we stood in line for our Thailand exit stamps. After journeying over the Friendship Bridge across the Mekong River and into Laos, we exchanged two photos and $35 U.S. for a thirty-day visa. A stoic official in a Soviet-style uniform inspected our bags, then waved us through to the other side, where we teamed up with a few other tourists and negotiated a cheap passage into the city. Forty-five bumpy minutes later, our van veered off the dusty highway and onto a sunny, tree-lined boulevard.

Rolling into downtown Vientiane, we were met by an enchanting blend of French Provincial architecture and Eastern religion. Fresh-faced vacationers sipped cappuccinos at sidewalk cafés, shopkeepers charmed new arrivals with handmade silks and intricately carved Buddha statues, and monks with freshly shaven heads and tangerine robes streamed from golden temple gates. Everything and everyone around us moved with a warm, syrupy tempo as if time had slowed. Following suit, we strapped our packs tightly to our backs and began a leisurely glide down the main road, returning the stream of resident grins and warm *"Sabaydee"* greetings.

Our first order of chillness: sampling traditional cuisine at Makphet ("chili pepper"), a snug eatery with ivory floor tiles, lime green walls, and open glass doors. Settling at a hardwood cherry table, we were immediately greeted by not one but three friendly servers in pinstripe aprons who presented us with tall glasses of ice water with fresh mint leaves and an extensive menu of popular local dishes, all prepared fresh daily.

"Hey, look at this, all of the salads come with a bacteria-free guarantee. And they have rice pudding. I love this place," Amanda said.

Amanda knew as well as I did that after months of brushing our teeth with tap water and sampling endless street cart cuisine, our stomachs were coated with cast iron. But the dessert part was a definite plus.

"I know. It's adorable. I'm so excited we decided to come. And I can't wait to explore this town," I said, taking a much-needed sip of the cool drink.

"This is your first time in our country?" the most smiley of the waiters (if that was possible) inquired. "We very much welcome you to Vientiane. I am Sommai," he added, asking us our names before taking our order.

We soon learned from Sommai that there was more to Makphet than met the eye. Run by Friends International, the restaurant trained homeless youths to cook and wait tables as well as afforded them an education and other necessary skill sets. Having learned that Laos was one of the poorest countries in Asia, we were happy to splurge on a multicourse meal and leave an extra-large tip. A tiny gesture, sure, but rather than give money to beggars—something guidebooks and travelers generally warned against doing—we much preferred putting our tourist dollars to good work through reputable nonprofits. In many developing nations we'd visited, it was fast becoming a trend for guesthouses, retailers, and cafés to double as charitable organizations, so any time the girls and I could sleep, shop, and eat for a good cause, we did.

After an unhurried feast of noodles with bean sprouts and bell peppers, pork-stuffed cabbage with chili sauce, sweet mangoes, and flavored *kah-feh nyen* (iced coffee) drinks, Amanda and I hit the warm and welcoming streets in search of lodging. We strolled past stands of dangling bananas, flower garlands, and vibrant watercolor elephant prints until we found a charming cottage with teal clapboards that advertised doubles for 50,000 kip. We'd yet to procure local currency from the one ATM in the entire country (which was fortunately in Vientiane), but the owner was happy to give us a room key explaining that to "rest now, pay later" would be fine. For the bargain price of about $5 U.S., we were given a surprisingly tidy and spacious abode with floral curtains, matching bedspreads, and a sidewalk view.

Sprawling across one of the twin mattresses, I closed my eyes for a few seconds. When I opened them, Amanda was gone. Fumbling through my bag to find my watch, I stared at the dial for almost five minutes before my brain finally churned out the correct time zone. Wow, I'd been asleep for an hour. I sprang to my feet, in a panic until I remembered there was nowhere I had to go and nothing I had to do. Man, I seriously love my life, I thought, walking over to the window to pull up the shade. Soft rays of light streamed in, illuminating a note next to my pillow that I'd missed: "Jenny B, Didn't want to wake you. Went to get money and check out the town. Be back in an hour or so! ☺ AP"

Content to wait in the cozy room, I piled a few pillows against the headboard and pulled out my latest obsession from a secondhand book exchange, *But Inside I'm Screaming*, about a broadcast journalist who has a nervous breakdown on camera and checks herself into a four-star psychiatric center. Lost in a world of delusional outbursts, bed checks, and pill cocktails in paper cups, I didn't notice the lock turn.

"Dude, wait till you see the wad of cash I have," Amanda said, bursting through the door.

"Jesus! You scared the hell out of me."

"Oh, sorry. But you've gotta look at this," Amanda replied, pulling a stack of blue-and-white bills out of her purse and splaying them across her bed.

"I seriously feel like a drug dealer," she added before dramatically pulling her sunglasses down over her eyes, falling on her back, and rolling around in the money.

Though she'd probably withdrawn max $200, kip notes were dispensed only in small denominations, which created quite a conspicuous cash flow scenario for Westerners.

I laughed. "Umm, looks like the pusher got into the goods again. Damn it, Pressner, didn't we discuss that it's bad for business when you do that? What *have* you been up to for the past hour, anyway?"

"Nothing," she said in a mysterious tone before leaping to her feet and jumping up and down on the bed, a signature Amanda move (along with dramatic poses in front of fruit stands and Michael Jackson's *Thriller* vs. *Ace Ventura: Pet Detective* dance-offs). While I'd seen her perform this ritual dozens of times—from our freshman-year college dorm to our first night in Peru—this particular encore symbolized so much more to me: my quirky friend was back and better than ever. It was such a relief to see her having fun and not rushing off to an Internet café to work.

In theory, Amanda, Holly, and I should've been able to pursue our own trip goals *and* peacefully coexist. But considering we ate, slept, breathed, brushed our teeth, and peed all within ten yards of one another, the reality of our on-the-road lives was that everything one of us did affected the other two. All in all, we'd done a remarkable job at balancing our individual needs with those of the group's, and 95 percent of the time we got along flawlessly. But my old habits of intermittent eye rolling and underhanded comments could not have died a slower, more painful death. It wasn't until our fight in Kenya that I had finally nipped my attitude problem in the bud. After all, it had been Amanda who'd orchestrated the trip and started our blog, so who was I to give her a hard time about working?

The irony was that somewhere between my ashram mini-awakening, the blissful Goa vacation, and my current love affair with Laos, I'd let go of my desire to control our trip priority list. I mean, who was I to tell Amanda and Holly how to live their lives? It wasn't as if I didn't have plenty of unresolved issues of my own. Maybe it was time I learned to stand on my own two feet a little. Use my year abroad as a chance to get over my fears

313

of being alone, maybe even travel solo for a few days (or at least a few hours). Just because Amanda was my best friend didn't mean we had to do everything together, right?

Sitting there in our sunny Vientiane guesthouse without a care in the world, I considered sharing my new outlook with Amanda. But then again, why ruin a classic bed-hopping moment with an intense conversation? So I did the next best thing: leapt up on my own mattress and jumped alongside her until we were both out of breath.

Before long, Amanda and I had melted into Laos's tranquil culture like marshmallows in hot chocolate, whiling away our first Vientiane days exploring sidewalk stalls for rattan and coconut shell jewelry and delicate camisoles, reading under the shade of sprawling bodhi trees, chatting with the owners of trendy boutiques, and snapping gleaming shots of the gilded stupa of Pha That Luang at dusk. Just when we thought life couldn't get any better, we discovered an unexpected path to paradise: massages.

Despite the abundance of cheap parlors on every corner, most expats and fellow travelers we'd met in town swore by an herbal sauna and outdoor massage center in the woods, where you could get a luxurious steam and sixty-minute rubdown for $4. Intrigued by their tales, Amanda and I flagged down a tuk-tuk (auto rickshaw) driver and asked him to take us to Wat Sok Pa Luang, the mystical forest temple (*wat paa*) that marked the "spa" entrance.

After a dusty thirty-minute journey past fields of flower and rice paddies, our "little motor vehicle that could" finally chugged to a stop at a gilded archway flanked by banana trees, and Amanda and I were on our own in the secluded countryside.

Following a convoluted series of hand-scribbled posters and several ambiguous gestures from resident monks, we wound our way down the long gravel road past modest huts, frayed hammocks, and the occasional barnyard animal. We'd just about given up when we heard a voice from above directing us where to go. "You want steam and massage? Come this way!"

Nestled thirty feet above us in the treetops was a makeshift wooden platform on stilts, packed to the brim with tourists in bathing suits and silk robes. Climbing slowly up a rickety staircase, Amanda and I fell into line behind fellow hedonists waiting to sign up for their treatments. A rosy-cheeked woman with a clipboard sat perched on a wooden bench near the rail doling out silk wraps. After ducking behind a curtain to change out of our clothes, we entered an attached outhouse structure that served as the sauna.

A wave of sweet, hot steam smacked us in the face as we blindly felt around for an empty bench, tiptoeing carefully around the hissing coals packed in pots on the floor and trying desperately not to sit on someone else's lap by mistake. We finally found an empty board and reclined back against the wall prepared to sweat off at least ten pounds. It didn't take long before we were puddles on the floor, infused from head to toe with a magic blend of kaffir lime, basil, lemongrass, rosemary, mint, camphor bark, and what smelled like a "special" herb to give guests an extra kick. Hey, who were we to deny the effectiveness of ancient Lao healing practices?

When we couldn't stand the scorching temperature any longer, we stumbled outside and flopped down on one of six massage cots squished inches apart on the back porch, doing our best to avoid the web of sweaty limbs splayed across the communal space. For the next hour, we were pulled and stretched like ropes of saltwater taffy by energetic young masseurs. Snaps, crackles, and pops filled the air as our body parts, made extraordinarily malleable by the steam bath, were adjusted one by one and then kneaded back into their somewhat original position. What looked and sounded like medieval torture was actually the most blissful and satisfying massage I'd received on the road— and constantly lured by the rock-bottom price tags in South America, Kenya, and India, I'd tallied quite a few. Pumped full of endorphins, I slurred a gracious thank-you to my therapist and floated over to the waiting area, where Amanda already sat sipping hot tea and chatting with one of the women who managed the place.

"That was so amazing. We have to come back tomorrow," I said.

"I know. I wish we'd found out about this place earlier. This is Noy, by the way. She was just telling me that her aunt, who is a Buddhist nun, was the one who created this spa."

Noy's cheeks glowed brightly, no doubt from the healing effects of the steam, as she continued to fold the spa's modesty sarongs against her slightly rounded belly.

"Hope you enjoy the massage," Noy said, motioning for me to help myself to a cup of tea.

"Sooo much. Thank you, uhh, *kop chai*," I replied, sinking down on the bench next to Amanda.

"We leave the money here with you, right?" Amanda asked, doing her best to air-dry the kip note she held in her hand.

"Yes, I take it. Thank you. And I have your address at hotel so breakfast at café next door in the morning. Eight-thirty is okay, then?"

"Sure, I'll meet you there," Amanda replied. Noy nodded and smiled before walking away.

"Hot date tomorrow?" I asked.

"Long story. I'll tell you later," Amanda said as Noy returned with our change.

After settling the unfathomably inexpensive bill, we joined

the crowd of other satisfied customers walking back toward the entrance of the monastery. As we stood waiting to hail a passing tuk-tuk, Amanda and I were pulled into a conversation with two local girls, a French couple and (much to our surprise) a cute American guy named Carter, who suggested we all grab a sundowner at a nearby outdoor bar.

Twenty minutes later, our new crew (including the tuk-tuk driver) was sitting cross-legged on bamboo mats at a waterside café, watching the sun melt into the Mekong River. As we slugged supersized bottles of Beer Lao, we performed the requisite backpacker meet 'n' greet: Where you from? Where have you been? Where you going? Carter, who'd been in Asia for a few months already, took an instant liking to Amanda, engaging her in conversation and whipping out his camera to show her his favorite travel shots.

Any time Amanda and I were in a situation where there was only one single guy (luckily a rare occurrence in the hostel world), we'd joke about flipping to see who flirted first. But the truth was, even though we liked similar "types," it was often clear from the get-go which of us got dibs: Soccer Player (me), Photographer (Amanda), TV Producer (me), Entrepreneur (Amanda), Film Fanatic (me), East Village Musician (Amanda), Boy Next Door (me), Sandy-haired Ski Bum (Amanda)—all easy layups. But even when it wasn't so stereotypically obvious on their end, our individual quirks generally stepped in to make the call. Although it'd been years since we'd both been single at the same time back in NYC, we had our on-the-road system down, from dutifully playing the wing woman role to gracefully exiting when the time was right.

So when sparks had started to fly between me and Adam, a cute British computer programmer staying at our guesthouse in Goa, Amanda's schedule had miraculously filled up with solo activities. Considering how long it'd been since I'd had any sort

317

of carefree fling, I was supremely grateful for her strategic absenteeism, but as her only on-the-road friend, I also worried that she'd feel left out. I'd vowed to tip the scale back in Amanda's favor the first chance I got. And now it was looking as if I might not have to wait long.

Later that night, as we cruised back to downtown Vientiane, Carter suggested that Amanda ("uhh, I mean you and Jen") accompany him to Vang Vieng, a tiny mountain town in the north.

"Seriously, you two really should come. It's this totally cool backpacker hideout where everyone goes river tubing all day and then parties at night," he added, running a hand through his shaggy auburn mop.

"Well, we'd planned to go to Luang Prabang in a few days, so I don't really know," Amanda said, glancing over at me with a hopeful expression.

"It sounds really fun," I interjected. "When are you going?"

"The day after tomorrow on the nine a.m. bus. Vang Vieng is actually on the way to Luang Prabang, so if you ladies want to make a detour, I'd love to hang with you. Seriously, it'd be totally cool, ya know?"

It was then that I realized just who it was that Carter reminded me of. It'd been bugging me all night, but suddenly it was so obvious. He was Amanda's ex-boyfriend Baker reincarnated. Of course, considering the tumultuous, multiyear relationship that had been, I kept my observation to myself. But now I was fairly certain we'd be on that bus.

Back at the guesthouse, as I dug through my pack trying to locate the least grungy items to wear to bed, Amanda wandered out of the bathroom, performing her nightly walk, talk, and toothbrush routine. As she worked her back molars, we discussed the possibility of taking Carter up on his offer. A quick peek at our Lonely Planet guide confirmed Carter's claims about Vang Vieng being "cool," so we agreed to play it by ear and decide the next night.

"We need to talk about tomorrow morning too," Amanda said, flipping off the bathroom light and climbing into bed. "You remember Noy from the spa?"

"Oh, yeah, your breakfast date? Well, you know there's no way in hell I'm getting up at eight a.m., but go right ahead and have fun."

"She might not even show up, but if she does, she said she'd take me to visit her aunt, you know, the nun who started the spa. So I'm not sure how long I'll be gone, and, well . . ."

Sensing the hesitation in her voice that usually preceded news she feared would disappoint me, I cut her off at the pass, explaining that she should stay gone as long as she wanted and that I was totally cool to hang by myself in town. Picking at the corner of her comforter, she rushed on to explain that she actually wanted to meet the nun to talk about herbal remedies just in case she decided to maybe, possibly, "but not if you'd be upset," accept a story she'd just been offered. It was the big enchilada, the mother of all assignments, a $3,000 piece on healing remedies from around the world. She'd pitched it months ago, when we were still in Kenya, but hadn't heard back from the editor until now.

"I'm not sure doing the piece would be the best idea, but either way, I thought it'd be cool to talk to the nun," she said.

"A-*man*-da. Do you really think I'd be upset if you took this? I just wanted you to enjoy the trip and not waste so much time in Internet cafés, but now that you have a legitimate assignment, you've gotta take it. It's your dream. You must follow your dream," I replied, trying my best to make light of the situation.

"Yeah, I guess, but the timing of this couldn't be worse. I mean I've been having so much fun just traveling, especially here. And things with us are finally really good, and I wouldn't

319

want to screw that up. Plus it's going to require a shitload of research."

I couldn't believe she was actually considering not taking this story partially because of me. I didn't know whether to be touched or to run and find the nearest monastery and beg a monk to wipe my guilty conscience clean. The truth was, even if I'd occasionally sat on the opposition's bench, when push came to shove, I would always be on Amanda's side. And knowing she might regret not taking her first big travel writing gig, I couldn't allow that to happen.

"Well, I'm telling you that you have to do this assignment. And that's just all there is to it, even if I have to go out and round up medicine men in every village to be your sources. So I don't want to hear any more arguments," I said firmly.

"All right, all right. I'll do the story, but on one condition," she said with a sheepish grin. "That we maybe meet up with Carter and detour to Vang Vieng first."

"But of course, darling. We gotta make sure you have some fun before you're forced to hole up with your computer," I replied, pulling the chain on our bedside lamp.

It had taken nearly six months, one subcontinent, and three full-size continents for us to get to this point, but here in Laos, everything finally felt right between the two of us again.

꒰

CHAPTER TWENTY

Amanda

LAOS
DECEMBER

The morning after Jen and I visited Wat Sok Pa Luang, I sat at a café in the historic district of Vientiane, waiting for the woman who ran the tree-house spa to meet me for breakfast. I'll admit that the New Yorker in me had been wary when Noy offered to shuttle me into the countryside to meet her aunt—Would she demand money later? Would I get stranded in a part of Laos where no one would understand me?—but I loved the idea of veering even farther off the trampled tourist circuit. Now, a half hour past our appointed meeting time, I wasn't so much worried about being taken for a ride as being stood up.

I'd just ordered my second cup of Lao coffee (a delightful concoction sweetened with condensed milk rather than cream and sugar) when Noy blazed up on her motorbike and flung herself into the seat across from mine. She catapulted a string of strident phrases at the waiter, who jumped in response, then turned around to give me her full attention.

"So sorry late, but big night!" she apologized with a guilty look on her face. "Too many Beer Lao . . . almost not wake up!"

I thanked her for coming in spite of her late evening and

asked how she could take the morning off work to act as a tour guide to an American she'd just met.

She shrugged. "Easy, place not open till two," she said, breaking the yolk on the eggs that the waiter had hustled to place before her. She was in no hurry to get moving, so I nursed my coffee as our conversation drifted from business (Noy was determined to save enough cash to open her own luxury spa in town) to family (her parents thought she was too independent and too career-minded to attract a man) to the universal topic that seems to bind women everywhere: relationships.

Though at twenty-seven she considered herself way, way over the hill, Noy loathed the idea of arranged marriages and hoped that someday she'd meet a guy who could keep up with her modern sensibilities and ambitions. I told her that lots of American girls, especially this one, could relate.

Maybe she felt comfortable enough to bare her soul or just figured she'd never see me again, but by the time I hopped on the back of her "moddah-bike" nearly two hours later, Noy was reaching deep into her personal file, revealing insider information even I'd need a glass of wine or two before spilling to a stranger. She told me about the different men she'd gotten involved with while working at the forest temple. Her current obsession was a middle-aged American guy named Alan, who'd promised to come back through town to see her. So far he hadn't. I wondered how often this story had played out before, how many men had showed up in the forest massage center and assumed that the masseuses—or at least the very friendly single proprietor—could ensure them some kind of happy ending.

I was surprised to feel my ire raised yet again over the treatment—and mistreatment—of local women we'd encountered on the road. Though I'd always been pro–equal rights for men and women, I'd never actually considered myself a feminist.

Almost as soon as I was old enough to learn what it meant,

I'd despised the term, hated the associations with unshaven, granola-crunching, crop-haired militant bitches and their unyielding man-hating ideals. Then, in my early twenties, as the guys I knew began expecting women to ask them for dates, to pay for them, and to be sexually liberated enough not to expect a follow-up call, I actually *blamed* feminism for ruining what had otherwise been a perfect system.

But the more I traveled and the more I'd learned about the roles of women worldwide and how powerless they were in many cases, the more I understood just how grossly naive and sheltered I'd been. Of course I hadn't grasped the importance of feminism, the century-long fight to win my right to vote, receive equal pay, be protected from harassment, and retain control over my own reproductive organs. Nearly all of the work had been done by the generations of women who had come before me.

As Noy flooded the gas and we zipped out of the touristy historic district, Vientiane no longer looked like the French Colonial village I'd initially found so charming. Car dealerships, repair shops, and liquor stores lined the main road. The traffic was terrible. Entire families were perched like carnival acts on the backs of motorbikes, with Dad driving in the front, Mom cradling an infant behind, and a toddler sandwiched in between. Wannabe tough guys stared as we zipped past. Noy shouted that I should keep my purse shoved between us, as locals had a nasty habit of snatching them. I did as she instructed, and for the next forty-five minutes, the wind made conversation impossible.

We passed acres of harvested farmland before finally reaching Wat Pahakounoy, the Buddhist temple where Noy's Aunt Meekow lived. As she entered the yard to greet her niece, I wondered if Noy had been wrong about her age. The tiny, bald woman with a dried apricot complexion and shriveled hands poking out from the yawning sleeves of snowy robes looked much older than sixty. Her face was stern, with no hint of a smile, and I couldn't tell if she was upset that Noy had shown up unannounced with a Westerner—or that the Westerner had worn a tank top and capri pants to a monastery. I retreated as the two women spoke, feigning interest in a kitten that had curled up on the brim of a bamboo hat.

Noy returned and ushered me toward the garden. "Okay, she say fine to show you around. After she make rice for monks, we return and she explain the herbs for the sauna."

Well, that was promising. At least she hadn't kicked me out.

Together we strolled through the dense wooded area, touring temples built several feet above the ground on raised platforms and crossing paths with monks who stared for a half second before dashing out of the way or averting their eyes. My immodesty seemed to be inducing a wave of panic among the holy men. I was kicking myself for spacing out on the rules of respectful attire when I noticed that Noy's thin white T-shirt and jeans did little to hide her curvy figure.

If anything was amiss, Noy didn't acknowledge it. She patiently guided me along the narrow dirt paths winding through the trees, pointing out the buildings used for study and meditation, identifying those meant for sleeping and eating. I asked her if she'd ever considered following in her aunt's footsteps and entering religious service.

"Me? No! Never could be a nun! Of course, is considered a very great honor, but not required for women. The boys, they must do one year of service, at least, when they very young." She explained that being a nun requires tremendous discipline. Though monks may eat one meal a day, food they receive from the villagers, the nuns eat whatever is left over after the monks are finished—if there is anything. Sometimes the women go for days without food, but they are expected to prepare the meals for the men.

"And you know what else?" she hissed, looking horrified. "No sex—ever."

She composed herself as our steps lead us back to the clearing where we'd started. Auntie was there waiting. She beckoned us up to a meditation platform built above a garden in vibrant, unabashed bloom. Though she was not quite smiling, her face seemed to have softened a bit, and she indicated that I was to sit down at her feet.

The nun looked at me but spoke to Noy, who translated. "She asked what you want to know, why you come here to see her."

Under the woman's steely-eyed gaze, I'd almost blanked on the reason, but my reporter sensibilities kicked in. Via Noy, I explained that I was writing an article for an American magazine and I hoped to learn more about the healing herbs used at Wat Sok Pa Luang. How had she come to know so much about the medicinal plants in the first place?

Noy explained that when Aunt Meekow was sixteen years old, she was a nurse in the "big war" and had fallen in love with a soldier. They had wanted to get married, but he was from a wealthy family and she was an orphan who lived in poverty. His parents refused to allow the match. Heartbroken, she decided to become a nun, but her uncle forbade her to do so. She was too young and too beautiful to give up on love, marriage, and children. But Meekow was not to be dissuaded. She trained for more than a year at school and proved her devotion by meditating every day for six months, sometimes up to twenty hours a day.

"Eventually she pass out from so much effort, so uncle realize that she mean business," said Noy. "He finally give her permission . . . and she become a nun."

It was only after Meekow apprenticed under one of the monks, however, that she learned about the medicinal proper-

325

ties of the plants growing in their gardens. When the monk had taught her everything he could, she went off into the mountains to live alone, collect more plants, and create a special mixture of herbs with tremendous healing potential. These plants—lemongrass, eucalyptus, mint, rosemary, kaffir lime, and holy basil—were among the ones now used to create the steam at the forest temple.

"Aunt say, monks have use herbal remedies for thousands of years for curing sickness, disease. Also make easier to relax and better for meditating."

"What types of illnesses can you treat using the herbs?" I asked, finally reaching into my purse to grab the tiny laminated pad and pen I used for stories. "Is there a way for someone to re-create the steam treatment themselves at home?"

Aunt Meekow stared at my hands as I wrote but didn't clam up as I thought she might. Instead, she went into great detail explaining how the plants could be used to treat everything from anxiety to reproductive issues.

Both women spent several more minutes indulging my questions, and the nun even allowed me to snap a photo of her. I wanted to give her, and the monastery, a small token in return for the time she'd spent with me. I reached into my purse to donate 60,000 kip, about $6. I hoped at least some of it would go toward food for the nuns.

Aunt Meekow accepted the bills and bowed toward me, the corners of her lips just barely curving upward into a small smile as she righted herself. I bowed back, trying to keep my own smile in respectful check, and started to rise to my feet.

That's when I felt the old woman's hand on my shoulder and looked up to see that her expression had flatlined once again. She indicated for me to sit and spoke to Noy for several seconds, gesturing in my direction. Suddenly I felt nervous.

Noy turned to face me and gave me an odd look. "So my

aunt ask me if you have been here before, and I tell her probably no. Right?"

"Yeah, this is my first time . . . I've never been here."

"My aunt say something about you familiar. This not be the last time you come here. You return, study with her, learn more about the medicines, herbs."

I smiled and bit my lip. Was this something that all spiritual advisers and healers in Southeast Asia said to tourists like me?

"She say she can see you have very strong will. Dedicated to work hard every day."

That much was true.

"She think it better you devote self to work, stay focus. Sorry to say, but men very bad for you, only bring trouble to your life. No good idea for you get married. Better stay away from men. Work hard. No get distracted by love and sex."

Aunt Meekow's words sucked the serenity right from my body. Work hard? No get married? Was she giving me advice— or predicting the future?

"Hey, hey," said Noy, no doubt noting the expression on my face. "No worry. Aunt always say men bad—for you, for me. Everybody. I never listen anyway!"

I forced a smile and tried not to overthink the exchange. Like most women I knew, Aunt Meekow was probably offering guidance based on her own experiences.

Looking up at the nun, I tried to imagine her as a beautiful young woman, the person she'd been before time and heart-break had etched themselves across her face. At first I'd thought it sounded romantic—she'd devoted her life to religious service because she had been denied the one man that she loved. Now the decision seemed almost reckless, and I could understand why her uncle had tried to talk her out of it. I wondered: Did she ever lie awake at night, reconsidering the choices she'd made as a teenager? Did she experience pangs of regret? Consider that her beloved might have moved on and married someone else while she'd been sequestered away from the world?

Somewhere nearby, I caught the chime of bells, and Aunt Meekow signaled that our conversation was over. She slowly rose to her feet, and I followed suit.

"*Khawp jai.*" I thanked her using one of the Lao phrases I'd learned. The slight smile returned to her face, and she nodded in response.

The two women descended the steps leading from the meditation platform to the ground and entered the garden. Noy stood with her aunt, talking softly as the old woman meticulously selected plants. She handed them to Noy, who placed them inside her canvas satchel and bowed respectfully.

"You ready go?" Noy asked me. "Getting late."

I was ready. The sun was at its highest point in the sky when we left the monastery through a stone archway and zipped past the farmers hard at the harvest. Noy and I didn't really talk much on the way back to Vientiane. Once again the wind made conversation impossible, and after Aunt Meekow's words, I was grateful to ride in silence. Today's warning against men hadn't been the first I'd gotten recently.

When Jen, Holly, and I had first revealed our travel plans to our girlfriends, several of them had become obsessed with the idea that one of us would hook up with some local guy, fall madly in love, and move around the world to get married and have ten thousand of his babies. They were sure it would be easier to find a halfway decent boyfriend in, say, French Guiana or Outer Mongolia than it was in New York City.

Only my ex, Baker, who'd finally returned to the States after years spent traveling in the Caribbean and Latin America, had anything negative to say about on-the-road romance. "Whatever you do, DO NOT have sex with dudes you meet in hostels! Just say NO!!" he'd warned me repeatedly via e-mail. I'd snorted and rolled my eyes at the computer screen as I read his assessment: As a group, backpacker guys were the sluttiest, dirtiest, most indiscriminate group of horn-dogs on the planet. They roamed in feral, salivating packs, moving from country to country, hostel to hostel, crawling into as many bunks and sleep sacks with as many girls from as many different nations as possible, all before returning home to the serious girlfriends they'd been Skyping the whole time.

I'd been tempted to blow off this obviously biased advice until I hit the backpacker trail myself and witnessed the massive, multilateral orgies taking place. At Loki, Mellow Yellow, or any hostel with an in-house bar, we were basically guaranteed to find a scene that looked like spring break, Mardi Gras, and MTV's *The Real World* all rolled into one. Since I had no desire to get naked in a hostel dorm or return home with the kind of souvenir you needed antibiotics to get rid of, I had begrudgingly adopted the "no shagging backpackers" law. Still, I was a romantic at heart. I knew I'd break the rule in a white-hot second if I met a guy who truly blew me away. And secretly, I'd been counting on meeting someone who would.

But by the time our sleeper car rocked and chugged its way up the coast to Goa and no worthy candidates had materialized, I'd started to feel churlish and not a little frustrated. What had happened to the extraordinary love I was destined to find this year? Where were all the exotic men begging me to run away with them?

As the Laotian countryside rushed past, it occurred to me that it had been weeks—no, actually, months!—since I'd been properly seduced or even simply held by a man. Sure, I'd had a few false starts. Back in Brazil, my fling with a gorgeous, brawny Irish guy at Mellow Yellow had gone awkwardly awry when he'd announced, in a reluctant whisper, that he had only one testicle and couldn't move past second base (even my insistence that it didn't matter couldn't charm the pants off him). Then later, in Diani Beach, Kenya, I'd spent a couple of seriously flirtatious nights hanging out with a hard-bodied British army lieutenant, but no sooner had things heated up than he'd had to leave with his brigade to build roads in northern Kenya. And of course, nothing at all had happened between Jason and me when I'd detoured through New York back in August. If I'd known that Carlos's invitation to have sex at his parents' place in Peru would be the closest I'd get to an on-the-road love affair, I might have considered the offer more seriously.

But now that things might be taking a more-than-friendly turn with Carter, I was actually glad that nothing else had worked out until this point. If given the opportunity, I intended to follow my heart and had no intention of listening to ex-boyfriends or Buddhist nuns. Clearly, both had ulterior motives.

The following day, I relayed my religious experience to Carter as he rode with Jen and me on the early-morning bus to Vang Vieng.

"So this woman thought you should come back to study with her at the monastery?" Carter asked as our bus climbed through the foothills just outside of Vientiane. "Would that make you, like . . . a nun in training?"

"I don't think that's what she meant," I said, laughing. "Besides, something tells me that I might be disqualified for nunship at this point in my life. She did have one very specific piece of advice for me, though."

"What's that?" he asked, his liquid blue eyes intently focused on mine.

"She said to stay away from men. Apparently, you're all bad news."

"Well, I'm glad you didn't take her advice," he said, not missing a beat. "It was a nice surprise to see you and Jen this morning. I wasn't sure you'd show."

I'd been thinking the same thing about him. Despite the sales job Carter had done for Vang Vieng, I wasn't sure he'd actually meet us at the Northern Bus Station at the time he'd suggested. Backpackers are notorious for making—then bailing—on the best-laid plans, but he'd been right on time. He braved the ticket kiosk on our behalf and helped us load our heavy backpacks into the belly of the bus.

Despite the unscheduled stops we made at roadside rice stands (a compulsory part of bus travel in Southeast Asia), it was still early when we rolled into Vang Vieng. It was a postage stamp of a town, just a few dusty streets crosshatched by even smaller alleys, hemmed in by the Nam Song River to the west. The entire area was nestled within a ring of emerald peaks that folded into one another like the haunches of sleeping dragons with clouds draped across their backs.

Most of the guesthouses and restaurants lining the main drag looked freshly built, the sharp metallic ping of hammers slamming against nail heads confirming that construction was still under way. This place had only recently come into its own as a backpacker destination, and the locals were doing all they could to meet the demand for cheap beds, food, and booze.

As we walked through the center of town toward our guesthouse, I could see into ground-level cafés where groups of slick-haired backpackers were curled up on cushions underneath wooden tables, mindlessly depositing French fries and crepes and glistening forkfuls of noodles into their mouths. Their eyes glazed over as they stared up at large projection screens playing endless episodes of *Friends, Family Guy*, or *The Simpsons*. All over the tiny town, American sitcoms and bootleg first-run movies were shown on a high-pitched loop, hypnotizing anyone who passed like a strong gust from a poppy field. Linger long enough

331

Amanda · Laos · December

to order a beer or pile of banana pancakes, and you'd be flat out until someone pulled the plug on the TV for the night.

We resisted the sitcom siren song in order to pursue the second, but no less addictive, reason to alight in Vang Vieng: extreme river tubing. During the previous few years, the locals had built a full-blown water park along a meandering stretch of the Nam Song, a cat's cradle of zip lines, rope swings, and make-shift bamboo bars that clung precipitously to the riverbanks.

For just 30,000 kip (about $3), you could rent a giant inner tube and waterproof bag, take a tuk-tuk or van ride a few kilome-ters upriver, and play bumper boats with other travelers as you floated slowly back in the direction of town. During the jour-ney, you'd hear an endless mix of rock music pouring through invisible speakers and the constant cry of "Beer-Lao-Beer-Lao-Beer-Lao!" Just motion with your hand or bat an eyelash, and one of the men standing along the riverbank would hook you with a pole and reel you in. Whether you were buying your first fifty-cent brew or your sixth, you'd be given unlimited access to the zip line or rope swing rigged up at that particular outpost.

The only real no-no here? Lighting up a joint. As Jen, Carter, and I rented our gear along with the other newbie tubers, we passed a sign that read TO SAVE MONEY, NO SMOKE MARIJUANA ON THE RIVER. THANKS!

"Get it?" said Jen, as proud as if she'd unlocked the riddle of the sphinx. "The sign doesn't say 'Stay out of jail!' or 'Avoid arrest!' It means you'd have to bribe the police to get out of trouble, so don't smoke."

"Gotta love the Lao," said Carter. "Always watching out for our wallets."

Depending upon how long we lingered at the riverside pubs, the ride ahead of us could take two hours—or five. We wasted no time in plopping our tubes into the river.

"Hey, everybody! Last one in buys the first round!" shouted

the boisterous Danish guy who'd shared our van upriver. Taking a running leap, he let loose his best Tarzan yodel before crash-landing into his tube and flipping it over, a feat that elicited cheers and wolf whistles from the other backpackers. We were on our way.

Our floating caravan hadn't made it a hundred yards down river when the first Beer Laos outpost lured us, dripping and thirsty, back out of the water again. After taking turns braving the zip line, we set off on our way again—only to get held up at yet another overwater pub with a longer, steeper zip line. The process of drink-climb-jump-dunk repeated itself at another shore bar two hundred yards down, and then another.

As we continued downriver, I felt a slight bump on my right and smiled, knowing without looking who'd brushed up, accidentally on purpose, against my inner tube.

"Hey, buddy, stay in your own lane," I joked, turning around to playfully push Carter away. But at the last second, just as our tubes were starting to drift apart, he caught my hand and pulled me back toward him. My gut immediately started doing its own version of the somersaults I'd just been practicing on the rope swing.

Squeezing my hand, Carter lay back in the tube and gave me the kind of half wink, half grin that only a sexy, scruffy dude can pull off so well. Taking his cue, I lay back too, turning my face toward the sky to catch the sunshine that flickered in strands of amber and honey through the trees above us.

It was turning out to be a languid, practically perfect afternoon, the kind I thought only existed in Country Time Lemonade and fabric softener commercials. We drifted hand in hand, lagging behind the rest of the group in the slowest part of the river. In the near stillness, I let my eyes fall shut and allowed my other senses to filter through. The layered sounds of splashing and laughter around me. The goose bumps that cropped up whenever the breeze picked up slightly. The points where Carter's palm pressed against mine.

I'd fallen into such a deep state of relaxation that when we reached our final stop—a granddaddy, multistory bamboo bar with blaring rock music, several barbecue grills, and a ginormous five-story rope swing—I almost didn't get out of my tube. But Carter and Jen insisted, so we all climbed ashore to grab paper cups filled with French fries and took a spot on the viewing log. We watched as other tubers ascended a ladder into the upper branches of a vertiginous tree. One bikini-clad girl leaned way out to grab a wooden crossbar and flung herself over the side of the platform.

Just imagining myself in her shoes (or rather, bare feet) made my heart pummel in my chest and my palms start to sweat. What if you slipped off the ladder or the platform and hit the roots at the base of the tree? Or landed badly in the river? I'd read that some travelers had perforated their eardrums by falling the wrong way, and the nearest modern hospital was a plane flight away in Bangkok.

There's no way in hell I'm going up there.

When I shared this thought with Carter, he interpreted my statement as a thrown gauntlet and pulled out all the stops— flattery, bargaining, and even bribery—to get me to change my mind. Finally, just to shut him up (or maybe to impress him), I begrudgingly agreed to make the leap.

My limbs were shaking as I ascended but had turned into gelatinous goo by the time I reached the platform at the top and looked down. *Holy shit.* Why had I agreed to do this? A man to my right used a hook to grab the crossbar and pulled it in toward me. I held on to a beam behind me as I reached, chest vibrating, for the wooden dowel in front of me. As my left hand jerked up to meet it, my weight dragged forward and I found myself moving toward the edge and flying over the water in a huge arc, my fingers desperately gripping the lifeline that suspended me above it.

Ahhhhhhhhh!

"Drop! Amanda, drop! Let go!" Carter called from the shore while Jen screamed her encouragement. Looking down past my feet to find the water, I did as instructed and landed with a forceful splash.

Yes . . . I made it! Popping up to the surface, I swam to the riverbank and climbed out, a goofy grin plastered to my face.

"That. Was. Awesome!" Jen high-fived me she walked by and toward the ladder.

"Killer jump!" Carter said, grinning as I approached. "Ready to do it again?"

I stopped in my tracks, water cascading down my ponytail and down my spine. "What? Are you nuts? There's no way I'd even think about—"

I didn't get the chance to finish my thought. Carter reached out to put his hand on the back of my wet head and pulled me in for an unexpected kiss.

"Sorry . . . I just couldn't wait any longer," he said before kissing me all over again.

I'd all but forgotten that we weren't alone when I heard clapping and whistling coming from the river. I opened my eyes and turned to see the remaining members of our floating wagon train drifting past us, offering their appreciation for our little show. Carter flashed them a thumbs-up and a smile before turning around to give me one last kiss—and this one, he definitely didn't act sorry about.

Later that night, after our group had gone to dinner at one of the Friends' cafés and attended a themed "astronaut space party" thrown by one of the bars (complete with tinfoil cone hats, plastic capes, and other impromptu costumes), I pulled Jen aside and asked her if she cared that I might go back to the guesthouse early with Carter.

"Don't be silly! Of course it's fine," she said. "Actually, I'm pretty sure I saw this coming before you did."

"But are you sure you'll be okay? I just don't want you to feel stranded if I leave."

"Amanda, the guesthouse is, like, a block and a half from here. But if it makes you feel better, I'll walk back with one of the girls from the group. And remember," she added, "I want all the details in the morning."

Carter was waiting for me near the entrance to the party. As he and I walked together, stopping every few feet to sneak another kiss, my brain rewound to my meeting with the nun a few days earlier. Her words, so startling at the time, seemed downright silly to me now. Stay away from men? How could I have taken that seriously, even for a second?

I looked up at Carter, the first guy I'd felt really drawn to in a long time, and allowed myself to be pulled into his arms. He wanted me to be here, and I wanted to be with him. As we walked back to the guesthouse hand in hand, I could feel my pulse racing. Carter let me into the darkened room before him, and I instantly tripped on the backpack he'd left at the foot of the bed. I vaulted through the air and came down, in a less-than-alluring fashion, on a brick-hard mattress. Carter, who noticed only that I'd assumed a somewhat horizontal position, rained down after me, swallowing me up in his athletic bulk and immediately pressing fast-forward on the seduction he'd started on the river earlier that day.

This is the part where I'm supposed to explain, or at least obliquely reference, how we sealed the deal, but to my own surprise—we didn't. Even as our clothes were rapidly evaporating, I found myself nervously yammering on about my "no sex with backpackers" rule and inquiring as to the recency of his last STD test. The latter was a standard question I always asked back in New York, but here, in a riverside hut in the middle of nowhere in Laos, it seemed a tad compulsive. As the words ejected from my mouth like bullets from a loaded handgun, I kicked myself for being such a neurotic freak. *Shut up! Shut up!* No wonder I hadn't gotten naked with a guy in so long!

Carter fielded my questions, then carried on as if I hadn't said anything at all, pressing me, but not too aggressively, to change my mind. When I didn't, we both fell asleep.

I figured that after that night, Carter might hop the next bus out of town, but the following morning, not long after I'd done the flip-flop walk of shame, he came by my room to see if he could take Jen and me to breakfast. And then later he suggested that we hit up the river for more tubing. And then he proposed we take a field trip to the caves north of town. That night, after Jen and I went off in search of a place that sold pancakes for dinner, Carter tracked us down and asked if he could pull up a floor pillow.

Jen hardly said a word when Carter decided that we'd be traveling as a trio to Luang Prabang. "Hey, as long as you're having fun," she'd said as we rerolled our clothes and wedged them into our packing cubes. "But just wondering . . . does he remind you of anyone?"

"Hmm . . . I guess he looks kinda like that actor from *Varsity Blues.*" I knew that's not what Jen was thinking, but I pretended to be oblivious.

There was something about Carter—his quarterback build, his sexy smile, the way he seemed right at home in any social setting—that reminded me of Baker. Once I'd realized it, my knee-jerk reaction had been to brush the comparison aside. After all, Carter was an entirely different person, and no way was I going to let the ghost of some relationship past prevent me from enjoying my present.

Before Jen could respond, or maybe shock me with her revelation, Carter arrived to hustle us to the bus stop. I glanced at his profile, and he turned to catch me staring.

L ong before the three of us made the dizzying ride through the mountains to reach the ancient royal city of Luang Prabang, we'd heard extensive accounts of its charms. Travelers spoke of the place as a kind of Shangri-la, a modern-day utopia where locals lived in perfect harmony in the cradle of the Khan and Mekong rivers, surrounded by ripples of velvety green mountains under a smudged pink sky. The townspeople walked through their day unhurried and somehow never seemed to age. Even the children spoke in melodic whispers.

In light of this effusive praise, I'd assumed that the town would be a total letdown, like an independent film that everyone's hyped so much that watching it can only disappoint. That wasn't the case. Few places I've ever visited, before or since, have been imbued with such a sense of exoticism and intrigue, mystery, and romance as Luang Prabang.

In the morning, the sun rose just as the monks and their novices had spilled from temple yards into the frangipani-scented dawn, the amber light warming the backs of the almsgivers who tipped rice and other offerings into their bowls. As the town stretched from sleep into waking, wafts of fresh-baked baguettes, chocolatey pastries, and roasted espresso warmed the air. The scent was a subtle reminder, as was the nineteenth-century architecture, that the country was once a French colony. Now an independent nation, Laos has held on to the civilized parts of European culture while cultivating its own traditional one.

As we strolled through town, men lounging against idling taxis suggested they'd be happy to take us anywhere we'd like to go for just a dollar per person. Women rode past on yellow bicycles or bright red motorbikes, their umbrellas held at attention to shield their skin from the light. Later on, they greeted us shyly as we approached to buy one of the mango-, pineapple-, or banana-flavored cakes they sold from pop-up card tables.

After dusk the main road through town transformed into a well-organized night market. Strings of neatly spaced bulbs ran down the length of it like the dips and arcs on a carousel; patches of fabric were placed end to end to form quilted sidewalks. Within their appointed squares, families sold silk scarves, elaborately embroidered robes, slippers with elephants and monkeys marching across them, hand-stitched pillows, duvet covers and throws, star-shaped lanterns punched with tiny geometric patterns, and hanging paper umbrellas that, when you stared at them together, looked like a school of pastel jellyfish floating upward into the night sky.

After shopping stoked our appetites, we filled our stomachs with all manner of delicacies—dumplings, curries, stews, noodles, rice cones, and other unidentifiable dishes—for just 50 cents a bowl. Then later, when the fatigue of the day set in, we collapsed into beds at one of the local spas and got an acupressure massage so powerful and restorative I almost cried from the release of toxins and uncorked emotion.

Once we'd all plunked down $3 apiece to sleep in a guesthouse that reminded me of a Swiss chalet, Carter and I shared dinner at an outdoor café overlooking a firestorm sunset on the Mekong. I decided this place was about as close to backpacker heaven as I might ever get.

And whether it was the spell that the town cast over me, a smoky haze of romance that clouded out my earlier apprehension, or just the patient, unhurried way Carter walked me back to his room later that night, I no longer felt any hesitation as we locked the door behind us. Tipping backward in his arms toward the bed and feeling his kiss on my throat, I knew I was finally ready to break the rules.

CHAPTER TWENTY-ONE

꽃

Holly

INDIA/SHRADDHA ASHRAM
NOVEMBER

I awoke shivering, drenched in sweat. Inside, the dorm was silent.
Outside, the wild dogs were howling as if it were a full moon.
My bed felt like a Tilt-a-Whirl ride at the state fair, and every time
I closed my eyes I feared I'd fall out and crash to the ground. A
kaleidoscope of color bursts exploded in front of my eyes.

The virus that had been spreading through the ashram must
have hit me as I slept. I considered waking Chloe or running
to find one of the swamis for help. I was suddenly terrified that
I'd die there alone in an ashram in India, thousands of miles
away from home and everyone I loved. Some part of me *knew*
I was being irrational, that I was just feeling ill and isolated in
the darkness in a foreign land. But my mind had its own force.
I didn't want to disappear in the dark on that lumpy mattress.
I wanted to matter to something. I wanted to matter to someone. In my feverish haze, a thought surfaced that I'd kept buried
deep: I feared I didn't truly matter to anyone. If I passed right
then in the night, would I be just like a ghost who faded quietly
away?

Managing to drag myself out from under my mosquito net,
I splashed cold water on my face and fumbled around in the

shadows for my uniform so I could slip out of my sweat-soaked pajamas. Then I crawled back into bed and lost consciousness.

The next thing I remembered was waking to sunlight streaming through the empty dorm. I'd let my overactive mind go to extremes in the dark, and felt silly in the light of day.

Sitting up in bed slowly to test if the dizziness was gone, I felt my breath stop when I saw a black tarantula—whose body alone was the size of my hand—poised menacingly at the foot of my bed. I didn't stop to think about whether it was a nightmare but could only react. My eyes were swollen and bloodshot from the virus pumping through my body, but pure fear jolted me with enough energy to jump out of bed and run down the length of the dorm.

I remembered in too much vivid detail seeing a similar hairy, eight-legged creature while cleaning the bathroom stalls, then hearing the sound of its body being squashed by the Indian woman in charge of karma yoga, who'd killed it with a rock after I'd screamed.

Before coming to the ashram, I'd known that learning to sit with myself, to meditate, to just *be*, would take discipline. It wasn't supposed to be easy. But throw in culture shock, a fever-inducing virus, and waking up to a tarantula, and I could almost understand the feeling an alcoholic might have when she hits rock bottom—spinning out of control.

After making sure the tarantula had moved on, I used all my remaining strength to drag myself back to bed, too weak to make a getaway. I didn't move for hours, until Chloe stopped by with tea and fruit after I didn't show up when she waited for me at lunch. Then I fell asleep again, as still as one of the yogis carved in stone by the lake.

B y day three of the illness I finally summoned up the energy to make it to a lecture. Sitting there on the floor, my body sometimes felt as if it were vibrating—and just thinking about doing a downward dog gave me a head rush. But I was improving, and at least I'd felt well enough to leave the confines of my bed.

The day's lesson was about karma. Yogis think the body is merely a vehicle for the soul, subject to reincarnation, until you finally get it right and reunite with the universal consciousness, or God. In yoga land, there's no such thing as instant gratification, and the road to cleaning up your karma can be long indeed, spanning dozens of lifetimes.

As I had been raised a Catholic, the concept of reincarnation was totally foreign to me. I had been taught that we get only one life before we hopefully make it to Heaven by the grace of God, following the teachings of Jesus, and making sacraments, such as confessing sins to a priest.

Still, I found comfort in that rather than looking to a priest to serve as a sort of middleman to God, my yoga manual said, "Self-realization is god-realization." That the whole purpose of life is to find your personal path that will help you connect to the spark of divinity everyone has inside him or her. I took this to mean that everyone has different gifts. Taking the time to figure out our passions is not selfish because once we find our calling, we'll feel that we have a solid purpose and a connection to something bigger. This helps bring peace.

"Regardless of your religion, your most important duty on this earth is to find your true self, and yoga's regime of self-discipline can help you get there," Swami said. "Only once you know yourselves are you able to know God, because the two are not separate but one and the same."

Once the swami finished his lecture, students with questions walked up to a microphone at the front of the prayer hall. Chloe rose to get up from her place next to me. "Swami, how would you explain why some people get diseases like AIDS and cancer and others don't?" she asked.

343

"People get diseases such as AIDS and cancer because they have impure minds or are paying off bad karma from a past life," he stated matter-of-factly. I'd consciously tried to be open to the ashram's lessons and reserve judgment until the end. How else was I ever going to learn anything new? But I wasn't going to listen to the swami try to say sick people are at fault. I thought of Esther being left on Sister Freda's doorstep with a near-deadly case of malaria. I was so angry, I was ready to walk out.

"What about this eye virus that's going around? What's the cause of all the people at the ashram getting sick?" Chloe asked.

"Can everyone who has *not* gotten sick please raise your hands?" the swami asked. When more than half of the students did so, he shrugged as if his point had been proven. "People get sick because of karma, or else everyone would become ill."

Feeling as though the ashram leaders saw me as a karmic leper, I walked outside to sit on the steps with my head between my knees. It was then that Vera, the bearded Indian man who served as kitchen master, came up beside me.

"Holly, how are you feeling? Like you have a weight on your head?" he asked, gently placing a hand on my shoulder. Even Vera had caught the virus and had spent the last week hiding behind dark sunglasses to veil his bloodred eyes.

"Vera, I have to leave," I said, the decision suddenly pouring out of me. I didn't know where I would go, I just knew I didn't want to stay here. I *couldn't* stay here anymore.

I felt Chloe sit down on the other side of me. "Holly, please, please don't go," she said, pleading. "You have only a week and a half left of the program. If you're going to be sick, you can be sick anywhere. You might as well recover here and at least have your teaching certificate to show for it."

Until then, the only treatment I'd received for the virus had been rosewater eye drops from the on-site ayurvedic clinic, which did nothing to heal and only stung my eyes, making them redder. Chloe offered to take me to the hospital so I could get some prescription meds to speed up the healing process, but Vera insisted that one of the staff escort me. As Vera helped me into the rickshaw, he whispered that he, too, had given up on the rosewater eye drops and had healed quickly after using prescription drugs.

B ack from the clinic a few hours later, with three different kinds of pills, ointment, and eye drops, I didn't walk straight back into the ashram. Instead, I spun in the opposite direction and sat by the lake to think. Why had I come? Why should I stay? Intentionally sticking with a situation in which I was miserable felt foolish, especially after I'd seen real hardship and knew how truly lucky I was to have so many opportunities. I wanted to run back out into the world, to be with other people and not just in my own head.

The lions roared in the safari park across the way, and Hindi music carried over the water's sleek surface from tinny radio speakers playing in one of the nearby shacks. My T-shirt clung to my back from sweat, and I tipped my face to soak up the sun's rays.

I felt broken from all the rebelling my mind and body were doing in the ashram. Using all my energy to try to control my impulses had left me feeling depleted and empty. Ironically, the sheer emotional exhaustion had left my mind more silent than when I'd been actively trying to rein it in.

Why did yoga school feel more like boot camp or an emotional breakdown? I suddenly remembered the old Alcoholics Anonymous saying "Let go, and let God." What if coming to the ashram was part of a larger plan, a lesson I needed to learn?

345

Would Sister Freda give up because she wasn't "happy"? Would she quit when she felt uncomfortable?

Sitting there, I recalled how the swamis had compared our minds to the lake: emotions such as worry, sadness, happiness, and desire created waves that kept us from seeing the bottom—our deeper, true selves. I could leave the ashram, but I couldn't keep running away from myself. I had to get to the bottom of my restlessness if I was ever going to be able to sit with myself peacefully.

I stared at the water, which was clear and blue. I saw sunlight glint off a school of fish far below the surface, their slick bodies effortlessly twirling near the lake's muddy floor. A flower floated by on the wind, maybe an offering carried away from one of the dozens of shrines peppering the ashram grounds.

Frustrated, I grabbed a smooth, flat rock and flung it at the water, watching the ripples radiate out from its center as it skipped once and then twice. I watched as the stone began to sink. Once it hit bottom, did it stay there forever, down in the darkness?

There's a metaphor in Buddhism about the lotus flower, which starts out growing on the bottom of all this muck and then rises through the swampy darkness into the light. When it finally gets there, it turns into what it was meant to be, opening up into something beautiful. But the flower doesn't open instantly; it has to go through the muck to get to the light. If I ran away from my own moments of darkness, would I never blossom into the person I was meant to be?

I recalled another Buddhist sentiment from a book of quotes I'd gotten back when I was a happiness editor: "There are only two mistakes one can make along the road to truth: not going all the way, and not starting."

I can't say exactly how long I sat there by myself, looking out at the lake. Picking up another rock and aiming it at the water, I lifted myself up without waiting for the rock to hit bottom. I was going to finish what I'd started—I was staying at yoga school.

E verything at the ashram became easier once I'd taken the prescribed meds and had gotten my health back. I hadn't mastered sitting still and quieting my mind, but my attitude had shifted. I wasn't going to fight myself—or the swamis—anymore. I began to suspect that the rigid schedule, the two meals a day, six hours of sleep a night, and four hours of yoga, was as much about pushing students toward their breaking point in order to reveal their real, raw selves as it was about discipline. But was the road to enlightenment supposed to be so uncomfortable? As the rest of the students filed out after class, I walked toward the stage where the swami was sitting in his standard lotus position.

He looked up at me and smiled gently. "You look like you're feeling better, Holly." Telling him I was back to my old self, I went ahead and asked him the point of all this self-discipline.

"You're telling us that we have to learn to control our bodies and minds in order to know our true selves and to know God. But our instincts and senses are essentially pro-grammed to lead us away from the divine—indulging in food and sex and sleep feels good. Why would God hardwire us this way?"

His luminous gray eyes softened. "That's an existential question, really," he said. I suddenly felt sorry for him—he had a tough job of drilling self-discipline into all of those critics.

"We're not talking about living a life without flavor. What we're saying is that attachments and desires diminish pleasure, because you can't fully enjoy something that you fear losing." I wasn't sure if it was really possible to fully love something or someone without being attached. Did Elan understand this, and that was why he had let me go on my own journey? Had my own attachments to my relationship kept me from being fully present on the road?

I went to sit in the prayer hall to let his answer sink in. For the first time, I saw the point. The swamis weren't saying that we had to live an austere life in order to connect with God. It wasn't about forgoing fun and sidestepping love and banning rich foods forever. Rather, it was about diving fully into all of those things without holding back out of fear that they'd end. Because, inevitably, everything comes to an end.

I thought I'd learned that lesson already on the road. Hadn't I felt more alive when I'd stopped to buy postcards from Padma outside the Taj than when I'd tried to shut out the beggars? Even anxiety held meaning if I simply paid attention to it rather than pretended it didn't exist.

When we were just two days away from graduation, I plodded into the dark prayer hall for morning meditation and sat cross-legged on the floor, just as I'd done almost every other morning for a month. Incense filled the air, and everything was silent. Except, of course, for my mind.

I prepared for another hour of sitting with myself. Not silently and not comfortably, but I guess that's why they call it a meditation "practice"—because it's not perfect. Instead, I simply listened to my breath coming in and out. I'd given up trying to force anything to happen while I sat there. I'd just accepted that I'd devote myself to sitting, and the acceptance somehow made it feel less tough. I'd stopped struggling. I let go, and I let God.

Suddenly I fell into myself. I don't know how else to describe it. There were no flashing lights or tingling feelings. I was aware

that the world outside my mind kept turning, but for the brief-
est of moments, I felt blissfully still and was wrapped in a light,
peaceful sensation. I felt myself smile from the inside, feeling
that nothing outside myself would make me feel complete, because nothing was missing.

꒐

CHAPTER TWENTY-TWO

Amanda

THAI ISLANDS

DECEMBER

So . . . then what happened? Did you guys finally do it?"

I was sitting with my friend and New York City room-mate Beth on an AirAsia flight headed from Bangkok to Phuket. I'd been relaying the story of what had eventually transpired between Carter and me in Laos in hushed tones between the beverage and food services. Gotta love the foreign government-subsidized airlines—even on hourlong flights, they ply you with booze, hot towels, and grub.

"C'mon, what happened?" she asked, her eyes wide.

"Yeah. We did, but . . . oh, Beth, it wasn't what I expected." I sighed, cringing as I recalled how things had played out. "I held off for so long, waited forever to meet someone, and then when I did . . . when we did . . . it was just . . . *awful.*"

Beth looked appropriately horrified. I explained that Carter must not have had many long-term relationships, or else his last girlfriend had been a blow-up doll, because otherwise he would have understood that the wildly enthusiastic, over-the-top sex tactics so prevalent in porn films didn't do anything for a real live woman.

"I actually stopped him in the middle and asked him to

slow down," I said. "That lasted for all of ten seconds before he cranked it right back up again."

I'd felt blindsided. Nothing about Carter's incredible kisses or sweet, protective nature could have prepared me for our rough, emotionless liaison. As soon as he'd passed out, I'd silently crept back to my own bed. There was just no way I could sleep next to him after that.

"Did he say anything the next day?" Beth asked. "I mean, he had to notice that something was wrong if you cut and ran in the middle of the night."

Jen stirred from her semislumber and joined the conversation. "Actually, that's the weird part. He really didn't seem to think anything was wrong, other than the fact that Amanda suddenly didn't want to hang out with him anymore. The whole time we were in Luang Prabang, he followed us everywhere . . . found us no matter what we did. We went to breakfast, and there was Carter at the next table. We'd go on a hike, and Carter was on the same trail. Getting a foot massage at the spa? Carter's in the chair next to us. He went from zero to stalker in point eight seconds. It was crazy. But you remember. This kind of stuff just seems to happen to Amanda."

Beth nodded. During the time that we'd all lived together, she'd experienced the full force of random exes coming out of the woodwork to call or text me incessantly. I'd decided there must be some aspect of my personality that attracted guys who never gave up, took any communication from me—even demands to get lost—as a sign of encouragement.

Of course I wasn't unique in this; every one of my girlfriends had a type. Some were drawn to wounded birds that required endless coddling; others were catnip for lazy bastards who took advantage of their good nature; a few couldn't escape those conceited Wall Street types looking for a trophy girlfriend. I considered myself one of the lucky ones. At least my men were consistent and could be counted on to call—and call, and call.

Though normally I'd try to lie low and ignore all stalker communications, this had proved impossible in Luang Prabang. Enchanting though it was, the small town offered only so many places to hide. After Jen and I escaped for a quick two-day hike and kayaking tour through the Hmong mountain villages north of town, we returned to our guesthouse to find Carter brooding on the porch, mechanically feeding pieces of stale bread to an owl the owners kept in a cage outside. He looked as if he hadn't eaten or even moved since we'd taken off. He glared under his brows at Jen and me as we quickly removed our shoes and left them in the cubbies at the foot of the stairs.

Feeling a stab of guilt for giving him the silent treatment, my resolve broke and I decided to just talk to the guy, to explain what had gone wrong. Maybe he'd even appreciate hearing the honest female perspective. We went upstairs to his room, and I apologized for taking off without a word. He grumbled some acknowledgment and wanted to know exactly what he'd done to make me run. Sitting on the edge of the bed, I tried, as delicately as possible, to explain how uncomfortable I'd felt the other night.

"Well, why didn't you just tell me at the time?" he asked, clearly insulted. "I would have done something, I would have fixed it."

"I *did* tell you. More than once. You listened to me for, like, a few seconds, and then it was back to . . . um . . . well, you remember. I mean, it's like I wasn't even in the room."

"C'mon, it wasn't that bad," he said dully.

"Are you kidding me? Were you there? It was *terrible*."

I knew I'd taken the whole honesty thing one step too far. Carter decided to share that I had to be frigid or mental or have some bizarre sexual issue, because I'd been the only girl to ever tell him that he'd been anything less than stellar in the sack.

"And just so you know, because I'm *sure* you'll want to . . . the last woman I slept with was a Thai prostitute," he said almost proudly, letting that fresh piece of info linger in the air for a second. "And she told me I was incredible. The best she's ever had."

My entire body turned to ice, and I couldn't feel my hands or feet. My brain, on the other hand, raced at Mach 12, rocketing past the other unpleasant details of our night together to fixate on the only thing that seemed important right then and there.

Oh, God. Thank Christ. We'd used a condom.

Now it was Carter who knew he'd taken it one step too far. Staring at me, then back down at his feet, he asked what I was thinking.

I just stood there, unable to turn my emotions into coherent sentences. Eventually, when I forced out the words, I demanded to know how he could have kept that information from me.

Carter was instantly defensive. Seriously, it wasn't *that* big of a deal. After all, Asian prostitutes used condoms and they were probably better protected against STDs than the average New York woman who sleeps her way around the city. Plus, a million other guys had done what he did, just never admitted it to their wives and girlfriends. It had happened before we'd even met. What difference could it possibly make now?

As I wheeled for the door, Carter reached out to grab me, to pull me back. My expression must have been enough to convince him to drop my hand. "I'm sorry, Amanda. Maybe I should have told you, but . . . don't go like this. Let me explain."

Carter was still talking as I flew downstairs. Slamming the door to my room, I started shoving clothes into my pack and informed Jen that we had to get the hell out of Shangri-la.

B y the time I'd disclosed the final detail to Beth and our plane had touched down on the shimmering asphalt runway, I'd decided that I just wanted to put the whole thing behind me. Considering I was in an entirely new country, with a thousand miles between Luang Prabang, Carter, and me, it seemed almost possible to do. I tried to look forward to our winter vacation.

Months earlier, Jen, Beth, and I had decided to spend the Christmas and New Year's holidays in the Thai islands. The same friends who had raved about Luang Prabang had vehemently recommended that we skip the resort destination of Phuket, saying that its natural beauty had already been choked out by crass commercialism, but we'd decided to check it out for ourselves.

During the forty-five-minute drive from the airport, I could see that the area had been fully colonized by multinational corporations, the original thatched huts replaced by more profitable businesses. The narrow streets were flanked by sprawling superresorts—JW Marriott; Sheraton; Novotel; Banyan Tree; Hilton—each one fortified by massive concrete walls. As formidable as these barriers appeared, even they hadn't been strong enough to hold back the deadliest and most unexpected of invaders.

Our driver, Ying, told us that the 2004 tsunami (which had claimed more than 4,000 lives in Thailand and more than 230,000 in the region) had done some serious damage to the resorts in Phuket, particularly those on the western and southern parts of the island.

As we gazed out at the Andaman Sea throwing diamonds of light in front of us and nary a petal out of place across the well-pruned landscapes, it seemed almost impossible that a twenty-

354

foot wall of seawater had hurtled ashore like an unstoppable freight train, obliterating everything in its path. I remembered watching in horror the video clips, the endless loop of CNN coverage showing people clinging to street signs as the deluge surged and sucked around them, the hysterical parents desperate to find their missing children, the villages that had been leveled or washed out to sea. Virtually every country bordering the Indian Ocean had been touched—and in some cases decimated—by the force of the strongest undersea earthquake recorded in modern history. How had the people here salvaged what was left, started their lives again, when some had so little to start with?

"Very terrible. Many, many Thai lose family, lose job." Ying shook his head. "But everything in Phuket built fast-fast, make good again. Need *farangs* come here, buy hotel, use taxi, eat in restaurant, visit girlie bar. They come back, we start over."

As we pulled through the grand porte cochere at the Chedi, a place that could have been ripped straight from the pages of the glossy travel magazines I so loved, the driver jumped out to assist us with our bags. I handed him the fare, plus 50 extra baht as a tip, and he thanked me profusely, saying that just by being here, and by coming to Phuket and spending our money, my friends and I were helping the local people. Ascending the steps of the luxury hotel we'd chosen to splurge on for Beth's arrival and accepting a tropical welcome drink offered by a young Thai woman, I hoped that—at least in some small way—he was right.

355

F rom where we sat on the veranda of our bungalow, a tree house perched high above a sliver of beach shaded by coconut groves, it was tough to see why so many people had warned us to steer clear of Phuket. True, it wasn't exactly an undiscovered paradise, but that hardly seemed enough to inspire the rancor of the ranks. What exactly was it, then, that had turned people off?

Even the most cursory of Google searches would have answered my question, but I'd been spending every spare moment trying to finish my article on "Healing Secrets from Around the World." While Jen and Beth sat by the pool, sipping pastel drinks adorned with hibiscus buds and fruit slices, I logged onto the Wi-Fi in the open-air lobby and slogged through the piece as quickly as I could. Somehow, the idea of being a glamorous international reporter, dashing off to foreign lands and filing stories from halfway around the globe, hadn't exactly panned out as I'd hoped. My editor didn't seem to understand that I wasn't sitting in front of a desk all day, with a phone and a high-speed connection at my disposal. She'd been making greater demands with each revision ("Do you think that you could go back to Laos and get better shots of the nun you interviewed? She looked kind of, you know, *mean* in her photo. Oh, and could you track down a different Kenyan traditional healer, someone we can call to fact-check the story? Great—thanks!"). More important, my heart was no longer in the game.

I was sitting there with rivulets of sweat pouring from under my arms, down my back, and beneath my knees instead of hanging out with the friend who'd schlepped halfway around the planet to see us. I found myself wishing I could jump into a time machine and delete the pitch I'd sent in Kenya. What had I been thinking? I sent off the latest (and hopefully final) draft of my article just as the sun was going down.

It wasn't until later that night, when Jen, Beth, and I hopped into a shuttle bus to explore the legendary nightlife in nearby Patong (a scene that our hotel manager cryptically described as "all shiny and glittery, with lots of the blinky-blinky lights and sounds and constant activity") that we finally learned about

Phuket's alter ego: it was an unapologetic, in-your-face, X-rated amusement park of prostitution.

While initially the restaurants, coffeehouses, souvenir shops, T-shirt stalls, and DVD stands along Beach Road appeared moderately legit (Starbucks, Häagen-Dazs, and McDonald's have all set up camp here too), things made a lascivious turn once we veered onto the pedestrian thoroughfare of Bangla. The wide arcade was heavy with foot traffic, and night had been blasted into fluorescent-tinted day by neon marquees, hanging lanterns, scarlet stage lights, and an enormous sign welcoming visitors to Patong in green, red, and amber Christmas lights.

In doorways and out on the street, Thai women costumed in bandeau tops, microscopic hot pants, schoolgirl kilts, and half-buttoned white shirts used singsong baby voices to call out to potential customers: paunchy, sunburned Europeans, nervous-looking college boys clutching cans of Singha beer, wide-eyed young couples, Japanese businessmen, and old men who looked like forgotten war veterans. Inside the dozens of beer halls, go-go bars, and dance clubs lining Bangla and the smaller side streets, girls pirouetted, ground their hips, giggled, and did their best to act provocative. Some danced with their arms and legs hooked around poles, while others worked the seamier, darker corners of the floor. Several appeared to be having fun, hamming it up for guys taking video, while others didn't do much to hide their boredom.

Back on the street, gorgeous half-dressed transvestites, also known as lady boys, or *katoeys*, catwalked through the red-light district. Even as I watched, a lady boy in an enormous tulle prom dress approached a group of guys, all wearing matching Same Same but Different T-shirts, and requested that they take a group photo together. Clearly, the guys didn't grasp that the lady was really a dude, because when she turned around and lifted her crinolines they all freaked out—the moment captured forever on someone's digital camera.

As disconcerting as that revelation had been (at least for the straight men involved), I didn't find it nearly as hard to witness as some of the "love connections" being made all around us. Very young girls, some of whom didn't appear much older than fifteen or sixteen, were draped around or pressed up against much older men, guys who could have been three or four times their age. For the most part, the partners in these May–December affairs looked totally in their element. The girl—or girls—flirted and giggled; the old men looked ecstatic, as if they couldn't quite believe they'd stumbled into a real live version of their pornographic fantasies.

We'd later learn that Patong is actually one of three renowned spots in Thailand (the other two being Bangkok and Pattaya) where international tourists can engage the services of prostitutes without fear that they'll be judged or arrested. Dozens, if not hundreds, of Web sites explain exactly where to hook up with a Thai "girlfriend," how much you should expect to pay for "short-time" and "long-time" sexual services, and how to avoid being drugged or duped by a girl looking to take a *farang*, or Westerner, for all he's worth. Apparently, according to the sites, these devious young women are master manipulators who see their clients as walking ATMs. Be careful, the sites warn, because a girl will say or do just about anything to extract more cash from your wallet: manufacture tears, pretend her mother is dying of a terminal illness, or promise to stop working in the bars if you wire her money every month. Of course, she tells the same story to every other client she manages to get an e-mail address from.

Based on the overt nature of the sex trade in Patong, one might assume that prostitution is legal, but it's been outlawed since the 1960s. But though selling your body, or purchasing someone else's, is technically a crime here, the local police turn a blind eye when the people involved are above the age of consent: That's fifteen years old if you're a "normal" Thai girl and eighteen if you're a sex worker. Sure, this might seem a little contradictory, but considering the huge amounts of cash the industry rakes in every year (one report puts that number at $4.3 billion a year, 3 percent of the Thai economy), no one's trifling with minor details.

Despite the general seediness of Bangla and its side streets, Jen, Beth, and I didn't feel unsafe there. Other than the occasional lady boy shrieking at us in passing or a Muay Thai boxing tout trying to get us to watch a match, no one paid us a whit of attention. There were far too many pretty faces and too much unchecked flesh for us to warrant more than a passing glance. Still, walking these streets, with their over-the-top carnival atmosphere and false laughter ringing out in stereo sound, made me feel uneasy.

Eventually I asked if we could stop and sit in one of the better-lit beer bars to figure out what to do next. The three of us had been walking around Bangla for only about an hour, but already I'd seen enough. Sitting there sipping her beer, Beth was completely quiet. I realized that this was the first time she'd really witnessed anything like this. Unfortunately, Jen and I had seen it before.

We'd gotten our first crash course in the pervasiveness of prostitution in Diani Beach, Kenya, right after we'd finished our volunteer program at Pathfinder. My friends and I had spent our first night in town at the guidebook-sanctioned Forty Thieves bar, trying to figure out why two local girls at the next table were hanging out with two unattractive balding Germans, one of whom had an obnoxious laugh and a mole the size of a bottle cap.

"Well, they might already know each other," Holly had said, giving them the benefit of the doubt. "Those women could be their girlfriends."

"C'mon," said Irene in a low voice. "No way. They're hookers."

359

We'd tried not to stare as the girls stood up and left with the men, only to return an hour later to strike up a conversation with another set of males at the bar. As the night had worn on, we'd witnessed similar transactions taking place all around us. Though the bar didn't rent rooms—drinks, cigarettes, and entrees such as the aptly named Bang-Bang Chicken were the only items on the official menu—Forty Thieves clearly doubled as a brothel.

Scandalized, we'd paid our check, with Irene venting on the matatu ride home about how horrible and disgusting men could be—how dare they exploit these women?

But it wasn't until the next day, when we saw several European women soliciting the services of Diani's ubiquitous "beach boys," that we were all stunned into silence. On the stretch of pristine sand, blue-haired ladies with flesh bursting out of their skirted bathing suits walked arm in arm with sinewy locals sporting baby dreads and six-pack abs. By the pool, twenty-something blond girls with cornrows and sunburned scalps accepted tanning oil applications from bare-chested Kenyans with bright smiles and a way with words in six different languages. We even ran into the famed octogenarian sex kitten who accepted sexual favors from several different beach boys, then tried to pay them with English toffees instead of cash. Sex sold in Diani Beach— and apparently, both the men *and* the women were buying.

As shocked as I had been by the whole scene, I was more baffled by the idea of arranging a "sexcation." Why would a foreigner fly to another continent—especially one where HIV had already claimed the lives of millions—for a few ill-gotten and risky orgasms?

Apparently, experts at the United Nations were just as baffled. Rachel, a twenty-five-year-old Kenyan we'd met at dinner one night, confided that she'd volunteered for the United Nations when it had been conducting a study on sex tourism in the area. Her role had been to infiltrate clubs and bars along the coast and learn the "ins and outs" of the business: What were the average rates for the various services? How did the men and women get started in the industry? In what ways did they try to protect themselves from disease?

Through Rachel's covert ops, she learned that many of the female prostitutes were from very poor villages and had entered the business as an extreme stopgap measure to feed their children after their husbands had left them or had passed away. The money they could make in a few nights as a prostitute would be more than they'd earn in a month back home, if they could even get work. Some men also found it easier to scratch out a living by working the beach, rather than by traveling around to look for jobs as a laborer.

According to Rachel, the sex workers were well aware of HIV and were much more diligent about using condoms than the average Kenyan. They were paid precious little for their services ("The Germans say that for the price of touching a boob back at home they can get the whole body here in Diani") and conducted their business out in the open rather than in some sleazy back room. But though the women required volume sales to stay afloat, men were often hired for an entire week to give the "relationship" time to develop. Sometimes they wouldn't even be required to have sex, as their clients were often more interested in companionship. They were also generally paid more for their services than their female counterparts. At the time, this disparity seemed unfair, and my compassion went out to the women. I tried to imagine how desperate a Kenyan girl would have to feel in order to compromise her body, to sell it off as her last precious commodity. I'd thought of Naomi and the struggle she'd face to become an educated Kenyan woman rather than a victim of circumstance.

Now, as I clutched a sticky pint glass in Phuket and stared

out at three young girls performing a striptease on a stage in the street, I no longer felt flooded with compassion or empathy. I just felt a clench of sadness, a curdle of disgust. Not toward any of the women, precisely—I figured the ones in Patong probably came from circumstances similar to those in Diani Beach—but in general, at the entire spectacle of it all. Thailand is called "the land of smiles," but even from here, I felt as though the ones plastered on the faces of the women were false, clownish in their excessiveness.

I also wondered: Was this the place that Carter had come to the week just before meeting me?

It was still well before midnight on the first night of Beth's vacation, but when I suggested leaving, no one put up a fuss. We caught a cab and left the blinky-blinky lights of Patong in the rearview mirror. I slumped down in the polyester seat and reminded myself, as I'd had to do many times during the trip, not to make snap judgments about what I'd seen. It was merely a postcard view of a situation, a one-dimensional reality that I couldn't begin to understand in a single visit.

That was part of the trouble with traveling from place to place so quickly. You hardly had time to get acquainted with the layout of your guesthouse, let alone the tangled inner workings of an entirely different culture, before you had to leave again.

Still, while I was willing to acknowledge my wide-eyed Western naiveté, I was fairly certain of one thing: places like Diani Beach, Patong, and countless others could not exist if the Johns (and the Carters) of the world didn't fuel the demand that kept them alive and thriving.

The following day, Jen, Beth, and I sequestered ourselves within the pristinely tended sanctuary of the Chedi Phuket, planting ourselves on terry-draped deck chairs and ordering drinks that we (or at least Jen and I) couldn't really afford. I knew my friends and I were insulating ourselves from the world beyond the walls, pretending that the garish, neon-lit, bass-pumping spectacle in Patong existed in some parallel universe, not fifteen miles down the beach. For my part, I was attempting to forget that it had, in some small and scary way, touched my life.

Looking past the onyx-tiled pool, through the precisely spaced white canvas umbrellas to the curve of confectioner's sugar sand, and out at an ocean that graduated from turquoise to cornflower to lapis like ombré silk, I realized that were it not for the musicality of Thai voices in the background, my friends and I could have been anywhere else in the world. And just for a second, that's exactly where I wanted to be.

CHAPTER TWENTY-THREE

꽃

Holly

BOSTON, MASSACHUSETTS/CAMBODIA
DECEMBER–JANUARY

I stood frozen on the sidewalk, mesmerized by how the concrete was studded with ice like diamonds and bordered by fir trees dressed in Christmas lights. On the streets, traffic adhered to perfect order: cars heading in the same direction all stayed in one lane rather than swerving into the opposite to avoid wandering cows or wayward rickshaws.

I hadn't expected to feel such awe earlier that day when I'd swiped my debit card at one of the many ATM machines lining Huntington Avenue. Without a glitch, it spit out a pile of crisp twenty-dollar bills, the familiar image of Andrew Jackson with his bouffant hair falling neatly into my hands. Between Indian rupees, Brazilian reals, Peruvian soles, and Kenyan shillings, I'd started to feel like I was playing with Monopoly money. It was comforting to be back in my homeland with mainstays such as baseball, cranberry sauce, and working traffic lights. And when I'd ducked into a deli that morning to order coffee with a splash of milk, that's exactly what I'd gotten—no need to flip through a pocket language guide first. I'd forgotten how easy life could be.

But I worried that other, more important things wouldn't

slip back on as easily as a pair of well-worn mittens. The crunch of boots over snow on the sidewalk behind me broke into my thoughts and sent me hiding from my pursuer, and I flattened my body inside the doorway of a wine shop. Now I was on the run. I only hoped that I'd moved fast enough to lose the man close on my tail and remain undetected.

Crunch, crunch, crunch. The footsteps were almost upon me. My entire body shook and I held my breath, trying unsuccessfully to suppress the laughter threatening to explode from my lungs. I pressed my hands against my mouth to hold it in, and woolly fuzzies from my gloves stuck to my peppermint-flavored lip balm.

Crunch, crunch, crunch. A shadow from the awning overhead fell across my face, and I could see that it was a couple, not the curly-haired man I'd been running from, who passed me by. They were bundled in fluffy scarves and earmuffs, the woman's arm linked through the man's in order to keep her from slipping on the ice.

I stuck out my head, craning my neck to look down the block. In the same instant, Elan's face materialized from behind the shield of another doorway twenty yards down, and his eyes locked on mine. I snapped my head back, but it was too late. The laughter I'd been trying so hard to contain erupted, and I was left gasping for breath and holding my sides. The tears that spilled from my eyes began to form icicles in my lashes.

In the span of a few seconds, Elan sprinted down the block and pounced on my giggling, bent-over form in the doorway. He wrapped his arms around my waist, twirling me on the sidewalk until the lights and the trees and the shoppers and the snowflakes all melted into a wash of color. The couple in front of us stopped to stare, smiling. A few others also turned to see what the commotion was about: Just two people in love, acting like giddy children, playing hide-and-seek in darkened doorways.

Holly • Boston, Massachusetts/Cambodia • December–January

As Elan put me down, his arm secured around my waist, I stood on my tiptoes to kiss his cheek; his cold, smooth skin made my lips tingle. I wanted to stay inside that protected snowy world, but sadness clouded my happy moment. Soon I'd be back in the blistering heat, exploring ancient ruins straight out of an Indiana Jones movie, while he'd be meeting with his agent and going on countless auditions. These little moments could be perfect, but the big picture was flawed. The dichotomy of our lives was driving us apart. E-mail and Skype were no substitution for a relationship, and the divide between Elan and me had grown deeper than distance alone.

After graduating from yoga school and spending a few days celebrating with Chloe and Marta on the beaches of Kovalam—indulging in ayurvedic massages and scarfing down any dish made with onions or garlic—I'd flown from Bangalore to spend the holidays in Boston, where Elan had gotten a role in a Chekhov play.

While part of me felt that returning home was cheating on my year abroad, the other part knew I'd be cheating only myself if I didn't make an effort to see Elan again—to lie beside him, breathe him in, and listen to him tell me about his day. And when my parents offered to split the price of a plane ticket between them as my Christmas present, I considered the decision made.

Standing here, wrapped in Elan's arms, I couldn't help but think about the old question "Can you go home again?" Home, I now knew, for me wasn't a place. It was with the people who mattered most.

But if people change, does that mean home is never permanent either?

I'd been pretending that the space between Elan and me didn't exist. I pretended that the evenings spent sipping mulled wine in candlelit cafés and kissing in the streets meant that time and distance couldn't diminish our love. I tried to believe that falling asleep with my head on his chest to the rhythm of his heartbeat was the way it was always supposed to be.

But while I'd been exploring the world, Elan had turned into a poster child for the term "struggling actor"—eating peanut butter and jelly sandwiches for breakfast, lunch, and dinner; waiting tables after auditioning all day; pooling loose change from the glass jars on top of our refrigerator to just barely make the rent. So if I sensed a bit of resentment, I figured I'd deserved it. If he couldn't come visit me during my year abroad, well, *I* was the one who'd left.

So many times during my visit, I found myself wondering: Was leaving wrong? Would remaining have been more wrong? I worried that staying in perpetual motion would keep me from finding answers that I was seeking—hadn't I just learned at the ashram that the truth is more likely to reveal itself in stillness?

I couldn't make that decision for my entire future, but I knew what I wanted right now. In the middle of that icy sidewalk, I grabbed Elan's hand, pulling him to a stop midstride. I buried my head in his chest and simply stood still.

A few days, a couple long flights, and a lonely layover in Bangalore later, I finally arrived in Bangkok to be reunited with Jen and Amanda. We'd been apart for more than a month. Deep down, I think they were a little surprised (and relieved) that I hadn't stayed back in the States.

"We were worried you wouldn't want to come back after seeing Elan!" Jen joked when I rejoined them at Big John's hostel.

Glancing at their faces as they poked their heads out of their bunks—faces I now knew as well as my own—I also understood just how dedicated you had to be to travel with two other people for a year of your life. In some ways, this trip required just as much commitment as my long-term relationship. It meant doing what I said I was going to do. It meant sticking with them even when a place lost its luster, even when we didn't agree, even when we felt like screaming. The second I walked into our tiny, windowless triple and felt relief at seeing their smiles again, I knew that my home, at least for now, was on the road, with Jen and Amanda.

As usual, the three of us had more time than money to spare, so we boarded a bus rather than a plane to make the five-hour journey from Bangkok to Cambodia. Apparently, taking the cheap route was going to cost us.

"I have an entire page with room for the stamp!" Jen said, stating the obvious to the Cambodian border patrol officer. He returned her passport unmarked after flipping through it and pausing with raised brows at the hodgepodge of stamps. From an outline of Machu Picchu to a rectangle containing the words "Good for Journey to Kenya," multicolored ink blots tattooed most of her pages—except for the last one. Jen kept her finger planted in the spine of the little blue book, holding it open to the empty page, which just beckoned for a fresh splash of ink.

"No, cannot stamp last page." The officer adamantly shook his head. The logic of this eluded us: if there was physically room for the Cambodian visa stamp, why couldn't he just use the free space?

Amanda and I stood guard on either side of Jen. Both of us had two blank pages left—the result of more efficient (or overlapping) stamping techniques used by officials at Brazilian customs. "Man, I didn't see anything about blank page quotas in the guidebook," I said to the girls, fully aware that Jen might not be let into the country at all. And that would mean, of course, that Amanda and I would be going back to Bangkok with her.

Hoping an apologetic approach might work better, I turned to the officer and said, "*Sohm to* [I'm sorry]. What can we do?"

"Must get more passport pages in Thailand," he said, unwavering. Dust coated our hair and sweat soaked our T-shirts. We'd been prepared to unload our backpacks from underneath the bus and lug them across the border to Poi Pet, one of Cambodia's overland entry towns, but we hadn't accounted for the possibility of enduring the bone-jostling, sports-bra-requiring, multihour trip *back* to Bangkok—if we could even find a bus to take us.

Amanda let her backpack drop to the ground with a thud and then sat on top of it. If we were ever going to get through Cambodian customs, it was obviously going to take a while. "But we're so excited to see your beautiful country," I tried again. After all, it was true.

"Okay, you pay," said the officer, crossing his arms over his chest.

Though flattery might get you nowhere, bribery could get you anywhere—in this case, across the Cambodian border. Jen pulled a guidebook from the flimsy fabric purse she'd bartered for in India, opened it to the bookmarked section, "Useful Khmer Phrases," and said, "*Th'lai pohnmaan* [How much]?"

"Ten dollar."

"I have only three," Jen said, slipping a trio of crisp greenbacks printed with George Washington's face from her money belt. Knowing she was bluffing, I wondered if the officer would pull out the handcuffs, attempt to haggle, or simply turn us away.

He peered at the bills for a full minute, then folded them twice before tucking them into the pocket of his button-down shirt. He looked left and right and spoke in a low voice. "Okay, but must get more pages at embassy in Phnom Penh. And must write note for permission to stamp last page."

He ripped a sheet of lined paper from a tattered notebook and slid it across the desk toward Jen. She grabbed a ballpoint and promptly penned a "Get out of Thailand (Nearly) Free" card:

> Dear Cambodian Border Patrol,
>
> I give the Cambodian government permission to stamp the last page of my passport.
>
> Sincerely,
>
> Jennifer Baggett

The officer took the signed permission slip and tossed it into a desk drawer, where it would probably be lost forever, before dismissing us with a wave of his hand.

"*Awk koun!* [Thank you!]" we said, all together. Then Jen and I helped Amanda slip on her backpack as automatically as if we were brushing a loose strand of hair from our own eyes. We didn't say a word as we hefted the load onto Amanda's shoulders, grateful that we had safely dodged yet another one of those random travel roadblocks we never saw coming.

With stamped passports in hand and the sun scorching our scalps, we moved deeper into a new land. Giddy that we'd successfully bribed a corrupt border official, I cheered us on as we crossed over the border. I'd come a long way since that morning in Brazil when I'd tried to separate from Jen and Amanda in the party dorms, when I'd worried that the whole trip would turn out to be one big happy hour.

Africa had humbled us, made us appreciate one another more, and strengthened our bonds after sleeping head to toe to escape a cockroach infestation. At no time had the strength of our friendship been clearer than when walking to a mall next to one of the world's largest slums in Nairobi. We'd stopped our usual chattering abruptly as a deafening *Bang! Bang! Bang!* had shaken the ground beneath our feet.

Before we could figure out if the noise was gunshots, an explosion, or something else, the locals scattered like gazelles being hunted by a lion. Following the herd, the three of us took off running as women held babies close to their chests and men dropped their flip-flops so they could move faster. In the mass panic that ensued, the three of us separated at a fork in the road—Jen sprinting in a zigzag pattern (she said she figured it lessened the odds of being hit by a bullet) to the right and Amanda diving left, crouched low to the ground with her hands shielding her head (she reasoned the lower you are, the safer you are). I'd sprinted ahead to grab Amanda and direct her toward Jen. In that second, choosing right or left wasn't an option—I had to pick both to make sure we were all together and no woman was left behind.

The danger turned out to be imagined. As our six feet slapped the pavement simultaneously, the Kenyans suddenly slowed to a stop and collectively let out a nervous laugh ("Only fireworks," one young mother said with a weak grin as she removed a blanket from her baby's head). As terrified as I'd been moments earlier, I was relieved to discover that my instinct under fire was to keep the group together.

Now, after more than a month apart, I'd made my way back to the group again and was surer than ever that we were all headed in the same direction. We'd been friends to start, but after good times and bad, our relationships with one another had deepened more than I'd ever expected. Sure, Jen and Amanda might have gotten into a screaming match or two over working on the road, and I'd had to step in to break it up. And maybe I'd escaped from conflicts a time or two by going for a run instead of hashing out exactly *why* I couldn't spend one more second listening to Jen and Amanda debate how many fat grams were in a spring roll. By the time we'd (barely) made it over the Cambodian border, any romantic notions we'd harbored about our around-the-world vacation, or about one another, had long since been discarded by the roadside. In their place was a real, perfectly imperfect group of friends.

The woman knew she was going to die soon, but still she smiled. Her puffy eyes pierced mine from behind the glass-protected photograph at the Tuol Sleng Museum of Genocide, one of hundreds of black-and-white faces staring out from the display case.

We'd arrived in Cambodia's capital of Phnom Penh earlier that morning after a few days spent biking around the ancient ruins of Angkor Wat. I'd never before heard of Tuol Sleng but knew about the nearby Killing Fields from the famous movie of the same name. The city of Phnom Penh, which grew up around a Buddhist monastery, had been transformed into a gruesome site for mass murder in 1975 by the Communist Khmer Rouge party. The Khmer Rogue had ordered the city evacuated and used one of its high schools—renamed Tuol Sleng—as a prison/torture chamber for thousands of people. Today the city is very much alive, although a place of extremes. Thriving drug and prostitution rings can be found on one end and quaint riverside cafés on the other.

After checking into a hostel, we'd immediately hired a tuk-tuk to take us to the killing fields. Our driver, a soft-spoken, gentle man named Sok, expertly dodged the mayhem of pedestrians, cyclos, and cars zigzagging through the streets and handed us masks to help block the clouds of pollution threatening to choke us. Once we were outside the city limits, the world whizzed by in clips of green rice paddies, onyx-haired children splashing in puddles, and simple wooden shacks.

As we watched kids chasing one another near the roadside, it was almost possible to forget that war rather than peace had so recently prevailed across Cambodia. My high school world geography class covered little about the country, but I'd gotten a kind of CliffsNotes version of its history by reading through our guidebook. But visiting the area was teaching me more than any book or class ever could.

A weak country sandwiched between more powerful ones such as Thailand and Vietnam, Cambodia had been repeatedly invaded for decades by other nations hoping to strengthen their influence over the Indochinese peninsula, including Thailand, France, Japan, and Vietnam. Americans had ravaged the land with bombs during the Vietnam War. But all the conflicts and wars that Cambodia experienced paled in comparison to the bloodshed of 1975. The Khmer Rouge party had taken over, and its leader, Pol Pot, had ordered the murder of more than two million Cambodians.

When we arrived at the Killing Fields, an outdoor museum that had once been an orchard and an old Chinese cemetery, Sok waited patiently outside. After the Khmer Rouge had taken control of the country, the land had been converted into a mass execution center to exterminate "traitors" thought to be opposed to the Khmer Rouge's Communist agenda. Among those the Khmer Rouge had seen as a threat were doctors, professors, diplomats, and other educated people, as well as anyone who wore glasses.

After I waited my turn in line to light incense at a shrine in front of the memorial—a glass-enclosed stupa filled with about eight thousand human skulls—our guide recommended we head to the Tuol Sleng Museum of Genocide as soon as we got back to the city. That was the first I'd heard of the high school turned

373

prison where Cambodians had been interrogated and tortured before being shipped off for execution. We knew it would be a lot for one day, but when we left the Killing Fields, we asked Sok to take us Tuol Sleng.

The museum was eerily silent as we wandered through classrooms converted into prison cells where captives had been locked to single beds with shackles. Bullet holes and bloodstains speckled the walls in ghoulish patterns.

After an hour, Amanda and Jen waited outside on a bench in the courtyard enclosed by a barbed-wire fence, but I couldn't stop myself from staying longer to look at every single one of the victims' photos on display in an act of remembrance. The Khmer Rouge had used the pictures, along with recorded biographies, to prove they'd captured their "enemies." Now these documents serve as a reminder of the atrocities inflicted by man. As I walked past the pictures, I examined each and every face. Every so often, I would come across a captive who stared boldly into the lens and smiled ever so slightly at the camera.

If these people realized they were about to be tortured, raped, or murdered, how and why did they smile? I can never presume to know what they were thinking or feeling, of course, but staring into their rebellious eyes, I imagined them saying "You can take my clothes, take my home, take my life. But there is nothing you can do that will ever break my spirit." Their smiles struck me as a final act of defiance, a legacy to those still living, proving that we all have a part of ourselves that no one can ever steal.

I walked outside to join Amanda and Jen on the bench. We sat in silence for a few minutes, kicking at the dirt beneath our flip-flops.

"You ready to go, Hol?" Jen asked. I just nodded and we crossed through those barbed-wired gates to where Sok was waiting in a whirlpool of car exhaust, street touts, and tuk-tuks.

"Where I take you now?" he asked as we climbed inside. Where do you go after seeing such horror? What do you *do*? Everything seemed so trivial, as if nothing really mattered.

When none of us said anything, he asked, "Maybe you like to eat? I know good restaurant."

I didn't have any appetite but couldn't stomach going back to the thin-walled hostel room, with only a bed and a dangling lightbulb, to stare at the cracked ceiling. Jen, Amanda, and I looked at one another, and I nodded. He was probably going to take us to a friend's eatery in order to bring him some business, but that was okay with us.

"Yes, let's go there." Before Amanda could even finish the sentence, Sok revved the tuk-tuk engine and flowed into the river of traffic.

I saw food carts, children hawking books, and a man selling papers. I watched life happening all around, people moving along, moving on from the past. In a matter of minutes we were near the National Museum in the city center. Sok pulled to the side of the road just as abruptly as he'd pulled onto it and pointed to a sign that read MITH SAMLANH RESTAURANT. Outside the French Colonial building was a courtyard packed with tables and decorated with red, blue, and yellow murals that looked as though they'd been painted by children. It seemed cozy and safe.

"The name mean 'Good Friends Restaurant' in English," Sok said. He explained that the eatery was part of an organization that used profits to house Khmer street children and train them in hospitality and cooking so they could start careers. Most of its staff were former street kids who worked as waiters, cooks, and managers. "You go. I wait here," he said.

We walked inside, and a boy no older than sixteen seated us at an outdoor table. Everywhere we heard glasses clinking. Waiters carried out spring rolls and salads delicately arranged on pristine white plates. I overhead a teenage waiter asking a diner if he could practice his English with him and then asked, "Why say 'raining cats and dogs'?"

The restaurant was like a pocket of hope in a country where history's wounds are still visible, raw, and real. We'd passed more than one child on the street with a missing leg, the victim of a land mine accident. And we'd noticed the absence of elderly people, because so many had been killed during Pol Pot's rampage only a generation before. It was easy for me to feel depressed at the horror, and I was just a visitor passing through. But these kids lived with daily reminders of the violent past and had no choice but to carry on. Again my mind traveled back to Esther and Sister Freda, who showed me that it's possible to transform ourselves into something greater than our suffering, how life forges on despite pain.

I excused myself to go to the bathroom. Then I stood at the edge of the room and watched the Cambodian teens going about their business. I imagined them wanting the same things that I wanted: To feel safe in an unpredictable world. To work toward something that mattered. To know love. To belong. I watched them from my place on the outside, standing still.

When we later paid the bill, we left to find Sok waiting for us, smiling. "Would you like to go to my friend's shop?" he asked.

"Yes, Sok, we'd like that very much," I said.

CHAPTER TWENTY-FOUR

Jen

SAPA, VIETNAM

JANUARY

Huddled in a frozen mass on the mattress, I peeled the woolly throw from my face just long enough to ask Amanda how her current fire-building attempt was going.

"Well, the wood is damp, there's a draft from the flue that keeps blowing out the flame, and I've lost all feeling in my fingertips. Otherwise, it's awesome," she said, readjusting her ski cap to fit more snugly over her ears.

"All right, we just need something dry to use as kindling," I replied, gathering up my cocoon of blankets and trudging out the door and back to the front desk to collect a pile of hotel literature. Catching my reflection in a hallway mirror, I groaned at the sad girl who looked like death *not at all* warmed over.

It's not that I wasn't thrilled to be in Vietnam, but between the flurry of overland bus trips and whirlwind tours Amanda, Holly, and I had packed into the past few weeks, we'd neglected to do our homework. So we were in complete and utter shock to encounter hearty gusts of wind and fleece-worthy temperatures when we stepped off the plane in Hanoi. Apparently, unlike our first stop in Vietnam, Ho Chi Minh City (formerly Saigon) in the south, the northern part of the country actually gets cold

during the winter months. We'd gotten so spoiled by the seemingly endless summers that we'd chased thus far across the globe
that the girls and I were ill prepared to handle even the tiniest
bit of Jack Frost.

But after spending a couple days pounding the pavements
looking for essential cold-weather attire in Hanoi's bustling Old
Quarter and resting our travel-weary bones in a cozy B & B, we
were eager to take one of the excursions that had drawn us to this
region of Vietnam in the first place: a spectacular trek through
the misty mountains of Sapa, a quaint frontier town near the
border of China. So we booked a four-day trip offered through
Kangaroo Café, one of Hanoi's most reputable tour operators
and, incidentally, one of the few places in the city that serves huge
mugs of coffee (as opposed to the thimble-sized teacups that are
the local standard). Not only would we squeeze in some hard-core
hiking, we would also have the unique opportunity to stay with a
local Hmong family in one of the tribal villages along the trail.

Happy to trade the city smog for country fresh air, we packed
small weekend bags, stashed our big backpacks in our guesthouse storage area, and boarded an eight-hour train to Lao Cai,
where we'd catch a van transfer to Sapa.

Compared with many of our previous rail trips, the ride
through northern Vietnam was a breeze. Our cozy little sleeper
car came equipped with real pillows, fluffy blankets, lamps with
actual shades on them, complimentary bottles of water, and,
most important, no cockroaches. Although we arrived at the
station at the ungodly hour of 5 a.m., we felt surprisingly well
rested and ready to explore the local village. Well, this was until
we actually stepped foot outside and realized that the "slightly
cooler climate" we'd been told to expect was actually closer to
that of a postapocalyptic Antarctica.

Melodramatic, maybe, but anyone who's known me for more
than five seconds can attest to the fact that when the tempera-

ture drops below freezing (which in my opinion occurs at 55 degrees), I transform to "Pure-evil Jen" faster than Carrie on prom night. And after spending the past seven months in countries where eggs could legitimately fry on the sidewalks, who could blame me for being a bit wimpy? But my thin skin would probably toughen up again after a day or so in our new environment. And even if it didn't, our hotel was sure to have a roaring fireplace and cozy heated rooms, right?

Unfortunately, the only source of (supposed) warmth in our double was a miniature wood-burning fire pit in the corner, covered in cobwebs thick enough to trap a small cat. Sprinting back to the room, I used one of five remaining matches to light the edge of a brochure that depicted an attractive couple drinking wine by a blazing hearth in our very same lodge. As their smiling faces went up in flames, I was hopeful. But the wood still failed to ignite.

"I've lit massive bonfires in torrential downpours at campsites up and down the Appalachian Trail and never had this much trouble," I wailed.

"Oh, yeah, well I used to walk a hundred miles barefoot through the snow to get to school," Holly said, appearing in the doorway. "So I finally got a fire going in my room, but unless you're sitting directly on the coals, it's not that warm. I figure the only way to avoid becoming a block of ice is to get out of here and move our bodies."

"Do you mean, you actually want to *exercise* right now? It's barely 8 a.m.," I protested.

"I guess it's better than turning into Popsicles here in the room," Amanda said.

"Definitely. Why don't we hike to the Cat Cat waterfall, which is only about three kilometers away. And then we can grab a huge breakfast. Pancakes, eggs—anything you want," Holly said.

Although I was still grumpy, the thought of food perked me up enough to agree.

"All right, as long as I get first dibs on the coffee, I'm in," I said before all three of us bundled up and headed outside.

Just after dawn the next morning, we were wrenched out of sleep by a sharp rapping on the door. The small fire we'd managed to build before falling asleep had long since crumbled to a pile of cold ash. Unwillingly cracking the shell of my cryogenic chamber with my two-ply wool feet, I stumbled across the room to see who was knocking.

"Morning! Hello! You to have your breakfast now. Then meet guide for hike, okay," sang the cheerful owner, whom we'd met yesterday at check-in.

"Oh, okay. Thank you. Uhh . . . *cam on*," I stammered in Vietnamese, but he'd already proceeded to Holly's room next door.

Quickly stuffing the few items we didn't already have on our bodies into our small daypacks, the three of us then climbed a long set of stone steps up to the lodge café. Although a few sheets of Sapa's dense signature fog had burned off at daybreak, an ominous rumble rippled across the charcoal sky and freshly squeezed raindrops were starting to form puddles in the outdoor stairwells. Snagging the wooden bench closest to the potbellied stove in the dining area, Amanda, Holly, and I sat sleepily clutching tin mugs of hot cocoa. We stared out the panoramic windows, searching the hazy skyline in vain for Fan Si Pan, the country's highest mountain and last major peak in the Himalayan chain.

"Are you Jennifer, Amanda, and Holly?" a bubbly voice called across the room.

Simultaneously turning, we were greeted by a young local

woman with a petite but sturdy-looking five-foot frame and striking facial features. She was dressed in a raven-dyed wrap dress, apron, and leg warmers, with silver bangles dangling from her wrists and colorful scarves and ribbons tied around her neck, her waist, and the top of her socks.

"I'm Tsu," she said. "I will be leading you on your trip."

With a near-flawless English accent, Tsu (pronounced Sue) gave us a quick briefing on herself. She'd been working as a guide for nearly three years, had grown up in a neighboring village, where she still lived with her family, had taken classes in hospitality and tourism at a city school, was presently single—but looking—and loved American movies and music. As her attire suggested, Tsu was a member of the Black Hmong, the Sapa region's most prominent tribal subgroup (there are also White, Green, Red, and Striped Hmong). One of the largest ethnic minorities in the nation, the Hmong are believed to have descended from the people of southern China who settled in the bordering regions of Vietnam, Laos, and Myanmar. In striking contrast to the Hmong villagers Amanda and I had encountered during a tour in Laos, Tsu had been around Westerners most of her life, and with her easygoing nature and wry wit, she was a favorite among the Kangaroo Café–sanctioned leaders.

After shoveling a few bites of omelet and bread into our mouths, we hit the now-rain-soaked streets and joined up with several other tour groups all prepped and ready to start the trek. Examining our clothing, Tsu suggested we make a quick pit stop at her friend's store to pick up some cheap rain gear, which turned out to be our saving grace. Our small daypacks stuffed beneath yellow plastic ponchos with only our heads peeking out from the hoods, Amanda, Holly, and I looked like a strange breed of mutant turtle as we splashed through puddles and slowly navigated the first of many steep climbs.

It didn't take us long to discover that a tortoiselike pace was

381

in fact a necessary survival tactic if we didn't want to pitch right over the edge of the path. After several steady hours of drizzle, the hillsides were frosted in thick, gooey layers of mud and the trail had been transformed into an obstacle course worthy of a *Real World/Road Rules Challenge Gauntlet* round.

A few wild arm flails, awkward hip shakes, and nosedives later, Amanda, Holly, and I had unintentionally invented a brand-new dance: the Sapa Slide. Unlike its cheesy predecessors, such as the Electric Slide, the Macarena, or Mambo No. 5, the Sapa Slide didn't require any lame music scores, choreography skills, or even hand/eye coordination. Success was measured purely on one's ability to (a) make a complete fool of oneself, (b) avoid sudden death or dismemberment, and (c) keep inevitable swearing under control, particularly considering the large number of impressionable youths who had latched onto our group.

"Now, remember, kids, we are trained professionals, so please don't try to re-create our moves at home without . . . adult . . . super . . . vision," I managed to utter before the root I was clutching snapped and I sailed three feet back down the trail.

Despite our best efforts to popularize our illustrious new dance moves, they didn't seem to be catching on with the locals. Everyone—from Tsu to the hordes of resident schoolchildren to the shrunken old grandmothers who'd joined our caravan—was able to work the trail like supermodels at fashion week. Strutting gracefully to the end of the path, they'd turn to offer words and gestures of encouragement, while politely attempting to stifle their giggles at our spastic attempts. As they effortlessly strolled along, some of the older girls even wove small toys and intricate crowns of freshly picked grass and thistles, without so much as breaking a sweat. But despite the obvious discrepancies in skill level, together we formed the perfect team: they helped us successfully navigate the slippery slopes, and we kept them entertained.

After an hour or so, Holly, Amanda, and I found our groove and were eventually even able to carry on a conversation with our new Hmong friends *and* look up from time to time. With the rain finally tapering off and the gray clouds moving on to reveal bluer skies, the girls and I reached the top of one particularly slippery rise and surveyed the scene that had finally become visible before us. Vertical rice terraces rose skyward while vast paddy fields blanketed the lower slopes of the Hoang Lien Mountains. Scenery befitting a Hans Christian Andersen fairy tale stretched endlessly across the rolling hillsides. A powerful nostalgia sparked within me for a time when my banana seat bicycle could fly me anywhere, couch cushions were the building blocks of castles, and giants roamed freely in the backyard. Even at my present "adult" age, I half expected to see strange woodland creatures emerging from the mist or one of the many pigs indulging in an afternoon mud bath to sit up and start talking to us.

Blame it on a temporary midtrip slump, but in recent weeks, I'd become exhausted—and a bit jaded by backpacker life and the incessant claims of "once in a lifetime" adventures. But I was happily surprised, in that instant, to find myself feeling invigorated and appreciative again. Road weariness notwithstanding, this hike truly was a remarkable experience, one that I would undoubtedly long for after returning home. But as intuitive as it may seem, I had to remind myself to savor these ever-fleeting moments. Making a conscious effort to bask in my fantasy-inducing surroundings, I (for once) maintained relative silence throughout the duration of our journey.

A few hours later, the path leveled out and Tsu directed us to a small wooden farmhouse that would serve as our digs for the evening. Clearly accustomed to having Westerners tromp through their home on a daily basis, the host family barely flinched as we piled into the entryway, our boots tracking mud and water droplets spilling off our ponchos, forming puddles on the dirt floor. Assorted garden tools, baskets of plants and vegetables, and oversized burlap sacks filled with rice, corn, and grain lined the perimeter of the main room. Nestled in the rafters above was a large platform accessible by a ladder. Near the back wall, five young children and an elderly woman sat squished together on a threadbare sofa, their eyes glued to an incongruous satellite television set. Welcoming us in, the mother directed us into an adjacent shed, where the father and possibly an uncle or grandfather sat in the corner chatting with each other while chopping and preparing food.

After we settled down on three-legged stools around a small fire pit carved out of the earthen ground, Tsu introduced us to Hai, a young male guide, and his two charges, an Australian couple, Karen and David, who were on an extended honeymoon. I'll admit that my ideal postwedding getaway did not include barnyard animals of any kind, but I was envious of their ability to take a full month off work and awed by their knowledge of the local culture and the tenets of responsible tourism.

Ever since Amanda, Holly, and I had touched down in Peru, and encountered hundreds of tiny children hawking Chiclets and cigarettes, we'd wrestled with issues of social responsibility on the part of tourists. While it was a bit disconcerting watching my dollars spawn future MTV generations among ancient tribal Hmong children, according to David and Karen, the alternative was often much worse. In the absence of income from hosting homestay tours, many minority people relied solely on the corn and rice they harvested for food. And since rice is a labor-intensive crop with a single annual yield, residents of many communities were malnourished. Tsu agreed but also pointed out that many children were dropping out of school altogether to sell trinkets on the trails.

"It is fortunate that some tour companies create education programs to address this problem. And it really is much better that people like you come to villages like this," she added.

Supporting organizations that gave back to the local community and volunteering our time and money certainly was a start, but it didn't change the fact that at the end of the day, we got to return to our cushy middle-class existence, with its infinite opportunities, when most of the world's population didn't have ample food, clothing, or shelter. As I looked across the room, one of the kids got up off the couch and shuffled barefoot across the dirt floor to change the television channel.

Watching him, I remembered one particularly sweet little boy in the Hmong village Amanda and I had visited in Laos. He had been fully dressed on top with a long-sleeved shirt, sweater vest, and suit jacket, but no clothing to speak of on the bottom. Our guide had explained that because there were no viable diaper options, it was easier for parents to let their offspring go half naked so they could use the bathroom without having to be cleaned up afterward.

At first I'd been heartbroken and slightly baffled by the notion, but in reality, it seemed their solution was the most practical. And after spending the afternoon playing with the kids, I noticed that each and every one of them smiled and laughed and skipped around as if they didn't have any concerns at all. They happily played with sticks and rubber balls, and instead of rocking horses, they rode around on live turkeys, lifting them up and stretching their necks like Play-Doh with barely a gobble from the birds in protest. And though their parents and grandparents might have struggled to feed them, there was no shortage of love or hugs. Of course, my first instinct had been to immediately head back to town and organize a food and clothing

385

drive to benefit the families. But the experience did make me question whether our Western ideals really were superior to the values they'd already learned.

In fact, traveling in developing nations often raised questions such as this one in my mind, especially in places like Sapa, where tourists breezed through for a few nights, rarely staying long enough to see the fruits, or potential damage, of their travels. But as I watched our host family enjoy the same ample portions of fried potatoes, sliced beef with ginger, and a medley of garden vegetables as we did—rather than a small amount of rice or corn for dinner—it did seem that our presence had an effect that was more positive than negative.

After the residents had retired to their own quarters in a different part of the farmhouse, Amanda, Holly, and I lingered around the fire with David, Karen, Tsu, and Hai. The consummate cultural anthropologist, Holly peppered them with questions about their heritage, where they had grown up, how they had gotten started as tour guides, their families, and their criteria for marriage.

"We are allowed to date anyone that we would like and choose our own husband or wife. Mostly we meet people at the market, and then we go out to get a meal after. But I am usually with my friends only because there are not very many good men in my village," Tsu said.

"Tsu, we totally understand that," Amanda replied. "There aren't a lot of good men in our village either."

"That is why Hai and I love to give tours, because we meet so many other people that way. And now we must all have a special dessert," Tsu added, pulling a bottle out of her bag. Describing it as homemade rice wine, she and Hai poured us all shots and instructed us to gulp them down in one swift swallow. One part lighter fluid, two parts rubbing alcohol—so it seemed to our throats and stomachs, anyway—this popular local liquor burned away any residual chill left in our bones and probably put hair in places we didn't want it.

"Come on, you have to have more," Hai prompted, topping off our glasses. Good God, I was going to die right here, wasn't I?

Luckily, after several more polite acceptances of this seemingly lethal libation, our entire group was still alive and laughing up a storm. And the more we chatted with Tsu, the more she reminded us of our girlfriends back home. With her feisty disposition, razor-sharp sense of humor, and remarkable ability to throw back booze, she could have fit effortlessly into New York City life. In fact, her facial features and mannerisms were practically identical to those of my favorite producer from my past television life.

This wasn't the first time this sort of comparative recognition had happened to me on the road. But it never ceased to amaze me that no matter how far we were from home or how isolated the pocket of the planet we were exploring, people were inherently the same.

387

After a thoroughly satisfying home-cooked breakfast of high-altitude pancakes, which, though flatter than their sea-level counterparts, tasted just as delicious, we got an early start for what Tsu warned us would be a rigorous five-hour hike. No problem. The weather was clear, and we had the Sapa Slide down to a science anyway. Unfortunately, we couldn't have predicted the challenge that lay before us.

The previous day's storm had done serious damage to the trails, which were now a complete disaster. Broken tree branches, slippery stones, and even thicker layers of sludge stretched for miles. Even the locals were taking baby steps to get down some of the more treacherous inclines, many of them adopting the Sapa Slide as they tried to carry baskets of sticks on their backs. Just when I thought the worst was behind us—or rather, caked on our butts—we reached a sprawling rice paddy. Stepping onto the thin grass strip that was our only means across, Tsu motioned for us to follow. Perched precariously on the leafy ledge, Holly, Amanda, and I had only six inches of space to play with before we would become "one" with the watery crop below. Performing a delicate balancing act worthy of a circus tent, we stutter-stepped slowly along the makeshift bridge, lending a saving hand to one another during a few close calls. At one point Amanda and I slid into each other, nearly sending her camera to a watery death. Eyes fixed firmly on our soggy feet for the duration of the hundred-yard shimmy to safety, we finally reached the path that continued on the other side.

From that point on, we finally got the authentic trekking experience we'd been craving. The trail now wound around a series of steep but thankfully dry hills, through lush forests packed with bamboo, and over jagged rock formations. Despite our slippery start, we managed to finish the hike almost an hour ahead of schedule. Along with dozens of other hikers, our group settled around one of several small plastic tables set up in the middle of a field to dine on jumbo bowls of noodle soup and hot tea. Since Tsu and Hai were going to be continuing on foot to another village, we had to get all our hugs and tipping ceremonies in before our assigned van arrived.

"All right, my crazy girls. You enjoy your night in Sapa, and you should visit the market tomorrow. Maybe you will like the men there better than I do," Tsu said with a wink before jumping in with another group heading down the hill. A quick pit stop at the ladies' bush and we were ready to brave the bumpy two-hour ride back to town. Unfortunately, we still hadn't prepared ourselves for the arctic accommodations we knew were awaiting us in Sapa.

Unable to bear another night of subzero sleep in our guesthouse, we made a collective decision to sell out. We forfeited the few Vietnamese dong we'd spent on our current room and moved to one of the other cheap hotels on the block that provided their guests with space heaters. We'd already proven we could tough it out on the trail. Plus, Holly and Amanda wisely realized that it was in their best interest to take all precautions necessary against the emergence of pure-evil Jen.

After waking up in a warm, toasty room the next morning, the three of us practically skipped through the cobblestone streets, well rested and motivated to pack in as much as we could before nightfall. Entering the city center, we were swept into a bustling bazaar that stretched down the sloping street. The lifeblood of the local trade industry, the market was flooded with hundreds of Hmong, who milled around selling everything from traditional clothing and handicrafts to livestock and heaping baskets of plums and cabbages.

After browsing numerous craft stalls and making a few requisite jewelry purchases, we made our way up Thac Bac Road to find Baguette & Chocolat, a French-style villa that doubled as a boutique hotel and café, rumored to have the best bakery in town. Settling into a white leather sofa lined with plush pillows, we spent more than twenty minutes perusing the extensive menu before settling on a decadent order of iron-pressed paninis, gourmet salads, a chocolate raspberry soufflé to share, and a round of the signature homemade hot cocoa.

"Have you ever had this drink before?" inquired a quirky-looking young Frenchman with a shock of charcoal curls who sat alone at the table next to ours. "It is absolutely exquisite. My favorite in all of Sapa," he added, his accent confirming his nationality.

Seemingly plucked from the screen of an art house film, Emanuel was a fascinating character who soon became our

389

fourth dining companion. Immediately after graduation two years earlier, he'd accepted a position as a junior curator at an impressionist gallery in Hanoi, where he currently shared a house with five other expats. He was on a brief holiday to Sapa to visit some friends but was returning to Hanoi that night on the same train we were taking. Since our van was picking us up in an hour at our hotel, we offered to give him a ride to the station. While he dashed off to grab his bags from his hotel, we settled the bill. As it turned out, Baguette & Chocolat was founded as a vocational school to train disadvantaged youths and local hill tribe minorities in hotel and restaurant services. So, as we'd always done in the past, Holly, Amanda, and I made sure to drop a few extra notes on the table before we left.

Although I hadn't initially warmed to Sapa, as we made our way across the town square, which was now bathed in a soft gas-lantern glow, I couldn't help but feel an unexpected tug of affection for this frosty mountain town. It certainly hadn't been the luxurious escape I'd hoped it would be, but it had temporarily pulled Amanda, Holly, and me out of the mini-funk that had settled over us during our first few days in Hanoi. And though we still couldn't quite shake the weariness in our vagabonding bones, there was a reprieve in sight. In less than two weeks, the three of us would head back to Bangkok and then go our separate ways for a little while—Amanda and Holly jetting off to Myanmar to vacation with Amanda's family and me journeying across the Atlantic to visit my parents in their new Florida abode. It was a much-needed break that I knew would be good for us, but until then, Amanda, Holly, and I were going to lace up our muddy boots, hoist on our backpacks, and keep on trekking.

꒰꒱

CHAPTER TWENTY-FIVE

Amanda

HANOI, VIETNAM
JANUARY

The pavement under our feet was oily slick with rain as we disembarked the train in Hanoi, the sky above us a squid-ink black that blotted out the stars. At 4 a.m., the only light came from the long row of lamps running between the tracks. Their gaseous amber glow bounced back at us from the long, smooth panels of the train and up from the puddles below, flipping the world into an eerie darkroom negative.

"Ladies, it was a pleasure to meet you. We stay in touch, yes?" asked Emanuel, kissing us on both cheeks before running off to find his motorbike.

Outside the station, a group of men were clustered together, chain-smoking inside a milky blue haze. As we stepped into their line of vision, they hurled down their cigarettes and swarmed into action. They encircled and darted between us, shouting prices, grabbing at our bags, and trying to hustle us toward vehicles hidden on side streets. Emanuel had told us to find a driver who'd use the meter ("Otherwise, they rip you off—no more than 35,000 dong to get home, okay?"), but most flatly refused. Others acted offended that we'd dared mention the word.

Just as we were about to give in, one driver emerged from the shadows and agreed to use his meter. Falling down tired, we didn't even consult one another before agreeing, trailing after the man in the wilted beige button-down as he tore down an alley. He deposited my bag inside the trunk, slammed it shut, then jumped into the driver's seat. The three of us wedged ourselves in the backseat just as the ignition sputtered to life.

"Meter, right?" I confirmed, and he grunted in response, slapping the small black box perched above the dash. I watched transfixed as the glowing red digits began ticking rapidly upward, compounding, it seemed, every half second or 1/100 kilometer we traveled. 20,000 dong. 32,000 dong. 45,000 dong. Northward it spiraled, posting numbers that seemed nonsensical to me. Was that the price we were supposed to pay? In my fogginess, it didn't make sense, but Jen—arguably at her sharpest in the predawn hours—instantly put two and two together.

The black box had been rigged. We'd been told that unscrupulous taxi drivers often fixed their meters to spit out prices that were five, ten, even thirty times higher than the standard rate, but we'd yet to encounter the scam.

"Sir, we can see that your meter is incorrect," Jen said flatly. "You can either take us to our guesthouse for the fair price of 40,000 dong or let us out."

The guy didn't say a word. Instead, he jammed his foot against the gas pedal, sending the vehicle careening through the lattice of foggy one-way streets.

"Excuse me, sir, we'd like you to stop the car," Jen continued, making her voice more forceful. "Stop the car and let us out."

He ignored her, and I echoed Jen's request. No response. I peered outside, trying to figure out exactly where we were. In about two hours, cyclos, motorbikes, pedicabs, cars, buses, trucks, vendors, and pedestrians would pack every inch of this pavement, but now the streets were utterly abandoned. The tightly packed rows of buildings were shuttered and locked, gates clamped down over entrances like rows of steel teeth.

Jen kept repeating her request, over and over, her voice increasing in pitch as the cab picked up speed. To my right, a now-lucid Holly clutched the door, ready to evacuate the second the cab slowed enough to allow her to roll into the gutter.

"Listen, I know you can hear me!" shouted Jen. "Even if you don't understand my words, sir, understand my tone! Stop this car right *now*!"

She was screaming, and the message finally seemed to break through to the driver. But by the time he finally slammed on his brakes just off the centrally located Hoan Kiem Lake, our fare already exceeded 100,000 dong.

Just as Jen pulled 40,000 dong from her money belt, determined not to pay one bill more, it finally dawned on me that we had a problem. Every important document and valuable that I had was still sitting inside the trunk, tucked inside my overnight bag. The second Jen's cash hit the driver's palm, the man detonated.

"No, *no*! I say 100,000 dong! 100,000 dong! *You give me my money!*" He turned fully around in his seat, giving us a better view of the fiery lumps of coal burning in the sockets where his eyes should have been. This was no ordinary haggling situation. Jen, who'd seen enough TV crime dramas in her life to qualify for an honorary badge, later likened his behavior to that of a heroin addict crazed for a fix: the only thing standing in the way of his next high was our cash. Holly recovered quickly and yanked her door handle, ready to make a mad dash to safety.

"Wait, I can't leave my stuff!" I pleaded, sounding like one of those idiot girls in horror films who deserve to get offed directly after the opening credits. I would have abandoned almost anything in the bag—my money, camera, credit cards, travelers' checks, remaining plane tickets, even the damn albatross of a

393

laptop, but I couldn't and wouldn't relinquish the visa I needed to enter Myanmar.

Getting permission to enter the notoriously closed-off, military-governed nation had taken extraordinary efforts, not to mention a few white lies about my journalism background. I'd never be able to replace the sticker currently affixed to my passport in time. My family, who'd endured their own entry ordeal back in the States, would be flying halfway around the world to meet Holly and me there in less than two weeks.

Jen and I pressed the driver to release my stuff from the trunk, while Holly remained halfway outside the car, but the man was determined to hold the luggage hostage until we handed over the rest of the money. I'm still not sure why we didn't just toss the additional 60,000 dong (about $3.50) over the seat, grab my shit, and run, but at the time, giving in to a lunatic's demands didn't seem like an option.

Thinking like a Westerner, I suggested that we should find a police officer to intervene. That's when the driver went from ballistic to completely nuclear. Without a word, he whirled around in his seat and slammed the gas, driving us off into a shroud of foggy blackness.

"Oh, my God, we *have* to get out!" Holly screamed. "This man could be taking us anywhere! We're definitely *not* safe here!!"

Her panic infected all of us. The guy, utterly silent, shot down a pitch-black side street that might well have been a portal straight to Hell. While one man might not be able to hurt all three of us, he could easily be driving us somewhere to find people who could. He might radio ahead for reinforcements, drag us off under the remaining cover of night, and extract some horrible revenge for our attempt to cheat him out of his money. Holly leaned out of her open door; I yanked her back before she jumped out of the speeding car.

"Sir! You are scaring us. We want you to stop this car, right now!" Jen said. "If you don't stop, I will open up this window and scream as loudly as I can for help!"

The driver called her bluff, never deviating from his original path.

"HEEEEEEEEEEEEEEEEEEEEEELLLLP! HEEEEEEELP!" Jen used atomic lungpower I had no idea she possessed to alert every man, woman, and child within a thirty-kilometer radius to our predicament. The driver slammed on his brakes. He snapped around in his seat and tried to backhand Jen with his fist, which only made her scream louder. Stumbling out of the front seat, the driver yanked the back door open and pulled Jen out. She stood there, feet planted, her resolve and strength stunning both Holly and me.

"Open the trunk right now, *right now*, and let us get our stuff, and we will give you the rest of the money," she seethed, grabbing a fistful of bills and holding them up.

Visual confirmation of cash broke through the driver's insanity. "You give me money?"

Jen nodded, and he moved around to the trunk and sprang the lock. I grabbed the heavy bag and, without thinking, reeled backward up the street. The driver was either terrified that I was trying to run or just crazed for his cash. He took a running start toward Holly, who happened to be closest, and kicked a foot in the direction of her gut.

Jen and I snapped. With no clear plan in mind other than defending Holly, we raced toward the driver. Seeing two furious women bearing down on him, the guy reeled backward, then thought better of it and charged again, hawking a huge ball of phlegm in Jen's face.

Now it was Holly's turn to lose it. She jumped between Jen and the driver to block her. He leapt back, then darted in to spit at us again. Finally, the schizophrenically unstable driver raced back to his car and slid behind the wheel.

Amanda · Hanoi, Vietnam · January

We didn't stick around to see what happened next. Jen and I grabbed Holly, threw some bills over our shoulder, and ran like hell in the direction of the lake.

O ur showdown with the cabdriver rattled our cages, to say the least.

Holly, who strongly felt that we should have ditched the scene a lot earlier than we did, became distracted and withdrawn. Jen, who believed that we'd never been in any real danger, had no regrets that we'd stood our ground and gotten my stuff back. And I was grateful that both of my friends had stuck by me in a crisis, but I felt horribly guilty that I'd compromised their safety. I replayed the scene over and over again in my head, questioning how I could have done things differently. Eventually Jen told me to stop beating myself up. We'd gotten my stuff and everyone was safe, so we might as well put the whole thing behind us. And once we'd reinstalled ourselves in the Quanghiep Hotel and gotten a few fitful hours of sleep, that's exactly what we tried to do.

According to the carefully plotted Excel chart schedule that Jen had created, we had nearly two weeks to spend exploring Hanoi, the longest stretch of time we'd devoted to any major city since we'd started traveling. While smaller villages and rural areas appeal to me more than population-dense metropolises (there's a sameness to big cities, whether you're talking about Hong Kong, Nairobi, or New York), I was fascinated by Hanoi, a place that during its thousand-year history has served as the seat of the ancient Viet Kingdom, the crown jewel of French Indochina, an incubator of socialism, the headquarters of Communism, and most recently, the cultural and political capital of the Socialist Republic of Vietnam.

Like many cities across Asia, it's in the throes of transition.

Prior to receiving its current, somewhat unimaginative title of Hà Nôi (which means "inside the rivers,"), the city was called Thang Long, which means either "ascending dragon" or "to ascend and flourish," depending on where you place the accent. Either way, the title seems to fit. Modern-day Hanoi has risen from its war-ravaged, impoverished third-world past to emerge as one of the continent's most cosmopolitan, upwardly mobile cities.

It's also one of the youngest. Thanks to a baby boom after the end of the Vietnam War (called "the American War" in these parts), nearly half of the population is under the age of thirty and a quarter are under fifteen, a demographic shift that we spotted as soon as we left the Quanghiep Hotel later that afternoon for a walk through the Old Quarter.

Spiky-haired, fashion-forward teenagers were all around us—they roared past on shiny chrome motorbikes, chattered animatedly into microscopic mobile phones, crammed into cybercafés to play online dance and soccer games. They were even break dancing to the nation's own politically correct, cleaned-up version of hip-hop music in Lenin Square. The young people didn't even acknowledge old man Vladimir's towering presence as they threw themselves into gravity-defying, tendon-twisting moves at the foot of the square's twenty-foot-high bronze effigy.

As Jen and I watched the dancers, Holly got to chatting with Allen, a college professor on a field trip with some communications students from Maryland. He explained that the statue, along with hundreds of other monuments built by the Russians in the latter half of the twentieth century, had basically become a relic of Vietnam's political past.

Though the country technically stands behind its Communist ideology, during the past two decades it has granted an increasing amount of economic and personal freedom to its citizens. In the mid-1980s, the government instituted a series of reforms known as Dôi Mói (renovation), which essentially allowed people to have their own free-market businesses and conduct trade abroad. Not only did this help foster good relations with the capitalist West, it ultimately transformed the nation's economy into one of the fastest-growing in Asia, second only to China. Capitalism and tourism have exploded here in almost equal measure, with the number of international visitors quadrupling in the last decade.

As Holly, Jen, and I wandered through the maze of streets just north of the lake, we saw firsthand how quickly entrepreneurship had gone from being a dirty word to the name of the game. New businesses—hotels, guesthouses, nightclubs, bars, restaurants, art galleries, clothing stores, souvenir shops, tour operators, and travel agencies—had opened to service the flood of foreigners, and we got the distinct sense that everyone wanted a piece of the action. And why not? As Tsu had explained in Sapa, catering to tourists is often a far more lucrative enterprise than, say, rice farming or fabric dyeing. It makes good financial sense for young people to switch from trades their families have practiced for generations to ones that may pull in fifty times the profit. And therein lies the tourism paradox: the greater a destination's popularity, the less authentic it becomes.

In few places has the proliferation of tourism occurred faster than in Hanoi's Old Quarter, a warren of thirty-six tangled lanes and double-knotted passageways situated just above Hoan Kiem, or Lake of the Returning Sword.

Though the Old Quarter fills only a single square kilometer, there's more than enough humanity crammed into it to fascinate an observer for months, if not years. We had less than two weeks left to explore. So each morning, after getting scrubbed down and layered in our single set of mismatched winter gear, the three of us would step from the familial hubbub of our guest-house and into the freewheeling pandemonium just outside our front door. Blaring horns, bicycle bells, high-decibel shrieking, and the ever-present rush of traffic provided the sound track as we navigated through the jumble of passageways between our lodging and the lake.

In centuries past, this area—a trading hub strategically located between the Royal Citadel to the west and the Red River to the east—functioned as the economic heart and soul of the city. Skilled artisans and craftsmen worked shoulder to shoulder on specific streets that eventually took on the names of the goods sold there—shoppers knew what they were getting on Sweet Potato, Bamboo Shade, or Pickled Fish road. These merchants lived with their families in ultraskinny buildings, known as tube houses. Because the residents were taxed on the width of their properties, many homes and shops were constructed to be just nine or ten feet wide—but could be five stories tall and up to 150 feet deep.

Back then the streets were frenzied trading floors where salespeople hawked their wares at earsplitting pitches, negotiated rapid-fire deals in order to edge out next-door competitors, and replaced hastily displayed merchandise as fast as it was sold. Today, other than the threat of getting nailed by a wayward scooter or losing one's hearing from the nonstop honking, the only thing that has really changed is the variety of goods on hawk.

Rather than tracking down coffins, charcoal, fish sauce, and chickens on their respectively named streets, Jen, Holly, and I had an easier time finding knockoff handbags, fussy stiletto heels, bootleg DVDs, cheap plastic toys, bins full of fruit-flavored candies, tins of chocolate, paper fans and lanterns, kites, baseball hats, and piles of mass-produced sportswear separates that had likely migrated down from factories in China.

Amanda · Hanoi, Vietnam · January

Commerce congested every passageway. Pushcarts, stalls, and tables full of merchandise hogged space along the main arteries. Barbers offered haircutting services (complete with chairs, mirrors, and draping cloths) right on the pavement. Farmworkers in conical hats slipped through the crowd balancing slender wooden poles on their shoulders. Along the way, they tried to unload the produce—bananas, green beans, tomatoes, pineapples, and grapes—from flat bamboo baskets suspended from the ends of the rods. And, as I learned the hard way, if you want to take their picture, you have to don the pole and hat yourself, then pay for a few pieces of fruit.

What little sidewalk space wasn't taken up by parked bikes, motorbikes, and baskets was used to create makeshift cafés. Plastic kiddie chairs and miniature stools no bigger than a single butt cheek were organized around equally tiny tables under bright blue tarps. Nearby, men squeezed fish paste over strips of sizzling meat and chopped vegetables inside woks; women squatted over hubcap-sized pans of glutinous white rice and tended to enormous cauldrons of *pho bo* soup above open wood fires.

As they stirred, a beefy blast of steam, richly scented with cinnamon, cardamom, and cloves, swirled into the atmosphere, seducing anyone who happened to catch a whiff. Since we'd arrived, I'd become almost manic about getting my hands on soup as often as possible. I'd even started eating the stuff for breakfast, standard operating procedure for the Vietnamese.

Traffic lights were nonexistent, which made crossing the major streets surrounding Hoan Kiem into a daily death wish—if we waited for a break in the traffic, we might as well have waited forever. The only way to make it across safely was to step off the curb directly into a raging river of oncoming chrome and steel, staring down helmeted drivers, who would then part around our bodies as if we were Moses and they were the Red Sea. Every time we made it to safety without being hit or dragged under the wheels of the rampaging vehicles, it felt as if we'd experienced a miracle.

After our run-in with the heroin-crazed cabdriver (whose reputation had swelled to almost mythical proportions in the retelling), all three of us were now motivated to forge a more positive connection with Hanoi. In all our months of travel, we'd yet to meet a destination that we didn't like—or at least one that we couldn't get along with—but the harder we tried to get on Hanoi's good side, the more roundly we were rejected.

Still ill equipped for the freezing cold temperatures, we ventured to the city's discount-clothing district to layer ourselves in even more coats, sweaters, gloves, scarves, and pants. Initially, we had a blast sorting through the piles of fabric and outfitting ourselves in a ridiculously mismatched combination of colors, patterns, and textures, but I was taken off guard when the women working one stall refused to let me try on a pair of pants, indicating that my five foot four, 125-pound butt was far too enormous to yank them up. Considering that a goodly percentage of the ladies around me barely cleared five feet and might have weighed 90 pounds with their boots on, I could understand that they might worry that I'd stretch out, rip, or otherwise damage the merchandise. But when I finally tracked down a pair of size XXL workout pants, the stretchy Lycra kind that could safely contain an elephant's quivering saddlebags, one of the women snatched them away, shrieking a string of Vietnamese phrases at me as another held her hands out wide in front of my hips in the international sign language for "fat ass." Holly tried to reassure me that being called fat was a compliment in Vietnam ("Even though it's not remotely true! You look amazing!"), but my obesity had clearly affronted their sensibilities.

The fun didn't stop with clothes shopping. Vendors who'd set up wooden carts and stands along Ngoc Quyen Street completed rapid-fire transactions with local customers but often ignored me when I tried to place an order. One man stonily agreed to sell me two forlorn-looking oranges for several times the local price, but when I countered with a more reasonable number, he hissed at me to get away from his cart. Bargaining and negotiating, an integral part of public marketplaces worldwide, didn't seem to be universally accepted here. We knew it wasn't uncommon to charge locals one price and outsiders another, but here the discrepancy almost felt like a form of punishment, some retribution for our general pasty-skinned, wide-hipped, big-nosed offensiveness.

Though some vendors wanted nothing to do with us, others were dogged in their determination to sell us something, no matter how politely and repeatedly we declined. Each afternoon as we walked around the lake, laser-eyed men hawking stacks of illegally photocopied guidebooks and paperbacks would hustle into our path, using their copies of *Lonely Planet: Vietnam*, *The Killing Fields*, and *A Short History of Nearly Everything* to barricade our movements.

At one point, frustrated that she couldn't walk a hundred yards without being accosted, Jen set her chin and decided that she was going to stick to her route, no matter what. For a few seconds, she and one of the guidebook guys played chicken on a stretch of the sidewalk: he bore down on her, frantically rattling off the names of the paperbacks in one long unbroken string of words; she continued looking straight ahead, no more interested in buying them now than she'd been on her first three laps around the water. At the very last second, when they were just inches away from colliding and sending thousands of poorly photocopied pages directly into the lake, the tout flung himself left and hurled a few "fuck yous" in her direction. It was as if Jen had committed the vilest of offenses just by minding her own business. To my amazement, when we'd lapped the lake the next time, the same sales guy moved in to approach our group again.

We leapt off the path and called it an afternoon before it came to fisticuffs.

In each instance, the three of us wondered if we could possibly be imagining things—the undercurrent of hostility, the uncanny sensation that certain Westerners were tolerated as long as they were interested in parting with their greenbacks at every possible opportunity—or worse, if we were doing something to bring misunderstanding and misfortune upon ourselves. It was entirely possible. We'd been traveling at a breakneck pace for the last few months, crammed into tiny rooms on top of one another, and we'd all grown road-weary and snappish. The initial freshness and excitement of the trip had long since worn off, and the reserves of humor and energy we had so often used to deflect aggressive touts, money changers, tour operators, postcard salesmen, beach boys, T-shirt hawkers, and taxi drivers had been all but drained. We tried our best to blow off the bad apples, to remain calm no matter how frustrating the interaction, but we didn't always succeed.

We'd decided to stay in Hanoi for as long as we did in part to give ourselves a chance to rest and to rebuild our reserves before continuing with the trip. But we'd chosen to stay in the most highly trafficked part of the city, and one that we later learned is notorious for the prevalence and sophistication of its scam artists. Most attempts to get visitors to part with their money involve overcharging for rides, returning incorrect change, or rerouting travelers to a different restaurant or hotel from the one they intended to visit. Others were more direct: Holly's purse was slashed while she was walking through one of the markets.

"This women just kept bumping into me and bumping into me," Holly said later, retelling the story. "I remember feeling irritated that she was walking so close to me that she was actually hitting me, but I felt rude telling her to back off. Eventually, I just got fed up, turned around, and stared her straight in the eye. That's when she turned and ran. I didn't really know why—until a few seconds later, when I felt my wallet slip out of my bag." Apparently, the woman had been razoring through Holly's shoulder bag as she walked but hadn't been able to grab the contents before getting caught.

After that, we considered whether it was wise to continue trying to force-fit a relationship that clearly wasn't working.

"I mean, it's unrealistic to think that we're gonna love every single destination that we visit," Jen reasoned. "Maybe Hanoi just isn't our kind of town."

We chewed on that idea for a few minutes, and I felt a little defeated. Could we really have such irreconcilable differences with an entire *city*? The three of us quietly considered packing up our stuff and making our way back to Bangkok. And we might have done just that—retreated nearly a week ahead of schedule, trying the whole way home to rationalize our hasty departure—except that, as it turned out, Hanoi wasn't ready to give up on us.

That night, in pursuit of what might be our last meal in town, we stepped inside a mysterious little lounge we must have passed by half a dozen times during our forays in the Quarter. I was startled to find the place packed and steamy warm inside. Our eyes hadn't yet adjusted to the dimness of the room, which was barely lit by a few scattered candles, when I heard our names called out in the darkness. I could make out the silhouetted mop of rambunctious curls and the distinctive French accent long before I could see the face.

"Jennifer! Holly! Amanda! You're here? I thought you had already gone!" Emanuel shouted, throwing kisses in every direction. He'd tried to e-mail Holly, but the messages had kept bouncing back.

"But this does not matter now. You must come over to meet my friends," he insisted, pulling us over to his table and introducing us to a hip-looking crew of local Hanoians, a couple of his European expat roommates, and a cute American guy in a blue baseball cap. Emanuel explained that the group was celebrating the inaugural issue of a national magazine that his Vietnamese friends Ngoc and Tuan had helped launch.

"Yes, please, sit down," said Tuan as everyone shoved over to make room for the new arrivals. Several oversized issues of the magazine were spread out between everyone's half-empty pint and wineglasses, and I couldn't resist picking up a copy and flipping through the pages to examine the images of girls in deconstructed shift dresses and sexy interior shots of Hanoi's lounges and nightclubs. It hardly mattered that I couldn't read the fine print or even make out the Vietnamese words in the dim light. There was something thrilling about holding a freshly printed full-color glossy, a feeling I can trace directly back to the sixth grade, when I first got my hands on my cousin's copy of *Seventeen* magazine.

The promise that the pages held back then—that just by reading, you might discover the one critical nugget of advice that would transform you into an entirely new, prettier, more popular person—had blown my eleven-year-old mind. I didn't know who dispensed these powerful truths about life, boys, fashion, and lipstick, but I was pretty sure they must be all-knowing goddesses, tapped into a knowledge bank to which we mere mortals would never have access. It was only after getting my first assistant job in publishing years later and realizing that the women penning these extraordinary works of literature were twenty-four-year-olds like me that I felt a teensy bit hoodwinked. What next—*The Wall Street Journal* is written by college business majors?

Still, my fascination with the printed page and the people who created the stories had never entirely waned, and both Holly and I were dying to ask Ngoc and Tuan about their experience working in the publishing industry in Vietnam. They were equally as curious about our magazine jobs in America, whether working in New York City really was like *The Devil Wears Prada*. Almost before we knew it, the three of us had been pulled into the middle of the conversational mix, trading our tales of long hours and tough bosses and learning that things weren't really all that different on this side of the Pacific.

A couple of bottles of Tiger Beer later, I ended up getting sidetracked into a discussion with the boyishly handsome American guy in the backward baseball cap. Andy, who was an expat photojournalist from San Francisco, had been living in Hanoi on and off for the past few years and had been doing extended assignments for editorial heavyweights like *The New York Times*, *Newsweek*, and the *International Herald Tribune*. His work had taken him all over Vietnam, where he'd reported on social issues and, with the help of a translator, explored corners of the country that even most locals never got to see. He'd snapped photos of Agent Orange orphans, documented the conditions suffered by peasants in rural hospitals, and recorded the gruesome work done at Vietnamese slaughterhouses ("kinda tough to stomach for a vegetarian," he told me).

His face glowed in the digital display as he showed me picture after picture of scenes that he'd lain in wait to capture for hours, sometimes days. I found myself riveted—by his passion for his work, the abiding respect he had for the local people, his sense of quiet determination and purpose. This was one American who'd literally viewed Vietnam from thousands of different angles through the lens of his camera and had developed a deeper appreciation for it as a result. Andy admitted that even now, after years spent trekking all over the country, he still had a lot to learn about the culture, the language, the social interactions, and the people.

That made me pause. The girls and I had barely left the Old Quarter, and we'd already decided we'd seen enough of Hanoi to cross the border and leave early. Suddenly I realized what a mistake that could be.

Though we'd run into some bad luck here, we'd also made some pretty novice mistakes. We'd let exhaustion get the better of us. We'd taken cultural differences personally. And we'd been basing most of our assumptions about Vietnam on our limited experiences in the Old Quarter, a single square kilometer that probably revealed as much about Vietnam as Times Square does about the rest of America.

Even though we didn't have much time left (even by Jen's original Excel chart calculations), I hoped we could stick around Hanoi and give ourselves an opportunity to see another side of it. I figured that I might need to do a bit of a sales pitch to convince Holly and Jen, but to my surprise, they were both quick to agree that we should stay. While I'd been wrapped up in Andy (in his photographs and stories, I mean), Emanuel and his Scottish roommate Katie had given Jen and Hol a little perspective on our experiences during the last several days.

Katie confirmed that we weren't imagining the edge of hostility and said that when she'd first moved to Hanoi, she'd encountered a seriously cold shoulder. "As odd as this sounds, ya really can't take it personally. Young women, especially foreigners traveling with no husband or guy to speak of, they just aren't given much respect here. In a lot of the cases, men would still rather negotiate with another man. That's sad, but it's a fact."

"And if you look like a sloppy backpacker, you'll definitely get treated like one," added Emanuel. "The vendors here know the packers always try to haggle down prices below what stuff is actually worth, so they don't even want to deal with them. Regular tourists, they just charge them some crazy price hoping that they don't know any better."

407

The best way to earn respect in Hanoi, our friends explained, was to avoid looking as if you'd just rolled out of bed in your sweats. Dress up a little, smile politely at the person you're dealing with, and never, ever lose your cool. If you act as if the person is going to rip you off (and apparently, a lot of Westerners like us did), they'll probably treat you with an equal amount of negativity or just act as if you're not there at all.

And if you really want to get on equal footing with the locals, said Emanuel, rent a motorbike. "There's no better way to see the city, and avoid being harassed by random guidebook touts and postcard sellers, than when you have your own set of wheels."

He asked us to stick around town until at least the weekend, so he and his roommates could invite us to their house in the suburbs of West Lake, make us dinner, and show us another side of the city. "You'll be the only Americans around for miles," he assured. We promised him that we would come.

Early the next morning, we got up, put on the outfits that we typically saved for dressier occasions, styled our hair, and walked out into one of the warmest winter days we'd experienced since arriving in the city. We took a long walk south of Hoan Kiem Lake, leaving the Old Quarter for the first time, heading beyond the Opera House, past all recognizable landmarks, museums, and tourist attractions, bound for some distant, undetermined point. Block after block passed under our feet, and eventually the whine and rush of the traffic, a sound that filled my ears even at night, tapered to a low rumble. I could no longer pinpoint our exact position on the city map.

People on the street, sitting on the curb, and standing inside shops watched us as we passed. They peeked out of doorways, over chessboards and stew pots, their looks more curious than anything else. Maybe they figured we were lost, tourist refugees from some foreign country, but everyone left us to our own devices. Whenever we smiled at people—schoolboys, fruit vendors, bicycle mechanics, old women tending grandchildren—some people looked surprised, but a lot of them smiled back.

Later that afternoon, we passed a small boutique with silk dresses, scarves, and purses displayed inside the window. Just beyond the glass, two salesgirls were laughing and chattering as they folded up squares of jewel-toned fabric and set them out on a table.

"Can we go inside?" Holly asked hopefully, already heading for the door.

Tiny bells chimed to signal that customers had arrived. The salesgirls looked up.

"*Sin jow*," said Holly, "good afternoon" in Vietnamese. Emanuel had written down a few phrases phonetically spelled for us to supplement the ones in our guidebook, and we'd been trying to use them as much as possible.

"*Xin chào*," responded the girl wearing a white puffer coat.

"*Cay neigh gee-ah—*" Holly said, trying to remember the rest of the phrase for "how much is this?" as she motioned toward one of the dresses she'd seen in the window.

"*Cái này bao nhiêu tiên?*" The girl in the puffer coat walked over to see which item Holly was pointing at. She began speaking in Vietnamese, and Holly shook her head to show she didn't understand. The woman motioned for her to wait, then shouted something into a back room. A few seconds later, a young woman in a black blazer emerged.

"Hello. I am Lan. You—ah—need help with something?" she said slowly as she approached. Holly indicated that she'd like to try on the dress and showed her which one. The woman nodded, pulling a similar dress from a nearby rack and handing it to her.

"You Australian lady?" Lan asked. "U.K.? German girls?"

"Americans," Jen answered.

"Oh, yes? American?" she responded, sounding more curious than anything else. The girl in the puffer coat asked Lan something, and she translated the question. "You—three-ah-sista?"

We smiled and looked at one another. Since Jen and I had similar coloring and were the same height, we were often confused for sisters (and sometimes even twins, depending what country we were visiting), but no one had ever thought all three of us were related. I loved the idea that we were all part of the same family, but we confirmed to the women that we were just friends.

"And are you?" Holly asked, looking around at the young women. "You are sisters?"

Lan translated, and the other two burst into laughter.

"No, we are friend. Good friend. Like you."

I'd like to report that during our final few days in Hanoi the girls and I experienced one incredible life-altering event that forced us to see the error of our ways. We didn't. Instead, it was an ongoing series of simple, positive interactions, like the ones with our magazines friends Ngoc and Tuan, Andy the photographer, the women at the dress shop, the people we'd meet during our walks, and even Emanuel and his quintet of expat roommates, that subtly adjusted our original negative impression of the country and helped us feel a little more at home in a place that had initially seemed so unwelcoming.

By the time we left the city, the three of us wondered if we'd return someday. And if, after all we'd experienced, maybe we'd gotten it wrong. Maybe Hanoi was our kind of town after all.

⚘

CHAPTER TWENTY-SIX

Jen

For as long as I can remember, I've been a girl on a mission, the one with a never-ending supply of grand plans. When I was ten, I became obsessed with the idea of boarding school, so I called an urgent family meeting to discuss my possible attendance. Though I loved my parents, I questioned whether my suburban hometown could afford enough adventure to sustain me through high school. As always, my mom and dad were sympathetic to my latest plight but claimed they'd miss me too much to send me away. Oh, the burden of being the sole offspring and family entertainer. But with other ambitions on the horizon, such as trips with my camping group, drama club tryouts, and sports leagues, I forged ahead.

By the seventh grade, I was knee-deep in a promising soccer career and working toward a varsity position as a high school freshman. As a junior, I was devising an advanced placement curriculum to max my GPA. Throughout college it was an ongoing schedule shuffle to fit in soccer, sorority, my business major, and a long-distance boyfriend. Then with only a few suitcases and an air mattress to plop on Amanda's floor, I was off to New York City to pursue a television career. Soon I was plotting a path from sales to marketing, then from network to cable, followed by a GMAT course. Just when I thought I'd hit a wall, the round-the-world trip came up and I was back in business with the grandest plan of all.

But suddenly here I was, Bangkok-bound on a Boeing 757 jet, and it hit me: for the first time in nearly two decades, my future was 100 percent open, with no clear-cut path to follow. Unless a husband and two kids were waiting for me back in the States, there was no next phase to glide into naturally. I didn't have a clue where I'd be living or what I'd be doing a few months from now.

"So you'll be going back to Manhattan when your big adventure is through, I suppose?" my Irish flightmate, Daniel, asked. In the few hours since we'd left London—my stopover city from the States, where I'd just spent two and a half weeks visiting my family—we'd swapped mini–life stories, so he knew all about Amanda, Holly, and our world travels.

"You know, I'm not really sure," I replied slowly, visions of sleazy apartment brokers, a zero bank balance, no boyfriend, and no job zapping my brain like migraine waves.

"I was there once as a boy and loved it. And how exciting that you work in television."

"Yeah. It was exciting. Maybe I'll go back. I'm not sure, though," I said. Old snapshots of Brian and me meeting for lunch in our shared office building or swapping stories about projects and industry contacts over takeout suddenly flashed before my eyes, tempting me to activate the emergency barf bag tucked in the seat pocket.

"Hey, no worries. You'll figure everything out when you get home," he said, which was another sad reminder that my parents had recently sold my childhood house in Maryland to retire to Florida. "So, no sense in fretting now. And how could ya, when the attendant is giving us all these extra bottles?" he added with a grin, toasting my wineglass with his fourth whiskey mini.

Try as I might to stash Daniel's free-spirited attitude in my carry-on and transport it with me off the plane, our innocent Q & A session opened a Pandora's box of dormant neuroses. As I sat all alone in my Big John's Hostel dorm, my inner demons flew out in a fury. In less than four months our trip would be over, and then what? Where would I live? What would I do for work? How was I supposed to start my dating career at twenty-nine, when most of my friends were nearing the end of theirs? What if "The One" was a figment of my overly romantic imagination and I never got married and had babies?

I tried to tell myself that it was just my fatigue talking. Between the six-hour flight from Tampa to Gatwick, a bus transfer to Heathrow, a nine-hour layover, a twelve-hour flight to Thailand, customs, baggage claim, and the taxi ride to Big John's, I'd been awake and on the move for who knows how long. I'd lost track of time somewhere over Europe. But if I could just get some sleep, things would surely look brighter in the morning. Unfortunately, the morning on this side of the world wasn't due to appear for a while. It was barely 5 p.m., and I knew that the nearly deserted hostel would soon be flooded with backpackers returning from a day of sightseeing to pile onto hall couches and watch movies, hit the downstairs bar, or get ready for a night out.

So as much as I hated to wrench myself off my comfy platform bed, it made sense to push through for a few more hours and crash out with everyone else later. Besides, it'd probably be good for me to walk around and clear my head, maybe grab a bite to eat. Plus, I still needed to e-mail the girls to let them know I'd arrived safely and coordinate meeting up either with Amanda and her family the next day or with Holly in Koh Tao, where she was getting her scuba certification.

Once the layers of travel grime were scrubbed off my body and rinsed down the communal shower drain, I changed into my standard Southeast Asia uniform (tank top, diaphanous skirt,

413

and flip-flops) and headed outside to hit my favorite shopping pavilion up the street. Unlike Khao San Road, the infamous backpackers' ghetto where Leonardo DiCaprio acquires the map to *The Beach* and where most of Bangkok's budget accommodations are still found, Big John's was nestled in the upscale Sukhumvit neighborhood—a formerly seedy area that had been recently revitalized with modern offices, trendy restaurants, dance clubs, art galleries, and bridal boutiques, and sprinkled with intermittent noodle stalls, lemongrass-scented spas, and tuk-tuk stands.

Settling in a lounge chair on the al fresco patio of Au Bon Pain, which, along with Starbucks, was the preferred haunt of local artists and designers, I nursed an iced latte under a striped umbrella and watched the community's daily grind slow to a smooth churn. Well-heeled wives greeted their sharply dressed businessmen husbands for dinner, teens in the latest punk/mod attire browsed record store aisles, schoolkids nibbled on sweet banana skewers, and expats loaded groceries into parked BMWs and Mercedes-Benzes.

While the implications of Daniel's in-flight survey still pressed on the back of my mind, sitting in this serene pocket of the city, I felt much more relaxed and couldn't help but relish the quirkiness of my existence. Less than forty-eight hours earlier, I had been lying on my parent's sofa watching old movies, and now here I was in another country halfway around the world, chilling alongside a crowd of Thai hipsters.

"Excuse me, do you know if this is the right way to the Skytrain?" asked a slender blonde who stood a few feet away on the sidewalk, motioning down the street.

"Oh, um, yeah, it is," I said, realizing she was talking to me. "Just keep going until you get *all* the way to the end of the road and turn right. You'll see the tracks above you and a set of stairs up to the entrance."

"Ah, brilliant. You're a lifesaver. Thank you," the girl said.

Although Bangkok was an incredibly user-friendly city, the similarly named and numbered *sois* (streets) could be really confusing. It'd taken Amanda, Holly, and me a few wrong turns to get the city down, but at this point, even as directionally challenged as I was, I could navigate the public transportation system to most major landmarks.

Once I was caffeinated enough to stay awake for a while longer, I headed back to Big John's, where a typical hostel scene was already in progress: new arrivals crowded the lobby, tossing out questions about prices and facilities, regulars lounged with books or took advantage of the free Internet connection, a handful of guys was engrossed in a rugby match on TV, and the local staff delivered bottles of Chang Beer and Australian-style pies (think meat, not fruit) to tables of backpackers, then dashed back to the desk to distribute keys and promote packaged tours.

Without Amanda and Holly there as social buffers, I suddenly felt exposed and self-conscious, as if it were my first day at a new school and everyone was staring at me thinking "Aww, look at that nerd, she doesn't have any friends to sit with." Since all the lobby computers were currently occupied, I found a seat at an empty table and immediately snagged a menu, studying the dinner section as if it contained the secret to eternal bliss. During the torturously long wait for my meal, I tried to project the image of a mysterious loner. Yes, I lounged in golden wheat fields contemplating the tragic beauty of the universe. Yes, I poured my poetic angst into leather-bound journals while sipping bourbon in smoky speakeasies.

But after a few odd looks from the waitress, I assumed I looked more crazy than cool, so I gave up. Even after I had eaten a plate of pad Thai one noodle at a time, strolled to the reception to inquire about the cost of laundry, and scribbled a slew of useless travel to-do lists in my notebook, no one looked any closer to abandoning their keyboards, and I was running out of ways to appear busy.

Jesus, Jen, get a grip. You could run upstairs and grab a book, buy a cookie or maybe even . . .

"Is anyone sitting here?" asked a muscular guy with a slightly affected American accent. Whew! Saved.

"Nope, it's all yours," I replied in my most nonchalant tone.

"Cool. Thanks," he said, plopping down next to me and pulling an expensive-looking camera from around his neck. "Holy shit, I'm sweating. I should really go change my shirt. Hey, you know, supposedly there's a restaurant down the street with a garden and lots of fans and . . ."

"Oh, my God, Frank. You totally missed it. This tuk-tuk driver swerved off the road and almost hit that stand that sells coffee in plastic bags," gasped a petite girl with a mass of wiry curls who suddenly burst through the door, three guys and another girl following in her wake.

"Whoa, Libby, I leave you for a few minutes, and all hell breaks loose. Well, as long as my ladies there are all right," my benchmate replied. "Man, that's my favorite place to go in the morning. Have you been there? The coffee is the best. You have to try it," he directed at me.

In less than five minutes, the entire crew was piled around the table recounting their adventures from the day. There was Libby, an Israeli hippie who had grown up in Pennsylvania and recently graduated from UCLA. Dan, from Vancouver, who'd arrived in Bangkok from Cambodia the day before. Brad, who looked like a California surfer dude but was actually English and had befriended Dan on the bus ride into town. Charlotte, a blonde with wire-rimmed glasses and a thick Irish accent. Peter, a soft-spoken Brit who was on sabbatical from an engineering job. And hilarious Frank, an American who'd been teaching in China for the past few years but was taking some time off. Sur-

416

prisingly, aside from Frank and Libby, who appeared to be in the midst of a fling, no one else had any past knowledge of the others. They'd just randomly stumbled in at the same time and created an impromptu circle of friends. And being on my own, it seemed, gave me instant street cred with the singles crowd, because before long, I found myself privy to personal tales and past life tidbits.

In between the group's round-robin of showers, wardrobe changes, and beer runs, I discovered that Frank had never planned to teach in China, but during a vacation he'd fallen in love with a woman there and on a whim decided to stay. They'd broken up a year before, but he had no regrets. Peter was an alcoholic, and this trip marked his fifth year of sobriety. Charlotte, who used to be married but was now happily single at thirty-two, thought Brad was gorgeous and planned to flirt with him all night. And Libby had recently decided to postpone her return to the States for another few months because her existential journey would not be complete if she didn't make it to Sri Lanka—and it would piss off her stepmom.

Though taking a vacation by myself had always appealed to me about as much as a root canal, in the presence of people who clearly thrived on indie travel, I wondered if perhaps I needed an attitude adjustment. Earmarking a few days for mandatory self-exploration might, in fact, make me a stronger person. Help me conquer my fears . . . prepare me to face an ambiguous future with grace and dignity . . . rediscover that precocious child inside who'd begged her parents to let her go off on her own to some far-flung preparatory academy. Or, at the very least, help me master my mysterious loner look.

Considering that Amanda was knee-deep in coordinating a multimember family vacation and Holly was almost a full day's journey away via yet another long bus-to-ferry combo, now was the perfect time for me to try flying solo. If I could direct a lost

417

backpacker to a mass transit station, I could certainly find a way to enjoy being on my own in Bangkok for a week, right? Before I could chicken out, I sprang onto a freshly vacated computer and alerted Amanda and Holly of my plan, sealing my fate as a one-woman traveling show.

As is often the case with daring leaps, the universe found a way to reward the faithful. From the moment I committed to being a single gal in Thailand's vast capital city, any potential loneliness got quickly kicked to the curb. If I stuck around the hostel common area for more than twenty minutes, someone would inevitably plop down nearby and strike up a conversation. Any time I crossed paths with a member of my Big John's starter crew, they'd inquire about my plans and extend sincere invites to hang out with them, a gesture that might not have been so instinctive had I been part of a preformed group.

Don't get me wrong: Amanda, Holly, and I had met tons of other travelers during our trip, but a clique of three projected a totally different vibe. When we weren't in the mood to chat with strangers, we kept to ourselves. During our rare quiet times, we were as comfortable with one another's silence as an old married couple in parallel rocking chairs. But being on my own provided a greater incentive to put myself out there and try to make new friends, so I tackled this new challenge with the same vigor I'd used to throw into special projects at work.

Before long, I found myself with quite the burgeoning social calendar. Frank, Peter, and Charlotte became my most compatible sightseeing partners, and we did almost everything together. If it was a nice day, we'd hit our favorite jogging spot, Lumpini Park (named after Buddha's birthplace), and take a light spin around the lush green space, passing tai chi masters, spandex-clad aerobics classes, and street musicians who competed with public speakers blasting eclectic native melodies—and the national anthem at 6 p.m. daily. If we were feeling lazy, Charlotte and I would browse the stalls at Little Siam, an inconspicuous side street near the mega–shopping complex Siam Center for trendy urban ware and custom-designed jewelry at bargain-basement prices. And as often as we could, we'd all pop into one of the city's innumerable massage parlors advertising "60 minutes with scented oil for 250 baht," which was always the best $8 I ever spent.

On day three of my "solo" adventure, the four of us managed to peruse dozens of downtown shops, squeeze in a matinee screening of *Babel* at the Siam Center multiplex, and make the requisite pilgrimage to Khao San Road. While the labyrinth of seedy guesthouses and back-alley bars was still woven into the background, the veritable "Bourbon Street of Bangkok" was now splattered with brightly lit pubs, restaurants, travel agencies, and vendors hawking everything from bootleg DVDs and fake driver's licenses to discount antibiotics and incense burners. Though I was glad to be staying in our Sukhumvit sanctuary, there was nothing more old-school cool than Khao San Road.

By day four, I practically needed a Palm Pilot to keep track of my packed schedule. Amanda and her family had returned to the city the night before after a three-day trek near Chiang Mai, so I'd met them for dinner and ended up crashing at the foot of Amanda and her sister Jennifer's plush king-size hotel bed for the night. After a delightful four-star (and free) breakfast, I'd had to hightail it back to Big John's to meet Frank, who'd offered to treat me to coffee in a bag if I'd be willing to burn all the photos I'd taken of our group onto a CD since he'd accidentally wiped out his entire memory card the day before.

After that, I would be joining Peter and Charlotte to attend my first professional Muay Thai fight at Ratchadamnoen Stadium, then meeting up with this guy Mark, an American teacher

419

in Bangkok, who'd gone to college with my friend Stephany from Maryland. An avid globe trekker herself, she'd sent e-mails to some of her overseas contacts to let them know when I'd be in their neck of the planet. Once I'd decided to stay in the city alone, I'd figured it couldn't hurt to shoot Mark a note. Of course, when I'd sent the e-mail I'd never expected I'd be so busy that I'd just barely have time to squeeze in a quick drink, but I was always happy to meet a friend of Steph's. And as luck would have it, Steph was going to be joining me, Amanda, and Holly in Bali the following week, so I wouldn't have to wait too long to thank her in person for the Bangkok connection.

I arrived back at Big John's with an hour to spare before I was supposed to meet Mark in the lobby. After a quick shower and wardrobe refresh, I bolted back downstairs and settled onto a bar stool to wait for the "tall blond who would appear to be wandering around looking for someone," as he'd joked in his e-mail. Less than five seconds elapsed from the time I saw Mark walk through the door to when he noticed me across the room, but within that tiny sliver of time, I knew that this gorgeous stranger was about to turn my world upside down.

As he walked toward me, his eyes locking hopefully onto mine, my heart fluttered straight out my chest and hit the floor with an audible thump. *Oh, my God, I can't believe this is Steph's friend. I was not expecting this at all.* Confirming that I was, in fact, the Jen he'd come to meet, a deliberate and impossibly charming grin spread slowly across his face, almost as if he were thinking the very same thing. As we crossed the threshold into the sultry night, it suddenly felt less like a casual meeting and more like a first date, both of us animatedly reiterating how fortuitous it was that Steph had put us in touch.

Walking side by side down a warmly lit street, I still couldn't get over how drop-dead handsome Mark was with his thick mass of sandy hair, soccer jersey, and sun-brushed complexion (but not in that too-pretty, overly chiseled way that immediately turned me off of prototypical "hot" guys). At first glance, Mark was a striking combination of all-American athlete and rugged cowboy, but he also had that sweet, unassuming boy-next-door quality that I'd always been hopelessly attracted to (which my girlfriends referred to as my Bryan MacKenzie complex after my adoration of the fiancé in *Father of the Bride*). My God, Steph really should have warned me, I thought, as Mark and I settled at a two-top in a trendy jazz bar across the street.

Since Mark had to be up early the next morning for class, I'd assumed we'd swap some fun stories and call it an early night. But before I knew it, hours had slipped by and we were both still bursting to learn more about each other. A boundless stream of carefree conversation spilled out between us—everywhere we'd traveled in the world, all the places we still ached to visit, our college soccer teams, careers, friends, past lives in and out of the States, anything and everything we were passionate about. At one point we even relocated to the front patio to avoid having to shout over the live band, all the while continuing our intense discussion about the effectiveness of U.S. volunteer programs overseas versus locally run organizations.

Never in my life had I been drawn to someone so instantaneously and, rarer still, someone who challenged and intrigued me as much as Mark did. Not only had he been to nearly twice the countries that I had, he cared deeply about prosocial causes, loved kids, and just happened to be a star soccer player in his spare time. He was accomplished, kind, adventurous, and dreamy—the type of guy I didn't quite believe existed. But as Mark fervently shared his teaching experiences in both inner-city schools back home and more posh academies abroad, bragged about his nieces and nephews, and discussed his latest aspiration to start an orphanage in South America, for the first time in my life I knew that I was capable of falling insanely head

421

over heels for someone I'd just met. Because if given the chance with Mark, that's exactly what would happen. Sadly, I could feel the night slipping away, and it was all I could do not to rip off the tablecloth and hunker down on the sidewalk with him until dawn.

Somehow sensing my inner thoughts, Mark glanced at his watch disappointedly. He wasn't ready to leave yet, but in a few hours he needed to be freshly pressed and ready to wow his students, so he'd probably need to go soon. But . . . *yes, there's a "but"* . . . he added that he'd really like to see me again and wryly insinuated that I hadn't experienced the "real" Bangkok until I allowed someone who lived in the city—himself, for example—to take me out. At the sound of the words "really like to see you again," I'd already flashed forward to us holding hands and cuddling in a tuk-tuk, but there was no point in mentioning that little fantasy. The important thing was that this night spent with Mark would not be my last.

Throughout the entire next day, I felt like a kid on Christmas Eve, full of nervous energy and bouncing all over the place in anticipation of my downtown meet-up with Mark. Maybe it was silly to make such a big deal out of it, but I hadn't gone on any sort of first date in nearly half a decade and I was going to enjoy every second of the experience, even if it was the backpacker version. Either way, it was a fun excuse to retire my ratty Reefs for a night and break out my one pair of low-heeled sandals. And any embellishments to my typical on-the-road beauty routine of lip balm, sunscreen, and headband were bound to make me feel like a new woman.

The plan was to meet Mark across town at the Sala Daeng station near Lumpini Park, so after a quick dinner at Big John's, I hopped onto the Skytrain and headed west. Since I didn't have a cell phone, we'd resorted to the old-school tactic of designating a specific landmark and time. At 9 p.m. sharp, I arrived at the large fitness center Mark had described in his e-mail, and there he was, standing on the corner of Silom and Soi Convent, still just as adorable as when I'd left him.

We moved through the night with the giddiness of a young couple in the honeymoon phase, chatting and laughing and continuing to reveal more layers of our personalities. Although Mark was a humanitarian by nature, it didn't preclude him from having a quirky sense of humor and the perfect touch of sarcasm. Before I knew it, we were engaged in a full-scale competition to classify the dancers at our current Patpong location as either ladies by birth, ladies by surgery, or lady boys who took impressive concealment measures.

Originally established as the red-light district for U.S. servicemen in the 1960s during the Vietnam War, Patpong was now a bustling tourist hub famous for its night market and boisterous social scene. Packed with shops, restaurants, pool halls, live music venues, countless go-go bars, and dancing girls (or boys, or too-tough-to-tells), Patpong was a hilarious place for me to explore with Mark, who, after living in Bangkok for nearly two years, knew the area well and got a kick out of taking newbies there.

During the course of the night, the space between us had naturally compressed: Mark protectively placing his hand on the small of my back to lead me across the crowded street; me affectionately patting his arm during one of his funny stories. Each touch was more enticing than the last. As we sat on the outdoor patio of a popular café, our knees brushing under the table, the chemistry between us was as palpable as the balmy air. As our conversations escalated into passionate debates, so did our anticipation. Somewhere between the value of traveling to third-world countries, concerns about returning home, and needing to be around people who understood us, Mark's gaze intensified and he slid his hand across the table and placed it on top of mine.

Capturing my eyes with his gaze, Mark grazed his fingers along my jawline and pulled me toward him. His hands wrapped tightly around my face, and he kissed me, a deep, slow, fall-to-the-ground kiss. My breath momentarily froze, then drizzled down my throat like warm honey. Sliding my hands up his chest and around his neck, I melted against him, every clichéd sentiment I'd thought existed only in silver-screen romances crashing over me in unfathomable waves. The frenetic sounds of the city, people passing by, tourists laughing at the tables around us . . . it all evaporated away. Temporarily unlocking me from his lips, Mark looked at me and smiled.

"I hope that was okay, I just couldn't help myself," he said with a wink. It took all my willpower to construct coherent sentences after that, but somehow I managed to discuss a tentative plan that involved going back to his apartment, opening a bottle of Riesling, and sitting out on the balcony to watch the stars.

As if that proposal weren't enough to convert me into a full-fledged swooner, what Mark said next certainly did. We'd just settled the bill when he paused and explained that though he would love for me to come back with him to his apartment, it didn't mean that things needed or should go too far. Not that he wouldn't seriously be tempted. But he wanted to know that we were on the same page before we left. I just stood there stunned for a few seconds. Until he mentioned it, I hadn't thought very far beyond a sexy make-out session over a bottle of wine. But, hey, I'd never claimed to be a saint. And considering I'd spent the majority of the past decade in two committed long-term relationships, I certainly wasn't opposed to a torrid love affair with a gorgeous man in an exotic overseas destination.

But as unbelievably attracted as I was to Mark physically, he already meant more to me than a wham-bam-thank-you-ma'am fling. And even though we'd just met, I was completely captivated by him, by everything. The way he looked at me. How he touched me. His seriously sinful kisses. We could just do that all night, and I'd be more than satisfied. So . . . that's pretty much what we did.

With the bright lights of Bangkok flickering like tiny fireflies in the distant skyline, Mark and I lay together in his moonlit bed, discussing our pasts, our fears about the future, and what we yearned for out of life. I'd never felt such a powerful connection to another person so quickly, and I knew, deep in the recesses of my soul, that we'd been placed in each other's lives for a reason. Kissing, cuddling, beautiful moments of silence filled the space until dawn. My head on his chest, his arms draped around my back, we eventually drifted off. But right before we did, Mark smoothed my hair off my face and whispered that he'd try not to wake me when he was getting ready for school and that he was going to take me out to dinner that night. Comforted by the promise that I'd have to wait only a few hours to see him again, I finally gave in to sleep's grasp.

W here have *you* been all night, little lady?" Frank inquired coyly as I walked through the front door of the hostel with my bed head, rumpled clothes, and huge grin plastered on my face.

"Oh, that's right. You had your date last night. How'd it go? Really well, by the looks of it," Charlotte interjected.

"I can't even begin to describe how perfect it was. Seriously. It was life-changing," I said.

"Way to go, Jen. You're really moving up in the world. Doing the walk of shame back to Big John's. I love it!" Frank said.

"And you speak from experience, now, don't you, Frank?"

Jen · Bangkok, Thailand · February

Charlotte said, before adding that she had to head out soon if she was going to make her bus to Cambodia.

That's the weird thing about backpacker life. One moment someone's there, the next they're gone. Charlotte and I had already exchanged e-mail addresses earlier in the week, so there was nothing left to do but wish her good luck and help her out the door with her stuff.

"I just can't believe that it's my last day here in Bangkok. I'm actually really bummed," I said, returning to the table and pulling up a chair next to Frank.

"Aw, man. I didn't know that. When are you leaving?"

"Our flight's actually not until 3 a.m., so my friends and I are just going to hop in a taxi from here around midnight. They're going to be here around 6 p.m., but I'm supposed to meet Mark for dinner later, so I should probably try to pack at some point."

"Mark? Life-changing guy, right?" Frank said. "Well, hurry up and pack, and let's go out and celebrate. It's not every day that you meet someone life-changing. Believe me, I know. I mean, shit, I moved all the way to China for a chick I'd just met."

"All right, you convinced me. Meet you back here in forty-five minutes?" I asked. "And hey, maybe we can even play tourist and do something really cultural for a change."

After a quick shower, I set aside an outfit for later, shoved everything else into my backpack, and headed downstairs to check my e-mail. Waiting in my inbox was a note from Mark confirming our dinner and suggesting a meeting place, which sent me into a giddy tailspin all over again. So this was what it felt like when a guy you really like "calls" you back to ask you on a second date?

"It's a good thing we're going out to sightsee, because I have way too much pent-up energy right now," I said to Frank while quickly dashing off a response to Mark that I, too, was really looking forward to our night out.

Frank had suggested we go to Wat Pho, the largest and oldest temple in the city and home of the Reclining Buddha, which meant we'd have to travel downtown to the central pier and hop on a water taxi. Amanda, Holly, and I had taken one of those canal (*khlong*) boats to the Flower Market, a delightful fairyland of blooms located near the Memorial Bridge on Thanon Chakphet, and I'd relished the experience. Considering that Bangkok had been nicknamed the "Venice of the East" it's certainly the most authentic way to travel, plus you get a little bonus sun and spray while you ride. After speeding down the banks of the Saen Saeb, we hopped off at the Tha Tien pier and went in pursuit of the big man on the temple campus.

One of the city's most visited landmarks, the Reclining Buddha measures forty-six meters long and fifteen meters high and is designed to represent the passage of the Buddha to Nirvana, which likely explains the serene smile on his face. With a body decorated entirely with gold plating and mother-of-pearl engravings on his eyes and soles of the feet, the Reclining Buddha, who lies on his right side, is an impressive sight to behold. Frank and I spent hours at Wat Pho, trying to digitally capture all the Buddha's wide angles and snapping as many shots as we could of the more than one thousand Buddha images on the grounds.

As the day flew by, I was continuously struck by the bittersweetness of my impending departure. I'd grown so fond of the mini-life I'd carved out for myself in Bangkok. For the first time since leaving our students at Pathfinder in Kenya, I was genuinely sad to say good-bye to a place and, more important, to the people I'd met there.

On the upside, I *was* really excited to see Amanda and Holly and get back on the road again, especially since our next stop was Bali. It was strange to think that after one week in Indonesia we would leave "hard-core" foreign travel behind and enter an English-speaking country for the first time in nearly nine months. From that point we had just four weeks in New Zealand, eight weeks in Australia, and it would all be over. I could hardly believe how fast the trip was flying by. In a way, it seemed as if we'd been gone forever, but at the same time, I could remember sitting on the airport floor in Peru waiting for Holly's lost luggage as if it were yesterday. There had been so many extraordinary moments throughout our journey that I longed to freeze-frame, rewind, and replay them forever. And the second I saw Mark again later that night, I added another one to the list.

I'd arrived at our agreed-upon meeting place a few minutes early, so I sat down on a nearby bench to wait for him. In a sea of petite locals, it's hard to miss a strapping six foot blond guy, so I noticed Mark when he was still about fifty feet away. Like the first time he'd walked into Big John's, my heart leapfrogged toward my throat. When he saw me, he grinned and accelerated his pace. Perpetuating the movie moment, I stood and walked quickly toward him, and when we reached each other, he swept me up into a kiss, my arms around his neck, feet dangling in the air just as they should. With a soccer bag slung over one shoulder, his face freshly shaven, and his hair still wet from his postgame shower, he was disarming in every sense of the word.

Since we'd both been experiencing withdrawal symptoms from going too long without Indian food, Mark had picked a place nearby that he said served a mean chicken masala. It was still fairly early for dinner, so aside from a handful of local patrons, we were the only two people in the room. Splitting a bunch of dishes on the menu, we stretched dinner over several hours. Compared to the nervous anticipation that had bounced between us the night before, it suddenly was the most natural thing in the world to be out at dinner together in Bangkok, holding hands and having "How was your day, dear?" chats.

Too soon the gold Ganesh wall clock indicated it was time for us to leave. But before we did, I had the waitress snap a quick photo of us with my camera. That way, when I woke up the next day in a totally different country thousands of miles away from Mark, I'd have proof that I hadn't just imagined him. That he and everything we'd done together had been real.

As we walked hand in hand to the Skytrain, I couldn't get over what a difference a week had made in my life. I hadn't magically shed all my worries or uncertainty about returning home, starting all over again, and finding the man I was meant to be with, but knowing that there was someone out there like Mark made me trust that it *was* possible. While the hopeless romantic in me had desperately wanted to believe that every Juliet had her Romeo, I'd started to lose faith that it could happen to me.

But suddenly there I was, standing in a train car in Bangkok wrapped tightly in the arms of a man who'd completely swept me away the moment we'd met. It had taken me 28 and $^5/_6$ years to experience that elusive notion of love at first sight, but my God, was it ever worth the wait. And I knew now that I could never settle for anything less.

As the car sped along the tracks, Mark leaned back against the door and held me against his chest. Before I knew it, the train began to slow. As we approached Mark's stop, he looked down at me and smiled.

"You know something, Jen. I'm not sure when or where in the world it will happen, but I have a strange feeling that our paths will cross again."

With that he pulled me in for one last delicious kiss before the doors slid open and he stepped out. As I watched Mark's silhouette fade away in the distance, I knew that he was right.

429

✻

CHAPTER TWENTY-SEVEN

Holly

BALI

MARCH

After our whirlwind tour of Southeast Asia, none of us was motivated to move for days. We'd competed for hostels and dodged street vendors at every "must-see" spot from Angkor Wat to Halong Bay. When you find yourself staring at etchings worthy of the term "world wonder" and thinking "*Another* carving of that elephant-faced god guy?" you *know* you're doing something wrong. We needed to stop before we could keep going, and the beaches of Bali were the perfect place to do that. We'd actually gotten this stopover as a free bonus when we'd booked our round-the-world tickets with a San Francisco–based company called AirTreks, and it couldn't have come at a better time.

After only a few days of relaxation, our hotel room in Kuta Beach looked like a college dorm in the aftermath of finals. Magazines fanned across the wooden floor like haphazardly scattered tiles. DVDs towered on the TV like blocks in a game of Jenga. Discarded bags of popcorn, Snickers wrappers, and cans of Diet Coke littered the bedside table. Twisted sheets and limp pillows topped the two twin beds. The only thing missing was an empty keg.

"Time check!" Amanda yelled from the bathroom, and I heard her shake the bottle of mousse she used to tame her curls.

"We have ten minutes until Jen and Stephany get here. But I can be ready in five," I said. Our threesome had turned into a twosome: Jen's high school friend was serendipitously in Bali on business, and she'd held Jen "captive" the night before in her fancy hotel in Nusa Dua. Soon enough, however, we would become a foursome.

I pulled from the top of my backpack the orange cotton sundress that I'd bought for $5 in one of the stalls lining the main street. Paired with my rubber shower shoes, I would've definitely made *Glamour*'s list of fashion don'ts. "This is my fifth day wearing the same outfit. I may break the trip record for going the longest without changing clothes," I said to Amanda.

"I broke the record for staying in bed the longest," Amanda said. Since I'd reunited with the girls after yoga school, a part of Amanda seemed to have died and been reborn—as if she'd managed to outrun the relentless striving that had plagued her. Even her temper, once quick to ignite whenever strangers showed the first hint of taking advantage of us, had been extinguished. She claimed to have given up working after her dream assignment had turned out to be a time-sucking, research-loaded monster. I was amazed, but still I wasn't convinced.

"So you're not going to pitch any more stories for the whole trip *ever*?" I'd asked when she'd first made the announcement, staring her straight in the eye to gauge any hesitation.

"Nope," she'd promised. That word alone wasn't enough to persuade me, but her actions spoke louder: She stopped crafting blogs every night. She abandoned spending afternoons holed up in an Internet café, her station sprinkled with to-go coffee cups and a handful of tattered notebooks. Instead, she had crashed long and hard, sleeping off any lingering itch to be productive, rising only to take surf lessons.

431

And Amanda wasn't the only one who'd transformed while we were apart. Jen had not only surprised us by willingly flying solo in Bangkok but had also let go of her fear of never finding love after falling hard for Stephany's friend Mark. We could be talking about anything, and she would find a way to work Mark into the conversation—when I'd mentioned my sister would be coming to visit in Australia, for example, she'd thrown in "*Mark* has a sister!" She couldn't even say his name without smiling. It was as if both of my friends had been plunged into healing waters and emerged as lighter versions of themselves. As for me, I was still waiting to get home to Elan.

"Jen, Amanda won't wake up," I'd noted on the third day in Bali, surprised, after coming in from an afternoon run, to find Amanda still wearing her eye mask. "What do you think we should do?"

"Let's have a movie marathon!" Jen suggested.

"Okay."

Jen stopped, now surprised herself. "Really? You don't want to go climb a volcano or something?"

I grinned. "Nah, I need to start on that list of movie classics you wrote out for me so I can get up to speed on pop culture. Besides, why climb a volcano when I can watch Indiana Jones do it better?"

While I'd spent a lot of my time educating myself on health and fitness stuff, pop culture had never been my strong point—and my ignorance always showed in awkward exchanges at dinner parties or office meetings. I'd stare blankly after someone quoted a movie or sitcom that everyone but me seemed to know. I traced it all back to my childhood—my mother used to tell my younger sisters, Sara and Kate, and me that the television was broken from June through August. (It was really only unplugged, but we obviously weren't the quickest kids on the block.) Then she'd *pay* us to read books.

I'd much rather have been using my imagination to transport myself into characters' heads than zoning out in front of the television and would have read for free. By the time I'd hit my teen years, I couldn't have cared less about TV and instead passed hours and hours reading contentedly by the fire, even when the TV wasn't broken (or "broken"). I had no complaints, but still, being the only person who didn't understand a single *Seinfeld* reference was getting a little old.

So—for a day at least—I'd been happy to follow Jen and rent a DVD player.

"Hey, Pressy and Corby!" Jen said now, strolling into the room with a beach bag slung over her shoulder and a woman I presumed to be Stephany in tow.

"Hi, Stephany! I'm Holly. Nice to meet you," I said, going in for a hug. She was about half a foot taller than me, with dark blond hair, brown eyes, and a thin face flushed red from the sun. Amanda, who'd already met Steph when she'd visited Jen at college, chimed out her greeting as she emerged from the bathroom.

"What was it like living in luxury for a night?" I teased Jen. I'd imagined a cloud bed and windows facing the Indian Ocean. Maybe she'd had banana pancakes in bed courtesy of room service before getting a massage by the pool. Jen responded by handing me one of the chocolates that five-star hotels sometimes leave on your pillow during turndown service.

Steph had invited all of us to hang out beside one of the dozens of pools at her resort later that week, but today we were going sightseeing—finally. We walked past the swimming pool lined with flowers, through the gates, and into the street. Herman, one of the smiling Balinese salesmen stationed across the street from our guesthouse, was sitting in his usual spot on the steps outside of his family's single-room office. He was relaxed and friendly. With him, we didn't feel we had to be on guard to keep from being scammed.

Hanoi's terrifying cabdriver experience had administered a shot of caution to all three of us. While no one had been hurt (except for maybe the driver's eardrums after Jen's deafening screams), we'd each gone through our own sort of grieving process to make sense of a situation that had been part blatant trickery, part cultural miscommunication, and part unwarranted violence.

Though I'd had nightmares about the episode like someone suffering a mild case of post-traumatic stress disorder, I knew that incident was only one small wrinkle in the fabric of events that wove our trip together thus far. Rather than muddying my faith in people, our journey proved that for each person trying to take advantage of you, another stepped in with a random act of kindness.

No country we'd visited had illustrated that as clearly as Vietnam. When one young woman had manhandled me before slashing my purse in the markets lining Hanoi's Old Quarter, another elderly woman had swooped in to my rescue. As the would-be thief dissolved into the crowd (I'd managed to scare her off when I made eye contact just as I caught my wallet before it crashed to the ground), the elderly woman had gasped in outrage before grabbing my elbow. She was about four feet five inches tall with hair that shined silver, and she'd led me past shelves quivering with baskets, lacquerware, and hand-embroidered purses. She'd handed me a cup of tea, stitched up the jagged slit in my purse as effortlessly as she breathed, and apologized over and over again in Vietnamese. I was grateful to her for her kindness and because she was a much-needed reminder that the darkness cast by some gives others the chance to let their light shine.

I didn't experience the same blatant push-pull with the people in Bali. Instead of the slight undercurrent of resentment toward backpackers I'd felt in Hanoi's Old Quarter, hospitality was all I felt in Bali. From the housewives placing flower offerings on cars to smiling salesmen such as Herman to giggling children skipping through alleys, the Balinese's overall attitude seemed light and airy—like powdered sugar or fresh whipped cream. Of course, this one-dimensional view brushed over the hardships they might face, whether it be struggling to feed a family or care for a sick parent. But I'd been awash with gut-level impressions of people whenever I'd first stepped into a new country. From the outside the people in Bali seemed calm, balanced, and graceful.

Seeing us approach, Herman grinned, his mocha skin crinkling at the corners of his eyes.

"Good morning, Charlie's Angels! You have a new friend with you today!" A picture of the Hindu holy trinity (Brahma, Vishnu, and Shiva) peered at us from his boxlike office window.

"*Selamat pagi* [good morning], Herman!" After introducing Steph, I asked how much it'd cost to drive us around the island.

"What would you like to see?" Herman asked.

"Are there any temples we can hike to?" I asked.

Amanda explained to Steph, "Holly likes to do something active whenever we're sightseeing."

"That's fine with me. I could use some exercise," Steph said happily.

Without pausing to think, Herman said, "I could take you to Pura Luhur Uluwatu, one of Bali's most holy temples." He explained that the temple was dedicated to the spirits of the sea and set high on a cliff overlooking the Indian Ocean.

Herman told us to come back in an hour so he could pick up the jeep from his brother. We went to grab breakfast, Steph easily falling into step beside us.

Adding a fourth person to our threesome was like holding up a looking glass: we began to see ourselves more clearly through the reflection in the outsider's eyes. The three of us had grown so accustomed to our idiosyncrasies that we no longer noticed them. With Steph visiting, the roles we'd each adopted to help us travel more efficiently and the habit we had of dissipating tension with humor came back into focus.

K uta Beach, the eight-mile ribbon of sand, markets, and massage parlors where most tourists settled on the island, disappeared behind the jeep in a wisp of exhaust. Forgoing the air conditioner, we rolled down the windows to let the damp, salty air tickle our faces, the sun's rays burning our cheeks as the yellow orb climbed higher in the sky. "Hips Don't Lie" shook from the radio speakers, and we sang along to the radio until we arrived at Pura Luhur Uluwatu temple.

While climbing the steps to the holy site, I watched a monkey leap from a tree, land on a woman's head, and grab her sunglasses. The woman spun around like a whirling dervish while her boyfriend screamed and ran in the opposite direction. So much for chivalry, I thought.

A few seconds later, a different monkey attacked me from behind, smacking my hand and waiting for fruit to fall. People feed the animals in hopes of divine rewards, which turns them into mischievous divas. Bali is the only Hindu island in the Muslim-dominated archipelago of Indonesia, and monkeys are considered sacred in Hindu culture as representations of the monkey god, Hanuman. I hoped devotees were reaping the benefits in exchange for their generous feedings, because the monkeys looked pretty fat to me.

"Holly, get closer to the big guy so I can get a picture!" Amanda was poised on the steps above, her camera pointed in my direction.

"Are you *crazy*?" I was mistrustful of monkeys—they had

already stolen my mangoes in Kenya, grabbed my hair while I had been walking the 777 steps to the temple on Mount Popa in Myanmar, and nibbled my shoulder in the Amazon like deer on corn.

I sprinted up the stairs toward her just as another monkey grabbed her hand and almost succeeded in stealing her camera. "Karma is a bitch!" I exclaimed with a laugh as Amanda squealed and surged past Steph and Jen.

We didn't stop for a breather until we reached the top, but we all froze once we arrived. The sun was flamingo pink and sinking behind craggy cliffs that pierced the sea, the light bouncing off waves as pointy as a sea urchin's spine.

"I've never seen such an amazing sunset," Steph said, her eyes glowing. "I wish I could travel with you for the rest of the trip. Every day must be one big adventure!"

"Come with us, Steph!" I goaded.

"Well, first I'd have to quit my job, and then I'd have to convince my husband to quit his, too," she said, taking one last wistful look at the sunset. I froze for a second. Why had no person or thing tied the three of us to home? Steph turned to face us, her hair whipping wildly in the gusts rising from the ocean. Leaning against the ledge of the stone railing, she asked, "What are you going to do when you get back?"

Glancing at one another, we stiffened and stood a little taller. For the first time that day, we weren't all talking over one another to get the words out. We'd come on this trip looking for insight into what to do next, but even though the trip was more than half over, we still couldn't answer Steph's seemingly simple question.

We'd slept under the stars in the Andes Mountains. We'd chanted as the sun rose over an ashram in India. We'd sailed past limestone pillars in Vietnam. We'd prayed in the killing fields of Cambodia. We'd scuba dived among the islands of Thailand.

437

Now, as we stood on top of a temple in Bali, the future seemed like the most distant place of all.

H ow old are you?" asked the petite Balinese woman who'd introduced herself as Nyoman, while pouring me a cup of coffee. I was sitting at a restaurant table in a garden courtyard. Wide leaves protected me like a parasol from the already hot sun.

"I'm twenty-nine," I answered.

"Are you married?"

Not that question again. Instead I smiled and said, "No, but I have a boyfriend at home in the States."

She looked relieved that I wasn't wandering this earth completely unattached. Family is the thread that binds Balinese society together, with each member shouldering specific roles and duties according to gender and birth order. The eldest brother, for example, traditionally plans all the religious ceremonies not only for his own wife and children but also for his younger brothers' families. It's the women, though, who make the offerings to the gods in those ceremonies.

And the impression I'd gotten was that the Balinese preferred doing most things together, from the crowds congregating at the *warung*s (traditional family-run restaurants) every afternoon to the packs of housewives wandering the markets together each morning. A lone woman traveling without a husband must have seemed like a lost soul. Many islanders deemed it their duty to relieve me of my solitude, as they struck up a conversation whenever I'd separated from Jen and Amanda.

After a little more than a week in Kuta Beach, we'd only just arrived in Ubud, Bali's cultural center. The girls had chosen to linger in bed that morning, but I'd been too excited to sleep and wanted to explore the town, which was bordered by chartreuse-colored rice paddies and flanked with art galleries.

"Are you married?" I asked Nyoman.

"Yes. I live with my husband and his family, and we have two sons," she answered. Balinese women typically move in with their husband's relatives, living in a compound that also houses his parents, his brothers, his brothers' wives, and their children. She likely also worshiped his ancestors at the family's temple constructed inside the compound walls. I wondered how long I would last living in such close quarters with my in-laws.

"You look at menu, and I'll be back," said Nyoman. I was relieved that the menu offered English translations for dishes such as seafood omelets, fried rice topped with an egg, and vegetables in coconut-milk curry.

Songs spilled from an invisible speaker like a metallic stream of wind chimes, gongs, and cymbals, known as Balinese gamelan music. Sipping my coffee, I watched Nyoman stand in front of a stone shrine at the edge of the courtyard. She lit a stick of incense and waved it around as if in prayer before placing it inside a bowl beside a pile of bananas. The smoke billowed skyward and married with the scent of frangipani, jasmine, and gardenia.

439

The small acts of daily devotion performed by the Balinese captivated me even more than some of the major monuments of faith—from the temples of Angkor Wat to the ruins of Machu Picchu—I'd seen in the past year, maybe because seeing people actually worshiping made faith seem more tangible. When I'd first arrived in Bali, I'd tripped over the piles of flowers, coconut leaves, rice crackers, and incense dotting the roads and sidewalks. They appeared too beautiful to be trash but too random to be sacred, and I'd heard nothing about them while studying Hinduism at the ashram in India. So I'd approached Herman, who had been sitting on his steps as usual, to ask what they were.

"They are called *canang sari*—offerings to guard against the evil spirits and bring luck from the good spirits," Herman explained matter-of-factly.

I'd since discovered that the Balinese practice Hinduism with a nature-worshiping twist. They believe that the world houses both good and bad spirits that can be kept in balance with rituals such as fruit offerings, dancing, and paintings. To stay in harmony, the Balinese believe, you have to keep good relations with the spirits, other people, and nature. I felt a surge of warmth and protection while watching the Balinese house-wives communing with the divine every day, placing offerings at family shrines. And regularly stumbling upon those home-made piles of devotion reminded me I was wading through an island of believers.

After making her offering to the spirits, Nyoman approached my table, balancing a steaming plate of fried bananas. "It's a gift for you to taste," she said.

"*Matu suksama* [thank you]." The caramelized sweetness tickled my tongue. An elderly woman hobbled over with a baby cradled in her arms.

"This is my husband's mother," Nyoman said. "She watch my son while I work, but I must feed him now." One of the perks of living with your in-laws is built-in day care. For what com-munal living lacks in privacy, it makes up for in cooperation, cocooning family members with the security of not having to struggle through life's challenges alone.

I poured sweetened condensed milk into my coffee and watched the whiteness swirl into the blackness, creating the shape of a blooming lotus flower.

It was the balancing of darkness and light that seeped into every crevice of life in Bali. I could only hope I'd be able to demonstrate the same balance myself—on a bike. I'd read the roads carved into the hills surrounding Ubud made for pictur-esque rides with sweeping views of the rice paddies. Besides, I wanted to see what life was like outside town and figured pedal-ing around would let me cover more territory than I'd be able to by jogging. "Do you know where I could rent a bicycle?" I asked Nyoman when she returned.

"My husband's brother rents them. If you walk Monkey Forest Road, you will find them parked."

After finishing up my breakfast, I paid my rupiahs, pushed back my chair, and wandered outside. The storefronts's paintings were awash in primary colors and textures splashed across hundreds of canvases. Painters sat on the steps in front of their shops, fluttering their brushes with the soft touch of a butterfly's wings. Even the concrete walls bordering the maze of alleys were decorated with art like mounted tie-dye, transforming an otherwise mundane space into something beautiful. Shadows moved across the walls. I looked up to see clouds blowing across the sun and noted that the air smelled heavy, like rain.

Not wanting to linger with a downpour threatening, I easily found the line of parked bikes among the rows of art galleries, organic food stores, and meditation centers. For $2, I had two wheels for the day.

Sliding onto the banana seat, I slung my purse strap across my body diagonally so it wouldn't slip off. I felt like my childhood self, hopping on my bike to seek out the secrets of foreign lands: the school playground, the church parking lot, my grandmother's garden. I was free again, belonging to no one.

With the wind tickling my ears and making my eyes water, I pumped my feet, mud from the tires speckling my legs. I rode away from Monkey Forest with its divine divas awaiting gifts of bananas. I passed a temple at the edge of town whose stone pillars were crisscrossed with carvings and shaded with palm fronds. I rode up a steep hill, past houses where children kicked balls around in the yard, stopping to yell "Halloooo!" as I approached. Men lounged on the front steps of their thatched-roof houses, eating balls of rice with their hands. Women carried jugs of water, laughing together as they walked.

I pedaled faster and faster as the sky darkened, trying to out-ride the rain. I'm free, I repeated to myself with every breath. The houses grew farther apart, and the rice paddies transformed the landscape into a layered green wedding cake. Palm trees dotted the grassy shelves, and a river ran through it all.

I'm free. Children's laughter poured from a lone compound, and I turned my head to see a woman placing a stick of smoldering incense inside her family shrine. I pedaled faster.

BOOM! Thunder exploded a few seconds before lightning tentacles formed glowing fissures in the clouds.

A sane person would have turned back toward town to avoid potential flash floods—especially when biking in a foreign country where she had no idea where she was going and no one else had any idea where she was. Instead, I was compelled to surge forward to beat the lightning. I tightened my abs and pushed down on the pedals so fast that the world melted into streaks like the tie-dyed paintings I'd admired in town.

I'm free. Raindrops fell, washing away the sweat streaking my forehead. I can do anything, go anywhere, I thought as I crested a hill and started to pick up even more speed on the descent.

What are you going to do when you get back? Stephany's question blew through my mind like a cold draft as the world breezed by.

I'm free.

Steph had also asked, while we were walking home from an Irish pub, giggling and sweat-soaked from dancing on her final night on the island, "What really made you go on the trip?"

I'd offered my standard answer. "How could I *not* go? I had two friends willing to travel the world with me and a little savings in the bank. It wasn't really a choice." I saw her examining my face out of the corner of my eye, sensing she wasn't entirely buying it.

"Yeah, but you said you were happy with your job. And it sounds like you're totally in love with your boyfriend—you don't even look at other guys. And you *live* with him in a cute apartment. Seriously, why did you decide to leave for an entire year?"

I should have known the answer, or else why *had* I traded my 401(k) plan for credit card debt, my closet for a backpack, and my bed with the man I loved for a different cot every night? Amanda wanted to jump-start her travel-writing career, and Jen was escaping a relationship with the wrong man. Me, I was in it solely for the adventure. Or so I'd told myself.

I'm free, I repeated my mantra, pedaling faster still. Stephany couldn't travel for a year because she was tied to her husband. Nyoman would never be able to go on a bike ride in the middle of the day, because she had a job to do and a baby to care for. I was tied to no one. I was free. And I was alone.

I heard Elan's voice echo in my head as my tires turned over pebbles in the road. "I'll miss you, Hol." I remembered how happy I'd been, laughing as he spun me around in the snow on that Boston sidewalk. I thought about how safe I'd felt on those nights when we'd fall into our bed but stay up talking until the sky turned from black to gray. I pictured the way he'd helped me slip into my loaded backpack for the first time and then watched me from above on our patio as I climbed into a cab on my way to the airport to begin my journey.

Then, quicker than a lightning bolt shooting across the clouds, I didn't want to be free anymore. I didn't want to travel through my life alone.

Swish, swish, the sound of the pedals slicing through the air undercut the sound of the rain pelting the ground.

I'd picked up so much speed that I'd finally stopped pedaling and put on the brakes, sending my bike into a near tailspin. Along with drinking the water and flashing expensive electronics in public, biking rural roads in a rainstorm sans map was probably listed as a Lonely Planet warning about what *not* to do when traveling.

Before my bike could sail into a ditch-turned-river, I regained my balance. At the same moment, a sliver of sunlight cracked through the clouds. The rice paddies were iridescent, rhinestonelike raindrops studding the greenery as if the spirits had taken a BeDazzler to the landscape.

I slowed enough to put one foot on the ground and then turned back in the direction from which I'd come.

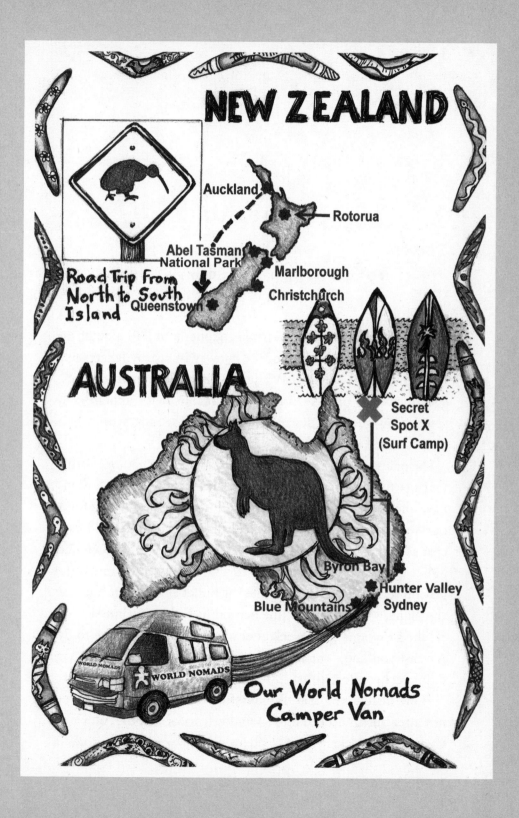

⁂

CHAPTER TWENTY-EIGHT

Amanda

NORTH ISLAND, NEW ZEALAND
MARCH

Six days after we flew Garuda Indonesia to Bali, one of the carrier's planes overshot the runway in nearby Jakarta and burst into a ball of flame. While 118 people escaped the wreckage (including one Australian cameraman, who unbelievably rescued his gear and started shooting footage for Sydney's six o'clock news), 22 passengers weren't so lucky.

Needless to say, none of us was clamoring to get on another Garuda flight in order to continue our journey, but we didn't have much choice. Even if we could get a last-minute refund, one-way fares to New Zealand on a different airline would have cost as much as our last six flights combined. We had a choice: either carve out a spot in Bali's thriving expat community and stay on the island forever, or bite the bullet and get our butts on the plane. A passenger in line behind us had an optimistic take on the situation: "The week after a crash is the best time to fly. At least you know the pilots won't be sleeping on the job." We didn't feel comforted.

Fortunately, the trip was blissfully uneventful. We arrived just after dusk, checked into a windowless dorm at the Auckland Central Backpackers hostel, and proceeded to enter a sleep coma until the alarm of one of our dormmates went off just after 7 a.m. Jen and Holly barely stirred, but I couldn't convince my brain to doze off again. I yanked on a pair of running pants, laced up my ultragrungy trail sneakers, and sneaked out of the room.

I wasn't prepared for the full-force blast of early-morning brilliance outside the front door: the sky was so saturated blue and cloudlessly dazzling, it almost hurt my eyes to stare into it. The sun was rising through the city skyline, and Auckland's wide streets were starting to fill with early-morning commuters. A bank's digital clock flashed the temperature, 17°C—about 68°F. I'd emerged into one of those impossibly perfect early-autumn days that makes you stop, draw a breath, and feel humbled that you're alive and able to experience it (particularly when you've been a Garuda passenger).

I didn't need the map I'd stuffed into my windbreaker to find my way to the waterfront. As I moved past the shipping containers at the industrial port section just north of town and emerged along the peacock blue waters of Judge's Bay, I felt my steps lengthen and my body pick up speed. About a mile in, I realized that I'd actually forgotten to turn on my iPod. Why bother now? I'd heard every song and every playlist a gazillion times before. There was greater novelty in the silence.

As I ran, I thought about Jen and Holly, either still asleep at the hostel or starting their morning rituals. By now I knew them almost better than I did myself—their personality quirks, their mood shifts, their penchant for silliness and capacity for kindness. They were my left and right arms, my compass and guidebook. We'd become the tightest of teams. Yet sometimes I wondered just how differently this trip might have gone had I—or any of us—chosen to go it alone.

Though there definitely was strength in numbers, being in a group sometimes made us less likely to reach out to new people. Or for well-intentioned strangers to connect with us. I was intrigued by solo travelers, so flexible and autonomous, always bursting with stories of freshly forged friendships with locals who'd housed them, fed them, introduced them to extended families, and invited them to weddings. They had to work a lot harder to do all of the tasks that Jen, Holly, and I usually split up (nailing down train schedules, securing rooms at hostels, negotiating prices, lugging toiletries and electronics), but their trips ultimately seemed more rewarding for the challenges.

Holly had been a solo traveler at one point in her life; she'd backpacked alone in Costa Rica for several weeks after grad school. She pointed out that while traveling alone can be liberating, doing it for an extended period of time requires some seriously sharp instincts and a willingness, particularly as a woman, to take considerable risks. You couldn't always throw money at a problem by staying at a nice hotel or taking taxis everywhere. By necessity, you had to put your faith in strangers, so you'd better have a knack for reading people.

Despite the potential drawbacks, I'd been thinking more and more about the possibility of extending the trip past our predetermined end date and organizing an adventure somewhere in Australia—on my own. I knew that both of the girls, especially Holly, wanted to head home on time, but now that I'd finally made good on my promise to stop pitching articles and writing and just *travel*, rushing back to my old life was the last thing I wanted to do.

When I hobbled back through town forty-five minutes later (unlike Holly, I was in no shape for full-out morning marathons), I found myself smack in the middle of Auckland's morning rush hour. It was a misnomer, really, considering that nobody actually seemed to be in a hurry. Cute, closely shaven men in impeccably tailored suits strolled up Customs Street, while adorably accessorized women breezed out of Starbucks with to-go lattes in hand. People laughed and made conversation with their friends or coworkers. No one stepped into the crosswalk until the signal instructed them to do so, and if they bumped into someone moving the other way, they apologized. It looked like an artist's rendering of some pristine, well-organized city of the future, a place where smartly dressed people look thrilled to be sharing communal spaces. Except this wasn't a sketch or a digitized model; it was the largest and most populous city in New Zealand.

Y ou're kidding me. You actually *like* it here?" said our local Kiwi pal Carmi when she picked us up the next day in her gunmetal gray Toyota Marino.

We'd met the twenty-four-year-old in cyberspace after she'd stumbled upon our blog. When she learned that we'd be in New Zealand, she'd e-mailed to ask if we'd like her to play chauffeur and tour guide during our stay in her city. Our response: a unanimous "hell yeah." We'd planned to stay in Auckland for only four days—long enough to spend some time with local friends of Holly's—but that was three days too long in Carmi's book.

449

"What do you like about Auckland?" she asked in utter disbelief.

"It just seems like such a *livable* city," said Holly. After spending our first day exploring, we'd all been impressed by the sheer amount of land devoted to parks, paths, and outdoor spaces—not to mention the waterfront views. The city had been built on a narrow stretch of land threaded between two harbors dividing the Tasman Sea from the Pacific. Every bay and cove was filled to bursting with gleaming white boats, from tiny skiffs to yachts. It wasn't hard to guess why it had been nicknamed the City of Sails.

What we couldn't figure out was why the locals seemed to have such a neutral impression of their own hometown. They voiced the same complaints as most other city dwellers: too much traffic, skyrocketing home prices, the fact that so much urban sprawl had developed in recent years. How could Aucklanders be so unaware of their city's awesomeness relative to everyone else's?

"Wait till you start traveling through the rest of the country," Carmi said. "Then you'll see why you shouldn't have spent so much time here."

She explained that the North and South islands were jam-packed with extraordinary natural wonders of IMAX-worthy proportions. Rain forests, redwood forests, deciduous forests, electric blue glaciers, limestone karst, knife-edged mountains, bubbling volcanoes, deeply cut fjords, steaming sulfur pools, and crystalline beaches rimming aquamarine waters had all been crammed into a landmass smaller in size than Italy. A total of 4 million people live in New Zealand, a third of whom are in Auckland, which makes this a nation of small towns and one of the least densely populated countries in the world. You can actually leave your front door unlocked in most places. Sheep outnumber people ten to one.

"Hey, d'you guys think you'd ever try something like that? I've never been, but I'd heard it's sweet as," said Carmi, pointing up at the Auckland Sky Tower. It looked distinctly like the Seattle Space Needle, except, according to our walking guidebook, Jen, it was 471 feet taller—the tallest freestanding structure in the Southern Hemisphere.

"Sweet as what?" Holly asked, squinting up at the tiny figures leaping off the side of the tower in a feat that looked like BASE jumping with a rope instead of a parachute.

"Sweet *as*. It's an expression, and you'd better get used to it. Kiwis say it a lot."

"Hey, Amanda, let's do it! Want to go this afternoon?" Jen asked eagerly, always ready to fling herself off something if it involved an adrenaline rush and bragging rights.

450

"*Hell* to the no," I said. Jen had been trying to talk me into doing some kind of famous bungee jump in the South Island, and I'd had a similar response. My days of seeking out crazy near-death experiences were just about over.

"Holly?" Jen asked.

"Sorry—at this point, I think my credit card company would decline me just on principle."

"Okay, so now that that's settled," Carmi said. "Where would you ladies like to go?"

"Oooh! I know! Let's go shopping!"

Holly, who anticipates visits to foreign grocery stores the way religious disciples look forward to their pilgrimage to Mecca or the Wailing Wall, requested that our first stop be the New World supermarket we'd passed on the way into town to check out all the unusual and exotic foods consumed by New Zealanders.

"Is she being serious?" Carmi asked me as Holly slid into the backseat.

"Completely. It's a borderline addiction."

After a quick spin through the aisles, Holly purchased a few essential rations and we struck off to find some real culture in greater Auckland. We made it to most of the spots on Carmi's hit list, including the "superflash," newly renovated Auckland Museum, Viaduct Harbour, and the Queen Street market, rocking out between stops to a mix of songs she'd created for us with local artists like Brooke Fraser, Dave Dobbyn, and her personal favorite, Fat Freddy's Drop.

"New Zealanders really *live* for music," she said passionately. "We savor every song. And our bands can rival just about anyone else's in the world. We're good at making music but even better at celebrating it."

As it turned out, Carmi was a wellspring of information about all things Kiwi. As we made our way to Mission Bay, a

451

beachfront strip of trendy restaurants and cafés, Holly peppered her with the same questions about marriage and relationships she'd been asking women the globe over: "How do people meet here? How old are they when they get married? How old are they when they have kids?"

Lobbing the answers back with the speed and precision of a tennis pro smacking balls over a net, Carmi kept us riveted with her revelations about New Zealand culture.

On gender roles: "After decades of proving that women are equal to men, relationships between guys and girls are very progressive. You'll usually see the men looking after the babies, putting them in prams, and taking them for walks while the mum goes off to work and earns the living."

On meeting guys: "We definitely don't go on 'dates' here like you girls do in the States. None of this *Sex and the City* stuff. It's not like a guy will come up to you in a bar and ask you out. You usually just meet someone through friends and get together. That's it."

On matrimony: "You'll find lots of couples who've been dating for years and years and live together but don't get married. Marriage itself doesn't really seem to be as much of a priority as it used to be."

Listening intently, we chewed on this information and filed it away for future reference. In the event that any of us ever defected from our New York lives in order to pursue a future in Kiwiland, this was exactly what we'd need to know.

L ater that afternoon, Carmi dropped us off at the home of Nora and Eric, a couple Holly knew through a friend of a friend from high school. Even though they'd never actually met Holly, they'd already offered to let all three of us stay with them for a couple of nights.

Nora and Eric had what appeared to be a pretty idyllic (and by Carmi's standards fairly prototypical) New Zealand relationship. They'd recently opened a Pilates studio in a trendy Auckland neighborhood, moved into a snug two-bedroom bungalow a block from the beach, and had an adorable one-year-old girl with platinum ringlets named Madison. We wondered if they were married or if Nora just hadn't taken her husband's name (maybe it was one of those independent Kiwi girl things?), but she quickly set the record straight.

"Oh, Eric and I aren't married. Well, not yet," she said as she cheerfully installed Holly and me in their guestroom. "We've tossed around the idea, but with everything else going on—you know, the baby, the studio—we just haven't gotten around to it."

She turned to smile at the angelic blond girl on her hip. "Isn't that right, my little darling? Mummy and Daddy are just sooo busy!"

Madison stared at her mom for a second before bursting into giggles and reaching up to pat her cheek. Nora handed the baby to Holly so she could grab a stack of towels.

"So are you girls all set, then? Jen, we'll make up a bed for you tonight on the couch before we all go to sleep. Oh—one more thing."

She pointed out a small red button on the wall near the bedside lamp. "For some reason, the last people who lived here installed this alarm just in case anyone tried to break in. But don't worry. Auckland's so safe, touch wood, we should never need to use it. Just try not to hit if you're getting up in the middle of the night."

We promised we'd be careful and thanked Nora again for her hospitality.

"Oh, don't be silly." Nora waved her hand. "We're always thrilled to have guests. And Eric's doing up a little dinner tonight, so get ready. He's a good cook."

The "little dinner" turned out to be a feast, and Eric and Nora had even bigger plans for our stomachs the second night. Their friend Ryan from Texas and his very pregnant wife, Kim, were throwing a dinner party for some other couples with kids, and we'd been invited. I was starting to think that Kiwis weren't just friendly to visitors—they actually competed to see who could be more accommodating.

"Don't worry, you won't be the only unattached guests there," said Nora. "Ryan says he'll invite his single friend Cameron so you girls can chat him up if the rest of us get sidetracked with boring baby stuff."

Ah—the token single male. I suddenly had a flash of Mark Darcy in a ridiculous reindeer sweater at the Christmas party in the first Bridget Jones movie. Except in our version, there'd be two sad singletons to scrap over him.

"He's mine, ladies," I joked. "Don't even think about it."

"Back off, Pressy," said Jen. "I already claimed him, like, five minutes ago."

As it turned out, the mysterious Cam was nothing like the frumpy, uptight Mark Darcy. He was a handsome Paul Rudd look-alike who was playing with all the kids when we arrived. I wondered if Jen or I really would want dibs on the guy; besides being supercute, he seemed incredibly sweet.

The hostess, Kim, on the other hand, acted edgy and hormonal around us from the second we walked in the door. We didn't take it personally—the woman was near-to-bursting pregnant—but I was a little surprised when she immediately put us to work in the kitchen slicing up sausages, bread cubes, and cheese.

"Oh, and d'you mind washing up the dishes afterward?" she asked, not waiting for an answer before turning and stalking off.

"Hey, whoa, are those American accents I hear?" Judging from the drawl, I figured the voice belonged to her husband,

454

Ryan, who tracked us down in the kitchen. He lounged in the doorway with a beer while we sliced. I'd spent half of my childhood in Texas, and this was truly a Lone Star good ol' boy—big, brawny, and loud. I could easily picture him spending late nights drinking at the kind of place where peanut shells on the floor were considered fancy decor.

"So, tell me, ladies. What brings y'all down under? How'd you find yourselves here?"

I'd wondered the same thing about him. A Kiwi-Texan mash-up seemed most unusual. After catching us up on all he missed about his home state ("Real barbecue sauce. And Whataburger fries. Oh, and bars that stay open past midnight"), Ryan walked over to the fridge and asked, since we already had our hands dirty, if we would mind seasoning his meat. We all stared blankly as he pulled out a three-pound slab of steak and slapped it on the cutting board near the sink.

He laughed at his own joke and promised that he'd do it himself. But overhearing his comment from the other room, Kim instantly reappeared to let us know that actually, we should probably mingle with the other guests in the living room.

By now all of the couples had arrived, and we hung out with the young moms and dads, who for the most part seemed interested in hearing our stories from the trip.

"C'mon, fill us in on all the juiciest bits," said Alice, whose three-year-old son, Kieran, was tearing around the house like an airplane. "We're all mommies and daddies now, so we really don't get the chance to—"

She stopped short as we all heard a crash, followed by a wail. "Oh, crap. Sorry . . . be right back."

We soon sat down to dinner, a gourmet multicourse food orgy complete with wines, salads, creamy side dishes, grilled and sliced meats, and a fluffy meringue dessert known as Pavlova. The Kiwis at the table made us promise, when we headed

455

to their larger neighbor across the Tasman Sea, that we wouldn't believe any of those "Aussie bastards" who tried to say they'd invented the dessert.

"It's always been ours. They keep trying to claim it," said Alice's husband, Ted.

"Ah, enough with that old Pavlova rivalry!" bellowed Ryan, who was sitting across the table from us next to Cam. With each course (and number of beers consumed), he'd gotten progressively louder and more vocal about expressing how much he missed the "good ol' U.S. of A." Now he turned his attention to our personal lives. "What I want to know is . . . which one of you girls doesn't have a boyfriend?"

"Honey . . . *please*," said an exasperated Kim, who'd been shooting us sidelong glances for the past two hours and now looked ready to evict us. Or murder her husband. Or both.

"What? What's wrong now? I'm just asking these nice ladies a question on behalf of my good buddy Cam here, who by the way is *totally available*," he said, nudging his friend, who blushed and shrugged as if to say, "Sorry, I don't actually know this guy."

"I have an idea." Kim ignored his comment, hoisting herself with some effort into a standing position. "I think it's time that we all switch the groups around so everyone gets the chance to talk to everyone else. I mean, there's no need to have all of the Americans in one cozy little cluster on one side of the table. C'mon, everybody—up."

Everyone stared at Kim for a second, unsure whether to follow her instructions. Kim repeated herself, and after the group slowly stood, Ryan told us to sit back down. He wasn't going anywhere, he said. Kim switched tactics, coming to our end of the table and wedging a chair between Ryan and Cam.

"So, *ladies*, I really want to know more about you, too. None of you are married, right? Wow. How old are you again?"

Holly provided our ages, and Kim continued grilling—about our lives back home, Jen's breakup, and Holly's long-distance status, whether we worried that taking a yearlong trip might set us back a few years in the dating-and-mating game.

"I mean, you *do* want to have kids, don't you?" she asked, now incredibly concerned for our welfare and health. "You know that it gets riskier the longer you wait, right?"

After several long minutes spent trying to produce inoffensive answers while a drunk Ryan mocked his wife, Eric and Nora came over to rescue us, saying that they really had to get home to put Madison to bed.

"Well, I can drop the girls off at your place later. Really, it's no problem," Ryan drawled, insisting that the three of us continue our night with him and Cam at a bar up the road. I couldn't even look at Kim.

We declined the offer (several times, in fact). Cam gave us each a hug and said that if we ever came back through town, to look him up. Kim paced behind her husband in the living room as we walked out and piled in with Madison in the backseat of the car.

"I think that went well," Eric joked as he pulled out of the driveway.

"I'll call her tomorrow," said Nora, and that was the last we spoke of dinner.

Later that night I fell into a fitful sleep in the guest room and dreamed that I was in a race chasing after Cam, desperate to win him so he could father my children. I eventually caught him, but when he turned around he'd somehow morphed into Kim, who was furious at me for trying to have an affair with her husband. I woke up sweating and reached over to fumble for the light, only to hear the high-pitched wail of sirens fill the house. Holly shot up in bed next to me and ripped off her sleep mask. "What's happening? What's going on?"

Amanda · North Island, New Zealand · March

Eric shot into the bedroom, pulled open a panel on the wall, and killed the noise.

Somehow, despite Nora's warnings, I'd hit the panic button.

After that, we decided that Carmi was right. It was time to get moving. We thanked Eric and Nora for their hospitality and started planning our road trip.

After some serious deliberation, we decided against the hop-on, hop-off backpacker bus tour through the North and South Islands (otherwise known as the "Kiwi Experience") in favor of renting our own set of wheels. The bus cost a little less, but the car would offer more freedom and flexibility. No more bus, train, and plane schedules for us, no sir. We couldn't wait to be on the open road, in charge of our own destiny.

And once we made the four-hour drive from Auckland to the volcanic village of Rotorua, we realized we'd made a wise decision. Checking in at the Hot Rock hostel, we watched as an enormous green monster of a bus pulled into the parking lot and sixty bedraggled high school– and college-age backpackers spilled out, straining under the weight of their backpacks, day packs, and plastic bags filled with chips, cereal, candy bars, and loaves of bread. It would have seemed like a dream road trip situation the summer after college (or, um . . . a few months ago?), but the whole concept just didn't sound quite as appealing to me anymore.

Most backpackers spend about a day or two at most in Rotorua. We'd scheduled four. "Too long! Keep moving!" I could practically hear Carmi shouting, but Jen, Holly, and I were done with blowing into and out of places at warp speed. As we'd learned during the latter half of our Southeast Asia trek, putting too much on your must-see list is the fastest way to ensure that you'll be exhausted and miserable and totally miss the point.

One of the first things we noticed as we approached Rotorua: the town and everything within a ten-kilometer radius smells like the bottom of a diaper pail. We soon learned that the entire area is located on a volcanic plateau, and the same underground forces that fart out a sulfurous rotten-egg smell from deep within the earth also produce geysers, steaming fumaroles, gooey mud pools, boiling waterfalls, and bubbling hot springs.

After a few days spent exploring the mud baths and voluntarily soaring over the world's highest navigable waterfall in a river raft (Jen's suggestion, of course), Holly decided that she wanted to join up with a crew of backpackers heading over to the Maori Twilight Cultural Tour. Jen and I opted out. It wasn't just that we disliked prepackaged song-and-dance shows. I wanted to talk with Jen about next year—and what she thought she might do after we returned to the States.

We'd planned to walk around Lake Rotorua, but the lack of a path and the overwhelming stench of sulfur forced us to turn back. After chatting with a couple also out for a walk, we learned that there was a far more scenic—and less malodorous—national park just ten minutes' drive from the town center.

The Redwoods Whakarewarewa Forest turned out to be an utterly breathtaking 700-acre world's fair of trees cut through with miles of hiking and biking trails. Jen and I had intended to walk, but after a brief check of the trail map and a glance at each other, we took off running. We sailed up, over and around the gentle curves on the leaf-strewn track, slowing down only to drink in a particularly stunning view through a break in the forest.

"Man, Holly's gonna be . . . totally crushed . . . that she . . . didn't get to see this," I said, gasping for air when our footsteps slowed to a crawl. Orange-gold slivers of light shot through the trees as the sun sank progressively lower in the sky.

459

Amanda · North Island, New Zealand · March

"I know. Maybe we can . . . take her here . . . tomorrow?" Jen suggested, although we both knew that we probably had to get on the road again.

We walked in silence for a few minutes, catching our breath, and then I finally broached the topic of "going back" with Jen. Returning to the States still seemed pretty far away, but I knew the time would pass in the blink of an eye. After New Zealand, we had just Australia left and then—what next?

"Oh, man, I don't know," she said, slowing her steps even more. "I've been thinking a lot about that ever since Thailand, ever since Mark. That whole experience with him . . . it just really opened my eyes, you know."

"In what way?" I said, yanking off my long-sleeve shirt and tying it around my waist. The air under the canopy was cool and slightly damp, and revived me like a chilled compress against the back of my neck.

"Well, meeting him made me think twice about whether I want to go back to Manhattan. It's a great place to build a career, to claw your way up the ladder. Not a great place to find the love of your life, to settle down," Jen tugged off her ponytail holder and reworked the hair into a wispy knot on top of her head. "Not once in New York did I ever meet someone who really just blew me away the way that Mark did. Not once in five years."

"But you had Brian," I pointed out as Jen paused, then chose the left-hand fork at a spot where the trail divided in two. "You weren't in the position to be blown away."

"Yeah, maybe. But it says something that I stayed with him for so long. I knew, deep down, that he and I weren't right for each other." She studied the ground directly in front of her feet, then eventually glanced over at me with a sad, almost apologetic expression. "It's just that I watched all of my girlfriends experience total hell dating in the city, and I didn't want to go through that. I chose the safe route."

"Well, that's not necessarily a bad thing," I said, trying to reassure her. "You've had two healthy four-year relationships under your belt, and you've gotten some serious practice in making things work. The only relationships I ever had crashed and burned, big-time."

She slowed for a second, unscrewed the cap of her water bottle, and took a sip. "Yeah, but you've *dated*. Really, really dated. You've seen what's out there and had the chance to figure out what you do like and what you don't. Other than my two boyfriends, I've never really been asked out by anyone."

"But you will when we get back," I said, taking a slug from my own bottle. "And besides, where did all of that dating get me, anyway? We're in the exact same spot now."

"Yeah, I guess."

I looked up at the patch of sky that I could see between the trees and realized that it was starting to get dark—and quickly. Wordlessly, we picked up the pace.

"Well, what do you want to do? Are you ready to go back to the city? Or are you thinking about somewhere else?" Jen asked.

That's what I'd wanted to talk with Jen about. The very idea of reentering my life in New York right now made me want to turn tail into the redwoods and start a new career as a recluse.

We'd come this far around the world, and I felt as though I'd *just* begun to explore a different side of myself, to establish an identity beyond my résumé and business card. For so long I'd been afraid that I might be wasting my life if I didn't achieve something tangible, accomplishments that would earn me respect in the eyes of others. Now I was starting to understand that my all-work attitude might leave me one very lonely lady in a decade or so. All the bylines and résumé bullet points in the world wouldn't make up for the time I'd miss with family, friends, a guy . . . or just hanging out with myself. They ultimately wouldn't make me happy. A sense of true, authentic satisfaction—the kind I'd first felt as a gymnastics coach and then years later with the girls at Pathfinder—didn't really come from some external place.

Finally accepting that realization was what made me feel so conflicted about returning to New York. I told Jen that earlier that day I'd gotten an e-mail from an editor I'd worked with as a freelancer asking if I might be interested in coming to work for her after I got back to the States—if I planned to come back. There was a good chance that she'd have a senior-level position open in late summer, and she'd like to talk to me about filling it.

Old personality traits die hard. Her suggestion absolutely thrilled me—it would be a *huge* promotion, about four steps up the editorial ladder, and I'd never have to be an assistant again!—but it also terrified me. I knew how easy it would be for me to get sucked right back into my old overachieving ways. I didn't want to find myself chained to a desk chair again at twenty-nine . . . and then thirty . . . and thirty-one. As grateful as I was to have a job lead at this point, I wasn't sure how Manhattan would fit into my life or how I'd fit into Manhattan. Could I have a career—and everything else I wanted too?

I hadn't acknowledged my feelings until now, but they hit me full force: I was ready for something more than just a job. I wanted what most women secretly (or not so secretly) want deep down—to fall in love, to be a girlfriend or wife, to come home to someone who wanted to come home to me. I'd never really made much space in my life or my heart for those things before. And though I didn't know where I'd live after the trip was over, I was sure of one thing: I wanted my life to look a whole lot different than it had the year before I left.

Jen brought me back to the present by asking me when the editor job would start.

"Not sure," I said, relieved to spot an open patch in the trees ahead. "She didn't mention a date."

"Well, it sounds like you've got some time to think about it. Don't turn her down just yet," Jen urged, her steps growing even more purposeful as we moved toward the trailhead.

I breathed out a small puff of relief. It looked as if the fork we'd taken earlier had been the right one.

"I won't," I promised. "I just wonder sometimes if it's really possible to strike a balance in New York. Don't you ever ask yourself if some things might just be easier—finding a great guy, a nine-to-five job—in another city?"

Jen laughed. "*All* the time. I bet it's easier to find those things in *any* other city."

I grinned. "Yeah. Back when I used to go to the health and nutrition conferences in Chicago, I could swear the whole place was crawling with gorgeous corn-fed boys just itching to get your number and ask you out."

463

"Totally . . . and what about Denver? One of my coworkers told me that not only are there tons of sexy weekend warrior types but that people bike to work and leave the office at five on the dot," Jen added.

By the time we'd reached the clearing and made it back to our car, Jen and I had worked our way through all of the cities that might have a romantic or work-life edge over New York: San Diego, D.C., Boston, Austin, Portland.

"Hey, forget picking one city," I said, now totally caught up in the idea of moving somewhere else. "Since we've already uprooted our lives and are travel professionals at this point, why don't we just do a tour of *all* the good places before we settle on one?"

"I love that! We could call it Crossing State Lines for Love or New Yorkers Beyond Borders," Jen suggested.

"No, wait, I got it!" I said, unlocking the doors and sliding behind the wheel. "Finding a Mate in the Fifty States."

"Hey, that's pretty good," said Jen, flashing me a grin as she slid into the car next to me. "Maybe you could start a career as a writer."

"I've been thinking about it."

464

✣

CHAPTER TWENTY-NINE

Jen

SOUTH ISLAND, NEW ZEALAND

MARCH–APRIL

Amanda, Holly, and I had been walking along the coastal track of Abel Tasman National Park for nearly four hours when we reached a fork in the road. Tamped down in the soil was a sign warning us of a tidal crossing ahead. The instructions were straightforward: GO LEFT DURING LOW TIDE (40 MINUTES). STAY RIGHT DURING HIGH TIDE (1.5 HOURS).

"Umm, I think I forgot my tide schedule at home. Should we assume that it's high or take our chances?" Holly said.

"I don't know, and it doesn't say anywhere," I replied, kneeling down to inspect every square inch of the sign on the off chance that we'd missed a timetable.

"Well, both paths lead to the same place. One just winds really far out of the way," Amanda added, perusing the crumpled trail map she'd stuffed in her pocket. "I guess we shouldn't have cut it so close to dark."

Since entering this richly painted paradise via a water taxi named Vigour, we'd made it a point to stroll at a leisurely pace, taking the time to appreciate the azure waters, emerald forests, and golden sand beaches that saturated all 360 degrees of our panoramic setting. But now, neck and neck with twilight, we decided it made more sense to take the shorter route and hope the tide was still at a safe distance from the shore. We set off in a mad dash down the path's west wing. But, as we'd soon discover, we had chosen unwisely.

In less than thirty minutes, we reached a clearing in the path and could see the entrance to the campground about two hundred yards ahead. Unfortunately, the rocky inlet that carved the section of coastline between us and our desired destination was already flooded with waves.

"Well, I guess we know what time the tide comes in," I said, scanning the area to see if there was an alternate route.

"Oh, man. What should we do? Turn around and go back the other way?" Holly asked.

"I don't think we have time. It'll take at least two hours to retrace our steps and follow the low-tide trail to the end and I don't love the idea of us walking so close to the edge of the cliff with only our headlamp light," Amanda replied.

"Yeah, you're right. And the cabin is right there too. It doesn't look *that* deep," Holly said, walking to the edge to inspect the water. "I'll go across if you two will."

"There's no way to know how far down it goes in the middle, but it's only two or three feet here. So I say let's go for it," Amanda said, glancing at me for approval.

"What the hell. Worst case, we turn around," I said, bending to unlace my hiking boots.

Since Amanda, Holly, and I had created our own tour package, combining an independent trek and an overnight campout with a guided kayak excursion the next morning, the only clothes in our possession were the outfits currently affixed to our bodies and an extra set tucked away in our small day packs, meant to double as both pajamas and a boating ensemble. It wouldn't have been a crisis if everything got soaked, but it wasn't ideal considering the increasingly cooler climate. And in view of the miraculous fact that my iPod was still going strong after nearly a dozen countries and countless planes, trains, and auto-rickshaws, I wasn't about to sacrifice it now. All three of us in agreement, we ducked behind some rocks, stripped down, and changed into our bathing suits. With everything else stuffed into our bags or lashed to the outside by the straps, we began our slow creep across.

"I love how we were the only ones left on the entire trail and somehow managed to get ourselves stuck in freezing cold water during high tide. It's so perfectly 'us,' I swear," Holly said, always the first to laugh off our latest in a long and distinguished string of screwball predicaments.

"Don't worry. We can do it, girls. I believe in us. 'Chariots of Fire' is playing," Amanda replied, pulling out one of her classic trip mantras. "Just be careful in this section. It's really slippery," she added as the water rose from her hips to above her waist.

"Oh, this is so *Stand by Me*. It's awesome," I said. "Except with no leeches, thank God. Hey, did I ever tell you about the time I found a leech on my foot at summer camp?"

"I think we might have heard that story a few dozen times," Holly teased. "But I'm so happy I get to live one of your movie montages, Baggy."

The girls had grown to expect my consistent stream of analogies, relating certain moments or events to scenes from my favorite films, and they always responded with the appropriate amount of sarcasm. But during our time together on the road, we'd learned to appreciate one another's various methods of creative expression for what they were, a vehicle for viewing the world.

Of course I had plenty of my own original interpretations of our travels. But when I was placed in a situation that seemed epic or nostalgic enough to warrant a spot on the silver screen, I felt more alive somehow. And oddly comforted. As if I were a character in a romanticized version of my own life story and someone or something bigger than myself was watching and rooting for me. As a child, I'd incessantly fantasized about embarking on a life-changing journey into the wilderness with my best friends, as in Stephen King's coming-of-age classic. And now here I was, wading through a stream with Amanda and Holly, living out an even greater adventure. Sure, my ass was totally numb from the frosty waters and the bottoms of my feet were being poked by razor-sharp pebbles, but it was a movie moment nonetheless.

"And darlin', darlin', stand by me," I belted out. "Ohh, stand by meee . . . ouch, shit, killer rock ahead, watch out!" I yelped as I pitched forward and my bag started slipping off my head.

"Okay, you're not allowed to sing if you're going to drown in the process," Holly said, simultaneously grabbing my stuff to save it from falling in the water, before we both cracked up.

"Yeah, and Jen, don't you know that's not our theme song today?" Amanda said. "It should be . . . 'In high tide or in low tide. I'll be by your side. I'll be by your side,'" she sang with an affected Bob Marley accent as the three of us continued splashing our way through the water until we finally reached the other side.

Laughing at the sight of ourselves shivering in bikinis, our feet caked in mud, we trudged up the grassy incline toward the communal barracks where we were to bunk for the night. It was then we realized we weren't the only ones laughing. A gang of fellow trekkers, who'd clearly taken the higher and drier route to camp, had been watching our manic tide crossing from a picnic table under the trees. As we approached, they erupted in cheers and claps.

"Well done there, girls. We weren't sure if you three were going to make it across there for a second," an older man with a white beard called out with a chuckle.

"Oh, we knew we'd make it," Holly said. "And it was a good substitute for a shower too."

"Right you are. And definitely more fun than the way we came around," he replied. "Well, anyway. Glad you're here. There are still a few more beds inside. No electricity. But there's a kerosene burner for cooking if you need it."

After drying off with our shared hand towel and changing back into our semidry hiking clothes, we pulled out our food stash and constructed a dinner of peanut butter and jelly sandwiches, soup, apples, and chocolate bars. Surprisingly, many of our roommates had long since eaten and turned in for the night, so we relocated to a far-off corner of the common area so we wouldn't wake anyone.

Huddled in a semicircle, headlamps in place, we entertained ourselves per the usual, rotating one magazine around the table and chattering away about anything and everything that came to mind. You'd think that after ten months of traveling together, we would've run out of things to talk about, but we hadn't. Sometimes our conversations were inane: Six Degrees of Kevin Bacon and the "Would you rather" game (". . . sleep with ten huge spiders or one large rat?"). Other times the topics were more serious: Could we start a nonprofit organization focusing on women's and children's issues? Debates about the environment and the Kyoto Protocol. Reaffirming our vow to take a vacation together once a year for the rest of our lives and "arguing" over our first post-trip destination. But tonight was reserved for our favorite pastime: quizzing one another on the random details and personal stories that we should all know at this point.

Amanda: "Name two jobs Holly had in college." *Ding.* Me: "Pizza delivery girl and driving the lead paint detection bus." Correct!

Me: "What was the ridiculous name Amanda came up with

469

for her childhood cat that was white? Bonus points for correct spelling." *Ding.* Holly: "What is W-Y-T-E-K-A-T?" Correct!

Holly: "Amanda. What cartoon character did Jen most look like growing up?" *Ding.* Amanda: "Annie?" Holly: "Wrong! Ha! She wanted to *be* Annie, but she *looked* like Strawberry Short-cake." Correct!

More amazing still than our ability to entertain ourselves anytime, anywhere was how—without even trying—we'd gotten to know all the silly details about one another that on the surface seemed insignificant but as a collection represented who we were as people. Amanda and I had always said that even though we hadn't become close friends until our twenties, in our collective memory, we'd been pals since the playground. And at this point, Holly was fully painted into that scene with us, racing to the swing set to claim the best seat, then deciding all of a sudden that mine looked more fun than hers and asking me to trade.

Before the trip, I'd known Holly as the gorgeous, athletic, bright, and bubbly girl who everyone claimed was one of the nicest people they knew. And while she still was all of those things, I'd grown to understand her as an extremely passion-ate, conscientious, and unfailingly patient and sympathetic confidante who stood strong by her convictions and had an uncanny ability to see the best in everyone and find the sunny side of almost any situation—a trait that did not come as easily to me. To this day, it still amazes me that Holly had stuck with the trip even after all the stumbling blocks, like maintain-ing a long-distance relationship, having her magazine column crash, and then barely having enough funds to get the whole way around the globe. But Amanda had been right that day at the Indian consulate in New York when she'd said that the trip wouldn't work without Holly, that Amanda and I needed her to balance us out. And that when it came to our round-the-world adventure, three Lost Girls were definitely better than two.

We'd foiled the dastardly plans of bag slashers, defended one another against maniacal cabdrivers, convinced embassy officials to put a '"rush order" on visa applications, and raced to clinics in the middle of the night to assuage fears of parasites. So crossing an inlet together as the waters of high tide rushed in to greet us? It was all in a day's work. And I couldn't wait to get up and do it all again tomorrow.

Though we'd certainly tallied an impressive number of badass activities during our time in New Zealand—rafting over a twenty-one-foot waterfall, sliding down the steep volcanic slopes of Mount Tongariro, attending an Abel Tasman pirate party, and hiking the legendary Franz Josef Glacier in the Southern Alps—I hoped to up the ante during our next stop: the country's adventure capital of Queenstown. Sailing down the scenic State Highway 6, the three of us were poised in our typical road trip stance: me at the wheel belting out radio tunes, Amanda riding shotgun, feet propped on the dashboard, harmonizing with me—though considerably more on key—and the earplugged, eye-masked Holly power napping in the back.

Upon arrival in hostel rooms, it generally took about 8.5 seconds before the contents of our backpacks exploded across the floor, bed frames, doorknobs, pretty much every available surface. To be fair, we treated our car equally. Wet clothes were strewn across the back windowsill, drying in the sun; rolls of toilet paper and bottles of hand sanitizer overflowed from seat pockets; a collection of half-empty soda bottles, assorted snack bars, and lollipop wrappers was sprinkled on top of muddy sneakers, guidebooks, and some weird Maori tribal tongs (possibly for salads, who knew?) that Holly had just *had* to buy in

Rotorua. To us, this scene epitomized the freedom of the open road, which we reveled in after months of public transportation slavery. And with hours of uninterrupted bonding time came impromptu pit stops, moments of pure goofiness, and frequent conversations about the state of our precarious futures.

"So I know we were just kind of joking around that day in the redwood forest, but I'm seriously starting to wonder. Maybe living in another city after the trip would be good for me," Amanda said, turning the volume knob until the music faded to a low background hum. "I mean, if we went to Colorado, life would be full of hikes and skiing and rafting. Just like it is here."

"I know. It'd be amazing. As much as I love big cities, I really miss being outdoors and having some semblance of a well-rounded life. I mean, the entire year before we left on the trip consisted mainly of working late, eating disgusting amounts of take-out dinners, drinking too much at happy hour, which prompted ham, egg, and cheese hangover sandwiches the next morning and lazing around Brian's apartment in sweats. I was *gross*," I said, rolling down the window to inhale the intoxicatingly pure air.

"Well, at least you had a boyfriend and made some time for friends. Until I met Jason, I just sat at home and wrote articles and totally neglected all social invitations. I seriously can't let that happen again," Amanda said, pulling her windblown curls up into a loose bun. "Do you remember our list? We need to make another one."

The list was a sheet of notebook paper we'd hung on the fridge of our first shared Manhattan apartment, covered with all the fun things we wanted to do that summer in the city, plus a few future life goals: Take a jazz class at Broadway Dance Center. Get half-price tickets to *Rent* and *Les Misérables*. Join the Niketown running club. Have drinks at the Rainbow Room.

Score an invite for a weekend in the Hamptons. Volunteer for New York Cares. Get promoted in less than a year. Go on a date in Central Park. The list had gone on and on, and aside from a few items, we'd accomplished everything and continued to add more. But sadly, that piece of paper had disappeared years ago.

With powder blue lakes and cloud-ringed mountains painting our view, and Holly snoozing in the backseat, Amanda and I tossed around the logistics of possibly moving to another city and starting all over again. Would we need to buy a car? Could we even afford one after spending all our money? We had such an amazing circle of friends in New York. Would it be foolish to give that up? Would there be enough job opportunities in our field? Maybe we could just spend a summer somewhere else . . . and so on.

"Oh, my God, you two are hilarious," Holly said, stirring from her slumber. "I've been half awake for the past fifteen minutes listening to you talk, and even my head is spinning from all your scenarios."

"I know, surprise, surprise that I would be a tad neurotic," Amanda said. "But we're mainly just having fun fantasizing. I have no clue what I'll want a few months from now."

"Believe me, Hol, if I had a boyfriend and an apartment to return to like you did, I'd run back to New York with open arms, but right now it just seems scary," I said.

"Well, you never know what's going to happen when I get home. But I know that if you both do come back to New York, yes, please for me"—she grinned—"you will get everything you want. It's more of a challenge, for sure, but once I switched magazines and moved to Brooklyn with Elan, I felt like I was living in a whole different city. So you'll just reinvent yourselves, and it will be amazing. We can have barbecues on my back patio, you can join my street hockey team, which has tons of cute guys on it, and we'll force each other to leave work at six p.m. every day

473

and go running in the park. And you'll find the loves of your lives and we can all buy apartments in the same building."

Every time Holly went off on one of her enthusiastic list tangents, it always made me feel so much better, as if somehow her confidence in me guaranteed a successful and happy future.

"Well, if you say so, Hol, then I believe it," I said. "I just have to figure out how to date since I've never really done it. You two will have to teach me how."

"Okay, Jen. Well, I promise to share all my infinite pearls of dating wisdom with you if you do me one favor." She paused. "Pull over at that apple stand," she said, leaning forward between the two front seats and pointing to the ORGANIC APPLES road sign.

After picking through the huge bin of New Zealand's finest Fiesta and Akane apples sold to the passing public with an on-your-honor money jar and a 3-FOR-$1 sign, we hopped back into the car and continued on to Queenstown, the stereo pumping full blast and the three of us singing at the top of our lungs.

F umbling around in the dim light of dawn, I tried to locate a pair of jeans and sweatshirt from the pile on the hostel room floor without waking Amanda or Holly. Today was the day I was attempting my most daring adrenaline feat yet, a triple-header bungee jump. My heart was already pumping with anticipation. While Queenstown offered an endless supply of action sports and adventure activities (more per square meter than any other similarly sized town in the world, as we'd learned) to all those courageous enough to take on the challenge, those same brave souls also needed to come equipped with a bulging wallet. Everything from jet boating and canyon swinging to white-water rafting and river surfing came with a hefty price tag. And considering we were barely squeaking by on $50 a day (nearly twice our pre–New Zealand budget), we had to choose our splurges wisely.

Since Holly had the least money left, she'd opted out of any costly experiences but had designed a schedule of free hiking excursions and cheap off-roading jeep tours to make up for it. But as much as I cajoled, needled, and begged Amanda to join me for this once-in-a-lifetime set of leaps, she hadn't budged. I was standing in front of the bathroom mirror, slathering on a layer of sunscreen, when I heard a soft knock at the half-open door. Amanda stood there in a rumpled set of PJs and half-cocked sleep mask.

"So I decided if you're going to seriously do this, you can't go alone. I'm coming with you," she whispered.

"Really?" I squealed softly in disbelief.

"Yes, but if I die, I'm holding you responsible."

"Absolutely. But you know, Pressner, if you want the ultimate rush, you gotta be willing to pay the ultimate price."

"All right, now is not the time for *Point Break* quotes, Baggett. I'm kinda freakin' out," she said, reaching across me to grab her toothbrush off the counter.

"Okay, sorry. I'll stop. But I seriously think you're going to love this. It'll change your life, swear to God," I said, slipping out of the bathroom before she could administer a death stare.

Being Amanda, she'd somehow managed to score us a discount coupon from someone at the tourism office for nearly half off the price of AJ Hackett's Thrillogy combo package, which delivered three unique bungee experiences back-to-back in a single day. Along with dozens of fellow rush junkies, we boarded a bus at the main company office and headed out to our first location, Kawarau Bridge, the world's first and most famous bungee-jumping site. At only 43 meters (141 feet), it was a baby leap compared to the next two, but it was a good warm-up to get our juices flowing. And with the option to graze the water below or even to be fully immersed, it was an early-morning wake-up call I was actually looking forward to.

After signing away our right to sue AJ Hackett in case of accidental death or dismemberment, the friendly attendant weighed us, wrote our kilograms in permanent marker on our hands so the experts at the ledge could adjust the rope properly, and instructed us to go outside and across the bridge to wait in line with the other jumpers.

"I think I'm going to pass out. I don't know if I can do this," Amanda said as we moved up through the line.

"Yes, you can. Just look straight ahead. Walk to the edge, and before you overthink things, just let yourself fall off. I promise you, you'll be so hopped up on endorphins by the time you bounce back up that you'll want to do it again immediately."

"All right, seriously. Where did you come from? And what did you do with my friend Jen? I mean, you're not even scared at all. How is that possible?"

Although Amanda wasn't exactly right (I did have a tiny bit of nervous energy), my lack of true fear didn't surprise me. Though I'd always been innately petrified of my house catching on fire or a tarantula coming within even ten feet of me, ever since I can remember, I'd craved a healthy dose of thrill-induced adrenaline like a junkie jonesing for a fix. But none of the most extreme highs I'd racked up in my life (skydiving in Switzerland and numerous Xtreme Skyflyer drops at amusement parks) had been done in Amanda's presence, so I could understand her disbelief.

"Look, it's okay to be nervous, but you'll watch me go first and you'll see how fun it is," I said as the hottie AJ Hackett staffer tightly secured my harness. Considering that the company had been founded by *the* Father of Bungee Jumping, Alan John Hackett, and had an impeccable safety record, I figured we were in the best hands we could ever hope to be in during such an adventure.

When I was all geared up and my rope was adjusted to allow me to skim the river with my fingers, I shuffled out to the edge of the platform and, without hesitation, flew. The second I saw the water whizzing toward my face, I got the jolt I'd been waiting for.

"Whoooo hooooo!" I screamed as I sprang a quarter of the way back up the way I'd come. After a few more wicked bounces, two men on a raft rowed over and extended a line for me to grab. Pulling me slowly down into the boat, they unlatched my harness and sent it back up for Amanda. I felt like a proud parent as my little Pressner soared out into the clear blue yonder for the very first time. And though her shrieks were noticeably more deranged-sounding than mine, she braved the jump all the same.

"Holy shit, I'm shaking," she panted, coming up the stairs to the viewing platform to join me. "I can't believe I just did that."

"You were so great. I'm so proud of you, seriously," I said, grabbing her in a hug. "Wasn't it amazing? Are you excited to do it again?"

"I haven't decided yet, but I'll let you know when we get to the Nevis."

My pulse quickened at the very thought that I was about to do something I'd dreamed about since we'd first decided to come to New Zealand. While I was a die-hard *Lord of the Rings* fan, the themed tours that cropped up across the islands were not for me. Rather, after seeing Orlando Bloom hurl himself off the legendary Nevis Highwire Bungy during one of the DVD special features, I'd vowed that I would follow in his righteous fling-steps if I ever got the chance. Finally, the moment I'd been waiting for had arrived.

Unlike your standard bungee adventure, where you walk up to the edge of a bridge or the top of another sturdy landmass,

477

the Nevis experience requires boarding a special pod that carries you across a vast canyon, sliding along cable wires to a suspended platform in the center. Dangling 440 feet in the air, the Nevis provides a mind-blowing 8.5-second free fall through a breathtaking river valley. And though it's not the tallest jump in the world (another brainchild of A. J. Hackett, the Macau Tower in China, is a staggering 760 feet), the Nevis certainly holds its own.

By the time we were next in the pod line to go, I'd long since stopped trying to persuade Amanda that bungee jumping was the best thing ever. At this point, I just hoped to stop her from hyperventilating. I have to admit, as thrilled as I was to take the ultimate plunge, the Nevis was seriously intimidating. Even more nerve-racking than actually going over the edge was hopping up to it. With a pretty brisk wind whipping through the ravine, you felt like a sitting duck standing out there, with the potential to blow sideways off the ledge if you lost your balance for even a second.

Luckily, I'd made it past the point of no return. With my heart thumping in my ears, I waited for the signal, spread my arms out wide, and let myself get carried away by the breeze. A lot can go through your mind in nine seconds (what if the rope snaps?, my cheeks are seriously flapping, pay attention or you'll miss the scenery), but the one thing that stuck out in mine was that this was the closest I'd ever come to flying. For some reason, watching the water below speeding closer to my face was way more thrilling than scary. And with such a long fall, I got an exhilarating rebound and went sailing back toward the sky. Soaring upward, I reveled in the temporary feeling of weightlessness, at the same time mentally prepping for the technical portion of the fall.

Before you jump, the guides instruct you to do a mini–abdominal crunch on your second bounce, reach up, and yank a special cord attached to your foot. This serves to turn you upright, so that you're sitting in a swinglike harness with your legs dangling down toward the water and your head in the direction of the cable car. One poor guy who went before me had failed to follow instructions properly so was upside down, blood rushing to his head, the whole ride up. Though it wasn't unsafe to ascend that way, I was determined not to. Luckily, when I swung myself upright, I felt the line in my fingers and pulled, which was a much more beautiful and enjoyable way to float back up. Plus it gave me extra time to fully soak in the view before being lifted back onto the platform by the attendants.

Once again Amanda courageously followed suit, and with only a few minor outbursts, she plummeted headfirst out of the pod. Though she confessed to having been utterly terrified, she grinned proudly and posed in a genuine hard-core stance during the group photos we snapped after returning safely to terra firma.

At that point, we had a two-hour break before our final jump, so we caught the bus back to town and had a light picnic lunch before heading over to the Ledge Bungy, the only urban jump in the heart of Queenstown. After Nevis, it was nice to give our adrenal glands a break, although the downside of the wait was the inevitable comedown from being amped up. But a few Diet Cokes and a 400-meter gondola ride above the city, and we were back in business. As we neared the top of the Skyline complex, which housed a restaurant, gift shop, private events spaces, and conference centers, we spotted Holly waiting for us at the entrance.

"Hey, crazy ladies. You survived," she called out.

"Just barely, but it was pretty amazing," Amanda replied. "But how on earth did you manage to find us?"

"Oh, I have my ways," she teased.

"Well, I'm so glad you're finally here to protect me from this one," Amanda added, nodding in my direction.

"Please. You kicked ass, Pressner. And just one more left, and then we can go out and celebrate. Dinner and drinks will be on me."

"Yes, mine too?" Holly asked, which, in my state of bliss, I agreed to.

Nestled among pine trees with panoramic views of Lake Wakatipu, the long platform to the bungee served as a veritable runway for fliers to strike their own original poses. Complete with a special harness that allows for flips, twists, and other innovative moves, the Ledge Bungy promised a totally different experience from the first two jumps and the perfect end to my perfect day.

"You can also turn and face the guide and go off bum first," one of the staff said as we waited in line to get geared up.

"Yes. That's awesome. I'm totally down for that," I said.

"Right on. Just tell the guy when you get to the front, and he'll set you up good and proper. And what about you?" he said, directing his question to Amanda.

"I'm lucky I made it this far. I don't think I can handle not knowing what's ahead of me," Amanda replied.

Attribute it to the intense shots of adrenaline that had been coursing through my veins all day, but standing up there with Holly and Amanda, looking out at the endless skyline, I felt the weight of the world temporarily lift off my shoulders. Even though I wasn't quite ready to pledge my commitment to return to New York immediately after the trip, I knew that what Holly had said in the car was true. No matter where we all ended up, we always had the power to steer the course of our lives in a new direction. To take all the lessons we'd learned on the road about who we really were, or hoped to become, and what we wanted most, and try to carve out a new and improved path for ourselves. Maybe it wouldn't work out the first or even tenth time, but we'd keep forging ahead until we got it right.

Until then, all we could do was take a chance . . . and jump.

※

CHAPTER THIRTY

Amanda

SYDNEY, AUSTRALIA

APRIL

With the scratch of wheels on tarmac in Sydney, everything changed. People scrambled into the aisles, as they always do the instant the captain turns off the FASTEN SEAT BELT sign, but Jen, Holly, and I stayed put. We all just looked at one another. This was it: the Last Stop.

During the year and a half leading up to the trip, and even for months after we'd left, I'd been convinced something would happen to keep us from completing the loop together. Amazing things like job offers, promotions, and marriage proposals. Scary things like health issues, canceled columns, or empty bank accounts. Even now, I couldn't believe we'd come this far and grown closer than I'd ever imagined was possible back in New York.

Several of the backpackers we'd met had seemed shocked—maybe a little skeptical—that we'd actually remained friends throughout the whole trip. How had we traveled for this long without secretly plotting one another's untimely travel-related demise? We'd explained that though our time together hadn't *exactly* been fight-free, we'd made it work simply because the alternative was unacceptable. No single issue was so important that the three of us would be willing to throw away a friend-ship—or the chance to complete this journey together—for the sake of being right.

But there was another, more important reason we got along so well: The Checklist.

Right from the beginning, we'd secretly tallied all the stuff we'd sacrificed as individuals in order to keep the peace as a group. For months, none of us had mentioned the "credits" we'd get for giving up the bottom bunk or sitting in the seat next to the guy with obnoxious B.O., but we'd all kept score in our heads (knowing Jen, she used Excel charts).

"C'mon, guys, you know we all keep track," Jen had finally pointed out in Vietnam. "And that's fine. As an only child, I never understood how siblings could fight over stupid little stuff, like who got more juice or who got to ride shotgun, but now I totally get it."

In some ways, we *had* reverted back to being kids. We'd been forced to share absolutely everything with one another—beds, bathrooms, train cars, battery chargers, breathing space—and still, we rarely wanted to separate. It wasn't just because we adored one another's company. We were all also worried we'd miss something really exciting if the other two went off without us for a day.

Of course, all of that togetherness could also be stifling. At times I battled the subconscious desire to compare my own be-havior to Jen's and Holly's and the slightly paranoid feeling that the other two might be assessing me. The flaws that I'd worked carefully to conceal back home—the fact that I can be impatient, forgetful, and neurotic and have weird one-sided conversations in my sleep—were totally unhidable in such close proximity.

But, I soon realized, so were my friends' slightly less lov-able character traits. By being so involved in Jen's and Holly's everyday, uncensored lives, seeing the women they are in

483

their amazing moments, average moments, and superlow, sleep-deprived moments, I finally understood the meaning of "nobody's perfect." And I mean that in the best way possible: appreciating their imperfections as parts of them made me realize that I could appreciate my own as parts of me.

The rest of the plane had emptied. And so the three of us finally disembarked from our last international flight before returning home. As we zigzagged our way through international arrivals, I started to imagine what my daily life would be like without Jen and Holly in it. Like it or not, the time was fast approaching when we'd be on our own again, making decisions and catapulting through the world without our two strongest lifelines to rely upon.

We'd no longer be The Lost Girls . . . we'd simply be ourselves.

Crossing the invisible line from the air-conditioned terminal into the warm, salty air of Oz, I felt enveloped with relief. We still had nearly two more months until that would happen.

T he light was rapidly draining from the sky as we stood in the alley behind Travellers Auto Barn, staring at what looked like a space-hogging double-decker camper van on an acid trip. The whole vehicle had been shrink-wrapped in psychedelically tinted cellophane and emblazoned with more international landmark and sponsorship stickers than a stock car.

Holly and Jen had bumped into the promotions director for the Aussie-based World Nomads insurance company nearly eighteen months earlier at the Adventures in Travel Expo. They'd struck what sounded like an unbelievable deal: the company would provide all three of us with a year's worth of travel insurance if we agreed to drive its fully loaded "Ambassador Van" during the seven and a half weeks we were in Australia, blogging about our experiences for the company Web site as we went. In addition to the free set of wheels, World Nomads would also hook us up with a brand-new laptop, a cell phone to stay in touch with our new bosses, and a special card that would guarantee us free Internet access in locations across Oz. The only catch? That there seemed to *be* no catch.

When Jen and Holly shook hands on the deal, all three of us were still in full-on multitasking New York mode. What World Nomads was asking us to do—blogging three times a week and posting video diaries on its site—seemed like a cakewalk. It wasn't until we'd arrived in Sydney a year and a half and about fifty thousand miles later that we finally grasped the full scope of the task—and the machinery—that we'd agreed to take on.

"That's the *van?*" Holly said as we all blinked hard at the hulking Day-Glo vehicle. "It's just . . . so . . . *big.*"

Behind us, a man snorted in amusement. "Well, you know, I hear that all the time. After a few go-rounds, you'll get used to it, I promise."

The voice belonged to Chris Ford, the publicity rep for Travellers Auto Barn, a man who swallowed up what little alley space hadn't already been commandeered by the van. At six feet, three inches, the guy was built like an army tank with a bulletproof chest and swollen arms where the heavy artillery should be. His comment barely fazed me. Just a day earlier, during a meeting with the World Nomads execs, the company's sales director had asked if we planned to hold naked pillow fights inside the van during our travels—and if so, could we please videoconference him in so the whole office could watch us in action? My gaze immediately shifted to Christy, the one woman who worked with this motley crew of guys. She cracked a smile and let the comment slide, so we followed suit. We'd been in Sydney less than forty-eight hours, but I was already getting the impression that the post–Clarence Thomas era of political correctness we took for granted in the States had yet to be ushered in here.

Christy had given us instructions to pick up the van from Chris Ford at the Auto Barn and to e-mail them with the list of the Australian destinations we planned to visit.

"Where do you want us to go?" I'd asked her, anticipating getting on the road again. "We're up for anything."

"Anywhere you want," Christy responded. "So long as you return the van in one piece, you can go across the outback to Perth and back for all we care. Actually, we'd probably prefer you do that—might make for better blog entries."

"You mean we shouldn't just stay here and drive it around Sydney till we go home?" Holly tossed out, half kidding.

It was the only time during our two-beer lunch that the executives didn't laugh.

By the time Chris finished showing us around the van the next evening, the alley had gone almost completely dark. He briefly explained the Auto Barn rules of the road:

The oil and coolant must be topped off daily.

No riding in the back.

No picking up hitchhikers.

"That last one's just for my own benefit. It'll help me sleep better at night," said Chris in a protective way that was kind of endearing.

And with that, we were ready to take off—except for one little problem.

"Hey, ladies, which one of you knows how to drive stick?" asked Holly.

I shook my head. I'd barely driven an automatic since college graduation and had never learned to use a stick shift. Jen unenthusiastically volunteered that she'd done it a few times as a teenager but had probably forgotten how by now. So the buck stopped with Holly, the one of us least inclined to operate electronics, machinery, or anything else sold with an instruction manual. Holly even turned to Jen or me when technical difficulties with her camera or iPod cropped up. But now, as the only one of us who'd ever gotten a basic stick shift education, she had to climb behind the wheel of the psychedelic aluminum beast.

Chris looked mildly apprehensive as he flipped the keys to Holly. "You guys signed all of your insurance forms, right?"

We assured him that we had. Holly gave him a thumbs-up, tentatively started the engine, and managed to stall only once as we pulled away.

B osses, jobs, and attention-hogging vehicles weren't the only responsibilities that we took on during our final months on the road. We also scored ourselves a two-month sublet with Simone, an Australian who'd used to date one of my ex-boyfriend Baker's close friends, Jeff. I'd met Sim for the first time nearly two years earlier, after she'd sent me an out-of-the-blue e-mail asking if she and Jeff, who lived together in the Cayman Islands, could be "terribly cheeky" and ask to shack on my futon in New York when they came up for vacation.

I'd met Jeff only once or twice before, and was entirely unacquainted with his new girlfriend. Impressed by this chick's ballsiness (and perhaps to show Baker that his friends still wanted to hang out with me even after we'd broken up), I not only prepared the futon for my houseguests but also planned an extensive weekend of dinners, parties, and social events for them. I knew almost instantly upon opening my front door that I'd love Simone. She was a gregarious, charismatic force of nature who'd spent the previous six years living in various glamorous locations around the globe. She was organized and pulled together in every way that I wasn't and had a passion for travel that matched my own.

Over the next several months, I visited Simone and Jeff in the Cayman Islands and then again in Vegas for Simone's twenty-seventh birthday. Though the couple split not long after our trip to Sin City, she and I stayed in constant e-mail contact, joking that if they'd done nothing else, we could thank our exes for bringing us together. And when she'd heard that our paths would cross again in Sydney, where she now lived, she wouldn't hear of us staying anywhere else. "My flatmate will be moving out just as you arrive. It's fated!"

When she offered to rent us the spare room in her apartment, where all three of us could sleep on a pair of air mattresses, we agreed to the deal straight away. Even through the rent was $1,000 per month (a staggering amount compared with what we'd been paying to sleep in Southeast Asia), we could justify splitting it. It would be cheaper—and infinitely more comfortable—than hopping between $30-per-night hostels in Sydney.

It wasn't until we'd had the meeting with World Nomads' execs that it dawned on me that we had a problem. If we paid Simone the two full months' rent that we'd promised her and took full advantage of our living situation by sticking around Sydney, there would be no way we could make good on the assignment to drive and blog across Oz.

At this point, we all had a cash flow shortage. Holly was so far in the red that she'd almost turned magenta, Jen had depleted far more than she'd actually saved for the trip, and all three of us were depending on credit cards to bridge the financial gap. Writing a check to Simone and shelling out more cash to camp up and down the continent would push us way beyond our budgetary boundaries. At this rate, we wouldn't even be able to afford our flights home.

Backing out on Simone wasn't an option. She was counting on us to make her rent. But we couldn't just give the van back to the World Nomads team either. Not for the first time, we were torn between settling into city life and our desire to hit the open road.

The longer we sat at Simone's kitchen table trying to figure out the best course of action, the tenser things got between us. A low-grade level of stress radiated within our group. We tried to pretend that we weren't completely freaked out by the fact that we'd somehow managed to take on a sublease, a massive vehicle only one of us could operate, an ongoing writing assignment, a cell phone, and yet another laptop two months before we'd even thought about reentering our "normal" lives—but we couldn't.

Finally, after a few friction-filled days, we came to a compromise: we'd stay in Simone's apartment for six weeks (but pay her for eight) and use World Nomads' van to take long weekend trips to locations in New South Wales and one final road trip up to Byron Bay. It wasn't ideal, but we'd just have to hope that our Pulitzer-worthy blogging skills could make up for the fact that we'd fall 2,030 kilometers short of Alice Springs (the unofficial capital of the Australian Outback) and a full 3,300 kilometers short of Perth.

I was disappointed that we'd come so far around the globe only to skip the continent's most iconic sights, but there was an upside: once we made our decision to break up our Sydney stay with short road trips, everyone seemed to snap out of the funk we'd fallen into. Jen began organizing urban-based adventures with renewed vigor ("We can blog about the Sydney Harbor Bridge Climb, right?"), Holly jogged down to the Bondi Junction shopping center twenty minutes away to check the cost of gym memberships ("If we're gonna be city girls again, we might as well take advantage of the amenities—plus, they're offering a big discount this month"), and I did my best to track down which tourist offerings were authentically Australian.

One evening, after we'd finished a tour of the Sydney Opera House and passed row after row of souvenir shops selling Aboriginal art watches, boomerang key chains, stuffed koalas, and Crocodile Dundee hats, I suggested that we follow Simone's advice to visit the famed Australian Heritage Hotel, a historic spot where you could order a pizza topped with kangaroo, saltwater crocodile, lamb, or emu. Holly couldn't bear to sink her teeth into a formerly cuddly, antipodean version of Bambi. So instead we took our appetites over to Sushi Train, a restaurant where seaweed salad and four-piece rolls traveled past our outstretched hands on a giant conveyor belt.

It wasn't exactly exotic or particularly Australian. But as I plucked a California roll and then a Boston roll off the revolving chuck wagon, I decided that for tonight at least, it was fine to have a taste of something familiar. Sydney was no longer just another destination we were visiting—for the next several weeks, it would be our home.

It wasn't long after we'd hung the meager contents of our backpacks in the closets at Simone's place that I started to notice that something was going on with Holly. I wasn't sure what it was, but she wasn't acting like herself.

Holly was one of the most laid-back, easygoing women I'd ever known, but by now I'd also learned that our eternal sunshine optimist was a still water whose emotions ran deep. Though she allowed the world to see her brilliant smile, her genuine kindness and compassion, she rarely shared the darker states of anger, depression, or disappointment. I knew she processed her feelings differently from Jen or me, who liked to talk and express and share until we'd exhausted our emotions (and those of everyone around us) and were ready to move on. It was only because I'd spent so much time with Hol in the past year that I recognized that she was going through something now. And I suspected that whatever it was had nothing to do with squeaky air mattresses or empty bank accounts.

Worried that she'd be missing out on our last weeks of freedom, I hoped she might feel like talking about it. I asked if she wanted to do the coastal walk from Bondi to Bronte. The 3.5-kilometer stretch between the two popular beaches is arguably the most spectacular in Sydney and, if the travel guides can be believed, one of the most picturesque in the world. Built in the 1930s as a government project, the path begins at the very top of Bondi's surfer-packed white sand crescent and winds its way south through limestone cliffs overlooking the Tasman Sea.

The beach's name comes from an aboriginal word that translates to "the sound of water breaking over rock." The title certainly fit. Even as we walked, I could hear the waves crashing against the shoreline, filling huge saltwater lap pools built directly into the cliffs. They also provided just the right amount of curl for surfers trying to catch a break all the way back to the shore.

I knew that Holly loved this walk. She'd told me that she felt revived by the sun warming her face, uplifted by the sight of young families spreading picnic blankets along grassy spaces in the public parks. She even got a kick out of the small tent city some hippie had built along the shoreline back in the 1970s, which lives on to this day. Due to a weird government-zoning technicality, the guy couldn't actually be kicked off the rocks. "Maybe we should ask to stay with him instead of paying rent at Simone's," Jen had joked the first day we'd all done the walk together. "He's got a stellar waterfront view and zero overhead."

Holly had been in great spirits then but was introspective now as we diverted from the path to check out the black-and-white photographs of lifeguards hanging in the Bondi Surf Bathers' Life Saving Club.

Swimming and surfing along Australia's 25,700 miles of coastline can be a risky endeavor—if strong currents or riptides don't drag you out sea, you could get an excruciatingly painful hug or a deadly kiss from a box jellyfish—so the formation of lifesaving clubs became absolutely essential here. Many of the techniques still used to prevent drownings today spring from those developed by the men—and later women—who served in Australia's lifesaving clubs.

As we walked past the turn-of-the-century portraits of cross-armed, serious-looking men in black-and-white candy-striped suits and matching skullcaps, I turned to Holly and casually mentioned that I thought she'd seemed a little distant lately. Was she doing okay?

Holly paused for several seconds to stare at one of the photos.

"Isn't it weird how in all of the old portraits, the lifesavers look really stern, almost pissed off?" she said. "But in all of the modern ones, they look over-the-top happy, like they don't have a care in the world?"

I peered at the photos and saw that Holly was right. The suntanned, red-and-canary-clad men and women from the current years looked as if they'd been splitting bottles of Prozac before every practice.

Simone had once told me that Australians adored the fact that outsiders viewed them as the happiest, best-adjusted people on Earth. Life down under, the world believed, was all about sunshine, surfing, shrimp on the barbie, and pursuing the endless summer. Nothing bad could happen in the magical land of Oz. "In reality, we have the exact same disappointments and heartbreaks that most people do," she'd said. "We're just better at hiding them than everyone else."

That was the closest Simone had ever come to alluding to how devastated she'd been over her breakup with Jeff. It was only after arriving in Sydney and watching the vivacious woman-an I'd come to know close off as she drank red wine by herself on the porch every night that I started to understand the depth of her hurt. Whenever I went outside to talk with her about it, her entire facial expression and demeanor would change. She'd perk up immediately and insist that everything was "just gorgeous, darling! Really!" and explain that she was just exhausted from a long day at work.

I never really pressed Simone about her feelings—I felt that it might be too intrusive for someone I was still getting to know—but I knew I needed to try again with Holly. Her nonanswer told me that there was more going on underneath the surface than I'd originally guessed.

I waited until we'd hiked up the stairs that rose above the Bondi Icebergs Winter Swimming Club and made our way along the path to the sandstone cliffs at Mackenzie's Point. From there we could take in the full sweeping curve of Bondi and catch our first glimpse of Bronte, a calmer spot a kilometer or so in the distance. This time Holly quietly confirmed that everything was okay—she'd just been feeling a little lonely lately, which, she hastened to explain, "has nothing to do with you or Jen."

I knew I could be treading on awkward ground, but I took the conversation one step further and asked her about things back home—and had she talked with Elan lately? Jen and I had noticed that since she'd returned from Boston after the New Year, Holly had brought up his name in conversation less and less, other than to report the headlines about his latest audition or the movie he'd just started filming in Chicago.

"It's just so tough with him on location and me not being able reach him on Skype," Holly explained, saying that she got little more than static when she tried to call him using our laptop. "And with the time difference between Sydney and the

States—we just haven't had a really good, long conversation in a while."

During the past few weeks—maybe even the last few months, she admitted—Holly had been wondering if she and Elan would ever really reconnect in the same way as they had when they'd first met. At times she'd felt more in sync with him than she'd ever thought it was possible to be with one person. Lately, though, they couldn't even agree on a time to schedule a phone conversation.

I thought back to the morning before our initiation into the Maasai tribe in Kenya, when Holly had shyly admitted that she'd thought Elan might actually be the man she wanted to spend the rest of her life with. It was a powerful realization for her—she'd kind of assumed that she'd be one of those independent girls who might not get married until later in life—but after nearly four years together, they'd never had a solid conversation about marriage and kids.

That had shocked Jen and me (again, not an emotional stone was ever left unturned with the two of us), but I also understood Holly's rationale. As a closet traditionalist, she wanted Elan to pursue her, to pin her down, to be the one to convince her to settle into adulthood at last. But thus far—he hadn't. Like Holly had been at twenty-seven, he was focused primarily on achieving his own dreams and creative ambitions.

From what I knew of Elan, he was truly in love with Holly, so much so that he'd given her his full support when she'd decided to travel. I remembered when he'd proudly showed me the full-color map he'd purchased and mounted on tackboard in order to follow Holly's route around the world. I'd told Holly just before we'd arrived in Sydney that I yearned for what she had: a loving, evolved relationship, a snug apartment, and a shared vision of the future.

Except that now, from what Holly was telling me, she wasn't

sure the last element in the equation was still in place anymore.

"Don't worry, Hol," I said, hugging her just before we walked down the steps to Bronte Beach. "Once you're back in New York and under the same roof, you'll get to know each other again. And you'll fall in love all over again."

I hoped that she'd agree or at least confirm that that's what she wanted, but she fell silent again as we descended to sea level. Finally she turned and gave me one of her winning Holly smiles, the kind that usually convinced our friends that she was doing fine and, in fact, on top of the world. Except that by now, I'd gotten to know Holly a whole lot better than that.

Within a week of picking up the World Nomads van, we'd broken all three of Chris Ford's rules. We hadn't topped off the oil or coolant (none of us remembered how to). Because the front seat was built for two and an insanely tight fit with three, we all took turns hanging out on the couch in the back ("If we're just driving on side streets, maybe it's not a big deal?"). And we'd just slowed down to pick up a hitchhiker on the side of the road during our first out-of-town excursion to the Blue Mountains.

Okay, Adam didn't exactly qualify as a hitchhiker. Holly had met the tall, brawny firefighter in the airport on the way to Sydney, and he'd offered to give the three of us a tour of the national park just outside his hometown of Katoomba. Since he didn't have a cell phone and insisted that it would be complicated to give us directions to his house, he'd made us agree to pick him up right on the side of the highway.

"Maybe this is how they save time in Australia?" Holly remarked as she slowed down near the drifter in washed-out cargo pants and a tight black tee who was waiting near one of the exits.

Amanda · Sydney, Australia · April ✳

"Or he's got a live-in girlfriend," Jen said slyly.

"You were right—it's absolutely impossible to miss this thing," Adam said, laughing as he jumped in the back of our rolling billboard. As we got closer to our destination, he gave us the backstory on what we were about to see.

In 1788, a group of eleven ships nicknamed the First Fleet sailed from Great Britain to Australia with 1,400 people aboard, more than half of whom were convicts. A penal colony was established in what is now downtown Sydney. In order to deter the prisoners from trying to escape west through the Blue Mountains, a rumor was planted that the range encircling the settlement was completely impenetrable. For at least ten years, the story stuck—until a freed convict named John Wilson returned to Sydney to report that he'd found a way through the supposedly impassable mountains. Over the next decade or so, the government conducted several expeditions to confirm the best route through the mountains and on to the more fertile lands on the opposite side. Incredibly, just twenty-six years after the First Fleet landed in Sydney, convicts constructed a road that cut through the foothills in the same general direction we were headed now.

As Adam shared the history of the country where he'd grown up, I listened with the intensity of a kindergartner sitting in the front row at story hour. I'd always loved learning the backstory of the places that we visited, but there was something about Oz's inauspicious beginnings that I found really compelling. So much about this young, rough-and-tumble country reminded me of my own.

Both the United States and Australia started out as British colonies that were still relatively unexplored at the time they were founded (at least by the settlers). They're also staggeringly large, and the same pioneering, self-reliant spirit that drove American settlers to spread west all the way from Plymouth

Rock to the Pacific was the same one that led Australians to throw down stakes in desolate, critter-infested outposts where no sane person should dare to tread. The early Aussie and American settlers had both pushed the boundaries of what was possible, taking a leap of faith—and oftentimes huge risks—in the hope of realizing some unknown reward. And though the journey that Jen, Holly, and I had just taken could hardly compare, I understood the mentality that had caused them to hit the trail in the first place.

I wasn't ready for that journey to be over.

After our first few strategy sessions in Sydney, I'd learned that both of my friends were planning to return home in early June, just less than a year after our original start date. I knew that it probably made sense to book a plane ticket at the same time. But something told me that I needed to stay in Australia, for a few weeks at least, on my own.

It wasn't that I craved solitude or wanted to be here without my friends. Exactly the opposite was true. I couldn't bear the thought of saying good-bye to them, helping them hoist their backpacks one last time before watching them disappear into the terminal. It's just that I felt that the personal journey I'd taken this year wouldn't truly be finished, and the lessons of the trip fully realized, until I'd handed off the laptop to Jen and Holly and struck out on the road alone.

Did the idea of being as far away from home as possible with no assignments to frame my day and no professional mission to accomplish still scare me? Not nearly as much as it would have the year before we left. Actually, a part of me couldn't wait to see what happened when I traveled without an itinerary, a goal, or a backup plan. Once that happened, it would be just me and me, kid—no distractions.

When Jen and I had traveled to Europe after college, my father had tried convincing me to stick around the continent as long as my budget would hold out. I refused, 100 percent sure that "all the good jobs would be gone" if I didn't scramble to New York by the time summer got under way. Now, seven years later, I didn't want to make that same mistake again.

We left the van behind and followed Adam's lead to Echo Point, a viewing platform perched several thousand feet above the floor of the Jamison Valley. The three of us had taken in some pretty stunning landscapes during our trip, but something about this one rendered all three of us silent—for a few minutes anyway. I started to reach for my camera and then thought better of it as I stepped toward the railing to soak in the scene. Capturing the full scope of the panorama—the velvety ripples of forest tumbling across hundreds of thousands of acres of low mountain foothills—would have been impossible anyway.

Approaching the edge, I thought of the first time my mom and her longtime boyfriend Bruce had taken my sister and me to see the Grand Canyon. They'd helped us climb up onto a railing just like this one and held us tightly from behind as we stared out into the gap carved in the earth by the flow of water over millions of years. I remember as a nine-year-old kid feeling overwhelmed by the sheer scope of it all, as if realizing for the first time just how vast the world truly is and how very tiny I was within it. Standing here now, pressed along the railing with Jen and Holly at my side, I experienced a similar feeling of humility and a sense of connectedness with the earth.

Adam pointed to a rock formation I'd noticed to our left, three limestone towers that rose dramatically from the ground and narrowed to a point like spires on a church.

"That's known as the Three Sisters," he said, leaning out over the rail. "According to an Aboriginal dreamtime legend, they were once real maidens from the Katoomba tribe who'd fallen in love with three brothers from the neighboring Nepean tribe."

Tribal law wouldn't allow any of them to get married, he explained, but the brothers wouldn't take no for an answer. They decided to capture their brides, which sparked a major battle between the two sides. Because the lives of the women were in danger, a witch doctor took it upon himself to turn the three sisters into stone to protect them from harm. Unfortunately, the doctor was killed in battle before he could reverse the spell and return the women to their former beauty.

"And so here they are to this day. Even though they're stone, they're still pretty beautiful, I'd say." Adam smiled, almost to himself. "I always liked that story as a kid—I figured if I used magic, or at least wished hard enough, I'd be able to turn them real again."

We laughed and teased him a little about that, and he shrugged, eager to change the subject. "Why don't we take a little hike and see them up close?"

The four of us walked as a group to the archway fronting the Giant Stairway, a series of eight hundred steps and runways that led to the valley floor, right past the Three Sisters. Adam motioned for us to go ahead. As we got closer, I could see that the individual formations were so tall—nearly a thousand feet each—that there was no way they should be able to stand on their own. But somehow, they must have supported one another, keeping the group upright while the rest of the rock around them had eroded away.

Jen and Holly, who'd already bounded down the narrow set of stone steps etched into the rock, paused, waiting for me to join them. I walked the last few steps to where they were standing. Once again in our own formation, we walked the rest of the way together.

✗⁄

CHAPTER THIRTY-ONE

Holly

SYDNEY, AUSTRALIA

APRIL

Despite its distance from home, Australia felt unexpectedly familiar. Well, "same same but different," as they say in Thailand. It was "same same" because everyone spoke English. People lived in houses and mowed their lawns and walked their babies in strollers rather than carrying them on their backs. Amanda, Jen, and I joined our newfound circle of friends at happy hour. We were strangely enthralled when we walked through the automatic doors of air-conditioned grocery stores to find *refrigerated* eggs for sale. We drank the tap water again without getting sick. And by renting a room at Simone's apartment, we technically weren't backpackers anymore. We had a home base.

Australia was "different" because the stars were upside down. The seasons were reversed. Cars drove on the opposite side of the road. People said "heaps" instead of "a lot." They preferred to have their toast with Vegemite (a salty, malty-flavored paste) as opposed to jam. The cities had funny-sounding names such as Katoomba and Maroochydore. The animals also had funny-sounding names, as if they belonged in a Muppets performance: wombat, platypus, wallaby.

Differences aside, Australians' lives seemed very much like Americans': people went to work, took their families to the beach on weekends, and used holidays as a time to get together with friends and loved ones. Though we'd be missing Memorial Day back home, we were able to celebrate an Australian national holiday, ANZAC Day.

"Is it named after a type of cookie?" Amanda asked Simone when she first heard of it, her eyes glistening at the prospect of a day reserved for eating the confectionary creation of rolled oats and granulated sugar.

"Dah-ling, don't be silly. It stands for Australian and New Zealand Army Corps," Simone said, explaining that the holiday honored soldiers who lost their lives in World War I. Australians turn the day of remembrance into a festivity that goes beyond Americans' typical backyard barbecues or picnics at the beach. Gambling is a mainstay in Australian pop culture, with casinos, racing, and "pokies" (electronic slot machines) as common as Starbucks in New York. In fact, Aussies lose more money to gambling than any other country in the world. So it's only fitting that to celebrate, a lot—I mean *heaps*—of Aussies head to their local bar to drink beer and play an addictive game called two-up.

And that's why Amanda, Jen, and I arrived in the middle of mayhem at Bondi's Beach Road Hotel at noon on a Wednesday. Our plan had been to beat the crowd, but the madness was already well under way. Pushing open the doors, we were accosted by the yeasty scent of draft beer and the sound of rising cheers. The hub of activity wasn't at the bar but rather among a circle of people that swelled around empty space.

Men wearing beach shorts and thongs (flip-flops) and women in sundresses waved money above their heads as if bidding at an auction and yelled, "Twenty on heads!" or "Fifty on tails!" A guy with a microphone stood in the inner circle, balancing large coins atop a small paddle.

501

Tension crackled and silence ensued as the announcer tossed the coins high into the air. Acting as a single organism, the circle pushed forward, straining to see how the coins would fall.

"We have heads!" he yelled, and groans from the losers and howls from the winners erupted like thunder.

Just then, I heard Amanda apologize to a blue-eyed guy wearing a baseball hat she'd apparently bumped into.

"No worries. I like your accent. Where are you ladies from?" he asked.

"New York," she said.

"New York? Like *Sex in the City* New York? Like Carrie Bradshaw?"

At this point in the trip, we were accustomed to men linking a group of female friends from New York to the infamous HBO series and Amanda to Carrie with her lioness-like mane of curls.

"Something like that," Amanda said.

Suddenly a few men formed their own circle around us, probably curious about a group of Americans out to celebrate the Australian holiday. The funny thing is, travel had taught me as much about my own country as it did about the ones I visited—mostly because it let me see what Americans looked like through foreigners' eyes. We'd quickly learned that there was a bonus to having an accent, because Australian males were quick to buy us rounds of drinks and have a chat whenever we'd ventured into a local pub. Either that or chivalry still survived and thrived Down Under.

"Would you like to play two-up?" asked a guy with spiky blond hair who'd introduced himself as David.

"I'd love to, but I have no idea what I'm doing." I wanted to join the Australian tradition but didn't want to look like the silly foreigner that I was by making all the wrong moves.

David explained that two-up involves waving a bill in the

air, finding a partner who is holding up the same amount, and betting on whether the coins will land on heads or tails. If you guess right, you get to keep your partner's money.

It sounded easy enough, as if it were all luck and no strategy. "So I have a fifty percent chance of winning?"

"That's right," he said. "Bets start at five dollars. I'll bet against you for your first time if you'd like. Heads or tails?"

"Tails!" I said, pulling out a fiver and following him to join the outer edge of the circle.

The announcer recruited a volunteer to toss the three coins. One landed on heads, the other two landed on tails.

"I won! I won!" I screamed, waving for Amanda and Jen, who were talking near the bar, to come watch. "I doubled my money!"

The announcer heard my American accent, despite the ear-rupturing clapping. He pointed to me and asked where I was from.

"New York!" I yelled. More cheers erupted—quite the easy crowd to please.

"We have a New Yorker here! Would you like to toss the coins?" His voice resonated from the microphone. It seemed as though practically everyone in the bar screamed even louder, and I pushed through the masses to walk self-consciously into the center of the circle, all eyes on me. Amanda followed, video camera in hand, recording my first ANZAC Day and fifteen (or five) minutes of fame.

The announcer hammed it up for Amanda's video recorder, raising his hands in the air as he yelled, "Woooo!"

"You're on *Candid Camera*, baby!" she said.

He turned to me. "All right, are you ready?"

I nodded, placing one hand on my thigh, lowering the paddle with a deep breath, and then releasing the coins in a giant arc. They landed as if in slow motion, then seemed to speed up,

503

spinning erratically. The people in the first layer of the circle jumped back, their eyes following the coins as they rolled away before scattering outside the bounds.

The crowd groaned impatiently. I definitely wasn't going to be cheered on for my lack of hand-eye coordination. "We'll have to roll again," the announcer said.

He whispered a few quick tips about tossing the coins lower so they'd stay within the circle as another player collected them to hand back to me. I took another deep breath and gingerly flipped the coins off the paddle. They landed cleanly this time, front and center.

"We have tails!" he announced, and the crowd was awash in the rustling of money exchanges and guzzling of beers.

"Nice job, New York," David said, patting me on the back.

Amanda and Jen held up their bills and walked across the crowd to exchange bets, making half a dozen new friends in a matter of minutes. Online dating has nothing on playing two-up—it's the simplest, least awkward way to meet new people that I'd ever encountered.

It was warm inside the beach bar, but a comfortable, cozy kind of warm. As the sun sank lower outside, the stakes grew higher inside.

"How are you doing, David?" I asked, eyeing the growing wad of cash in his hand.

"I'm up $750." He grinned when my eyes widened in shock. "It's a very good ANZAC Day indeed."

Mundane stuff that once felt like a chore, such as grocery shopping, washing dishes, and folding laundry, became unexpectedly comforting as Jen, Amanda, and I had settled back into domestic life at Simone's apartment. We stocked the freezer with cookie dough ice cream, carefully hung the few items of wrinkled clothing we had in a closet, organized by color, and arranged our sunscreen on the bathroom shelf as if displaying pieces of fine art. There was even a mirror above the sink, where I'd placed my hydrating eye cream, vanilla-scented lotion, and strawberry-flavored lip gloss.

Shamed by my extravagant nonessentials, I had long let those goodies remain in the crevices of my backpack. The girls had staged repeated load-lightening interventions at airport weigh stations, their purist packing approach clashing with my philosophy: you should carry whatever brings you comfort on the road. For me, that's books and toiletries. (The girls *did* manage to wrangle my rather ironic copy of *How to Pack* from my bag's zippered pocket, which shaved off approximately two ounces.) There was just something about brushing a stroke of emerald liner near my eyes or a dab of peachy shimmer across my cheeks that makes me feel clean and pretty—no matter how dust-covered I might be. And now I didn't have to hide them anymore. Simply being able to wake up and brew coffee with our very own coffeemaker (well, Simone's coffeemaker) and then to cup a steamy mug in our hands while watching the morning news felt as special as Christmas, New Year's, and Easter all rolled into one.

After all the times I'd exercised in a windowless gym after a day spent inside the office—only able to dream about running on a beach or hiking in the mountains—I was surprised I'd wanted to convince Jen and Amanda to sign up for a gym membership at the Westfield mall near Bondi Junction. I mapped out a weekly schedule of classes and taped it to the refrigerator as a reminder. Joining the groups of exercisers in the mirrored classroom, with its rows of yoga mats and ruby-colored exercise balls neatly lined up against the wall, felt safe to me rather than confining. Our return flight to New York was taking off in just six weeks, and I was shocked to discover that I wanted

505

to do "normal" stuff when my "normal" life loomed so close. I hungered for the normalcy that I'd so gleefully bid good-bye to when we'd first embarked on this around-the-world journey.

And it was with the same desire for the familiar that the girls and I enthusiastically accepted an invitation to join Simone's friends for their monthly book club party. It was one of those sparkly Sundays that seemed typical in Sydney. The water in the harbor shimmered under a butterscotch sun. We sat at a wooden picnic table on the deck of the yacht club in Rose Bay, which offered surprisingly cheap food and drinks despite the fancy-sounding name.

I couldn't tell you the name of the book the women were meeting about, because it was never actually discussed. We arrived with Simone to find half a dozen women in their late twenties seated on the opposite sides of two picnic tables. They were wearing sunglasses with lenses so large they covered their entire cheeks. Two bottles of wine were chilling in gleaming silver buckets.

After Simone introduced us, Jen, Amanda, and I took our places in the empty spaces between the women. Rather than sit together, the three of us dispersed, each easily falling into conversation with the new person next to us.

For the greater part of a year, our social circle had consisted of the lucky number three. And in a way maybe similar to a marriage, we'd fulfilled roles for one another that went well beyond the frivolity of casual courtship. Traveling through foreign countries had morphed us into one another's accountants, counselors, organizers, nurses, and bodyguards. We'd also become slightly codependent.

This became clear once our "real" lives loomed close, as each of us tried to absorb the fact that, soon enough, we'd return to making choices solely for ourselves, not based on the good of the group. Even the most mundane decisions, such as what to make for breakfast, would again become solitary activities with no need for group compromise.

I sensed we were each branching out, trying to sink our roots deeper into our individual worlds and stake out a plot of land that was uniquely our own.

I planted myself next to Leonie, a dark blonde with steel blue eyes and a raspy voice that sounded both effervescent and sexy. "Would you like a glass of wine, love?" she asked. "I usually prefer red, but we ordered white because it's so warm today."

I nodded, and she pulled a bottle from the ice bucket, filling an empty glass with the pale liquid. "We have heaps of wineries in Australia. You should visit Hunter Valley for a wine tour," she said.

I told her that the only distinction I'd been able to make between types of wine pretrip was whether one was red or white. While biking through wineries in New Zealand, though, I'd discovered what an art form it was to grow grapes ripened to just the right sweetness and to blend different varietals.

"I was in New Zealand when I went backpacking, too," she said. "I didn't go on any wine tours while I was there, but I *did* shag a hobbit."

She said this just as I took a sip, resulting in a coughing fit. Leonie calmly handed me a napkin.

Leonie quickly explained that her liaison hadn't been with a *real* hobbit, but with an actor playing the role. She'd just happened to be on the North Island when *The Lord of the Rings* had been filming, met a worker from the set at a bar, and agreed to help with costume fittings to earn extra cash on the road. It was probably her charisma that had gotten her invited to the wrap party afterward, where the hobbit had invited her back to his hotel room. "That was after many glasses of wine, of course," she said.

"The free wine at wrap parties can be a dangerous thing. My

507

boyfriend is an actor," I said, thinking of Elan at the first mention of acting.

It was Leonie's turn to pepper me with questions: How long had we been dating? Did we live together? How were we getting along with the distance between us? What was he doing now?

"He was supposed to go to L.A. while I was traveling because there's more acting opportunities there, but things didn't work out as planned. He ended up doing a play in Boston and filming a football movie in Chicago," I said, knowing as I spoke just how much I'd lost touch with Elan, with his daily life, with who he was becoming (and vice versa). A wave of sadness made me shiver despite the heat from the sun overhead.

Was I wrong to follow my dream of traveling the world, leaving behind the man I loved? Had I abandoned him when he needed me during that transition from graduation to working in the real world? Or was giving us time apart something that might make our relationship more resilient in the end?

It was then that Simone, who'd been tied up in conversation with Amanda, leaned across the table to refill Leonie's wineglass. Then she paused and announced, "Ladies, I'd like to make a toast. Leonie and Mike are *engaged*!"

I glanced down to see a diamond glinting in the sun on Leonie's ring finger. She grinned broadly as we raised our glasses and took a swig, then set them on the table to clap our hands in congratulation.

"You're going to be such a yummy mummy!" Simone exclaimed, the decibel level of her enthusiasm ten points higher than the average person's. It was infectious, actually. There was no way you could see the glass as half empty with Simone around spreading her cheer.

Jen asked to look at Leonie's ring. "Would you like to try it on?" Leonie asked.

Jen's eyes sparkled brighter than the diamond itself as she

took Leonie up on her offer, sliding the gem onto her ring finger and holding it at arm's length to admire. "I used to want a princess cut, but now I'm thinking maybe a cushion cut would be better." It always amazed me how Jen could speak as if she were directly quoting from *Modern Bride*.

"What's a cushion cut?" I asked. Jen glanced my way and laughed.

"Hol, you crack me up! You've really never thought about what kind of diamond ring you want?" she said.

"I don't really want a diamond," I admitted, and Jen's eyes nearly bulged out of their sockets. I realized I hadn't given it much thought, but it just didn't make sense to me to spend thousands of dollars on a piece of jewelry when that money could be spent exploring the world—and my partner—on a honeymoon adventure. Or could be invested in a down payment on an apartment. I wouldn't necessarily turn down a big ring, but I didn't need one to impress my friends or as proof of a man's love for me.

As Leonie's ring passed around the circle of women, each trying it on for size and examining it in the light, I thought about how something so small could carry such powerful symbolism. But what it symbolized, exactly, was different for different people. For many it symbolized love. It might also represent belonging and the achievement of arguably adulthood's biggest milestone. A ring could mean a promise. It could mean commitment. It could mean security. It could serve as a placeholder in a relationship. I'd encountered women who wore rings given by their boyfriends in an effort to buy time after years of dating, not ready to walk down the aisle or to let go. One woman's ring might mean a lifetime of freedom found in someone's arms, another's might be a shackle that holds her back from becoming who she might have been.

The ring had come full circle and was now to me. I tried to

509

hand it back to Leonie, but Jen said, "Holly, you have to at least try it on!"

I can't explain why, but a wave of panic washed over me as I slipped it on, as if one of the women had handed me her newborn baby and I didn't know exactly what to do with it. I didn't know if I was ready to have all that meaning fitting snugly around my finger or if sliding on that ring felt so funny only because it wasn't meant for me. Mike had given it to Leonie, and Leonie alone.

I leaned against the metal pole of a streetlight, hoping to absorb some of its coolness while waiting for the guy with frayed shorts and a beer can to finish using the pay phone. I hadn't thought anyone besides me used pay phones anymore.

It'd been almost a week since I'd spoken with Elan, and calling him on Skype from my laptop in Simone's apartment resulted only in static. I didn't mind walking down the street to buy a phone card from one of the minimarts near the beach. The early evening was warm, and I wanted to take myself out of earshot of my roommates (as I liked to refer to Jen and Amanda now that we were stationary) so I could have a little privacy.

The sun had already sunk below the horizon, but surfers continued to bob up and down as dusk fell, floating on their boards on an ocean that stretched beyond the skyline—maybe even stretched on forever. I watched sea foam frost a wave as it crested, then spill over itself, spreading thinner along the sand like beach glass until the larger force of the tides sucked it back to rejoin the body of water from which it had come.

I'd watched a similar scene, but with a different ocean and different sky, while sprawled in the sand next to Elan in Hawaii three years earlier. Or maybe the ocean and the sky were all the same. I remembered them as being the same color—the water midnight blue and the sky canary yellow and dotted with darkening clouds as dusk fell. The surfers had looked just as serene back then, floating on their boards, comfortable in their solitude, waiting patiently for the right wave.

We'd flown from New York to Oahu for Elan's mother's wedding and celebrated afterward by camping on the beach. Her new husband, Randy, was an expert fisherman. He'd built us a fire with pieces of driftwood we'd helped him collect before he grilled his day's catch, seasoned with garlic. We'd eaten it sitting in lawn chairs with plastic forks and paper plates, and it was better than any dish I'd ever eaten on fine china in a fancy restaurant.

Elan and I had walked off our dinner on the beach and plopped down in the sand to watch the waves roll in. We'd stretched our legs out in front of us, and he'd grabbed my hand.

I'd looked down to see that our skin was washed bronze by the sun, but our nail beds remained white. I'd looked up at him from the corner of my eye and smiled, his dark curls matted with salt water from a day spent body surfing. When I'd tilted my face back, the warm wind had touched my skin as it traveled across the ocean and over the land.

"Elan?" I'd said.

"Yeah, Hol?"

"I'm really happy right now." He'd just smiled in response and put his arm around my shoulders, his sun-scorched skin radiating heat and giving me goose bumps.

The first stars had been popping into the sky, like points of light pushed through blue velvet by a needle. One light had broken free and blazed a path in the darkness. I'd squeezed Elan's hand and made a wish while it grew fainter before it disappeared. I wondered where it had gone. Then we'd sat there and looked at the sky in silence, together.

Bang, bang, bang. I turned to the source of the noise and saw

Holly · Sydney, Australia · April

the phone receiver dangling limply from its cord in the breeze and hitting the metal booth. The man had abandoned his conversation, and I'd been too caught up in my daydream to notice.

Where was my phone card? I dug into the Eagle Creek purse, sifting through leftover Vietnamese dong and Kenyan shillings. I dialed his number, and the phone began to ring. Please be there, I silently prayed.

Ring. Ring. Ring. Ring.

Just as I was about to hang up before it went into voice mail so I wouldn't be charged, I heard his voice: "Hello, Hol?"

"Elan? Yeah, it's me! I'm calling you from a pay phone."

"Hey, what's up?"

What's up? I suddenly felt shy and didn't know what to say. Should I tell him that I'd learned to play two-up or that I'd seen a kangaroo or that I'd tasted Vegemite for the first time? Or should I simply tell him that I missed him? And say that I couldn't wait to put my head on his shoulder again?

Instead, I said, "Nothing much. We have an apartment now!"

"That's great, Hol." He sounded distracted.

"How are things going at our apartment? How's your brother?"

"Good, good. Everything's good. Evan and I started a garden on the patio . . . Look, there's something I wanted to talk to you about." His tone was serious.

"Sure. What's going on?"

"I've been thinking a lot about it lately, and I need to move to L.A. now."

My stomach fluttered when he used the word "I." He didn't say "we." He wasn't thinking about "us." I felt blood pumping through the veins in my throat. I only half listened as he reasoned that he'd have a better shot at an acting job if he moved to Hollywood, that he could stay on his friend's couch to save money, and that now was the time for him to take a chance, while he was still young. He didn't want to stick around New York, doing odd jobs to cover rent, when he could be going out on auditions that might actually lead somewhere.

I knew it all made perfect sense for his career, but it was as though my feelings had left my body, evaporating in a poof of smoke. I couldn't breathe. After my year of being a nomad, I'd thought of home not as a physical place but as being with him.

I suddenly remembered the summer years earlier when he'd first asked to move in with me, temporarily subletting his own apartment until school started again in the fall. When autumn had come and the leaves had turned from green to gold, he'd moved back to his old place. I'd laid on my bed on top of the covers, alone in the space, not wanting him to know I'd cried. He'd returned a few days later, saying, "Hol, can I move back here? My home is with you." And he had. And it was.

His voice crackled through the receiver, "What do *you* think about L.A., Hol?" His voice sounded far away, as if it were coming from the other side of a tunnel whose end I couldn't see.

An icy numbness had traveled through my brain like a snake, squeezing it tight and cutting off my thoughts. Before the emptiness could take over, I was hit with the truth I wanted to ignore: I couldn't go with him, and I had to let him go. So I agreed that he had to go to L.A. but asked that he wait a few weeks, until I got back, to leave.

I had no well-formed, rational thoughts. I had only the feeling of knowing that he'd allowed me to live my dream. Now it was time for me to let him live his. I would never let myself be his shackle—I loved him too much.

I can't remember how the conversation ended, only the sound of the receiver hitting the metal booth as it dangled in the wind and seeing a shooting star break free to fall from the sky.

513

Holly · Sydney, Australia · April ✻

The thing was, I'd thought that when I'd returned from the trip, I'd have my future mapped out—I'd have Elan and our apartment to return to. Unlike Jen and Amanda, I'd believed my around-the-world journey would end exactly where it had begun.

✻

CHAPTER THIRTY-TWO

Jen

HUNTER VALLEY, AUSTRALIA

MAY

Rocky-road fudge, cocoa-dusted marshmallows, cream-filled truffles. Holly was crouched in front of the glass case in the Hunter Valley chocolate shop, giving me a detailed assessment of which handmade confections she deemed most worthy of sampling. We'd get anything Holly wanted, I thought. I was just happy to see that old familiar sparkle in her eyes.

"Ladies, you're going to be really excited to hear this," Amanda said, snapping our group cell phone shut and rejoining us at the counter. "I just spoke to the woman at the Balloon Aloft office, and we're all set for a hot-air balloon ride tomorrow morning . . . and . . . she's giving us a discount for Jen's birthday!"

"You guys, my birthday was forever ago and you already threw me a pretty-in-pink party," I said. A few weeks earlier, I'd stumbled out to the living room in my normal anti-morning state and found the entire space decorated with pink balloons, streamers, and confetti. Holly was in the kitchen baking me muffins, and Amanda handed me a goodie bag filled with candy, fuzzy slippers with PRINCESS embroidered in, you guessed it, pink, a *Rough Guide to Chick Flicks*, and a stack of my favorite movies rented from the video store. After Amanda's bash in Lima, Peru, and Holly's dinner and dance party in Hanoi, Vietnam, it was our third and final on-the-road birthday.

"I know, but it's our prezzie to you," Amanda replied.

"Yes, definitely. It's the perfect way to end our Hunter Valley vacation. *And* I am so excited that we get to stay in a real hotel tonight too," Holly said before turning her attention back to the chocolate.

"Well . . . okay, if you girls insist," I said grinning. I'd *always* wanted to take a hot-air balloon ride. But really, as long as we were all together and having fun, I didn't care what we did.

Since we had arrived in Australia's renowned wine region two days earlier, the subtle shadow over our trio had vanished. When we'd originally designated the majestic land of Oz as our last stop, I'd assumed it would be smooth sailing, the perfect storybook wrap-up to our epic adventure. But with Holly in the throes of a complicated and tumultuous situation with Elan and all of us struggling, often unsuccessfully, to quell our anxieties about returning home, our happy ending was dangerously close to unraveling.

Even when Holly put on a brave face and insisted she was okay, Amanda and I could sense the pain and uncertainty lurking behind her smiles and attempts at silliness. We tried our best to rally around her, making the executive decision that it was high time to break the seal on our *Lonely Planet: Sydney and New South Wales* and do what we'd come on the trip for in the first place: travel. And not just on a day trip to the Blue Mountains and back; we needed something more substantial.

Lured by promises of rolling vineyards, scenic bushwalks, wine tastings, horseback riding, and gourmet restaurants, we hopped aboard our trusty Technicolor steed and left the bustling city for the tranquillity of the wine country. Stocked with brochures, maps, and local events schedules, we spent the first couple of days soaking in our idyllic surroundings, sampling world-class Semillons, picnicking next to lush grape fields, and watching kangaroo boxing matches at sunset. We'd even received an official Wine School certificate for our impressive knowledge of growing techniques and aroma wheels. And now, uplifted by a substantial chocolate high, we headed back outside and left in hot pursuit of a popular vineyard nearby.

It was another clear, glorious afternoon in Hunter Valley as Amanda, Holly, and I cruised happily along in our tripped-out World Nomads camper van. The sun was shining, the birds were singing, locals greeted one another with huge smiles and "G'day, mate". Even wild dingoes realized the error of their ways and graciously returned stolen babies. And to top it all off, I'd mastered the delicate art of driving with a stick shift in less than a week and was operating our rainbow beast on wheels like a pro. Yep, in that moment, life was pretty perfect.

Now I just had to figure out exactly where I was going. We'd arrived at one of the vast resort properties that dotted the valley, and somehow I'd gotten a bit turned around.

"Okay, I'm confused. How do I get out of here?" I asked Amanda, who was riding shotgun with the map. "Oh wait, never mind. I see," I said as I realized that all I had to do was follow the gravel road around the front of the nearby hotel and out of the gate. I whistled happily as I shifted into second, preparing to cruise gently under the wooden portico and around the circular driveway.

Crash, boom, shudder, shake, splinter, crack!!!!

Oh, my God! What was happening? Suddenly the entire roof was caving in on us. As Holly and Amanda screamed and covered their eyes with their hands, I gripped the wheel tightly, trying to keep the shaking van straight and praying we'd come out the other side in one piece. Huge chunks of wood rained on the vehicle as fluffy bits of fiberglass floated down on our heads like snow. In that instant, the sun went behind the clouds, the birds stopped singing, dingoes started stealing babies again, and I realized that in less than five seconds, I'd royally destroyed our only mode of transportation and our picture-perfect day.

As the dust cleared, I managed to pull myself together long enough to turn the van off and spill out of the door in a pool of shame. The hotel owner came running outside to confront the crazy tourist who'd defaced her property. Maybe it was my shocked expression or sputtering series of "Oh, my God, I'm so sorry." But she immediately took pity on us, asking if we were okay and trying to make me feel better. Since I was bordering on catatonic, Amanda took charge and followed the woman inside to exchange contact information before returning to snap a few photos for insurance purposes. Holly stood next to me, her arm across my shoulders.

"It's okay, Jen. If I'd been driving, I would've done the same thing, seriously. And it doesn't look that bad. I'm sure we can just get the dent pounded out, no problem."

I stared at the wreckage like a deer in headlights. "I just can't believe they didn't have a clearance sign. I mean, the van isn't even that tall, and it seriously didn't look that low," I stuttered, fully aware that the damage far exceeded anything that could simply be banged back out. Although for a moment I was hopeful. I even got into the van and pushed as hard as I could against the ceiling carpet, which now hung down like a pouch. But it wouldn't budge.

"Maybe I could say that a rogue kangaroo jumped down from a bridge and landed on top of the van," I said as one of the groundskeepers walked over to us.

"You ladies all right? Banged your roof up pretty good, I see. You know, you're not the first one to hit that cover. Happens all the time. So try not to feel too bad."

Apparently low-clearance signs are about as popular Down

Under as Foster's beer (which is to say, surprisingly *un*popular), because I could not for the life of me figure out how other people had rammed into the roof and they hadn't posted any warnings. I tried my best not to scowl at the man.

"All right, well, don't let this ruin the beautiful day," he said as Amanda returned saying that we were all set to leave and that she'd gotten directions to our hotel.

"We'll just go there now, check in, and chill out for a bit before we decide what to do," she said. I nodded and muttered a soft "okay."

Sensing that I was in no shape to get back behind the wheel, Holly hopped into the driver's seat and steered us away from the scene of my crime and back onto the main road. We'd only gone a few miles when visions of hundreds of dollars in deductibles and the shame of confessing to the World Nomads reps that I'd wrecked their van began tormenting me and a panic attack set in.

"Stop the car!" I shouted. "I'm freaking out!"

Holly immediately pulled over to the side of the gravel road. She and Amanda sat there, patiently allowing me to vent. I'd never been in an accident in my life that was my fault. I wasn't one of those crazy chicks who couldn't drive. Even my guy friends could attest to that. We were having so much fun and I'd ruined it . . . and blah blah blah.

"Jen, when we signed those insurance forms, it listed our deductible as four hundred dollars, and that's in Australian dollars, so it's even less. Really, it's not the end of the world if we have to split that," Holly said.

"No. No. No, that's not true. There was another column, I specifically remember, that listed nine hundred dollars. And I'm pretty sure it was either for certain major damages or anything where the driver was at fault," I replied, fumbling around the glove box, now desperate to determine my worst-case scenario.

"Yeah, but I really think we were covered under the four-hundred-dollar plan," Amanda said, taking the book from my trembling hands and flipping through it. Pausing on one page, she scanned it several times and fell silent. "Okay, so it says here that damage to the roof or undercarriage of the vehicle isn't covered, but technically, this isn't *really* the roof. It's just an extra camper top piece, so we may still be all good. Either way, I really don't think it's going to cost a lot to fix this. It really isn't that bad, Jen. Everything will work out, I'm sure."

I almost started to hyperventilate. What if this cost thousands of dollars? I'd be paying off this stupid van until I was forty. Despite their own obvious concerns, the girls continued their attempts to calm me down. "This story will add flavor to our reign as World Nomads ambassadors, right?" "Worse case, we go with the kangaroo story." "One day you'll look back at the whole thing and laugh," they said.

With a roof that practically brushed our heads and slits of sunlight shining through gaping holes of ripped fiberglass, I found it hard to find the humor in the situation. But Amanda and Holly were being so supportive about the whole thing that I tried to force a smile onto my face. On the upside, at least I'd timed the van accident to coincide with the one night we'd splurged on a hotel.

After parking our freshly crunched vehicle in the farthest parking space from our lodge, we checked in and headed to our room. Continuing to maintain control of the situation, Amanda placed a call to the World Nomads office to face the music on my behalf. Holly and I were silent, listening to the "uh-huhs" and "okays" and "no, it's just *sort of* dented" with bated breath. When Amanda hung up, she reported that they hadn't sounded too concerned and had instructed us to bring the van back to Auto Barn body shop as soon as we could and they'd have a look.

"Guys, no," I said. "We have to take it back now. We can't

just keep driving it like this. This whole thing is my fault, and I'll totally pay so we can rent a car for Holly and her sister. I'm so sorry I totally screwed up our vacation." Holly's sister was scheduled to fly into Sydney the next week to drive around with us, which I'd now ruined. I sucked.

"Jen, don't be ridiculous. We'll all just pitch in some money and work something out. We really can't worry about it now, though," Holly replied.

Of all the things that most amazed me about Holly was her ability to breeze through an emotional situation with grace. As my parents can attest, I'd been quite the little dramatic actress since birth. I admit that I do have a propensity to, maybe, sometimes, overreact just a bit, but those instances are pretty few and far between. Of course, it always helped to have a calming force like Hol when they weren't. And if calm didn't work, I had Amanda to step in and regulate. When we'd first become friends, I remember thinking, Wow, someone who can go head-to-head with my feisty disposition. Either we'll be the best of buddies or we'll strangle each other. And it had worked out perfectly so far: generally when I freaked, Amanda chilled, and vice versa.

"Yeah, I agree with Hol. In fact, I say after our balloon ride tomorrow, we sweep out the van and go on a camping trip in one of the national parks that we passed on the way here. It's the weekend anyway. Auto Barn can wait," Amanda said.

She had a point. I really wasn't ready to go back to Sydney yet. And if I had, God forbid, screwed up our chances of doing a final road trip up the coast, at least we'd have one last night of fun. So I agreed to their proposal—on one condition: that they drive the entire way back.

Though rising before dawn was the last thing I'd normally want to do on vacation, floating above the clouds in an open-air basket provided a huge incentive. So at 5:30 a.m. on the dot, we arrived at the Balloon Aloft office, eager to take flight. Clutching a paper cup of complimentary coffee, I gazed at the glossy photos of other hot-air heroes that hung on the wall, which provided even more of a pick-me-up than the caffeine.

"So, you guys, if we write a blog about this for World Nomads, I totally know what we should call it," I said. "The Wizards of Oz. Get it? 'Cause in the movie, the wizard floats down into the emerald city in a hot-air balloon and Australia's called Oz. Oh, I am hilarious." I nodded approvingly at myself, impressed by my early-morning wit.

"Uh, that's worse than lawn moo-er, dude," Holly replied, referring to my clever naming of the cow in Kenya that always lingered outside our hut loudly chomping grass.

"Yeah, but if that'll make you care less about the van, we'll do it," Amanda said.

Ridiculous pun or not, I was feeling better about the whole debacle. But unfortunately our bad luck hadn't quite run out. We'd been warned by the owner that there was a slight chance of inclement weather, so they'd been monitoring the winds all morning to make sure it was safe to go up in the air. After waiting around for nearly two hours, it was still a no-go, so, much to everyone's disappointment, they canceled our ascent. As we begrudgingly made our way outside to leave, we noticed a few Balloon Aloft employees were gathered around the van, inspecting the damage.

"Is this your handiwork?" one of them asked with a smile.

"Guilty," I replied. "Hey, you wouldn't happen to know how to pop the dent back out, would you?" The guy was wearing a blue, mechanic-like jumpsuit, so I figured, what the hell.

"No, I think you're going to need a professional to do that, but in the meantime, you do know there's a good chance of rain, right? We were just talking about how you should probably at least patch up that large tear in the front there." He pointed.

Oh, shit, I hadn't even thought about that. If it did start to sprinkle just the tiniest bit, the interior of our van would be flooded, and that, I was sure, was not covered by our insurance. This time even Amanda and Holly looked panicked.

"What should we do?" Amanda asked. "Maybe go buy a tarp or something?"

"Well, the storm is moving north, so I suggest you let us try to tape up the cracks and then head south straightaway. Hey, Aaron!" he called over to another of the employees. "Do we have anything in the office that might work?"

"You know what, don't we have duct tape?" Holly asked.

"Yes, you're right. I put my roll under the sink," Amanda replied, diving into the van to look under our mini–dishwashing station. "See, I told you this would come in handy."

Before we knew it, all three Balloon Aloft employees had sprung into action. Bringing a stepladder over for the out-of-reach areas, they formed an assembly line around the van, ripping and passing long pieces of tape off the roll and meticulously waterproofing the entire vehicle. My favorite patch by far was the jagged horseshoe strip that pointed down to the KEEP TRAVELLING SAFELY decal below the rear window.

"You're our heroes, seriously," I gushed, giving them all hugs. "I don't know what we would have done if you hadn't been here."

"Aw, don't be silly, we're happy to help. We've got a national reputation to uphold anyway, you know?" Aaron said.

With the rain fortunately still at bay, we headed out of town in pursuit of the perfect campsite.

H ours later, we pulled into a peaceful valley fringed by dense forest and rocky mountain peaks. Racing against nightfall, we immediately went to work building a campfire in the national park–provided sand pit.

523

Before long, a blazing inferno shot sparks into the midnight sky, crackling against the sound of the swaying trees. Uncorking a bottle of Sauvignon Blanc, we formed a semicircle around the perimeter, dangling marshmallows over the center until they'd roasted to a golden brown. With the soft flames licking our faces, we sat there for hours, reminiscing about all the incredible adventures we'd shared and pondering what lies ahead on the other side of our journey.

It's strange, but back when the trip was still just a pipe dream, a crazy notion that Amanda, Holly, and I had tossed out during our vacation in Argentina, I could envision us together on the road as clearly as if it had already happened. And suddenly it was just as easy to imagine us getting together to discuss new jobs, boyfriends, and thoughts about our lives over brunch back in New York. Giving toasts at each other's weddings. Group getaways with our husbands and kids. Taking vacations together, just the three of us. Maybe someday we'd even write a book about the trip, as we'd occasionally fantasized about doing. Who knew?

But though I couldn't predict the specifics of our future any more today than I could have before, I saw now how fast it could all fly by. Soon we would be returning to the States and the last chapter of this story would be complete. Although we'd hit some unexpected bumps during our final weeks in Australia, in a way it seemed befitting. Because it wasn't during those picture-perfect moments when I learned the most about myself; rather, it was during the most challenging portions of the trip, when the three of us stood side by side refusing to let one another fall. I certainly hadn't received all the answers I'd been seeking when I left, but as I looked across the fire at Amanda and Holly, I knew I'd found something even better.

Toward the start of the trip, I'd confessed to the girls that one of my greatest fears was that something would happen to my parents and I'd be left an orphan, with no siblings to shoulder the sadness. And though I'd been blessed with the most amazing friends I could ever hope for, deep down I would always feel alone until I had started a family of my own, people who put me as their number one priority above all else and vice versa.

But after everything the three of us had been through together, for the first time in my life, I wasn't afraid of that anymore. I knew I would never have to walk this earth on my own. Come what may, whether it was something as minor as a fender bender or as major as losing a loved one, Amanda, Holly, and I would always be there for one another.

Truthfully, I felt in many ways just as lost now as I had when we'd first set off on this adventure, but I wasn't lost alone. And I was going to sit there with my sisters until the last embers flickered out.

525

Jen · Hunter Valley, Australia · May ✂

✼

CHAPTER THIRTY-THREE

Holly

AUSTRALIA

MAY

C areening through the sleek sports cars that were gliding over the Sydney Harbour Bridge, our van was like a fat man at a beauty pageant—totally out of place. It wasn't just the splashes of paint splattered across it as if a rainbow had vomited or its hefty bulk. No, it was the lopsided crater on the roof and the gleaming silver duct tape holding it all together.

I'd gotten into so many fender benders myself that my father once asked if I'd mistaken the highway for a bumper car arena. I was actually surprised that it was Jen—rather than me—who had crashed the van.

Jen was sitting in the passenger seat beside me, looking totally stricken. "I can't walk into Auto Barn and face Chris after I mangled the van. And World Nomads is definitely going to fire us."

"Jen, accidents happen. If this is the worst trouble we've gotten ourselves into after a year on the road, then we're blessed," I said, trying to reassure her. "And don't worry about the deductible. Whatever it costs, we're in this together and we're splitting the money."

"Hol, you don't even have enough money left for a plane ticket home," she said.

"Details, details," I said before Amanda popped her head up from the back.

"Merge here! Auto Barn is up on the right," she ordered. I automatically jerked the wheel to the right, causing a few cars to swerve with an angry scream of their horns. Jen gripped the seat belt strap, her knuckles white.

"It should be up here on the left," Amanda directed.

As we pulled into the garage, Jen slid lower in her seat, her cheeks red from mortification. I have to admit, my stomach felt as if I'd ingested gasoline. We were supposed to be spreading goodwill, not demolishing the van.

"Do we have enough cash for a taxi?" I asked, fully prepared to unload our bags and find our own way back to Simone's apartment. Jen covered her face, and Amanda just nodded.

Narrowly making it through the garage door opening—all we needed was for me to dent the van even more upon returning it—I slowed to a stop. Awaiting us was a small crowd. Chris was there, as were Christy from World Nomads and the owner of Auto Barn and a few mechanics.

527

"Oh, man, they called for backup," Amanda whispered, looking nervous.

I turned off the engine, and the three of us climbed out of the van, preparing for an angry onslaught.

After the group took a few seconds to silently survey the van in all its mangled glory, they broke into applause. Chris pretended to jump out of the way, dramatically shielding his face from the imaginary crash. The three of us looked at one another, not knowing what to make of it.

"Well, you're not the first World Nomads ambassadors to get into an accident, but you certainly did the best at it!" Chris said, laughing.

"Is that . . . duct tape?" one of the mechanics asked incredulously.

"Um, yes?" Jen said. The group broke into another round of applause.

"How on earth did you manage to shave off the entire roof? Were you distracted by some strapping young man at the roadside?" Chris joked.

Jen immediately stepped in to apologize, saying that it was her fault and she alone would pay for the damage. As the mechanics poked around the vehicle, peeling back tape and running their fingers over the splintered fiberglass to estimate the damage, Chris enveloped us in a bear hug.

"I'm glad you ladies are all right!" he said. I looked over at Amanda. She just shrugged her shoulders. This was not the reception we'd expected.

Then Phil, Auto Barn's owner, who had kind brown eyes that crinkled when he smiled, broke in. "It looks like there's about eight thousand dollars' worth of damage," he said solemnly.

Jen froze, and I worried she might pass out. I squeezed her arm to comfort her. Eight thousand dollars was almost half her trip budget. With Australia being our last stop, that money had long since been spent.

Just as I was contemplating how I'd be able to increase my credit card limit, Phil added, "But all you'll have to pay is the four-hundred-dollar deductible."

"What?" Jen asked. I wasn't sure if I'd heard right either. Was this guy really letting us off the hook?

"If you pay the minimum deductible, we'll take care of the rest," Phil said. Now Jen appeared as though she'd been given a second lease on life.

Christy stepped in next and added, "We've already discussed the logistics. Chris will look into getting you another vehicle. One that's smaller—and an automatic."

I'd been prepared to grab my backpack and hail a taxi, but

instead our "employers" were *rewarding* us for ruining their vehicle? It didn't seem to make sense.

"You'd really do that for us?" Jen asked.

"So we're not fired?" Amanda asked at the same time, probably having flashbacks to her editorial assistant days.

"Yes, and of course not! We'll give you the car, but you'll have to keep blogging for us," Christy grinned. "You can't let a little accident stop you from exploring Australia. You just got here, and there's so much you have to see."

Aussies had a reputation for their laid-back, "no worries" attitude, and this was one stereotype that struck us as being true for the most part. Of course our saviors had their own motives for giving us another vehicle—they wanted us to promote their blog. But the humor with which they handled the situation, and the kindness they showered us with, showed that life can sometimes be as hard—or as easy—as one chooses to make it.

"I have a friend who runs a surf camp a few hours up the coast. I can call him if you'd be interested in staying there for a few nights," Chris offered. All three of us answered yes in the same breath. Our road trip was definitely taking a turn for the better.

"Okay, on one condition," Chris said. I knew there had to be a disclaimer, I thought. I looked at him suspiciously.

"You have to record a video of the wrecked van so we can put it up on the site."

It was a task that Amanda took on with zeal. As Phil positioned the camera to zoom in on the cracks crisscrossing the roof like the roots of a tree, Amanda joked, "If you're a foreigner and you can't drive, then call Auto Barn!"

So it wasn't literary skills or inspiring adventures that gave us our claim to fame on the World Nomads site. Rather, it was a photo of the van, captioned "The Ambassador van survived a crash by The Lost Girls."

529

The sun was melting into the ocean, and Amanda and Jen were floating on their surfboards beside me. Squinting my eyes to scan the horizon, I couldn't spot a single resort—let alone person—on the wide crescent of sand that curved around the rugged coastline into what appeared to be infinity. Besides the blue heron acting as a sentry on shore, it was only the three of us.

Chris hadn't revealed the surf camp's exact location at "Secret Spot X," which was somewhere north of Coffs Harbour and south of Byron Bay, until he called our loaned cell with directions when we were only a few miles away. I figured it was fitting for us not to know where we were going, given that the trip was almost over and, well, we didn't know where we were going. I didn't know what would happen with Elan, with our apartment, and with finding work when I returned home. It'd all unfold itself to me in time, and there was nothing that I could do about those things from across the ocean.

We were all grateful that the van collision had unexpectedly led us to surf camp rather than bankruptcy. My younger sister, Kate, had taken the twenty-plus-hour flight from Syracuse, New York, to meet me in our final destination. Though I sometimes felt like the little sister with Jen and Amanda's willful ways, with Kate I was the protective older one.

On the drive to surf camp, I'd looked in the rearview mirror at Kate in the backseat, a pile of guidebooks between her and Jen as they fortified themselves with Weetabix cereal. Though Kate's face had lost its childlike roundness now that she was almost twenty-four years old, I could still picture her as a little girl with coal-black eyes, rosy cheeks, and dark ringlets.

Even as a kid she'd been a spitfire, dancing for hours around the house and waving her arms dramatically to impersonate Bette Midler in the movie *Beaches*. She'd hated schoolwork, so

530

I'd made a game out of it by pretending to be her "teacher," giving her spelling tests with rewards of M&M's for each word she got correct. As a child, she liked to follow me wherever I went, so I'd carry her on my back through the fields behind our house, our yellow Labrador retriever, Corby, running in circles behind us. I hadn't realized how much I'd missed her until I saw her step off the plane in Australia.

Being near one of my real sisters, and the two women who'd come as close to being my sisters as I'd ever find, made me feel stronger. Besides Sara and Kate, I knew that Jen and Amanda would always be there. I laughed thinking about how I'd probably meet Amanda's real eighty-year-old self, whom I'd heard a lot about this past year, and Jen's, too.

At surf camp, the four of us fell into a cozy routine. As the sun made its way back to our side of the world, we'd wake to wash up in the communal bathrooms, join the other surf students in line for a breakfast of fried eggs and toast, and then hit the waves for our morning surf lessons. We learned about riptides and practiced jumping up on our boards on the beach before doing so atop the crest of a wave. In the afternoon, we'd play cards on towels in the sand or read in one of the hammocks hung beneath the teak trees. Kate and I would run barefoot on the beach, with Amanda and Jen walking behind us and talking the whole way. Time seemed heavy and moved slowly, like syrup. And we felt light.

When the air got cool, we'd grab our sweatshirts and line up for an al fresco barbecue, eating our burgers and coleslaw together at a picnic table under an A-frame awning. Then we'd gather around the bonfire, swapping stories with other travelers.

It wouldn't be long—maybe until the moon was halfway up in the sky—before the girls and I would slip away, content to burrow in our sleeping bags and keep talking. No childhood story was left untold, and I secretly marveled that a year had

531

gone by in which Amanda, Jen, and I had seen each other at our best and at our worst, and we were still in it together—and had so much left to talk about. The days when Jen had been only an acquaintance and Amanda only a coworker seemed like memories from another time.

We were in front of the bonfire on our last evening, and the sun was just beginning its downward descent. As it sank, the shadows from the fire grew taller, kind of resembling Aboriginal rock art. Kate was playing cards with some of the other surfers, and I'd plopped myself on the ground in front of two chairs where Amanda and Jen sat.

"Remember when we were camping on the Inca Trail in Peru? Australia seemed like a world away this time last year," I said.

"Uh-oh, Hol, don't go getting all sentimental on us on our last night here," Amanda said. As hard-nosed as she acted sometimes, I now knew she was really a softie underneath.

"Hey, guys?" Jen asked, her cheeks flushed from the heat of the fire. "I want to try to ride a wave one more time before we leave. Do you want to go?"

I hesitated for a minute, wondering if we should stay put where it was comfortable and warm. But the ocean was right there, and there was still enough light left to hit the water.

"Okay, let's go," I said, standing up and brushing the sand off my jeans. Amanda and Jen pushed back their chairs, leaving trails in the sand, and we went to put on the wet suits we'd already hung out to dry on a line outside the cabin's windows.

Then we tucked our boards under our arms and walked down to the beach to paddle out together. Our feet padded on powdery sand, then rock-hard sand, and then into the surf. The water and the air were almost the same temperature, and I waited for the cool liquid to fill my wet suit before my body heat would warm it up.

The three of us floated on our boards and stared at the water stretching toward the setting sun. It felt peaceful to be doing nothing but bobbing up and down on the waves there with Jen and Amanda. I'd always dreamed of surfing in Australia, but I'd never really believed I'd actually do it.

Dreams and memories. Memories and dreams. I was awash in a sea of them. The trip was over. After all my searching for something to believe in, what if taking the journey itself were the highest act of faith? Traveling anywhere that was foreign inevitably meant I'd have to rely on the kindness of strangers. To venture out into the world, I had to have faith in the goodness of people—and to be open to the lessons that every new person might bring. There was the Quechua woman again on the Inca Trail, handing Amanda back her lost wallet. The Brazilian woman taking my hand to show me the sunset. Esther waving good-bye from Sister Freda's lap. Chloe bringing me food when I was sick at the ashram. The street kids turned waiters in the Cambodian restaurant. And there were always Jen and Amanda, ready to share with me their beds, their clothes, their encouragement.

Floating there, I held on to faith. Because you can't know who might cross your path or who will take your breath away. You can't know what friends might actually become sisters because they stayed by your side. You can't know when there'll be an unexpected detour that'll take you to the place where you were always meant to be.

I glanced at Jen and Amanda, leaning back on their boards as the swells rolled on by. We lingered for a moment, soaking up that split second of silence that comes before the next wave breaks. Then the waves began to roll in higher and stronger. I looked behind me to see a swell rising and felt the momentum of it push my board forward. Time to go.

I turned to Jen and Amanda and said, "The sun's almost set. Let's ride this one back in."

Holly · Australia · May ✻

Epilogue

During the final days of our trip we made a promise—a pact, actually—that our explorations together could not and *would* not end with the punch of a reentry stamp. We swore that no matter where our individual paths led us, we'd go away together every year for the rest of our lives to guarantee that the bond we'd forged would remain strong. It took us longer than expected, but twenty-six months after we returned home, we dug out our old backpacks, double-checked that our passports had enough blank pages, and hit the road again. Our first post-trip destination: Santa Catalina, a fishing village turned surfers' paradise on the Pacific coast of Panama.

After a five-hour flight, six-hour bus ride, forty-five-minute cab ride, and ten minutes in the back of a cattle truck, we arrived at Oasis Surf Camp, a collection of rustic bungalows on an isolated volcanic-sand beach. Well, almost. As our driver pulled onto the sandy earth littered with twisted driftwood and broken coconut hulls, he gestured to the far bank. Because it was high tide, he couldn't go any further. We'd have to travel the rest of the way on foot. So, dry clothes and backpacks notwithstanding, we did what we'd always done in a situation like this:

we hiked up our shorts, hoisted the bags above our heads, and waded across the river.

After retrieving the keys to our triple—a small but clean room with bunk beds, concrete floors, and a cold-water shower—we did something we almost never do: we each claimed a mattress and immediately collapsed into a deep sleep.

T he afternoon had almost fully transitioned into evening by the time we woke to the sound of animated voices. Creeping outside, we were greeted by our next-door neighbors, Paul and Itzel from Miami and Juan, a local Panamanian who managed a 150-acre cattle ranch nearby. A little embarrassed to be rolling out of bed at 6 p.m., we explained that we'd just been in an accident.

Earlier that day, just three kilometers shy of Santa Catalina, our driver had jerked his taxi into the opposite lane—at the exact moment that another truck had whipped around a curve. By the time the three of us had realized we were going to be in a head-on collision, there was little we could do but send up the world's most abbreviated prayer, then brace for impact. Despite the sickening crunch, we—along with everyone else in the accident—had walked away with nothing but scrapes, deep bruises, and a mild case of whiplash.

We hadn't gotten two sentences into our story when Itzel interjected.

"Oh, my God, that was *you*?" Her face was aghast as she leaned forward in her white plastic chair. Although it had been only a few hours since it had happened, they'd already heard about the accident—apparently, everyone else in the town of 350 had too.

"Yeah, those cars were totaled," said Paul, echoing his friend's sentiments. "You girls are lucky to even be here right now."

Breaking out a bottle of rum, Paul suggested we toast to surviving the near miss—and to finding our way to Oasis. We all decided to contribute a few words—to our health and safety, to new friends, to continuing on with the journey, come what may. But it was Juan, making his toast in Spanish, who said it best. *"Hoy es el día que ustedes nacieron. Bienvenido al resto de su vida."*

Today is the day that you are born. Welcome to the rest of your life.

After our experience in the taxi that morning, it had been our knee-jerk reaction to want to hop the first flight back to the States, to retreat to the safety and familiarity of home. We resisted, and our trip turned out to be exactly the reunion we'd been anticipating. During the ten days that followed, we went scuba diving off the deserted Isla Coiba, explored hidden beaches, went horseback riding with Paul, and surfed each morning and night. We stayed, because if there was any resounding lesson that we took away from our year of wandering, it was that we would no longer make decisions based in fear. We wouldn't hightail it home at the first sign of trouble or remain in a stagnant situation simply because we were afraid to challenge the status quo.

Back when we first starting calling ourselves The Lost Girls, a tongue-in-cheek nickname we invented long before we ever stepped outside the country, we sort of assumed that the goal of the journey would be to get *un*-lost. We thought the trip would yield the kind of earth-shattering, value-bending, shout-it-from-the-mountaintop epiphanies that would help us discover just what we wanted out of our short existence on this planet. We thought the trip would instantly change our lives. We wanted to be *found*.

Looking back on it now, we might have been putting a teensy bit too much pressure on the universe—and ourselves. Though

536

we'd had some epiphanies along the way, we wondered: Had we learned enough? Did we really change? Would our new attitudes last after returning home?

As it turned out, yes.

After traveling solo for a month in Australia (and finally digging her electronics-free existence), Amanda returned to New York, confronting her fear of morphing back into a stressed-out workaholic. She accepted the senior editor position when it was offered but negotiated a more flexible schedule with fewer hours spent behind a desk. Thanks perhaps to this change in attitude—or maybe just the change of pace—she found that her heart was open to new friends, new passions and, shortly after her return, her next great love. After writing an article on a dance program benefiting young girls in Spanish Harlem, she decided to pick up where she left off in Kenya and now teaches and mentors through city youth programs.

Holly came back to her old apartment, but not to her old life. Though she and Elan reside on different coasts, they still keep in touch. To live more in line with her priorities, she began to spend more time with the people she loves and pursue the activities she cares about the most. She decided to turn down editorial job offers in order to take the less secure route as a freelance writer. She now spends her nonworking hours traveling to Syracuse to visit her family. She trained for her second marathon as well as her first triathlon and continues to practice yoga a few times a week. She remains in contact with Sister Freda in order to support Esther's education. She's also checked off more destinations on her travel wish list: hiking the Leaping Tiger Gorge in China; swimming with stingrays in the Bahamas, and visiting her seventh and last continent, Antarctica.

Despite her fears that Manhattan might be geographic kryptonite to single women, Jen returned to the city, where she threw herself headlong into dating. To her surprise, she quickly found romance . . . then didn't . . . then did again . . . then didn't. Until she finally chilled out and remembered one of the most important lessons she'd learned on the road: it's okay to be alone for a little while. Of course, once she accepted this, she found the real love she'd been searching for. In addition to immediately landing a dream gig at an independent film channel, Jen decided to devote a portion of her time volunteering with kids in inner-city schools. Though she still isn't a fan of Internet cafés or doing assignments on the road, she continues to create Excel spreadsheets and travel itineraries and is currently planning her next international getaway.

For all three of us, friendships have taken on a much greater significance—and not just between our trio. Instead of canceling plans, we started making them again, and we've been amazed to watch our circle of Lost Girls grow. The three of us, as impossible as it sounds, have become even closer on a new journey together: writing this book about our adventures. And those adventures aren't over—not even close.

As we were putting the finishing touches on this book, we learned that *A Tree Grows in Kenya*, the play we wrote with Irene at Pathfinder, has now been distributed across the country. Girls all over Kenya perform the play and have made Wangari Maathai, a woman all but unknown to them before, into a role model. That's something that couldn't have happened if we had stayed on the tried-and-true path in New York, if we'd never decided that our dreams were bigger than our fears.

Though we can't predict where the road ahead will lead, there's one thing we know for certain: uprooting our lives to take an unconventional detour was one of the most challenging things we ever did, but the experience taught us that getting lost isn't something to avoid, but to embrace. The only leaps of faith you'll ever regret are the ones you don't take.

Acknowledgments

W e'd be truly lost without . . .

Our parents:

April Baggett, my best friend: for inspiring my travel bug in the first place. Thank you for always being there to listen to me wherever I was in the country (or the world) and for however long I needed you; **Bruce Baggett**: my handyman hero, partner in crime, and dancing role model: for always fueling my imagination and teaching me the value of hard work. You once wrote to me, "follow your instincts and your heart," which are words I continue to try to live by; And to you both, **my ever-patient mom and dad**: for giving me faith that a marriage can last forever—and that raising a child on public television can lead them to places they only ever dreamed about.

Kathy Barone Corbett, for leaving the door to home always open, and showing me unconditional love. Anything I have or will ever accomplish in my life can be traced back to the lessons you've taught me.

Patrick Corbett, for always supporting my dreams without judgment. Whether helping me move to the city for the twelfth time or getting me a plane ticket home, you've never left me lost or stranded.

Maureen Pressner, for always supporting my writing career, even when I was working in crayon. Not everyone could give their mom chapters to edit, but you were a true professional, never judging the content of the book (or my character!) as you cheerfully gave me your notes. Thanks also for creating the gorgeous maps in this book!

Robert Pressner, for encouraging me to travel now, work later. And for advising me to "do what you love and the money will follow," then lending me a few bucks during the times it didn't.

Our superagent, **Kenneth Wright.** Thanks for taking a chance on three unknown writers and Lost Girls, guiding us through the often tumultuous process of publishing our first book, and finding it amusing (rather than annoying!) when all three of us talked over one another in meetings.

Everyone at **HarperCollins** who believed in our project, especially **Jonathan Burnham** and **Serena Jones**. And a huge debt of gratitude to our editor, **Stephanie Meyers**, for wholeheartedly adopting our project and allowing our individual voices to shine through.

All those friends who inspired us, counseled us, provided storage space in their attics and basements, offered us their futons to crash on, bought much-needed cocktails, read our drafts (even the roughest early versions), and/or eased our transition back into the "real" world: **Aimee and Mike Stafford; Bindu Swamy; Catherine Hanson; Chantel Arroyo, Courtney Dubin; Courtney Scott; Courtney Thom; Dean Arrindell; Jenna Autuori; Jenny Depper; Kateri Benjamin; Kristin Luna; Jessica Rosenzweig; Marco Antonio Palomino; Melissa Braverman; Mike Bristol; Nadji Kirby; Nyoman Neuva Reviannossa Suastha; Pierre P. Lizee, PhD; Sarah and**

Pete Wildeman; Steph and Danny Spahr; Stephanie Davis; Stephanie Sholtis; Stephen Bailey; and Trisha Posen.

The friends and "characters" who joined us on the trip and the new ones we met along the way: **Beth Frey; Carmi Louw; Chloe Douglas; Eric Pain and Nora Thompson; Hugh Williams; Irene Scher; Kate Corbett; Marlena Krzesniak; Sam Effron; Sarah Bailey; Simone Morgan; Stephany Foster Spahr; the Irish Lost Girls (Georgia, Suzie, and Sadhbh); and Paul Meyer and Itzel Diaz.**

The creative types, media professionals, and travel gurus who helped us launch LostGirlsWorld.com and supported us in our journey from the very beginning: **Alan Phillips; Jodi Einhorn; Mark Ledbetter; Molly Fergus; Nina Lora; Patty Hodapp; Patrick Sasso; and Tracy Schmitt.**

Shana Greene and all of those at Village Volunteers who devote themselves to helping others, especially **Joshua Machinga; Mama Sandra; Emmanuel and Lillian Taser; Sister Freda Robinson** and the remarkable men and women who support her medical clinic.

Chris Noble and Christy McCarthy at World Nomads and **Chris Ford** at Auto Barn. We appreciate that you forgave us so quickly for utterly destroying the roof of your Ambassador van, then subsequently provided a getaway car so we could hit the beach and shred at surf camp (and "keep travelling safely").

Lulu, the stinky but lovable Boston terrier and Lost Girls mascot.

Also a huge thanks from . . .

Jen:
To my consummate parental figures—**Sharon and Wes Andrews, Lil Slebodnick and Patrick Gibbons,** and **Nic and Brigitte Monjo**—for never judging me when I wore the same

541

set of pajamas for days on end and for making my self-imposed writing retreats a little less lonely. To **Kevin Brennan**. Who would have thought I'd travel around the world to find what I was searching for right across the Hudson River—who? Thank you for making the long journey so worthwhile.

Holly:

To my sister **Sara**, for being my accountant and therapist during my travels, and my sister **Kate**, for always meeting me on my journeys. My life is infinitely fuller because you are both in it. To **Meg Foye**, a fellow Lost Girl, for being the greatest editor and turning into an even better friend. Meg, you *are* the rock! To **Enver**, for teaching me how to love and let go. To **Sophie, Frank, Adam, and Barry Barone**, for reminding me that life is short and the time to live is now.

Amanda:

To **Jeff Cravens**, who stood by me through every step of the process. Thank you for sharing your energy, passion, and creativity. I couldn't have completed this chapter of my life without you. To **Jennifer Pressner**, my first-and-always best friend, my fellow adventurer. I might never have learned to explore (and certainly wouldn't have gotten into as much trouble!) if you hadn't showed me the way. To **Nadine Pressner,** who invited me to North Carolina so I could finish the really difficult pages and let me borrow Mia when I needed a buddy. To **Aunt Karen and Uncle Eddie**, who've repeatedly allowed me to store my worldly possessions in their basement and fed me heartily during my New York layovers. To **Bruce Kirk**, the role model who taught me everything from turning the perfect cartwheel to surviving in the desert. To **Jeff Baker**, who helped inspire my travels and has generously offered to edit anything I write, whether it be a novel or a grocery list.

542

About the Authors

Jennifer Baggett (left) never dreamed that she'd become a writer, but she's thrilled to have cut her teeth on *The Lost Girls*. Prior to the trip, she worked as a marketing and promotions professional and held positions at the Sundance Channel, VH1, and NBC Universal. A dedicated film buff, Jen has a passport full of stamps from destinations that she discovered while watching movies as a child. She hails from Bowie, Maryland.

Holly C. Corbett (middle) used to run laps around her block as a kid and now trains for marathons and triathlons. When she's not jogging, she's a freelance writer whose work has appeared in publications such as *Women's Health*, *Prevention*, *Seventeen*, and *Fitness*. Her adventures have taken her to all seven continents, where she's swum past icebergs in the Antarctic Ocean, slalom water-skied next to alligators in Florida, and hiked the Leaping Tiger Gorge in China. She was born in Syracuse, New York.

Amanda Pressner (right) caught the travel bug at age eight when she and her family did a cross-country trip in a camper van nicknamed the Blue Moose. Between trips abroad, she writes for such publications as *USA Today*, *Shape*, *Travel + Leisure*, and *Cosmopolitan*. While she's previously served as a diet and nutrition editor at *SELF* and *Shape*, she still believes the best reason to hit the road is to eat. She is a native of Tampa, Florida.

When they're not traveling the world, all three Lost Girls live in New York City.